The Origins of the Corinthian Christ Group

*Edinburgh Studies in Religion in Antiquity*

**Series editors: Matthew V. Novenson, James B. Rives, Paula Fredriksen**

*Edinburgh Studies in Religion in Antiquity* publishes cutting-edge research in religion in the ancient world. It provides a platform for creative studies spanning time periods (classical antiquity and late antiquity), geographical regions (the Mediterranean and West Asia), religious traditions (Greek, Roman, Jewish, Christian and more), disciplines (comparative literature, archaeology, anthropology, and more) and theoretical questions (historical, philological, comparative, redescriptive, and more). Deconstructing literary canons and confessional boundaries, the series considers and questions what we moderns call "religion" as a prominent feature of the human past and a worthy object of historical enquiry.

**Advisory Board**
Helen Bond, University of Edinburgh
Kimberley Czajkowski, University of Edinburgh
Benedikt Eckhardt, University of Edinburgh
Martin Goodman, University of Oxford
Oded Irshai, Hebrew University of Jerusalem
Timothy Lim, University of Edinburgh
Yii-Jan Lin, Yale University
Candida Moss, University of Birmingham
Paul Parvis, University of Edinburgh
Matthew Thiessen, McMaster University
Philippa Townsend, University of Edinburgh
Greg Woolf, University of California-Los Angeles

**Books published in the series**
Stephen P. Ahearne-Kroll, *The Origins of the Corinthian Christ Group: Paul's Chord of Gods*
Stanley K. Stowers, *Christian Beginnings: A Study in Ancient Mediterranean Religion*
Elena L. Dugan, *The Apocalypse of the Birds: 1 Enoch and the Jewish Revolt against Rome*
Megan S. Nutzman, *Contested Cures: Identity and Ritual Healing in Roman and Late Antique Palestine*
Matthew T. Sharp, *Divination and Philosophy in the Letters of Paul*

Visit the series webpage: https://edinburghuniversitypress.com/series-edinburgh-studies-in-religion-in-antiquity

# The Origins of the Corinthian Christ Group
*Paul's Chord of Gods*

Stephen P. Ahearne-Kroll

Edinburgh University Press is one of the leading university presses in the UK. We publish academic books and journals in our selected subject areas across the humanities and social sciences, combining cutting-edge scholarship with high editorial and production values to produce academic works of lasting importance. For more information visit our website: edinburghuniversitypress.com

© Stephen P. Ahearne-Kroll, 2024, 2026

Grateful acknowledgement is made to the sources listed in the List of Illustrations for permission to reproduce material previously published elsewhere. Every effort has been made to trace the copyright holders, but if any have been inadvertently overlooked, the publisher will be pleased to make the necessary arrangements at the first opportunity.

Edinburgh University Press Ltd
13 Infirmary Street
Edinburgh EH1 1LT

First published in hardback by Edinburgh University Press 2024

Typeset in 11/13 Bembo Std by
IDSUK (DataConnection) Ltd, and
printed and bound by CPI Group (UK) Ltd,
Croydon, CR0 4YY

A CIP record for this book is available from the British Library

ISBN 978 1 3995 3629 5 (hardback)
ISBN 978 1 3995 3630 1 (paperback)
ISBN 978 1 3995 3631 8 (webready PDF)
ISBN 978 1 3995 3632 5 (epub)

The right of Stephen P. Ahearne-Kroll to be identified as the author of this work has been asserted in accordance with the Copyright, Designs and Patents Act 1988, and the Copyright and Related Rights Regulations 2003 (SI No. 2498).

# Contents

| | |
|---|---|
| *List of Illustrations* | vi |
| *List of Abbreviations* | ix |
| *Preface and Acknowledgements* | xi |
| Introduction: Ancient Religion, Social Theory and Methodology | 1 |
| 1. Chords of Gods around the Mediterranean | 25 |
| 2. Chords of Gods in Corinth | 82 |
| 3. The *Pneuma* in Corinth | 113 |
| 4. Genealogy, History, Mythology and Cult of Paul's God(s) | 162 |
| 5. Reimagining the Early Days of Paul's Corinthians | 196 |
| 6. A Chord of Gods as a 'Tool' for Rupture | 213 |
| *Appendix* | 217 |
| *Bibliography* | 220 |
| *Index* | 240 |

# Illustrations

## Figures

| | | |
|---|---|---|
| 1.1 | Plan of Temple at Edfu. (Public domain) | 29 |
| 1.2 | Plan of Temple at Dendera. (Public domain) | 30 |
| 1.3 | Aerial view of Caesarea Maritima with harbour and Temple of Augustus and Roma marked. (Public domain) | 36 |
| 1.4 | Plan of the Sanctuary of Pan at Banias/Caesarea Philippi. (After Andrea M. Berlin, 'The Archaeology of Ritual: The Sanctuary of Pan at Banias/Caesarea Philippi', *BASOR* 315 (1999): 29, modified) | 38 |
| 1.5 | Sanctuary of Pan at Banias/Caesarea Philippi. Photo by Berthold Werner. Licence CC by 3.0 IT (https://creativecommons.org/licenses/by/3.0/). Enhanced resolution. | 38 |
| 1.6 | Plan of the Sanctuary of Asklepios at Pergamon. Welcome Images (https://wellcomecollection.org/works/u6pw5py4). Licence CC by 3.0 IT (https://creativecommons.org/licenses/by/3.0/). Enhanced resolution. | 43 |
| 1.7 | Plan of the Acropolis. Madmedea. CC-A-SA-2.0 (https://creativecommons.org/licenses/by-sa/2.0/deed.en). Enhanced resolution. | 49 |
| 1.8 | Relief of Xenocrateia and Kephisos, c. 400 BCE, at Kephisos. National Archaeological Museum of Athens. Photo by Jerónimo Roure Pérez. Licence CC by 4.0 IT (https://creativecommons.org/licenses/by-sa/4.0/deed.en) | 62 |
| 1.9 | Plan of the Forum of Augustus. Plan by Cassius Ahenobarbus. Licence by 3.0 IT (https://creativecommons.org/licenses/by-sa/3.0/deed.en). Enhanced resolution. | 66 |
| 1.10 | 3-D rendering of the Sanctuary of Fortuna Praenestae. (Purchased from Deposit Photos 26 October 2023) | 73 |

1.11  Lararium, House of the Red Walls VIII 5, 37 Pompeii Prowalk, first century CE. Photo by Mary Harrsch. Licensed under the Creative Commons Attribution-Share Alike 4.0 International licence (https://creativecommons.org/licenses/by-sa/4.0/deed.en). Enhanced resolution. 75
1.12  Fresco of lararium with a niche and altar, mid-first century BCE. Located in kitchen of Villa 6, Terzigno. Photo by Tyler Bell. Licensed under the Creative Commons Attribution 2.0 Generic licence (https://creativecommons.org/licenses/by/2.0/deed.en). Enhanced resolution. 76
1.13  Painted Roman lararium, House of the Vettii, Pompeii, first century CE. Photo by Patricio Lorente. Licensed under the Creative Commons Attribution-Share Alike 2.5 Generic licence (https://creativecommons.org/licenses/by-sa/2.5/deed.en). Enhanced resolution. 76
1.14  The Capitoline Triad (left to right: Juno, Jupiter and Minerva), 160–80 CE. Rodolfo Lanciani Archaeological Museum, Montecelio. Photo by Sailko. License CC by 3.0 IT (https://creativecommons.org/licenses/by/3.0/). Enhanced resolution. 80
2.1  Map of ancient Corinth. (From Steven J. Friesen, Daniel N. Schowalter and James C. Walters, eds, *Corinth in Context: Comparative Studies on Religion and Society* [Leiden: Brill, 2010], 516.) Used with permission. 83
2.2  Map of central Corinth. (From Friesen, Schowalter and Walters, *Corinth in Context*, 517.) Used with permission. 84
2.3  The Acrocorinth looking north. (Public domain) 85
2.4  Plan of the Acrocorinth. (Public domain) 85
2.5  Plan of the Sanctuary of Demeter and Kore on the Acrocorinth in the Roman period. Used with permission from the American Academy of Classical Studies in Athens. 88
2.6  Intact *pinakes* from the Acrocorinth Sanctuary of Demeter and Kore, both found on the upper terrace, from the late Roman period: (a) ΔΙΟΝΥΣΟΥ (Dionysou); (b) ΑΛΦΙΑΙΑΣ (Alphiaias). Used with permission from the American Academy of Classical Studies in Athens. 89
2.7  Plan of the Roman upper terrace of the Sanctuary of Demeter and Kore, where three temples are located: one to Demeter, one to Kore and one to an unknown god/gods. Used with permission from the American Academy of Classical Studies in Athens. 90
2.8  Plan of the Sanctuary of Poseidon at Isthmia. (Public domain; https://lucian.uchicago.edu/blogs/isthmia/files/2010/06/genplan.gif) 96

| 2.9 | Close-up plan of the Sanctuary of Poseidon and Palaimon. (Public domain; https://lucian.uchicago.edu/blogs/isthmia/files/2012/03/composite.gif) | 96 |
| --- | --- | --- |
| 2.10 | Temple of Melikertes on obverse of Marcus Aurelius coin. (Public domain) | 98 |
| 2.11 | Plan of the Hellenistic Corinthian Asklepieion. (Modified from Bronwen L. Wickkiser, 'Asklepios in Greek and Roman Corinth', in *Corinth in Context: Comparative Studies on Religion and Society*, edited by Steven J. Friesen, Daniel N. Schowalter, and James C. Walters [Leiden: Brill, 2010], 48.) Used with permission. | 100 |
| 2.12 | Medical box from Herculaneum with image of Asklepios and Hygieia, first century CE. (Public domain) | 103 |
| 2.13 | Typical Tiberian coin from Corinth: (a) obverse with image of Tiberius; (b) reverse with six-columned temple carrying inscription GE[NT] IVLI. Used with permission from the Ashmolean Museum of Art and Archaeology. | 107 |
| 3.1 | Pompeiian painting with *genius* at the centre of the top portion. Photo by ArchaiOptix. Licence CC by 4.0 IT (https://creativecommons.org/licenses/by-sa/4.0/deed.en) | 137 |
| 3.2 | Helios in a chariot drawn by four horses, from the Temple of Athena, Ilion, fourth century BCE. (Purchased from Alamy 26 October 2023) | 140 |
| 3.3 | Right side panel from 'Statue Base of Marcus Antonius', second half of second century BCE, showing sea thiasos for the wedding of Poseidon and Amphitrite. Detail of Nereids riding a sea dragon, and a Triton. (Public domain) | 141 |
| 3.4 | Altar with the goddess Luna, second or third century CE, Mithraeum, Mundelsheim. Licence CC by 4.0 IT (https://creativecommons.org/licenses/by-sa/4.0/deed.en) | 142 |

# Tables

| 4.1 | Thomas R. Blanton IV's version of the Friesen–Longenecker Economic Scale. Used with permission from Oxford University Press. | 144 |
| --- | --- | --- |

# Abbreviations

This book follows the abbreviation conventions of the *Oxford Classical Dictionary* and *L'Année Philologique* for journals and other work. The following are not in either of these reference sources.

| | |
|---|---|
| ANTC | Abingdon New Testament Commentaries |
| ADAIK | Abhandlungen des Deutschen Archäologischen Instituts, Kairo |
| ASCSA | American School of Classical Studies at Athens |
| ASOR | American Schools of Oriental Research |
| *AvP* | *Altertümer von Pergamon* |
| BASOR | Bulletin of the American School of Oriental Research |
| BNTC | Black's New Testament Commentaries |
| *BTB* | *Biblical Theology Bulletin* |
| *HTR* | *Harvard Theological Review* |
| ICC | International Critical Commentary |
| *IGR* | *Inscriptiones Graecae ad res Romanas pertinentes* (1906– ) |
| *IGUR* | *Inscriptiones Graecae Urbis Romae I–IV* |
| *ILTG* | *Inscriptions latines des trois Gaules* |
| *JBL* | *Journal of Biblical Literature* |
| *JSJ* | *Journal for the Study of Judaism* |
| *JSNT* | *Journal for the Study of the New Testament* |
| LCL | Loeb Classical Library |
| NIDNTT | *New International Dictionary of New Testament Theology*, edited by E. M. Blaiklock, 4 vols (Grand Rapids, MI: Zondervan, 1975–8) |
| NIGTC | New International Greek Testament Commentary |
| *NTS* | *New Testament Studies* |
| *RBL* | *Review of Biblical Literature* |
| *RECAM* II | Stephen Mitchell, *Regional Epigraphic Catalogues of Asia Minor, II: The Ankara District. The Inscriptions of North Galatia*, with the |

|  | assistance of David French and Jean Greenhalgh, British Archaeological Reports, International Series, 135 (Oxford: BAR, 1982) |
|---|---|
| *RICIS* | *Recueil des inscriptions concernant les cultes isiaques* |
| SBL | Society of Biblical Literature |
| *TDNT* | *Theological Dictionary of the New Testament*, edited by Gerhard Kittel and Gerhard Friedrich, translated by Geoffrey W. Bromiley, 10 vols (Grand Rapids, MI: Eerdmans, 1964–6) |
| TPSulp | Tabulae Pompeianae Sulpiciorum |
| WUNT II | Wissenschaftliche Untersuchungen zum Neuen Testament, series II |

# Preface and Acknowledgements

The origin of this book on origins can be traced to my first public presentation of some of the book's ideas at my installation as Sundet Family Chair in New Testament and Christian Studies in the then Department of Classical and Near Eastern Studies (now the Department of Classical and Near Eastern Religions and Cultures) at the University of Minnesota in the fall of 2015. Since then the Sundet Family Chair has been a continual source of support for this project, funding summer work and presentations at conferences along the way towards the creation of this book. I would like to thank the Sundet family for their generosity and foresight in endowing this chair many years ago to establish the permanent presence of the study of early Christianity at the University of Minnesota.

I would also like to thank Jennifer Eyl, L. L. Welborn, J. Albert Harrill, Stanley K. Stowers, Lee A. Johnson, Paul A. Holloway, Joshua Reno, Charles McNamara, Spencer Cole, Mattias Gassman, the anonymous reviewers and the organisers of the Society of Biblical Literature programme units Redescribing Christian Origins and Pauline Literature. They all gave me important feedback and resources along the way that tremendously improved the project. Kristi Lee and Sam Baker helped proofread and format the manuscript for publication, and provided me the time I needed at the perfect times I needed it. I would also like to thank the good people at Edinburgh University Press – Matthew Novenson, Paula Fredricksen, and James Rives (editors of this series) and Grace Balfour-Harle and her team of production editors – for the timely and beautiful production of this book.

Since 2015, a great deal has happened to me personally and to the country and world. Black Lives Matter was only two years old when I gave that first talk in 2015, the movement having been born in the wake of the murder of the teenager Trayvon Martin for wearing a hoodie, and the subsequent acquittal of his killer, George Zimmerman. Michael Brown and Eric Garner had already been killed by police, with no convictions resulting from the deadly actions of law enforcement. The movement exposed the police racism that Black and Brown people had known and experienced for many years, and it mobilized millions of people to protest this racism and police violence against Black and Brown people. After many more killings at the hands of police, the murder of George Floyd in Minneapolis in 2020 and the subsequent conviction of his murderer a year later were watershed, culture-defining moments for the country and especially for the Twin Cities, where I reside and teach.

The end of Barack Obama's second term came shortly after I gave that paper. His successor's inauguration in January 2017 happened in the midst of national protests by millions of women and their supporters against his obvious misogyny and sexism. Later in 2017, the #MeToo movement exposed the persistent sexual violence against and bodily violation of women by men, something women had known and experienced for many years.

In 2020, a worldwide pandemic developed, when COVID-19's rapid spread was quickened still more by the wilful denial of its potency and the consistent inaction and misdirection by the leader of the US federal government. Millions of lives were lost, and the education of a whole generation of children was forever altered for the worse.

In early 2022, Russia invaded Ukraine in the largest military attack in Europe since World War II. This unprovoked invasion has resulted in tens of thousands of civilian deaths, the displacement of millions of Ukrainians and the kidnapping and forced Russian adoption of thousands of Ukrainian children, which the UN has deemed a war crime.

And in 2023, a brutal terrorist attack by Hamas on Israeli civilians resulted in the death and kidnapping of approximately 1,500 Israelis and an ensuing response by the Israeli military that has caused the deaths of over 30,000 Gazan residents, according the to Gaza's Ministry of Health. The immense complexity of the situation makes it difficult for any one group to claim the moral high ground amidst all the bloodshed.

All of these events and many more that have occurred since I began the book in 2015 have irrevocably changed the world, my country, my family and my own outlook on the world. Thinking back on these events, some of which are ongoing, is overwhelming. And yet, we scholars strive to do our work and to do it at as high a level as possible amidst the turmoil.

I mention this context to put this book into perspective. Yes, I have worked very hard to write it, having read many books and articles and having analysed a wide array of evidence from the ancient Mediterranean world to construct a (hopefully) compelling argument about the earliest moments of Paul's interaction with the Corinthians. But the events I have just described should help us students of the ancient world gain perspective on the import of our scholarship. Our scholarship is certainly important in our little worlds, but we live in a much bigger world with much more important issues to deal with on a daily basis. As such, I do not overestimate the significance of my work and remain humble about the potential for scholars of the ancient world to say anything that accurately represents the way things actually were back then. We can make educated guesses based on the small glimpses of the ancient world that survive. This book is one of those educated guesses. Nothing more, nothing less.

Part of the reason why this book has taken so long to write is the presence of the chord of people who make good trouble for me: my children, Kieran and Marin, and my spouse and colleague, Pat Ahearne-Kroll. Many authors take this space to thank their families for their patience and understanding during the many days and weeks when writing and researching took them away from their families. On the contrary, my chord of people kept me away from my book, and I love them all the more for it. The joy and meaning that Pat and I have experienced by nurturing the growth of our children from preschool-aged at the start of this project to young teenagers at the end far exceeds anything I have derived from my writing. Their creativity, good humour, companionship and intellect have grounded me, inspired me and significantly delayed the completion of this book, and I would not have it any other way.

*For my beautiful family
Kieran, Marin and Pat*

INTRODUCTION

# Ancient Religion, Social Theory of Practice and Methodology

This book is about imagining the earliest moments of what later becomes Christianity. But it is not a general theory of Christian origins.[1] Instead, its scope is quite a bit more circumscribed, both temporally and geographically. I treat only Paul's initial interaction with the Corinthians, positing what I hope is a reasonable culturally grounded scenario for how the movement might have grown among Corinthian gentiles after Paul's first encounter with them. While many scholars over the years have focused on Paul's appeal to gentiles, few have considered socio-religious practice as a major factor in the growth of the movement, instead opting for more theological factors: promise of personal salvation through faith and not works, miracle-working, or Christ's atoning death, for example. The assertion that undergirds this book is that, for Paul's movement to grow, its purported uniqueness – theological or otherwise – was not the factor that made it compelling, if such uniqueness even existed. Instead, its cultural familiarity, especially with regard to social practice, was the driving force in creating and growing the movement. While the particular social practice on which I am focusing is likely only one among several social factors, I will argue that the culturally pervasive pattern of worship of small groups of gods provides the familiarity necessary for the Corinthian gentiles to join the movement. What follows in this introduction and the rest of the book is that educated guess that I mentioned in the Preface and Acknowledgements.

## Some Assumptions about Ancient Religion

My own genesis of inquiry regarding the beginnings of the Christ movement with respect to Paul's groups came mostly after encountering Paul in the

---

[1] Although I think that my scenario in this book with regard to Corinth can be adapted to other locations as a reasonable explanation for why gentiles were motivated to join the movement in those places.

classroom. I have taught about Paul and his letters annually since the spring of 2001 and, as each year passed, I became more and more confused. Certainly, Paul's letters can be confusing in their content; the last 150 years of scholarship would attest to that. But what troubled me most was why an average gentile would have ever been attracted to becoming a follower of Christ because of Paul's appeals.[2] Was it the inevitable call towards monotheism that Paul's Judaism began? Was it the promise of individual salvation that 'pagan religion' could not offer? Was it the charisma of Paul that drew them? Or did the 'truth of the gospel' slay Paul's audiences? The more I reflected on these and other options and learned about the ancient world, the more thoroughly modern they seemed and the more unsatisfied I became with traditional explanations for the growth of Paul's Christ movement.

Many scholars have argued that Paul and his movement were firmly situated in first-century Judaism,[3] however one describes that complex religious,

---

[2] 'Luke's evident interest in portraying a Paul eager to use the scriptures for proving the truth of the gospel is part and parcel of his overall theological project. The truth is, however, that people are not turned into converts by theological arguments, certainly not by arguments hurled precipitately at them by a stranger from abroad.' John Ashton, *The Religion of Paul the Apostle* (New Haven: Yale University Press, 2000), 162–3. Calvin J. Roetzel, *Paul: The Man and the Myth* (Columbia, SC: University of South Carolina Press, 1998), 63, says, 'A generation ago, Nils Dahl's exegesis of Rom. 3:29–30 showed that Paul's radical monotheism that forbade any distinction between Jew and Gentile owes something to a Hellenistic philosophical monotheism with strong cosmopolitan or universalistic tendencies. This universalizing tendency, however, when combined with the apocalypticism of Paul's Jewish heritage produced a hybrid that also generated explosive tensions between inclusion and exclusion, between boundlessness or universalization and boundedness or particularity. By Turner's model, Paul would have been a liminal figure between two worlds – one dying and one being born – and also on the boundary between two communities – one Jewish and the other gentile. And the tensions between these worlds were so great that the logic of Paul's gentile mission defied human understanding, as we see in Rom. 11:25–36, and its mystery was hidden in the mystery of the Godhead itself.'

[3] This trend was spearheaded by E. P. Sanders in his revolutionary *Paul and Palestinian Judaism: A Comparison of Patterns and Religion* (Minneapolis: Fortress Press, 1977), but it has continued with a growing number of scholars from both similar perspectives to and very different ones from Sanders's work: John G. Gager, *Reinventing Paul* (Oxford: Oxford University Press, 2000) and *Who Made Early Christianity? The Jewish Lives of the Apostle Paul* (New York: Columbia University Press, 2015); Pamela Michele Eisenbaum, *Paul Was Not a Christian: The Original Message of a Misunderstood Apostle* (New York: HarperOne, 2009); Joshua D. Garroway, *Paul's Gentile-Jews: Neither Jew nor Greek, but Both* (New York: Palgrave Macmillan, 2012); Albert J. Harrill, *Paul the Apostle: His Life and Legacy in Their Roman Context* (Cambridge: Cambridge University Press, 2012); Mark D. Nanos and Magnus Zetterholm, eds., *Paul within Judaism Restoring the First-Century Context to the Apostle* (Minneapolis: Fortress Press, 2015); Gabriele Boccaccini and Carlos A. Segovia, *Paul the Jew: Rereading the Apostle as a Figure of Second Temple Judaism* (Minneapolis: Fortress Press, 2016). Of course, the table was set many years earlier by Krister Stendahl in his ground-breaking article 'The Apostle Paul and the Introspective Conscience of the West', *HTR* 56 (1963): 199–215, an article originally delivered as a talk to the American Psychological Association, and then subsequently revised and published.

social, ethnic, cultural phenomenon in Greek and Roman contexts.[4] Paul may have reinterpreted his Jewish heritage in light of what he thought about Jesus, but the most convincing arguments about him keep him within Judaism. However, Paul describes himself as an apostle to the *gentiles* in his writings. Whatever one might say about the character of his groups ('Jewish',[5] 'Christian',[6] 'Jewish-Christian',[7] 'gentile',[8] 'gentile-Jewish',[9] 'ex-pagan pagans'[10]), we have to account somehow for his success among gentiles for these early years of development of the movement to make sense. So, as we begin our inquiry, it is important to sketch out the basics of how gentile religion worked.

Throughout this book, I am positing a situation that assumes a non-existent divide between what scholars have traditionally thought of as monotheism and polytheism.[11] With regard to the existence of ancient Jewish monotheism,

---

[4] 'This is a Paul who fits within his Jewish, Greek, and Roman contexts by way of conformation rather than contrast ... A Paul, in other words, who lived his life within his native Judaism.' Paula Fredriksen, *Paul: The Pagans' Apostle* (New Haven: Yale University Press, 2017), 175.

[5] While Daniel Boyarin does not treat Paul or his communities in his major work, he does argue for the New Testament to be counted among the Jewish writings of the Second Temple period. Daniel Boyarin, *The Jewish Gospels: The Story of Jesus Christ* (New York: The New Press, 2012). For his full treatment of Paul as an observant Jew trying to redefine Jewish identity of the first century, see Daniel Boyarin, *A Radical Jew: Paul and the Politics of Identity* (Berkeley: University of California Press, 1994).

[6] John Barclay and N.T. Wright both hold that Paul is a Christian theologian and that his communities are neither Jewish nor gentile but Christian. These are two of the most prominent biblical scholars in the field. John M. G. Barclay, *Paul and the Gift* (Grand Rapids, MI: Eerdmans, 2015); N. T. Wright, *Paul and the Faithfulness of God*, 2 vols (Minneapolis: Fortress Press, 2013). See Ann Conway-Jones, 'The New Testament: Jewish or Gentile?', *Expository Times* 130 (2019): 237–42, for a review of the role of Jewish scholars in New Testament studies and the 'correcting' effect that they have regarding Christian 'misunderstandings, distortions, stereotypes and calumnies to recover the various Jewish contexts of Jesus, Paul, and the early Christian movement' (237). However, she still uses the word 'Christian' to designate Paul and his communities and to differentiate them from other Jews of the time.

[7] Garroway, *Paul's Gentile-Jews*, 2, points to this designation, which is common in scholarship to describe Paul and Peter, Priscilla and Aquila, and early figures like them who were Jews who became followers of Jesus. See also Matt Jackson-McCabe, ed., *Jewish Christianity Reconsidered: Rethinking Ancient Groups and Texts* (Minneapolis: Fortress Press, 2007), for a good set of essays addressing this category in the study of the first century.

[8] Stanley Stowers's important work on Romans helpfully reoriented the field to read Paul's letters as directed to gentiles. Stanley K. Stowers, *A Rereading of Romans: Justice, Jews, and Gentiles* (New Haven: Yale University Press, 1994).

[9] This is Joshua Garroway's term. See Garroway, *Paul's Gentile-Jews*.

[10] Fredriksen, *Paul: The Pagan's Apostle*.

[11] Despite the fact that many scholars now think it can be assumed that monotheism did not exist in the first century CE, the writings of many major scholars with large followings in scholarly and popular circles (N. T. Wright and Larry Hurtado, for example) still do assume a monotheism/polytheism divide, and this divide is one that relies on a fairly simplistic and outdated understanding of how polytheism functioned. The fact that Peter Schäfer wrote

many scholars have convincingly argued that the concept of monotheism – the belief that Jews thought only one 'real' god existed for Israel – is simplistic if not completely wrong. Stanley K. Stowers says pointedly, 'Scholars should now know better.'[12] Peter Schäfer says, 'Among the most popular clichés not only in Jewish and Christian theology but also in popular religious belief is the assumption that Judaism is the classic religion of monotheism, and if Judaism did not in fact invent monotheism, then it at least ultimately asserted it.'[13] Paula Fredriksen has argued throughout her work, starting as early as 2005, that the term 'monotheism' should cease to be used, and says that it 'import[s] anachronism and distortion into historical descriptions of the cultural context of Christianity and its origins, in the end obscuring precisely the evidence that they mobilized to illumine'.[14] Many of the main scholars who have written influential works on the topic of ancient Jewish monotheism argue for a strong distinction between Jews and other ancient ethnicities along the traditional lines of monotheism (Jews) and polytheism (gentiles).[15] Even when there is an acknowledgement of mediating figures in early Judaism (angels, patriarchs, personified wisdom, for example), they are not gods but only divine agents and do not account for the claims of the divinity of Jesus in early Christianity. Schäfer writes that this 'results, as Larry Hurtado has stated with particular emphasis, exclusively from the cultic worship and veneration of Jesus, which is what comprises the "binary mutation" in Jewish monotheism that is characteristic of early Christianity'.[16] This sort of thinking sets the stage for a trajectory from Jewish monotheism to the divinity of Christ, to the identification of Christ with the Jewish god that finds its culmination in early church trinitarian doctrines and assertions about the coequal nature of the three persons of god.[17]

---

*Two Gods in Heaven: Jewish Concepts of God in Antiquity* (Princeton: Princeton University Press) in 2020 is a witness to the widespread scholarly assumption of ancient Judaism being monotheistic in nature, despite the evidence against it. The traditional monotheistic sentiment found in scholarship is understandable because the theological identity of modern Christians and Jews is certainly built on this idea. It is difficult to excise or nuance these assumptions when they have been so ingrained for so long.

[12] Stowers wrote this in 2018, but he gave a talk on the topic in 2012. See 'Why "Common Judaism" Does Not Look Like Mediterranean Religion', in *Strength to Strength: Essays in Honor of Shaye J. D. Cohen*, ed. Michael L. Satlow (Atlanta: Brown Judaic Studies, 2018), 250.

[13] Schäfer, *Two Gods in Heaven*, 1 (emphasis mine).

[14] Paula Fredriksen, 'Mandatory Retirement: Ideas in the Study of Christian Origins Whose Time Has Come to Go', *Studies in Religion/Sciences Religieuses* 35 (2006): 231. This article is based on a talk Fredriksen gave in 2005.

[15] See, for example, Richard Bauckham, *God Crucified: Monotheism and Christology in the New Testament* (Carlisle: Paternoster, 1998), and Larry W. Hurtado, *Lord Jesus Christ* (Grand Rapids, MI: Eerdmans, 2003).

[16] Schäfer, *Two Gods in Heaven*, 8.

[17] See ibid., 1–8, for a succinct but compelling summary of the trends in scholarship around the issue of Jewish monotheism and its relationship to developing Christianity.

However, the linearity of this schema does not represent the actual process or the reality of most ancient people, even elite writers in early Judaism and developing Christianity. The evidence against monotheism in the time of Paul is simply too great to adhere to the monotheism/polytheism divide that so many theologically oriented scholars of the New Testament assume.

For those who assume a sharp divide between monotheism and polytheism, the nature of polytheism tends to be built on incorrect or outdated notions of how 'polytheism', or simply religion, worked in the ancient world. Robert Parker says that everyday Greeks would rarely name a particular god when calling on them for help.[18] Yet where everyday Greeks (and Romans and indigenous peoples living in Greek and Roman territories) lived and interacted with the divine world – houses, villages, urban shrines and sanctuaries, sacred groves, ports, rural sanctuaries and so on – gods were identified by name regularly. The inscriptional and archaeological evidence across time and geographical location contains a long record of votive offerings to particular gods. Even if the sacred places and votive offerings do not account for all the evidence of how people interacted with the divine world, it is clear that particular, named gods played a large role in the life of ancient peoples.

Religion in these contexts, however, does not mean just belief in or worship of any and every god in the Greek or Roman (or other countless) pantheons. In reflecting on the nature of Greek religion, Parker says something almost in passing that was first noticed in the nineteenth century: Greeks 'typically prayed not to individual gods but to "chords of gods"',[19] namely, small groups of gods working together and connected to each other in ways based on local traditions.'[20] This idea of a chord of gods being the typical local configuration of gods found among Greeks in various places holds true across the Mediterranean for all sorts of ethnic groups and local populations. As we will see in Chapters One and Two, it is a ubiquitous feature of ancient religion in a variety of types of locations and levels of society – urban and rural, domestic and civic, elite and not so elite. These two basic notions of ancient religion – that there was no monotheism/polytheism divide and that ancients tended to worship and adhere to small groups of gods – are foundational to my argument.

---

[18] Robert Parker, *Polytheism and Society at Athens* (Oxford: Oxford University Press, 2005), 140. See Stowers, 'Why "Common Judaism"', 251, for the discussion.

[19] Robert Parker, *On Greek Religion* (Ithaca: Cornell University Press, 2011), 66.

[20] John Bodel calls this phenomenon 'divine menageries'; he notes that it was 'the common Greco-Roman cultural practice of ... conceiving of [deities] in various fluid combinations and groupings more often than separately and individually. This applied not only to the standard Olympian deities but also to those foreign gods whole legitimacy and place in Roman cult were more ambiguous.' See 'Cicero's Minerva, *Penates*, and the Mother of the *Lares*: An Outline of Roman Domestic Religion', in *Household and Family Religion in Antiquity*, ed. John Bodel and Saul M. Olyan (London: Blackwell, 2008), 255.

## Reconstructing the Early Christ Movement

Stanley Stowers's comments anticipate the kernel of what I will argue in this book:

> The key to the question of why the Corinthians gave some recognition to who Paul was, and what he did, and why they had some interests in him, is not that his message of a crucified Christ and the power of Christ's *pneuma* met a universal intrinsic need or was inherently intelligible or attractive. Rather, the Corinthians possessed fine-grained practical understandings, skill intelligibility, if you will, of most of the practices that Paul advocated, albeit differentiated in various ways, for example, by age, gender, free/slave, elite/non-elite. They therefore already had practical dispositions toward the genres of Paul's doings and sayings, but not necessarily toward his particular interpretations of these practices.[21]

The basic insight here rings true with how I wish to approach the topic of why Paul would have been received by the Corinthians in any sort of positive way. In short, it was because what he was advocating – adherence to and honouring of God the Father, the Lord Jesus Christ and the *pneuma* (for some)[22] – resonated with their local practice of adherence to and honouring of small groups of gods in and around Corinth. It is not just about Paul making an intellectual or theological argument, which is something that would have convinced only a small portion of his audience. It is also about a resonance of practice, namely, a practice familiar to the Corinthians that they also recognised in Paul's appeals. My primary focus will not be on whether Paul intended this resonance or not but on the plausibility of whether his calls to adhere to his god(s) would have been received by the Corinthians as a call to a familiar practice and therefore one that would have been compelling to them.

I am not the first to attempt a reconstruction of the genesis of the Christ movement, and I will not be the last. The scholars are too many to engage with in a productive way. But some of the most exciting work regarding the early decades of the Christ movement comes from a new generation of writers. These scholars are completely rethinking aspects of the movement in the first and second centuries to be much more contextual within the cultures of these centuries and comparative with relevant phenomena in these and

---

[21] Stanley K. Stowers, 'Kinds of Myth, Meals, and Power: Paul and the Corinthians', in *Redescribing Paul and the Corinthians*, ed. Ron Cameron and Merrill P. Miller (Atlanta: SBL, 2011), 128.

[22] In Chapter Three, I will treat the question of how the Corinthians might have understood *pneuma*.

other cultures, rather than driven by later theological and ecclesial concerns. For example, Joshua Garroway's *Paul's Gentile-Jews: Neither Jew nor Gentile, but Both* examines the long-standing question of the nature of Paul's groups: in particular, whether he is aiming to constitute a group of Jews who believe in Jesus as the Messiah or a group of gentiles who believe in Jesus as the Messiah. Rejecting the binary of Jew and gentile, Garroway argues for a spectrum that makes space for a more complex picture of ethnicity in the first century and one that ultimately allows Paul's groups to share characteristics typically described as both Jew and gentile.[23] Maia Katrosits's *Rethinking Early Christian Identity: Affect, Violence, and Belonging* is a fascinating reappraisal of several important texts from the late first and early second century through the lenses of affect and diaspora. She argues that these works are not about 'negotiating or generating a distinctly Christian self-understanding, belief system, or set of practices, but are thick with the dynamics of national haunting and ongoing and transgenerational trauma'.[24]

Giovanni B. Bazzana's *Having the Spirit of Christ: Spirit Possession and Exorcism in the Early Christ Groups* is both anthropological and broadly comparative in ways that help us understand Paul's claims of being 'in Christ' and 'having the spirit of Christ' literally, as a claim of actual spirit possession on Paul's part and as an assertion by Paul that the community is possessed by the spirit of Christ.[25] Daniel Ulluci's *The Christian Rejection of Animal Sacrifice* calls for a rethinking and recontextualisation of ancient animal sacrifice and therefore a reconsideration of why early Christians rejected the practice. He attempts a more thoroughgoing comparative model for understanding animal sacrifice in the ancient world and situates it within the wider cultural pattern of reciprocity and gift-giving.[26] And Jennifer Eyl's *Signs, Wonders and Gifts: Divination in the Letters of Paul*, which is also comparative but limited to ancient cultures, convincingly demonstrates that Paul's claims to have performed miracles, acts of power and prophetic utterances reflect typical forms of divination in the ancient world.[27] All of this scholarship follows previous generations of scholars who recast the early years of the Christ movement to be much more

---

[23] Garroway, *Paul's Gentile-Jews*; see also Joshua D. Garroway, *The Beginning of the Gospel: Paul, Philippi, and the Origins of Christianity* (New York: Palgrave Macmillan, 2018).

[24] Maia Kotrosits, *Rethinking Early Christian Identity: Affect, Violence, and Belonging* (Minneapolis: Fortress, 2015), 1.

[25] Giovanni B. Bazzana, *Having the Spirit of Christ: Spirit Possession and Exorcism in the Early Christ Groups* (New Haven: Yale University Press, 2020).

[26] Daniel Ullucci, *The Christian Rejection of Animal Sacrifice* (Oxford: Oxford University Press, 2012).

[27] Jennifer Eyl, *Signs, Wonders, and Gifts: Divination in the Letters of Paul* (Oxford: Oxford University Press, 2019).

contextualised within the social and cultural contexts of the first few centuries of the common era.[28]

While there are strengths and weaknesses of each of these books, all of them are highly contextual, situating the attitudes and practices of these early groups within the social worlds of their times. And they all draw upon modern social theory to ground their investigations, all with intriguing and interesting results that have shifted our understanding of the way in which the Christ movement developed and lived within the first and second centuries. *The Origins of the Corinthian Christ Group* aims to perform a similar type of contextual analysis, but it focuses on the ancient practice of worship of small groups of gods and the construction of the groups themselves. My research has been indirectly strengthened by the work of these scholars, even if I am studying an aspect of Paul's world that is parallel or correlative to their foci.

## Social Theory of Practice

*The Origins of the Corinthian Christ Group* examines the ancient Mediterranean human social practices of the worship of gods and the human construction of divine society. Although I am most focused on practice at Corinth in the first century CE, I will argue for a pattern of practice that stretched both backwards and forwards several centuries across the entirety of the ancient Mediterranean world at every level of society and in various worship contexts. This pattern of practice reflects not simply coincidental local activity but a pattern so widespread, ubiquitous and long-standing that it constitutes a true social pattern of practice akin to what Marcel Mauss and Pierre Bourdieu call *habitus*, and which later critics of Bourdieu's work like Brenda Farnell and Theodore Schatzki refine into more precise descriptions of social practice. The evidence that we have of ancient social life is scant when compared with what modern social theorists can access. But the insights of theorists can help describe some aspects of the evidence of ancient social activity, even if incompletely, and help scholars of the beginnings of the Christ movement redescribe the evidence and perhaps offer more plausible explanations of these originating years than has been offered to date.

What all these social theorists grapple with constructively and helpfully for our purposes is the way that patterns of human activity create social expectations and common understandings of these activities. Humans do not act in a punctiliar fashion, completely unrelated to what came before their actions or

---

[28] The work of Wayne Meeks, Dale B. Martin, L. L. Welborn, Stanley K. Stowers, Jonathan Z. Smith, Burton Mack and the many scholars of the Redescribing Christian Origins group at the Society of Biblical Literature come to mind as major influences for these scholars and for the present work.

to how others act around them. Instead, there is a continuity of activity that carries forward from past, long-standing local and regional customs (such as worshipping small groups of gods) and extends outward from the individual in ways understandable to, expected by and even shaped by other humans in that locality and region. Practices (in the technical sense I will describe below) are inherently social, understandable and repeated through actions by those who interact with each other. And there is an individual and group self-interest in practice, which allows us to imagine scenarios of understanding (or misunderstanding) among Paul and his Corinthian interlocutors based on practice. Why would Paul preach something radically unfamiliar and incomprehensible to his adherents and expect them to be attracted to it? Would his interlocutors have expected what Paul was asking of them to fit with their practices and have ends similar to those that had motivated them to carry on their traditions from time immemorial? For his adherents to be even mildly interested in or attracted to what Paul had to offer, would there not have to be some basic similarity between their practices and his, between their nexus of doings and sayings and his?

The insights of these social theorists, especially those of Schatzki, ground the argument in this book and allow me to examine the evidence for patterns of activity and discourse around divine–human interaction in the ancient world. They give me space to argue that Paul's practices (particularly his doings and sayings about a father god, his son (Jesus, Christ, lord) and *pneuma*) would have constituted a similar set of practices to ones known to his Corinthian interlocutors. They permit me to posit a scenario of attraction to Paul's initial solicitations to join the movement. And perhaps they can even help me to account for some of Paul's efforts to explicate and clarify his practices in light of some of the differences in the group's continued practices.

I use 'practice' as a technical term meaning a 'nexus of sayings and doings', as defined by Theodore Schatzki, but his work rests on and is a response to that of Marcel Mauss and Pierre Bourdieu, among others. Mauss formulated his notion of *habitus* by observing the varying bodily habits of different large groups of people – differing ways of running, swimming, marching, digging with certain kinds of shovels and so on across various societies. These are not just socially agreed-upon habits, according to Mauss, but are deeply engrained practices that are formed with extensive and explicit education in bodily techniques to create 'the art of using the human body'.[29] Mauss explains that one of three elements is usually used to explain the habitual actions of humans: the act of imitation, the psychology of the group, or the biology of the individuals. Instead, he argues, 'the whole, the ensemble, is conditioned

---

[29] Marcel Mauss, *Sociology and Psychology: Essays*, trans. Ben Brewster (London: Routledge & Kegan Paul, 1979), 101–2 (quote at 101).

by the three elements indissolubly mixed together'.[30] Embodied action, for Mauss, is thoroughly social in nature.

Bourdieu takes the notion of *habitus* further, wishing 'to account for the "practical knowledge" of social actors', as Brenda Farnell has put it.[31] Bourdieu's *habitus* points to the dispositions that give rise to action, dispositions that are 'structured structures, predisposed to function as structuring structures, that is, as principles of the generation and structuring of practices and representations' that are not based on 'obedience to rules'.[32] The *habitus* is a system of 'durable, transposable dispositions' that creates a common-sense world of actions that people and groups perform.[33] These actions are not consciously reflected upon by the group but are nonetheless deemed acceptable and 'right' (not in an ethical way but in a sensible way) or appropriate in a particular situation. Individuals do not think about their actions in these situations because the appropriate way to act emerges automatically from the *habitus*.[34] 'In short,' says Bourdieu, 'the *habitus*, the product of history, produces individual and collective practices, and hence history, in accordance with the schemes engendered by history.'[35] He envisions the habitus as self-perpetuating, describing it as 'a past which survives in the present and tends to perpetuate itself into the future'.[36] The *habitus*, in other words, is the social history of dispositions that shapes an individual's actions without predetermining them, and it underlies all social experience. In his theory of the *habitus*, Bourdieu tries to account for the social patterns of practice at the same time as he allows for individual actions and agency within those social patterns.[37]

---

[30] Ibid., 102.

[31] Brenda Farnell, 'Getting Out of the Habitus: An Alternative Model of Dynamically Embodied Social Action', *Journal of the Royal Anthropological Institute* 6 (2000): 401.

[32] Pierre Bourdieu, *Outline of a Theory of Practice*, trans. Richard Nice (Cambridge: Cambridge University Press, 1977), 72. One can see Bourdieu's indebtedness to structuralism and his desire to move away from it to allow for decisions that are not predetermined by structures. His *habitus* is the force in the middle ground between actions determined by structures and actions undertaken completely free from constraint. He further says, 'It is, of course, never ruled out that the responses of the habitus may be accompanied by a strategic calculation tending to carry on quasi-consciously the operation the habitus carries on in a quite different way, namely an estimation of changes which assumes the transformation of the past effect into the expected objective' (76).

[33] Bourdieu, *Outline of a Theory of Practice*, 72. The note attached to this quote says, 'The word *disposition* seems particularly suited to express what is covered by the concept of habitus (defined as a system of dispositions). It expresses first the *result of an organizing action*, with a meaning close to that of words such as structure; it also designates a *way of being*, a habitual state (especially of the body) and, in particular, a *predisposition, tendency, propensity,* or *inclination*' (emphasis original).

[34] See ibid., 80.

[35] Ibid., 82.

[36] Ibid., 82.

[37] See Farnell, 'Getting Out of the Habitus', 401–2.

There have been critiques of Bourdieu's social theory of *habitus*. Brenda Farnell points out that 'dispositions in the *habitus* are not grounded in any clear conception of human agency' because there is a residual Cartesian dualism in Bourdieu's thought, one that '*internalizes* . . . tacit knowledge at the level of the individual when talking of dispositions, and *externalizes* it when talking of the collectivity, because the *habitus* is also a social phenomenon'.[38] She argues that causal powers theory offers a way to avoid this residual Cartesian dualism. Causal powers theory is born out of the philosophy of science but its importance for social theory was articulated by C. R. Varela (among others), who argued that

> the ideas of substance, causation and agency are internally compatible with each other. In this light human agency entails both that the person is a real entity – a substance – and that the exercise of agency is a real event – a causal force.[39]

According to Farnell, the theory 'replaces the dualisms of individual vs. society and subjectivist vs. objectivist with the joint activity of empowered embodied persons using vocal and action signs'.[40]

An aspect or development of causal powers theory (which Farnell deems 'conversational realism') is constituted by the idea that human social order is brought into being through the managing of symbols: vocal signs and action signs grounded in biology (that is, the body) but not determined by it. The formulation of balance that Bourdieu sought between determinism and individualism is also noticeable in conversational realism and causal powers theory, but the two are brought together in the latter, whereas Bourdieu's theory keeps them separate, according to Farnell. The result is that causal powers theory sees the human as 'naturally cultural', and social order as created through the interaction (conversation) among humans. This aspect of causal powers theory can help us bridge the gap of the Corinthians' non-verbal reflections on their actions regarding small groups of gods and Paul's verbal appeals to the Corinthians found in his letters.

Theodore Schatzki critiques Bourdieu and other practice theorists who 'overintellectualize practices and actions',[41] a critique similar to that of Farnell who points to the abstraction and the lack of grounding of agency for the *habitus*

---

[38] Ibid., 406, 403. Emphasis original.

[39] C. R. Verela, 'Cartesianism Revisited: The Ghost in the Moving Machine or the Lived Body', in *Human Action Signs in Cultural Context: The Visible and the Invisible in Movement and Dance*, ed. B. Farnell (Metuchen, NJ: Scarecrow Press, 1995), 218.

[40] Farnell, 'Getting Out of the Habitus', 405.

[41] Theodore R. Schatzki, 'Practices and Actions: A Wittgensteinianism Critique of Bourdieu and Giddens', *Philosophy of the Social Sciences* 27 (1997): 285.

and the separation of the *habitus* from actions. Schatzki argues that Wittgenstein offers a way to avoid this over-intellectualising with his explanation of practical understanding and intelligibility in practice. Schatzki describes Bourdieu's *habitus* as a 'consortium of different senses' that are directly written in the body. This bodily, practical understanding is the basis for human activity.[42] But he points out that Bourdieu's theory does not account for the fact that people cannot explain their actions, so the content of practice can never be articulated for Bourdieu. Schatzki's appeal to Wittgenstein allows him to draw upon the concept of teleoaffectivity, defined as 'orientations towards ends and how things matter'. He goes on to say, 'The sole universal feature of teleoaffectivity is the omnipresence of affectivity: human activity continuously expresses the emotions, moods, and feelings ignored in Bourdieu . . . Teleology . . . is usually the prime organizing axis of activity.'[43]

Schatzki's focus on ends is important because he describes actions (human activity in the moment) as derived from practices (patterns of human activity over time), as Bourdieu does, but puts forth a threefold organisation of practices – practices which include religious practices as one of the major categories:

> Each can be understood to be an open-ended set of actions linked by (a) pools of practical understanding [knowing how to do something, identifying that thing, and responding to that thing[44]], (b) arrays of explicit rules, and (c) a teleoaffective structure . . . a field of right and acceptable combinations of teleoaffectivity-housing conditions of life.[45]

He adds a fourth component in a later work: general understandings.[46] Above all, for Schatzki, practices are inherently social, expressed 'in the *nexus of doings and sayings* that compose them, as opposed to the individual doings and sayings involved'.[47]

Interaction with and adherence to small groups of gods was a distinct and widespread pattern among ancient inhabitants of the Mediterranean, which I will describe in more detail in Chapters Two and Three. Elements of the modern social theories that I have briefly described above can be helpful for articulating the pattern of interaction and adherence as a practice – a nexus of sayings and doings – ingrained in people's cultural traditions for generations. Elements of these theories can also help describe the ways in which the

---

[42] Ibid., 295.
[43] Ibid., 301 (both quotations).
[44] Theodore R. Schatzki, *The Site of the Social: A Philosophical Account of the Constitution of Social Life and Change* (University Park, PA: Pennsylvania State University Press, 2002), 77.
[45] Schatzki, 'Practices and Actions', 303–4.
[46] Schatzki, *The Site of the Social*, 77.
[47] Ibid., 88 (emphasis mine).

Corinthians and Paul conversed with each other (in the sense that Farnell theorises conversation), with a presumed common understanding, at least initially, and the ways in which Paul might have responded to the Corinthians when the presumed common understanding actually turned out not to be so common. While the social theories of practice underlie the whole of the rest of this book, I will be explicit about how they ground the argument at particularly important points.

## Context and Comparison

What is also common to the newer scholarship that examines the first decades and centuries of the Christ movement is the contextualisation of different aspects of the movement. Contextualisation requires comparison of these aspects with those in the larger cultural contexts of the members of the movement, or comparison with cognate phenomena in other cultures from different time periods. As much as possible, I will be transparent about my contextualisation and comparisons, and I will limit them to the ancient world. But first it is important to clarify the terms 'context' and 'comparison' since they are so important to this project.

In *The Site of the Social*, Schatzki spends a fair amount of time discussing 'context' in ways that are helpful for my argument. At the outset, he says, 'Context, at bottom, is simply that portion of what that something is beholden to for its character and existence, the sum-total of everything other than itself that determines these.'[48] He goes on to name three aspects of context. (1) Context 'surrounds' or 'immerses' that for which it serves as a context: 'Things are entangled or suspended in contexts' and, obviously, contexts are larger than that in which something is entangled and includes more than one entity.[49] (2) Contexts determine that which they encompass and 'confer value and significance on entities and events in it'.[50] And (3) 'Context is its own composition . . . which varies with the entities and phenomena that exist in context.'[51] In other words, context has almost a symbiotic relationship with that which it contextualises. For our purposes, this means that we cannot think of Paul's divine figures separate from the greater context in which these figures exist. Whether that is Judaism or not depends upon whether Paul is the focus of our inquiry or whether the Corinthians are. With the Corinthians being the focus, the context should be the religious practice and discourse of Corinth, and Corinth as contextualised in the greater Mediterranean world.

[48] Ibid., 60.
[49] Ibid., 61.
[50] Ibid., 62.
[51] Ibid., 62–3.

Many traditional reconstructions of the earliest moments of Paul's work among the Corinthians and other groups have a common tendency to argue for what might be unique about the early Christ movement – what might have set it apart from other Jewish groups, gentile religious communities, or contemporary movements.[52] Uniqueness is not what we should be after. The great theorist and historian of religions Jonathan Z. Smith points out that the kind of comparison that seeks out uniqueness – only difference – is dangerously one-sided and can be used to justify purported superiority of Christianity over other religions.[53] In discussing the idea of uniqueness among those scholars with a Christian apologetic bent, Smith argues that comparison is simply a cypher to bolster claims of superiority, which actually undermines true comparison: '"Unique" becomes an ontological rather than taxonomic category; an assertion of radical difference so absolute that it becomes "Wholly Other", and the act of comparison is perceived as both an impossibility and an impiety.'[54]

If the historian of early Christianity wishes to understand this movement in comparison with other contemporary social groups, they must compare both the similarities and differences, and not just the differences. In a more focused way, to use Smith's classic formulation, we have to perform a scholarly comparison about phenomena in the ancient world triadically: '$x$ resembles $y$ more than $z$ with respect to . . .', where the 'with respect to' corresponds with a scholar's interest or main question.[55] To focus only on the differences leads to a portrait of early Christianity as exceptional, unique among the movements of the ancient world, thereby denying the complex social, cultural and historical dynamics that resulted in the development of this small movement into a

---

[52] See Jan Bremmer, *The Rise of Christianity, through the Eyes of Gibbon, Harnack and Rodney Stark* (Groningen: Barkhuis, 2010), 73: 'In its unity, exclusivity, social practices and religious beliefs Christianity offered a combination that was both unique and clearly highly attractive to the inhabitants of the Roman Empire, even though explanation of individual choices are hard to find.'

[53] See Jonathan Z. Smith, *Drudgery Divine: On the Comparison of Early Christianities and the Religions of Late Antiquity* (Chicago: University of Chicago Press, 1990), 25, where he concluded his analysis of the earliest scholars in the modern Western tradition who sought the origins of Christianity in the ancient world: 'the broader issues remain even when their apologetic context is less overt, when one term – the early Christian – is more highly valued than the other, as, for example, in the footnotes in biblical commentaries up to the present day'.

[54] Ibid., 38. As Smith further argues, unique as an ontological category usually falls along the lines of the Protestant/Catholic divide: 'One can formulate the principle of comparison that has informed the majority of scholarship in this area as follows: "Apostolic Christianity" and "Protestantism" are "unique"; the religions of Late Antiquity, most especially the "mysteries" and "Catholicism", are the "same" . . . Early Christianity is primarily to be considered as autochthonus' (ibid., 45–6).

[55] Ibid., 51.

widespread religious and political power within a few hundred years.⁵⁶ I would further argue, along with many others, that as much as we might like to think that the compelling nature of the early Christ movement resided in its uniqueness, its similarities to its context might have had just as much, if not more, power to attract its earliest followers.⁵⁷

As Giovanni Bazzana recently commented,

> The reality of the matter is that everything we write is methodologically grounded in exercises of comparison, even though we may be reluctant

---

⁵⁶ See ibid., 117. Along with *Drudgery Divine*, Jonathan Z. Smith's bibliography on comparison is both foundational to the study of religion and vast. I offer only a sampling: 'In Comparison a Magic Dwells', in *Imagining Religion: From Babylon to Jonestown* (Chicago: University of Chicago Press, 1988), 19–35; 'Differential Equations: On Constructing the Other', in *Relating Religion: Essays in the Study of Religion* (Chicago: University of Chicago Press, 2004), 230–50; 'What a Difference a Difference Makes', in *Relating Religion*, 251–302.

On the importance of comparison, John Kloppenborg, 'Greco-Roman Thiasoi, the Ekklesia at Corinth, and Conflict Management', in *Redescribing Paul and the Corinthians*, ed. Cameron and Miller, 189, says, 'My interests instead have to do with the process by which humans discover or create loci of meaning and the conditions under which various loci fail or perdure. This is inevitably a social process and one that includes both discursive practices and social arrangements bundled together. Such an interest makes comparison crucial, for the very act of assembling differences and similarities between groups with quite different origins, appearances, and fates helps to problematize particular aspects of the group under study, and to raise questions about what in the complex chemistry of social practice and belief helps to account for the success of one group and the failure of another.' Eva Ebel, *Die Attraktivität früher christlicher Gemeinden. Die Gemeinde von Korinth im Spiegel griechisch-römischer Vereine* (Tübingen: Mohr Siebeck, 2004), tries to make a very narrow comparison, but she focuses on the similarities between two associations (*thiasoi* or *collegia*) and the Corinthian assembly for her comparison.

Kloppenborg's extensive work on associations (see especially John Kloppenborg, *Christ Associations: Connecting and Belonging in the Ancient City* (New Haven: Yale University Press, 2019)) is more expansive and useful than Ebel's work, and it is certainly appropriate to compare these social phenomena to the Corinthian groups. But this comparison does not answer the question of the initial attractiveness or success that Paul and the other early leaders had in getting Corinthians even to pay attention to their appeals. Comparison between Paul's Corinthian group and Corinthian *thiasoi/collegia* is certainly a good thing and can yield a great deal of insight into the nature of the Corinthian group. But it assumes that there was already a formed assembly. I am interested in the attraction before the assembly was formed – if it ever was during Paul's lifetime. See Stowers, 'Kinds of Myth', 109: 'In my view, two things are very clear from the evidence of the Corinthian letters: first, Paul very much wanted the people to whom he wrote to be a community, and he held a theory saying that God had miraculously made them into a community "in Christ"; second, the Corinthians never did sociologically form a community and only partly and differentially shared Paul's interests and formation. In my estimation, it is very unlikely that "the Corinthians" ever had any more social organization than households that may have had previous ties with other households and, after Paul, a roughly shared knowledge that Paul wanted them to be an *ekklēsia* in Christ, and that he kept telling them that God had transformed them into one.'

⁵⁷ See Eyl, *Signs, Wonders, and Gifts*, 20–30, for a similar assessment.

to admit it. Could there be any analysis of ancient literary genres without comparison among literary productions across cultures and epochs? Could there be any study of inflation in the ancient economic world without comparison with the economic structures of more modern periods?[58]

Bruce Lincoln has likewise written copiously on comparison, and much of his work has included performing careful comparative analyses of texts from different cultures or within the same culture.[59] His most succinct formulation of the comparative method comes in his 'Theses on Comparison', where he both extolls comparison as the basis for understanding (as so many before him have) and warns against bias and overreach in comparison, with 'collegial criticism' as the necessary check against it.[60] Lincoln further delineates two types of comparison: strong comparison and weak comparison. He describes strong comparison as 'wide-ranging comparison', which 'has consistently disappointed' because it is limited to superficial analysis of a large number of examples and tend to reflect the imaginations of the analysts more than the data itself.[61] Weak comparisons, on the other hand, are 'more modest' but lend themselves to deeper analysis because they focus on a small number of *comparanda*. Key for our purposes are his last three characteristics of weak comparisons: (1) they 'are equally attentive to relations of similarity and those of difference';[62] (2) they 'grant equal dignity and intelligence to all parties

---

[58] Giovanni Bazzana, 'The Challenges of Comparison: A Response to Peter Struck', *Synergistic Pneumatic: A Syndicate Symposium*. Accessed 26 August 2022. https://syndicate.network/symposia/theology/synergistic-pneumata/

[59] As with J. Z. Smith, Bruce Lincoln's bibliography of comparative analyses is extensive, but some of the major collections include *Apples and Oranges: Explorations in, on, and with Comparison* (Chicago: University of Chicago Press, 2018); *Discourse and the Construction of Society* (New York: Oxford University Press, 1989; 2nd ed. 2014); *Myth, Cosmos, and Society: Indo-European Themes of Creation and Destruction* (Cambridge, MA: Harvard University Press, 1986). *Theorizing Myth* (Chicago: University of Chicago Press, 1999), although reaching beyond comparison, has at the heart of its methodology of myth analysis that of comparison of different versions of comparable stories. See ch. 7 for both Lincoln's definition of myth and his process for comparative analysis of myths.

[60] Bruce Lincoln, 'Theses on Comparison', in *Comparer en historie does religions antiques*, ed. Claude Calame and Bruce Lincoln (Liège: Presses universitaires de Liège, 2012), 99–110. Online version, https://books.openedition.org/pulg/8058, thesis 5, para. 6, hereafter the version cited.

[61] Ibid., thesis 6, para. 7. Lincoln lists 'the books of Lévi-Strauss, Dumézil, and Eliade ... Max Müller and Frazer as cautionary examples'.

[62] I strive to highlight both of these, especially with respect to the ways in which Paul may have tried to negotiate the differences between what he envisions for the Corinthians and what they are practising, presumably based on their traditions.

considered';[63] and (3) they 'are attentive to the social, historical and political contexts and subtexts of religious and literary texts'.[64]

Lincoln's insight into comparison is invaluable, but there are several aspects of it that need comment and perhaps modification as we embark on the main argument of this book. First, although the concepts of 'strong' and 'weak' comparisons are clear enough, the terminology is not intuitively matched with the concepts. 'Strong' is actually the less precise and more superficial comparison and 'weak' is the more precise and insightful. I think it might be more helpful to use the terms 'generalised' and 'localised' in place of 'strong' and 'weak', respectively, while keeping the content of Lincoln's categories. I prefer these alternative terms because they also lend themselves to a non-binary construction of comparison, thereby allowing consideration of modes of comparison as falling along a spectrum.

I will try to adhere to localised comparison as much as possible, but a key part of my argument relies on a widespread pattern of behaviour that requires a fairly superficial comparison of the evidence at a variety of locations across the Mediterranean in different times (see Chapter Two). This initial comparative work will necessarily resemble generalised comparison more than localised. But in order to avoid some of the pitfalls of generalised comparison that Lincoln points out, my comparative argument will not stop at generalised comparison. It will progress to more and more focused (that is, localised) comparison as I move from the wider Mediterranean to Corinth and then to Paul's writings (Chapters Three and Four). Second, Lincoln's method of comparison is focused almost exclusively on literary evidence. His work shines most brightly when comparing two or more versions of a story, or two or more literary expressions of a similar cultural phenomenon. But his comparisons do not usually venture very far beyond the literary, whereas the kinds of comparisons that I will perform later in this study will necessarily include a wide variety of evidence – literary, architectural, inscriptional, archaeological, art historical (statues and sculptures), numismatic and so on. This range of evidence makes comparison all the more difficult because I have to be sure that the evidence that I am comparing is legitimately comparable.

Without exclusively literary texts of similar stories to compare, I have to create somewhat abstract categories that are apparent in a wide range of evidence – categories that can accurately describe the practice and the meanings of the practice to argue for the pattern I wish to bring into conversation with Paul's writings. Ultimately, I am comparing systems of religious practice in Corinth and arguing for a fundamental similarity with respect to this practice between Paul's Corinthians and Paul himself. In Smith's terms, I am comparing

---

[63] I have kept this in mind when examining evidence not just from elite quarters of the ancient world but from as many social contexts as possible.

[64] Lincoln, 'Theses on Comparison', thesis 12, para. 13. This is really the backbone of my argument.

Corinthian religious practice to Paul's religious practice with respect to small groups of gods. In order to do this effectively, I have to consider particular categories to compare that will help me redescribe the similarities between the practice of the Corinthians and that of Paul. Therefore, these categories need explication and definition. Key to my argument is that the practices I intend to consider rely on small groups of gods being connected locally through genealogy, mythology (or myth), history and cultic practice.

## Intertwined Categories of Analysis

In order to make plausible the cultural similarities between Corinthian practice and Pauline practice, I need to define what I mean by several categories that are difficult to completely separate from each other, namely genealogy, mythology (or myth), history and cultic practice. **Genealogy** simply means the relationship between a god and his or her fellow gods at a sanctuary. Most often this refers to their familial relationship, such as the fact that Apollo and Asklepios are father and son. While there is abundant material evidence for Apollo and Asklepios being worshipped or honoured in Asklepieia across the Mediterranean, the material evidence does not usually express the relationship between the two gods. It is assumed by the sanctuary's local participants because there is a long tradition of these two gods being related as father and son. But we learn about this relationship in texts – mostly mythological texts. The problem with genealogy is that these familial relationships are often expressed in mythological terms.

Without going into the long history of scholarship on myth and mythology, which would take us way off course, it might help to discuss some recent scholarship, particularly that of Wendy Doniger, Bruce Lincoln and Russell McCutcheon. Their scholarship redescribes myth and mythmaking in ways that go beyond detailed genre description and talk more about the way that they fit within social discourse and formation. I begin with the line of inquiry that Wendy Doniger takes in *The Implied Spider* in defining myth, one that is thoroughly social in nature.

> In its positive and enduring sense, what a myth *is* is a story that is sacred to and shared by a group of people who find their most important meanings in it; it is a story believed to have been composed in the past about an event in the past, or more rarely, in the future, an event that continues to have meaning in the present because it is remembered; it is a story that is part of a larger group of stories.[65]

---

[65] Wendy Doniger, *The Implied Spider: Politics and Theology in Myth* (New York: Columbia University Press, 1998), 2 (emphasis original).

Notice how Doniger uses 'sacred' in this definition. Sacredness is not something that can be divorced from the people who read the story; a story is sacred *to* a group of people because it is 'shared' and 'remembered' and thus has enduring meaning. The story is not ontologically sacred but gains its sacredness in relation to those who remember it. The only thing that this definition does not account for is when authors change the stories they receive, and we can observe this change as it is happening, as in Paul's retelling of Israel's sacred stories in light of his purported experience of Christ. Later in *The Implied Spider*, Doniger reflects about the process of comparison as an art rather than a science, which she follows with these suggestive comments:

> After all, a novelist does not create *ab ovo, de nihilo*, any more than the spider (or mythmaker) can; the poet uses available words, with all their associations . . . The comparatist is not a painter but a collagist, indeed a bricolagist (or a *bricoleur*), just like the mythmakers themselves.[66]

Paul's activities as mythmaker would seem to fit into this idea fairly well, but Bruce Lincoln's notions about myth supplement Doniger's and perhaps make better sense of Paul. After writing and thinking about ideology for many years of his academic career, Lincoln builds off an intriguing element of Mauss's and Durkheim's notions of myth: 'Every mythology is fundamentally a classification, but one which borrows its principles from religious beliefs, not from scientific ideas.'[67] Lincoln calls their understanding of myth undeveloped and terms it 'taxonomy in narrative form'.[68] He notices that there is nothing neutral about taxonomy because of its inherent ordering of the elements classified. He says,

> Pursuing these lines of thought, I am thus inclined to argue that when a taxonomy is encoded in mythic form, the narrative packages a specific, contingent system of discrimination in a particularly attractive and memorable form. What is more, it naturalizes and legitimates it. Myth, then, is not just taxonomy, but *ideology* in narrative form.[69]

What I find useful about Lincoln's notion of myth is that it does not dwell on the generic elements of ancient or long-ago text forms. Instead, what makes the story mythic is the fact that its meaning is contingent on the historical moment of those who receive the text, especially when a tradition is modified

---

[66] Ibid., 77.
[67] Cited in Lincoln, *Theorizing Myth*, 271n17.
[68] Ibid., 146–7.
[69] Ibid., 147 (emphasis original).

by someone who transmits it in a modified form.[70] This is something that Russell McCutcheon develops in his short treatment of myth.

Following Roland Barthes and Burton Mack, McCutcheon redescribes myth as a thoroughly human activity, something that 'turn[s] the collective agreements of a people into truths held to be self-evident'.[71] He goes on to argue that mythmaking is fundamentally a process of social formation, and, with Barthes, Lincoln, Mack and Benedict Anderson, he concludes that 'by means of mythmaking local, symbolic worlds of significance are authorized and naturalized by being (mis)taken for or actively portrayed as universal, literal ones. This is the role of ideology in human affairs.'[72] So, processes of mythmaking are not just about the nature of the stories from long ago but '*historical processes of reinterpretation* [of] tradition' as J. Z. Smith says.[73] The line between myth and history really is blurred here because, with each generation of interpreters, the history is changed by the interpreter, who imbues it with meaning based on the interpreter's current situation. The writing and recalling of history becomes mythology or mythmaking. Willi Braun's excellent essay on the production of Christian history demonstrates this blurring well.[74] The activity of mythmaking happens in the present and is fundamentally based on the mythmaker's attempt to make sense of their present moment.

So, for our purposes, **history/mythology** or **mythological language** can be understood as the type of language that appeals to and (re)interprets historical traditions, grounds them in time immemorial, naturalises them by imbuing them with particular meanings important to the local population and/or uses them to justify a particular local religious practice. This language can be a story, or it can simply refer to a larger, universally accepted set of stories about a local group, sanctuary, or sacred site.[75] It is within this sort of language that we can identify genealogical or other important relationships between the gods that are important in a local setting. It is also where we can find references to stories where the gods act together in important ways with each other on behalf of local, regional, or universal human groups. The genealogical relationships and perceived collaboration of divine figures is a common pattern found throughout the ancient Mediterranean world, part

---

[70] Lincoln formulates his method for interpreting different versions of myths just after his definition of myth. See ibid., 147–59.
[71] Russell T. McCutcheon, 'Myth', in *The Guide to the Study of Religion*, ed. Willi Braun and Russell T. McCutcheon (London: Continuum, 2000), 201, quoting Mack.
[72] Ibid., 205.
[73] Smith, *Drudgery Divine*, 107 (emphasis original).
[74] Willi Braun, 'Amnesia in the Production of (Christian) History', *Council of Societies for the Study of Religion Bulletin* 28, no. 1 (1999): 3–8.
[75] For an excellent reconstruction of the myth that lies behind much of Paul's writings, see Stowers, 'Kinds of Myth', 123–4.

of the nexus of doings and sayings that constitute practices. It is one way that we can assume that gods at a particular sacred site are related, even if that relationship is not mentioned anywhere at the sacred site. For example, at the sanctuary of Asklepios at Pergamon, Apollo and Asklepios both feature in an inscription describing required actions of human participants in the sanctuary, but nowhere does the inscription speak of their relationship. Because we know something of their relationship from the history/mythology of Asklepios found in a wide variety of literary sources, we can assume that it was common knowledge for those humans who participated in the sanctuary.

Because the common pattern I am trying to demonstrate is not just about historical/mythological speculation but about the wider religious practice of local populations, cultic activity must also be considered an integral part of the pattern of practice of interaction with small groups of gods. As Daniel Ullucci has pointed out when talking about animal sacrifice (a kind of cultic activity), 'To understand sacrifice we must understand the complex social system of which it was a major part.'[76] Cultic activity of Paul's Corinthian assembly would only make sense within the larger social system of Corinth, but the Corinthians would not need to be guided by discursive explanations of their cultic actions within this larger system. They would know what to do as a matter of their 'practical intelligibility', in Schatzki's terms, defined as 'what makes sense to a person to do. [Practical intelligibility] governs action by specifying what an actor does next in the continuous flow of action.'[77] In other words, the Corinthians (and Paul, presumably) knew what to do without needing to justify it when it came to interacting with their gods. What they did was to honour their gods in manifold ways according to tradition as part of a larger ongoing relationship between humans and gods.

One of the popular misnomers about ancient religious systems like those of the Greeks and Romans is that the offering of animals or other substances (grains, liquids, possessions and so on) was done with the expectation of repayment by the god or gods. I give the offering and so the gods are then obligated to grant me my wish in return, so the thinking goes – *do ut des* in other words.[78] The type of exchange in this notion of ancient religion is

---

[76] Ullucci, *The Christian Rejection of Animal Sacrifice*, 15.
[77] Schatzki, *The Site of the Social*, 74–5.
[78] Two art historians, Beth Harris and Steven Zucker, use this characterisation of Greek religion in their video on the sanctuary of Apollo at Delphi (https://www.khanacademy.org/humanities/ancient-art-civilizations/greek-art/daedalic-archaic/v/delphi). James B. Rives, *Religion in the Roman Empire* (Malden, MA: Blackwell, 2007), 24, has a good reminder and qualification of the way reciprocity worked in one aspect of Roman religion, the vow: 'In a vow, the offering was part of a *quid pro quo* arrangement: the worshipper promised a gift to the god if the god granted his or her petition. It is tempting to think of this as a mere exchange, lacking any sense of awe and devotion appropriate to a religious act. But we must keep in

based on the idea of an exchange of goods relatively equal in value, where the first gift automatically results in the second. This is not the kind of giving actually at work in ancient religion. Instead, Ullucci argues that the proper social context for ancient animal sacrifice – and we can expand this to cover all ritual offerings – is that of reciprocity. In the logic of the system of reciprocity, gift-givers give because that is the proper thing to do to create an ongoing relationship between parties. While there might be pressure to return the gift, the gift-giver has no right to demand a gift in return.[79] It is an open-ended relationship.

There are several aspects of reciprocity that are important to highlight. First is the completely voluntary nature of gift-giving in the logic of reciprocity, even if both parties know that their mutual gift-giving has entered them into a certain kind of relationship based on the dynamics of reciprocity.[80] Second, reciprocal gift-giving creates long-term relationships that have *kharis* as a foundation in a Greek context.[81] Robert Parker puts it this way:

> The ideas of reciprocity and repayment are associated with *khari-* words, but not in a direct semantic way. One gift or act endowed with *kharis*, power to please, will call for another, which will in turn evoke yet another; but a *kharis* even when given in return for a *kharis* is not in meaning a recompense, however, it may be so in function.[82]

mind two points. First, since the formal exchange of benefits was something that characterized a wide range of social relationships in the Graeco-Roman world, it is not surprising that it also helped structure relationships between mortals and immortals. Secondly, the external form of a religious act is not in itself evidence for the worshipper's state of mind: we may reasonably expect that people who made vows did so with varying levels of emotional involvement and intellectual commitment ... In many cults sacrifices were organized on a regular schedule; people also made offerings in thanksgiving for particular benefits, even when these were not the subject of a previous vow.'

John Scheid, *An Introduction to Roman Religion*, trans. Janet Lloyd (Bloomington: Indiana University Press, 2003), 98, says something similar: 'Relations between mortals and immortals were founded upon the exchange of gifts and counter-gifts', but he goes on to describe the complexity and range of such gifts and the ambiguity of their meaning in many cases. What they both would have benefited from is grounding their understanding in a more detailed discussion of reciprocity, because statements such as 'exchange of gifts and counter-gifts' and '*quid pro quo* arrangement' could be understood as an equal and obligatory exchange rather than reciprocity.

[79] Ullucci, *The Christian Rejection of Animal Sacrifice*, 26.
[80] Ibid., 24–5.
[81] Ibid., 25.
[82] Robert Parker, 'Pleasing Thighs: Reciprocity in Greek Religion', in *Reciprocity in Ancient Greece* ed. Christopher Gill, Norman Postlethwaite and Richard Seaford (Oxford: Oxford University Press, 1998), 109.

The idea is that gifts are freely given, but the result is that the gift will be received with gratitude and reciprocated, which will then result in more gratitude and reciprocation, where the ultimate dynamic is that of a long-term and ongoing relationship. According to Parker, 'The fundamental conception at all periods is that of an unceasing interchange of delightful gifts and services, a kind of charm war.'[83] Correlative to this idea, which is based on Mauss's insight that the system of gift and counter-gift was a way of forming social relations between humans, is that the same thing happens between humans and gods. Gift-giving with *kharis* at its core establishes and maintains human–gods relationships reciprocally.

Third, reciprocity does not assume equality, either in the value of the gift or in the status of the giver, especially in reciprocal relationships between mortals and immortals. 'If one party gives much and the other returns little, this does not endanger the relationship.'[84] The power dynamics of this unequal relationship are complex, but the act of reciprocal exchange is what maintains the relationship for the long term. The idea of unequal but reciprocal exchange can be seen in the variety of votive offerings in Asklepieia and other sanctuaries, where the supplicant who is healed makes an offering of thanksgiving for the healing. The offering can range from very simple, inexpensive offerings such as simple wooden plaques with a message of thanks to an inscribed silver pig or statue of great value. Any value of offering was acceptable as thanksgiving.

Drawing on these notions of reciprocity, we can define cult or cultic activity as encompassing a wide spectrum of ritual activity that is given to honour a god or divine figure. In our case, **cult** means any ritual honour that is given to a god or divine figure that maintains and reinforces the relationship between the god or divine figure and the practitioner *and* among the local group of gods of a particular sanctuary. In other words, even when a cultic practice is focused on one god (ritual offerings to Asklepios at Epidauros or Piraeus, for example) that cultic practice is part of a larger ritual life at the sanctuary – ritual offerings or hymns sung to other gods (Apollo, Artemis, Mnemosyne and so on) that are necessary to honour all the gods working together at the sanctuary. Cultic activity directed towards one god finds its proper meaning and practice when contextualised and practised in concert with cultic activity to the other gods present in the group. The reasons why these gods are present together in a sanctuary and proper honouring is necessary is reflected in the genealogical, mythical, or historical relationship found in the local or regional traditions of the human group honouring them – hence the intertwined nature of these three analytical categories.

---

[83] Ibid., 109.
[84] Ullucci, *The Christian Rejection of Animal Sacrifice*, 26.

## Structure of *Paul's Chord of Gods*

The structure of this book is fairly simple. I will spend Chapters One and Two describing religious practice focused on small groups of gods – first across a wide variety of geographical locations (Egypt, Israel/Palestine, Asia Minor, Greece and Rome; Chapter One) and then in Corinth and the surrounding regions (Chapter Two). These chapters will form the basis for the relevant context of Paul's writings for my purposes of comparison between his appeals to the Corinthians and how the Corinthians might have received these appeals based on their context. Chapter Three will be occupied with an extended discussion of how the presentation of the *pneuma* in the Corinthian letters could be received by a heterogenous group of Corinthians. I argue that those who had some formal education were a minority in the group and likely would have understood *pneuma* with materialist philosophical understanding, however sophisticated that understanding might have been. But those who were marginally or not educated likely would have understood *pneuma* as a distinct, autonomous divine being. Chapter Four argues in detail that the Corinthian letters reflect a similar enough practice to what we found in Chapters One and Two that it would be reasonable for most of the Corinthians to have received Paul's appeals to adherence to god (father) and (lord Jesus) Christ – or (lord Jesus) Christ – and *pneuma* in the context of this practice. Finally, in Chapter Five, I will offer a plausible reconstruction of the early years of Paul's interaction with the Corinthians and what might have been his efforts to distinguish his appeals for a certain kind of practice from the Corinthians' practice, followed by some closing remarks in Chapter Six.

CHAPTER ONE

# Chords of Gods around the Mediterranean

Among scholars of the classics, the phenomenon of worship and cultic activity involving small but defined groups of gods will not come as a surprise. As noted earlier, the title of this book comes from Robert Parker, who wrote, 'Greeks typically prayed not to individual gods but to "chords of gods"',[1] and the same could be said of Romans, too. But Parker was only quoting the mid-nineteenth-century German scholar F. G. Welcker, who was cited by L. Preller in 1846.[2] So classicists have long recognised that worship of small groups of gods constituted a common and fundamental feature of various forms of Greek and Roman religious practice in different contexts from the classical period through to late antiquity. Scholars of the New Testament might understand Greek and Roman religion differently. Stephen Mitchell puts it well:

> Viewed from the perspective of monotheistic Christianity we may be perplexed by the diversity of pagan cults; but for an inhabitant of Roman Asia Minor [for example], the ubiquity and diversity of the pagan gods, which is implied by the bewildering mass of the surviving evidence, was a far simpler notion to grasp than the omnipresence of a single God.[3]

This chapter will focus on the phenomenon of worship of or interaction with small (and not so small) groups of gods across the ancient Mediterranean, with examples from a wide range of geographical locations, time periods and social

---

[1] Robert Parker, *On Greek Religion* (Ithaca: Cornell University Press, 2011), 66.
[2] 'Nicht sowohl einzelne Götter ... als ganze Accorde von Göttern.' L. Preller, 'Das Zwölfgöttersystem der Griechen', *Verhandlungen der neunten Versammlung deutscher Philologen, Schulmänner und Orientalisten zu Jena* (Jena, 1846), 49.
[3] Stephen Mitchell, *Anatolia: Land, Men, and Gods*, 2 vols (Oxford: Oxford University Press, 1993), 19.

situations that indicate the widespread nature of this phenomenon. By the end of this brief but representative analysis, it will be clear that the worship of groups of gods represents a widespread social practice as Schatzki has defined it: a nexus of sayings and doings. In this case, the sayings and doings revolve around the worship of groups of gods.

## Egypt

### Ptolemaic Religion in General

This section cannot do justice to the grandeur and complexity of Ptolemaic and Roman religious practice, but I hope to give a taste of it and highlight how groups of gods worked within it using the temples at Edfu and Dendara as examples.

Egyptian religion during the Ptolemaic and Early Roman periods continued ancient Egyptian traditions while adapting them under the rule of Greeks and Romans. The Ptolemies strove to present themselves as pharaonic in image and authority, for reasons that are debated by scholars.[4] The temple complexes that have survived from the Ptolemaic and Early Roman periods of Egypt not only show architectural continuity with ancient Egyptian temples but also provide 'a rich source of information about the mythical and ritual traditions of the temples' themselves.[5] This is mainly because of the durable remains of hieroglyphs inscribed on their walls: records of life in the temple, mythology, ideology, cultic practice and so on. Jan Assmann sees these temples and their inscriptions as foundational to the expression of cultural identity, a 'monumentalized memory' (*gebaute Erinnerung*), pitting this dynamic against the encroaching Greek influence of the Ptolemaic period.[6] But this is not a necessary conclusion to draw if the basic idea for the Ptolemaic rulers was to ground their authority in centuries of pharaonic ideology.

Scholars think that the design of the temple complexes and the key ritual practices within them aimed to continue ancient designs and practices that go

---

[4] Günther Hölbl, *A History of the Ptolemaic Empire* (London: Routledge, 2001); Stefan Pfeiffer, *Herrscher- und Dynastiekulte im Ptolemäerreich. Systematik und Einordnung der Kultformen.* (Munich: C. H. Beck, 2008).

[5] Ragnhild Bjerre Finnestad, 'Temples of Ptolemaic and Roman Periods: Ancient Traditions in New Contexts', in *Temples of Ancient Egypt*, ed. Byron Shafer (Ithaca: Cornell University Press, 1997), 197. Here she is referring to the temple of Edfu.

[6] Jan Assmann, 'Der Tempel der ägyptischen Spätzeit als Kanonisierung kultureller Identität', in *The Heritage of Ancient Egypt: Studies in Honour of Erik Iversen*, ed. Jürgen Osing and Erland Kolding Nielsen (Copenhagen: Museum Tusculanum Press, 1992), 15.

back to earlier eras of Egyptian history.⁷ Regarding the extensive inscriptions and reliefs on Ptolemaic temple walls, Finnestad correctly points out two important religious functions: 'They defined the space and the actions that took place there, and they made what they represented cultically present.'⁸ So the gods and practices within a temple complex can reflect both ancient traditions continued and updated ones for Ptolemaic and Roman times.⁹ But Dieter Arnold, following Sylvie Cauville, argues that the archaeological design of the pronaos of the temples is 'a symbolic space for uniting the gods of the two lands'. The columns of these temples have particular gods on them for each temple, and 'the distribution of these gods follows a complicated system of religious and geographical associations'.¹⁰ Reflected in this construction was a connection between the gods at various temples and the coming and going of gods around Egypt from temple complex to temple complex.

One other comment to make is that it seems that the religious life of Ptolemaic and Roman Egyptian temples was tied very closely to the mythological/ cosmological worldview articulated on the temple walls. Earthly (lilies, figs, palms, papyrus, lotus and reeds) and heavenly (sun, moon and stars) objects cover the walls and columns of temples, along with depictions of the gods and royal figures in action.¹¹ So we should not imagine a cultic life of an individual god as being separate from the overall ritual life of the temple, which was itself intertwined with the mythical/cosmological ideology expressed in inscription and relief.

---

[7] Finnestad, 'Temples of Ptolemaic and Roman Periods', 198. In disagreeing with Assmann, Finnestad says: 'It is unnecessary ... to regard the temples as defensive castles against Greek-Hellenistic traditions ... but the temple's role as codification of cultural identity and memory seems highly important. Such a role appears to have been ancient, even though its extensive reflection on the walls was a late phenomenon.' Katherine Eaton, *Ancient Egyptian Temple Ritual: Performance, Pattern, and Practice* (London: Routledge, 2013), 4, writes: 'In the Ptolemaic and Roman periods (332 B.C.E.–395 C.E.), temples continued to be built according to ancient Egyptian traditions already established in the New Kingdom, but by foreign rulers.' She makes this comment as the last in a pattern of similar comments about each era of temple building. The temple designs remained fairly consistent through the eras but the contexts in which the designs were executed changed dramatically.

[8] Finnestad, 'Temples of Ptolemaic and Roman Periods', 198. On the second point, see Jan Assmann, 'Die Macht der Bilder: Rahmenbedingungen ikonischen Handelns im Alten Ägypten', *Visible Religion: Annual for Religious Iconography* 7 (1990): 1–20.

[9] So a renewal effort on the part of the Ptolemies could be one way to think about these temples. An analogy could be drawn with the efforts of cultural elites in the Second Sophistic period: tapping into the cultural greatness of classical Greece and establishing it for a new era.

[10] Dieter Arnold, *Temples of the Last Pharaohs* (New York: Oxford University Press, 1999), 306–7. 'The two lands' refers to Upper and Lower Egypt. See Sylvie Cauville, *Le Temple de Dendera. Guide archéologique* (Cairo: Institut Français D'Archéologie Orientale de Caire, 1990).

[11] Finnestad, 'Temples of Ptolemaic and Roman Periods', 204.

These temples provide excellent examples of how complex religious practice around their gods did not fall into the neat categories of 'polytheism' or 'monotheism' but are better described as practices revolving around 'a chord of gods' or perhaps even 'chords of gods'. We should remember, however, that even the metaphor of 'a chord of gods' does not do justice to the complexity of religion in Egypt. What we can say is that it describes one feature that contributes to the overall logic of Egyptian religious practice during the Ptolemaic and early Roman periods and provides my first example of a common practice across the Mediterranean before, during and after Paul's time. The temples at Dendera and Edfu demonstrate how these groups of gods were present and working together in temple life.

## Dendera and Edfu

The Hathor sanctuary at Dendera and the Horus sanctuary at Edfu are intertwined with each other ritually and with respect to the divinities represented in each place.[12] But even to call them 'Hathor' or 'Horus' sanctuaries does not accurately represent the dynamic daily life present in each temple complex.[13] The temple at Edfu was begun in 237 BCE and completed in 57 BCE. The temple at Dendera has a long history, but the earliest extant building (the birthing house) goes back to the last pharaoh, Nectanebo II (360–343 BCE). The main extant Hathor temple at Dendera seems to have been started late in the Ptolemaic period, under Ptolemy XII, in 54 BCE and was completed under Cleopatra VII;[14] however, additions and expansions to the temple complex continued into the mid-second century CE under Antoninus Pius's rule (138–61 CE).[15] These late dates of construction relative to the early history of Egypt demonstrate the staying power of the mythological and ritual traditions embodied in the temples, and are a good example of how the Ptolemaic rulers wanted to continue these traditions in this new era. Figures 1.1 and 1.2 show

---

[12] Ibid., 205: '[The temple of Horus at Edfu]'s relationship with the temple of Hathor at Dendera can be taken as an example of the kind of close connection that could exist between temples. Theology and cultus of the two were coordinated. Horus of Edfu received attention in the cultus at Dendera, and the pantheon of Edfu was included in the Dendera cultus. A list of all the gods of Edfu is inscribed in the hypostyle hall at Dendera, and in the Edfu temple we find the festival calendar of Dendera. The two temples cooperated in celebrating the famous festival of the Reunion of Hathor and Horus.' See also Sylvie Cauville, 'Le pantheon d'Edfou à Dendera', *Bulletin de l'Institut Français d'Archéologie Orientale* 88 (1988): 7–23.

[13] Here I follow the analysis of Finnestad, 'Temples of Ptolemaic and Roman Periods', 203–19. See also Eaton, *Ancient Egyptian Temple Ritual*, and Cauville, *Le Temple de Dendera*, for more detailed treatments of the ritual life of Egyptian temples.

[14] Arnold, *Temples of the Last Pharaohs*, 212–13.

[15] Ibid., 324.

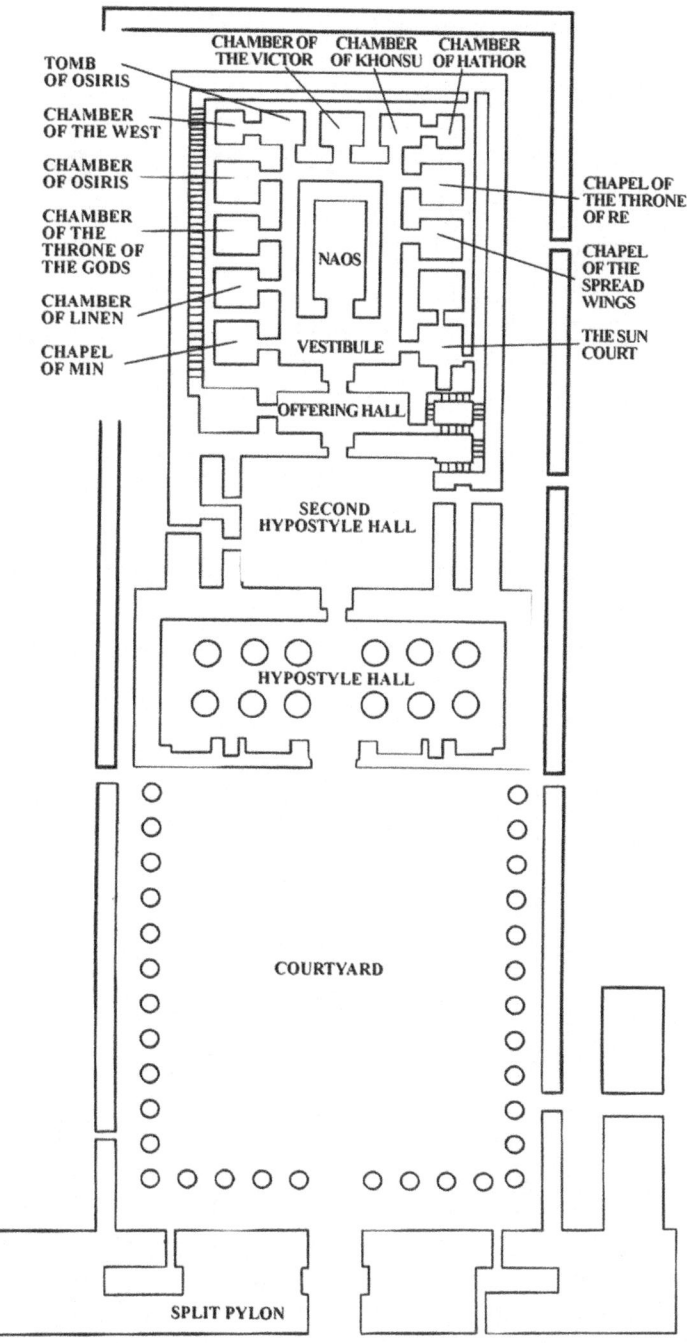

**Figure 1.1** Plan of Temple at Edfu. (Public domain)

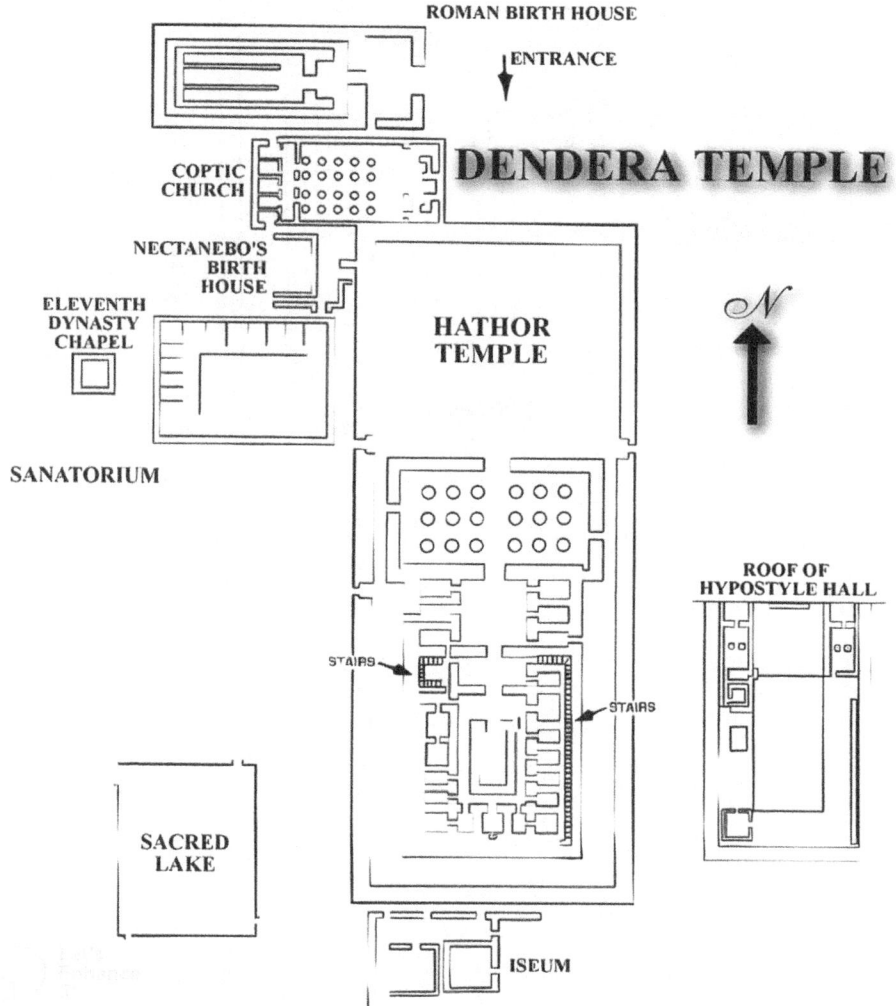

**Figure 1.2** Plan of Temple at Dendera. (Public domain)

the layout of each of the main temple complexes. The multifaceted nature of the Edfu complex is immediately evident, with dedicated spaces to Re, the Ennead (a group of nine gods), Khonsu, Hathor, Osiris and two past kings of Egypt. At Dendera, there was a bark shrine containing the barks of Hathor, Horus of Edfu, Harsomtus and Isis, along with the main space housing Hathor's statue, surrounded by a series of smaller 'chapels' dedicated to various gods, including Hathor/Isis, Osiris, Harsomtus, Horus and Re.[16] These and

---

[16] Ibid., 213: 'Along the surrounding ambulatory, eleven chapels served the cult of Hathor and her associates', but Arnold names only a few of the associates.

the other spaces were involved in various rituals or contained descriptions of the ritual life and Egyptian mythological/cosmological worldview (either local or regional).

While all temple complexes have a large number of inscriptions and reliefs as part of their architectural structures, Edfu is particularly well known for the vast wealth of inscriptions and reliefs throughout the structure – especially on the wall surrounding the temple – that communicate the rich life and thought world of those who lived in Edfu. The wall is approximately 20 feet tall and covered from top to bottom with inscriptions and reliefs – an amazing collection of evidence regarding the temple and religious life at Edfu. The inscriptions are still in the process of being translated, so the full extent of evidence remains unknown. Unlike Greek and Roman sanctuaries, where there is much guesswork about their inner workings, Edfu and Denera offer rich potential to understand the ritual life of Egyptians in the temple at a deep level.

Most major Ptolemaic temple complexes show evidence of a 'birthing house': a smaller side temple that memorialises the birth of the deity in question. Edfu and Dendera are no exceptions. Edfu's birthing house 'was dedicated to the triad Horus, Hathor and their son, the falcon-headed Hartsomtus (Somtus)' and was decorated with images of the fertility god Bes, who was also represented in the birthing house at Dendera.[17] In addition, these houses celebrate and mark the birth of Horus from Hathor.[18] Along with the main divine players, 'In the Mammisis of Edfu and Dendera are many attestations of Sopdu nb iAbt, "Lord of the East", together with Wadjet nbt imntt, "Lady of the West".'[19] Reliefs at Dendera show Trajan making offerings to gods in the birth house (Hathor, Ra-Harakhte), which raises the interesting question of the role of Ptolemaic and Roman royalty in the life of the temples.

Another important grouping of gods found in these temples is that of the Enneads, a Greek loanword meaning 'the Nine'. This grouping has a long history in Egyptian culture, perhaps going back as far as the unification of Upper and Lower Egypt in Dynasty I. The first attestation is that of the Ennead of Heliopolis, 'which served as the model for further enneads in the pantheon'.[20] While the number nine is mostly stable in the many manifestations of the

---

[17] Ibid., 202.
[18] Sylvie Cauville, *Offerings to the Gods in Egyptian Temples*, trans. Bram Calcoen (Leuven: Peeters, 2012), 178–9.
[19] Fatma Talaat Ismail, *Cult and Ritual in Persian Period Egypt: An Analysis of the Decoration of the Cult Chapels of the Temple of Hibis at Kharga Oasis* (New Haven: Yale Egyptology, 2019), 76. 'Mammisi' is the term for 'birth house'.
[20] Erik Hornung, *Der Eine und die Vielen* (Darmstadt: Wissenschaftliche Buchgesellschaft, 1971). Translated by John Baines as *Conceptions of God in Ancient Egypt: The One and the Many* (Ithaca: Cornell University Press, 1982), 221.

Enneads through the centuries,[21] which deities are included in the group is not. Pharaohs often included themselves in the list, as was the case with Sety I. The grouping of the gods is not random but usually based on genealogical relations,[22] and so the inclusion of pharaohs in the list is an interesting commentary on the authority and genealogy that the ruler claimed.

In describing the ritual life of Ptolemaic religion, I will focus on Edfu for the sake of simplicity, in order to give a sense of the complexity of the ritual life evident in Ptolemaic and Roman temples. Each day, three main rituals occurred: one each at morning, midday and sunset, corresponding to the solar path, but the morning was the most important of the three. A short description of the morning ritual gives a sense of the fluid nature of the deities being evoked and honoured in the ritual. Each morning with the rising of the sun, the 'rising', reconstitution and appearance of the solar creator was expressed through rituals that included music, hymns, incense, anointings, libations, processions, and words to make manifest the god 'in the entering sunlight and golden luminescence of statues and images'.[23] The solar creator was represented in statue form within a smaller shrine inside the temple complex; the priest would start the ritual by opening the doors to the shrine, revealing the statue and saying: 'You arise as Khepri as you come out of Nenet, and your rays spread over the world.'[24] The opening of the doors happened while hymns of adoration were sung, praise was given, and names and epithets were recited, all to 'invoke the divine presence'.[25] This act of revealing and seeing the sun god was the most significant part of the morning ritual, according to Finnestad, but she goes on to argue that other parts of the ritual held significance (for example, the bringing of incense and perfumes, and offerings of food and drink to all the gods of the temple).[26] The threefold seeing of the god, the appearance of the god and the coming out (or coming into being) of the god constituted a key part of the cosmology that purported that sunlight was 'the divine, vital, creative element in the world', repeating the cycle of a 'dynamic coming into being' that was marked each day in the temple.[27]

This coming into being was also marked by the many doors and gates of the temple, each signifying the existential transition from darkness and chaos

---

[21] There are some exceptions. The ennead at Abydos had only seven members, and the one at Thebes had fifteen. See Hornung, *Conceptions of God*, 222, especially n.22.

[22] Ibid., 222.

[23] Finnestad, 'Temples of Ptolemaic and Roman Periods', 216. I follow Finnestad's description of the morning ritual throughout this section.

[24] Finnestad, 'Temples of Ptolemaic and Roman Periods', 206. Khepri was the name of the sun god (represented with a scarab head) as he emerges from the night sky (Nenet).

[25] Ibid., 210. See also Jan Assmann, *Der König als Sonnenpriester. Ein kosmographischer Begleittext zur kultischen Sonnenhymnik* (Glückstadt: J. J. Augustin, 1970), 21, 48.

[26] Finnestad, 'Temples of Ptolemaic and Roman Periods', 206–7.

[27] Ibid., 207.

to sunlight and order. Near doorways throughout the temple were carved invocations and images related to the epiphany of the divine sun. The largest of these gates was the 131-foot entrance pylon, which 'heralded that the temple was a place of existential transition', showing that 'the coming of the Creator and ruler of the world confronted and overcame chaos and expanded the territory of cosmos'.[28] When these main doors were opened, the High Seat in the inner part of the temple received natural light, illuminating the Falcon-of-Gold image and uniting it with the images on the ceiling. The morning hymn declares that Horus 'comes from the night sky every day to see his image in the High Seat. He descends to his image; he joins his images.'[29]

While Edfu's main ritual marked the rebirth of the divine world each day as expressed through the arrival and departure of the sun gods (Nun and/ or Horus as a manifestation of Re, in this location), there were other aspects of the temple complex that included other specific gods. In particular, there was a close relationship between Horus of Edfu and Hathor of Dendera. The Edfu complex depicts the annual festival visit of Hathor to Edfu and Horus to Dendera to unite with each other as spouses. As with most Ptolemaic temple complexes, Edfu had an element that dealt with nonbeing and death – opposite to but interrelated with daily rebirth and regeneration. Thus, Osiris, too, is present in the temple; a leg of Osiris was kept as a relic of the god.[30] His story is depicted in several places, in particular in connection with Hedjhotep, a god originally associated with light or white things, but by the Ptolemaic era associated with weaving and divine textiles. Because the word from which Hedjhotep's name comes (htp) has the basic meaning of 'to rest' or 'setting of the sun', he could also be associated with the west. At both Dendera and Edfu, he clothes Osiris (the naked one) and crafts Osiris's mummy bandage; at Dendera, he is called the one 'who belongs to the place of Osiris'.[31]

As we can see, although the temples at Edfu and Dendera were dedicated to Horus and Hathor respectively, there was much more going on than worship of the individual gods. Instead, a host of gods – and within that host various subsets of gods – all contributed to the ritual and cosmological dynamics of these locales.

**Assessment Regarding Chords of Gods**

The architectural pattern of Ptolemaic and Roman era temples in Egypt has a large central sanctuary for the main god, surrounded by a series of rooms, some

---

[28] Ibid., 210.
[29] Ibid., 211; Sylvie Cauville and Didier Devauchelle, *Le Temple d'Edfou*, vol. 1 (Cairo: l'Institut Français d'Archéologie Orientale du Caire, 1984), 13.
[30] Finnestad, 'Temples of Ptolemaic and Roman Periods', 216.
[31] See Ismail, *Cult and Ritual*, 79, with the references cited there.

of which are dedicated to the ritual necessities of the temple but most of which are dedicated to other gods associated with the main god. This pattern was not wholly new but echoed older temple complexes like that of the Temple of Sety I at Abydos.[32] These associates are genealogically and mythologically connected, and their relationships are played out on a daily basis in the temple rituals that express the dynamic cosmology of Egyptian religion. Along with the Enneads and the group of gods represented in the birthing houses, we have a pattern of smaller subsets of gods acting together both locally and across Egypt, even if the divine figures in the temples vary.

While the 'pantheon' of Egyptian gods is represented in the temples at Dendera and Edfu, not all of the Egyptian gods are included. 'Pantheon' is a misnomer, I think, because the term assumes a collection of distinct gods, who are related but who do not necessarily fit together ritually, mythologically or cosmologically.[33] The gods in these Egyptian temples certainly do collaborate in the temples' ritual life, which in turn is an expression of the mythological and cosmological foundations of Egyptian society. The gods morph and intertwine and overlap, so it is very difficult to distinguish them completely, which, in turn, makes describing them in static terms somewhat artificial. So, while the list of gods is quite extensive in these temples, if one were to assemble a comprehensive list, a 'chord of gods', however artificial, can be used as an imperfect metaphor for what they are. But this term can work in the sense that they are strongly intertwined with each other and there are distinct purposes for their interaction. They are not a random collection, in other words; there is a logic and there is an identifiable grouping. They are not one, but they are also not indefinite in number. They are a large and complex chord, but a chord, nonetheless.

## Palestine

### Caesarea Maritima (Temple of Augustus and Roma)

From Egypt, we go up the coast of the Mediterranean to Palestine, the mythological homeland of Jews, Judaism and the god of Israel. But, as we will see,

---

[32] 'Originally, seven processional routes, often called "alleys", ran through the hypostyle halls out onto the terrace of the Second Court of the Temple at Sety I at Abydos, one corresponding to each of the seven barque chapels ... There are six panels of scenes, one between each set of doors leading into the First Hypostyle Hall. Along each alley the recipients of ritual depicted in the scenes generally belong to the family of the deity to whom the corresponding chapel is devoted. The group of deities along the alleys of Osiris and Ptah are larger, since they also serve the Osiris complex and the Nefertem-Ptah-Sokar complex, respectively.' Eaton, *Ancient Egyptian Temple Ritual*, 79–80.

[33] 'Pantheon' is really a term to describe a temple to all the gods, but unless it is referring to the Roman Pantheon temple, it is usually used as a term to describe all the gods of a particular group of people.

the Holy Land was not monolithically focused on adherence to the god of Israel. The presence of sanctuaries of Greek and Roman gods was abundant in this region in Hellenistic and Roman times, giving a very diverse picture of its religious culture, a diversity that existed for centuries in different forms.

As one entered Herod the Great's Caesarea Maritima via the harbour, the most prominent and imposing structure was the temple of Augustus and Roma, which stood at the landing of the harbour. Figure 1.3 shows an overhead view of the ruins of Caesarea, with the harbour and temple location marked. Most scholars believe that Herod's placement of the building at the back of the harbour was intended to allow the temple to be seen from a long way away, as a way of raising up the prominence of the gods.[34] But Holum has recently argued that this interpretation, based on a translation of Josephus's *Antiquities* 15.339, might not capture the scope of its prominence, and instead emphasises the temple complex's role as a navigational guide for mariners sailing along the coast.[35] The complex housed two divine figures, Augustus and Roma. Although there is some debate as to whether Augustus considered himself a divine figure or a god in his lifetime, there is less uncertainty for the Roman provinces, among which Caesarea is located.[36] So we are on safe ground asserting the divine status of Augustus in Caesarea, with the dedication of the temple to him and Roma.

Regarding the cultic life, there is little evidence for the particulars, but we can assume from other temples to Augustus around the empire that these were not simply monuments to the emperor to honour him but were fully functioning sanctuaries with a rich cultic life. There is one fragmentary inscription at Caesarea, likely from Vespasian's rule, that indicates the presence of *Augustales*, freedmen who dedicated themselves to imperial cultic

---

[34] Ehud Netzer, *The Architecture of Herod, the Great Builder* (Tübingen: Mohr Siebeck, 2006), 95; A. Schalit, *König Herodes. Der Mann und sein Werk*, 2nd ed. (Berlin: De Gruyter, 2001), 332.

[35] 'Putting aside for the moment doubts about this translation, and placing ourselves in the situation of the "performers" in this case, i.e. the mariners at sea, we find it easy to grasp an element of Herod's original intent. Herod's temple was to serve as a navigational marker. Indeed, even without the text it is obvious from the architecture, from the lay of the land and sea, and from the prevailing weather along this coast that mariners plying these waters would very much have welcomed the sight of Herod's temple towering above the nearly featureless terrain along the coast and would have rejoiced to know that they would soon be able to rest from their labors, and from the dangers of a sea voyage under such adverse conditions.' Kenneth G. Holum, 'The Gods of Sebastos: King Herod's Harbor Temple at Caesarea Maritima', *Eretz-Israel: Archaeological, Historical and Geographical Studies* 31 (2015): 60.

[36] What Holum, 'The Gods of Sebastos', 54, says in passing reflects this debate: 'Ehud Netzer did not care to speculate on the position of the main altar upon which sacrifices would have been brought to Roma and to or on behalf of the emperor.' The classic work on the imperial cult in the provinces is Simon R. F. Price, *Rituals and Power: The Roman Imperial Cult in Asia Minor* (Cambridge: Cambridge University Press, 1984).

**Figure 1.3** Aerial view of Caesarea Maritima with harbour and Temple of Augustus and Roma marked. (Public domain)

activities and *ludi Augustales*, games honouring Augustus.³⁷ How long these figures and games predated the time of Vespasian is unknown. Since Herod built the temple to honour Augustus and strengthen his relationship with the emperor, we can assume that this was part of the empire-wide efforts to build the mythology around Augustus as a living god, who was as worthy of divine honours as any other god. To build a temple complex that joined him with Roma, who was the embodiment of Rome as a culture and state, made a political and mythological statement about the place of Augustus in Rome's history and culture. The likely image of Augustus in the temple, along with the image of Roma, was intended 'to shape the emperor's person and to constitute the principal objects of a discourse on the divinity of the emperor'.³⁸ In other words, Augustus's presence as a cohabitant with Roma was not accidental but instead would have played a key role in mythologising Augustus as the embodiment of Rome alongside Roma.

## Panias

The cultic association with Pan at this site in northern Palestine at the mouth of the River Jordan is reflected in the name that Polybius gave to the rural shrine: 'the Panion'.³⁹ This connection with Pan lasted for about 700 years, from its initial stages in the third century BCE to its uneventful abandonment in the fifth century CE. In the course of these 700 years, the rural shrine grew to a city shrine associated with Caesarea Philippi, which Herod Philip founded in 2 BCE.⁴⁰ As the site grew from a rural Pan shrine to a city sanctuary, so did its complexity with respect to who was worshipped there along with Pan.

The remains of the site have been thoroughly excavated, most recently from 1988 to 1994 under the auspices of the Israeli Antiquities Authority, but the remains are still being interpreted for their significance and meaning.⁴¹ Figures 1.4 and 1.5 show the layout of the ancient sanctuary in the Roman

---

[37] Holum, 'The Gods of Sebastos', 65. For the inscription, see Clayton M. Lehmann and Kenneth M. Holum, *The Greek and Latin Inscriptions of Caesarea Maritima: Joint Expeditions to Caesarea Maritima*, vol. 5 (Boston: ASOR, 2000), 120 (#122).

[38] Dirk Steuernagel, 'Synnaos Theos: Images of Roman Emperors in Greek Temples', in *Divine Images and Human Imaginations in Ancient Greece and Rome*, ed. Joannis Mylonopoulos (Leiden: Brill, 2010), 243, following Price, *Rituals and Power*, 1984.

[39] Polyb. 16.18.2, 28.1.3; Josephus *AJ* 15.10.3; and Euseb. *Hist. eccl.* 7.17 also call the site by this name.

[40] Andrea Berlin, 'The Archaeology of Ritual: The Sanctuary of Pan at Banias/Caesarea Philippi', *BASOR* 315 (1999): 27.

[41] Berlin, 'The Archaeology of Ritual', and Elise A. Friedland, *The Roman Marble Sculptures from the Sanctuary of Pan at Caesarea Philippi/Panias (Israel)* (Boston: American Schools of Oriental Research, 2012), are two of the more interesting studies to focus on the remains of Panias.

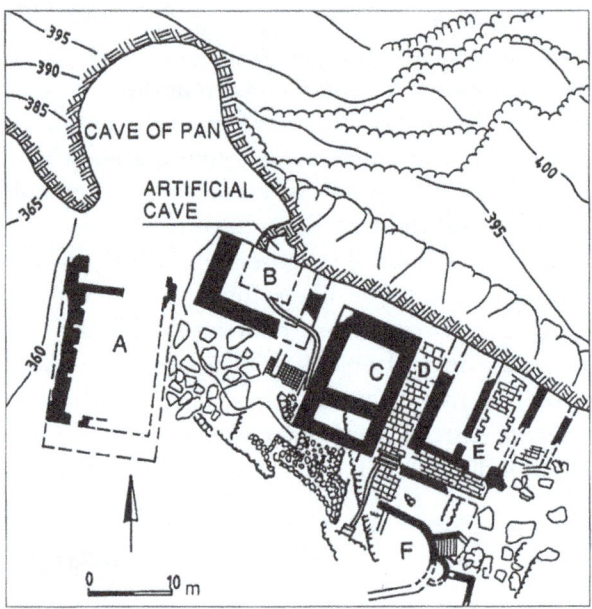

**Figure 1.4** Plan of the Sanctuary of Pan at Banias/Caesarea Philippi. (After Andrea M. Berlin, 'The Archaeology of Ritual: The Sanctuary of Pan at Banias/Caesarea Philippi', *BASOR* 315 (1999): 29, modified)

**Figure 1.5** Sanctuary of Pan at Banias/Caesarea Philippi. Photo by Berthold Werner. Licence CC by 3.0 IT (https://creativecommons.org/licenses/by/3.0/). Enhanced resolution.

period and its current state. Before the Roman period, the sanctuary was dedicated to Pan and the Nymphs and functioned as such from the third century BCE. But Herod decided to build his third temple to Augustus and Roma here, which would transform the site without negating the presence of Pan and his fellow deities.[42]

The large natural cave that lay at the west end of the sanctuary, behind one of the sources of the Jordan, and the carved niches along the cliff face were constructed as part of the Augusteum. The largest of the niches, Berlin argues, held cult statues for Roma and Augustus.[43] The terrace that stretched the length of the sanctuary was constructed from the late first century BCE onwards, and on top of the terrace a series of buildings were erected, the first of which was probably the temple of Augustus and Roma, right in front of the cave.[44] The other structures associated with gods that were present by the latest period of the sanctuary were (from west to east): (1) a court in front of an artificial cave identified by an inscription as the 'Court of Pan and the Nymphs'; (2) a temple dedicated during Trajan's or Hadrian's reign, called the 'Temple of Zeus and Pan'; (3) another court identified by an inscription as the 'Nemesis Court'; and (4) a shrine or small temple called the 'Temple of Pan and the Goats'.[45]

Berlin's 1999 analysis of the pottery finds in different periods in the lifespan of the sanctuary shows a consistent cultic life, starting with the areas where the Court of Pan and Nymphs and the Temple of Zeus and Pan were later located, before the courtyards and buildings were constructed. Most of the pottery from this stage was for cooking and eating, probably for dining purposes, likely brought to the sanctuary by the participants.[46] Since the sanctuary was rural, with very few inhabitants within a five-kilometre radius, this early stage of the sanctuary represents cultic dining practices (either formally as part of a ritual, or informally as a way of communing with the deities thought to be present there).[47]

In the early Roman period, Herod's introduction of the Temple of Roma and Augustus to the site transformed the sanctuary and surrounding region significantly. The decision brought resources to the area unseen in its history,

---

[42] The first was at Sebaste/Samaria and the second was at Caesarea Maritima. According to Suetonius, Augustus did not want any new temples in his honour unless they were dedicated to both Roma and Augustus (Suet. Aug. 52).

[43] Andrea Berlin, 'Herod, Augustus, and the Augusteum at the Paneion', *Eretz-Israel: Archaeological, Historical and Geographical Studies* 31 (2015): 1–11. See also Friedland, *The Roman Marble Sculptures*, 41–3, 51–2, 57, 75–7, for an analysis of the head of a colossal statue that she argues was part of the cult statue of Roma, which would have fitted in one of the niches.

[44] Berlin, 'The Archaeology of Ritual'.

[45] Ibid., 29.

[46] Ibid., 30.

[47] Ibid., 31.

and Herod's successor, Herod Philip, decided to build his new capital city, Caesarea Philippi, close by. The result was that the sanctuary became an urban cult rather than a rural one, and so the cultic life changed along with the landscape. Alongside a continuation of dining pottery, there was a marked increase in lamp dedications from this period, which seem to indicate both a continuity with cultic activity from the Hellenistic period supplicants and the introduction of a newer form of worship, probably from the city dwellers nearby.[48] Some traditional adherents to the sanctuary still preferred spending an extended amount of time at the sanctuary (indicated by the dining vessels), but others came for shorter times to honour the gods with simple lamp offerings.

By the end of the first century CE and into the second, the sanctuary was developed to include the Temple of Zeus and Pan, along with more niches being carved into the cliff wall, probably to display statues. Sculptures made of imported marble are among the finds for this time period; Friedland divides them into three categories: cult deities of the sanctuary (Satyr, Pan or Daphnis, Nymph, Zeus or Asklepios, Roma or Athena); visiting Olympian deities (Athena, Artemis Rospigliosi, Artemis of Ephesos, Aphrodite, Apollo or a Muse, Dionysos, Eros); and visiting semi-divine figures (Herakles, Kybele, Orpheus, Antoninus).[49] This division is based on inscriptional evidence that indicates cultic activity for particular gods. The 'visiting gods' show no other evidence of cultic activity, although there could very well have been cult offered to them.

While this categorisation of the gods present in the sanctuary is problematic,[50] the evidence shows that the sanctuary included a defined group of gods. Further, Nemesis can be included in this group, given the inscriptional evidence near the Court of Nemesis. The expansion of the sanctuary and the importation of expensive Italian marble sculptures shows how the patronage for the sanctuary had increased significantly over the previous decades. The pottery finds, or lack of them, during this period also seem to indicate that 'small-scale worshipers essentially abandoned the cult'. There were a small number of dishes and bowls but only one cooking vessel, perhaps indicating that these items were offered as gifts rather than used for sanctuary dining.[51]

---

[48] Berlin (ibid., 33) notes that the Hellenistic period finds in the sanctuary include only 7 lamps, whereas the early Roman period finds include fragments of 141 lamps, over half of which were imported from Italy, Cyprus and Syria.

[49] Friedland, *The Roman Marble Sculptures*, 50.

[50] For example, calling Artemis of Ephesos an 'Olympian god' is unnuanced at best, and misrepresents the local nature of this god. She is not an Olympian goddess but a particular manifestation of Artemis arising out of a long cultural hybridisation of local traditions and Greek traditions. There is very little about this goddess that is 'Olympian', whatever that means. And by the time that Herakles was represented in this sanctuary (well into the common era), he was not really thought of as 'semi-divine' but given the same honours that any full-blown god received.

[51] Berlin, 'The Archaeology of Ritual', 35.

The final building stage of the sanctuary before it was abandoned[52] was the third to fifth centuries CE, which saw the construction of two buildings on the easternmost side of the site, including the Temple of Pan and the Goats. The pottery finds show a marked increase in lamps, which Berlin argues indicates a shift in the kind of worship that occurred there. Comparable percentages of lamp usage around the Mediterranean correspond to mystery cults or oracular shrines. The shift in lamp usage probably evinces a change in the patronage from fewer wealthier adherents to larger numbers of less wealthy worshippers.[53]

The sanctuary's original configuration of gods, Pan and the nymphs – a traditional association, given Pan's connection to the wilderness where nymphs reside – gradually increased in complexity as the Roman period emerged, beginning with Herod's construction of the Temple of Augustus and Roma and continuing until a host of Greek gods were included too. The gods that were added to the sanctuary were not random but traditional groupings. Augustus and Roma were consciously linked together at the request of Augustus, as Suetonius indicated, probably to mythologise the place of Augustus alongside Roma as embodying Romanness, and therefore elevating him to being worthy of divine honours. Asklepios and Apollo are son and father, both foundationally healing gods, genealogically connected to each other through a long history of story and tradition. Artemis, of course, is the twin sister of Apollo, and she is famously associated with the wilderness, as is Pan.[54] Nemesis was often associated with the Roman military and the emperor cult,[55] giving her the connection with Augustus in the sanctuary. Aphrodite had a long history of being linked with Pan in classical Greece, going back to the fifth century BCE. From this time forward, representations of the two gods linked them as having similar spheres of influence when it came to sexuality, both in connection and in contrast to each other (one excessively beautiful, the other not).[56] There is clearly enough here to establish the pattern of small groups of gods connected by genealogy, mythology and/or history being worshipped in a single sanctuary.

## Anatolia

As we continue around the Mediterranean, our next region is Anatolia, where we will look at a major urban sanctuary – the Asklepieion at Pergamon – and

---

[52] Ibid., 41–2, where Berlin links it with the depopulation of Caesarea Philippi and the general decline of Upper and Lower Galilee.
[53] Ibid., 36–7.
[54] Friedland, *The Roman Marble Sculptures*, 52.
[55] Ibid.
[56] Ibid., 54, following Phillippe Borgeaud, *The Cult of Pan in Ancient Greece* (Chicago: University of Chicago Press, 1988), 75.

a rural context in Phrygia, mainly focusing on a pairing of gods – Hosios and Dikaios. Both sets of evidence predominantly reflect the second to fourth centuries CE, but in the case of Pergamon the traditions go back much farther.

**Pergamon Asklepieion**

The second-century CE Asklepieion at Pergamon was widely considered the most prominent of all the Asklepieia at that time. The architectural plan of the sanctuary reflects extensive building activity in that century. The sanctuary is situated below the Acropolis of Pergamon, set some distance from the main part of the city, as is typical of Asklepieia. The earliest evidence for building on the site dates to the fifth century BCE, 'and there was continual rebuilding throughout the Hellenistic and Roman periods (eighteen building phases have been identified in the pre-Roman period alone)'.[57] The emperor Hadrian visited Pergamon in 123/4 CE; following his visit, a major building programme commenced, lasting approximately five years, which expanded the sanctuary and added several new structures (for example, the theatre, library, Propylon and forecourt and rotunda). Included among these new structures was the temple of Zeus Asklepios. This temple supplemented but did not replace the Hellenistic temple of Asklepios Soter on the other side of the complex. The Hellenistic temple was functioning right up until Hadrian's visit (and thus in the first century) and was part of a complex of three temples, but the identity of the gods associated with the other two temples cannot be determined with certainty: the possibilities are two from among Hygeia, Telesphoros and Apollo.[58]

The expansion of the sanctuary in the wake of Hadrian's visit resulted in an impressive complex, as can be seen from Figure 1.6. Some scholars have viewed the sanctuary as a mixture of sacred and secular elements; Jones calls the library, theatre and gymnasium 'secular amenities' and claims that the sanctuary is a 'cross between a German spa and a research institute'.[59] But as Petsalis-Diomidis has persuasively demonstrated, the sanctuary 'provided an encyclopaedic, all-encompassing sacred framework for the whole spectrum of bodies on the one hand, and on the other for every aspect of the individual'.[60]

---

[57] Alexia Petsalis-Diomidis, *'Truly Beyond Wonders': Aelius Aristides and the Cult of Asklepios*. Oxford Studies in Ancient Culture and Representation (Oxford: Oxford University Press, 2010), 167.

[58] Ibid., 168, which has 'Kaliteknos' as the epithet for Apollo, but Petsalis-Diomidis has no reference to the inscription or evidence for this epithet, so it is unconfirmed.

[59] C. P. Jones, 'Aelius Aristides and the Asklepieion', in *Pergamon: Citadel of the Gods: Archaeological Record, Literary Description, and Religious Development*, ed. Helmut Koester (Harrisburg, PA: Trinity Press International, 1998), 65–6. See also J. M. Cortés Copete, *Elio Aristides. Un sofista griego en el Imperio Romano* (Madrid: Clásicas, 1995), 60–77.

[60] Petsalis-Diomidis, *'Truly Beyond Wonders'*, 170.

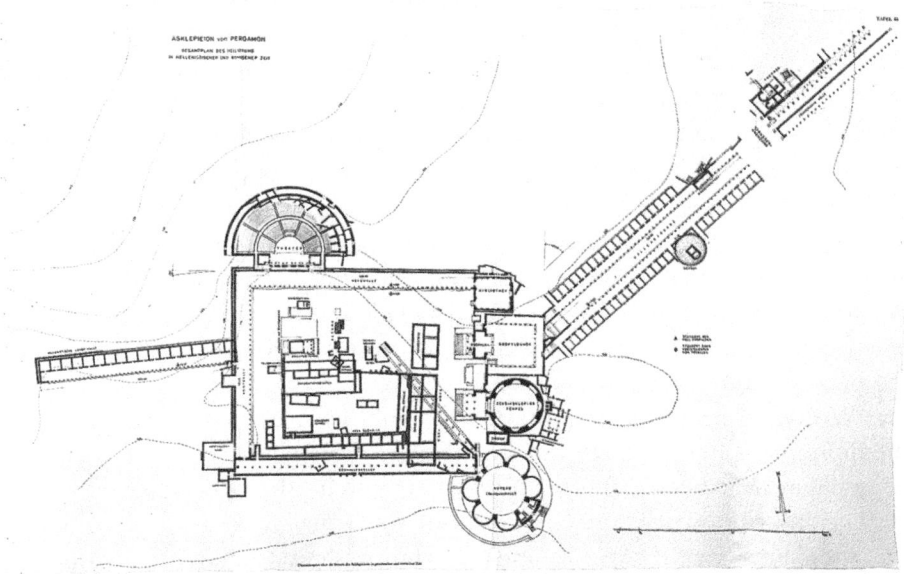

**Figure 1.6** Plan of the Sanctuary of Asklepios at Pergamon. Welcome Images (https://wellcomecollection.org/works/u6pw5py4). Licence CC by 3.0 IT (https://creativecommons.org/licenses/by/3.0/). Enhanced resolution.

Each element contributed to the sacred workings of the sanctuary, even the library, which contained a statue of the emperor Hadrian in its central niche. This statue depicts Hadrian nude, a common portrayal of Greek gods and heroes, and the inscription on the base of the statue reads, in part, 'The god Hadrian': the two together make a clear reference to the imperial cult, which was firmly established in the provinces by this point.[61]

A look at the Hadrianic temple of Zeus Asklepios confirms both the connection with the imperial family and, more importantly for our purposes, the fact that Asklepios was not alone in his sanctuary. The temple was modelled after the restored Pantheon in Rome, being of similar design (if on a considerably smaller scale), Petsalis-Diomidis calling it 'a miniature replica of the Roman Pantheon'.[62] Figure 1.6 includes the temple of Zeus Asklepios, the circular structure on the eastern edge of the sanctuary. A particular feature to highlight here is the alternating hemispherical and rectangular niches, which were thought to house statues of deities, although there has been no direct find to confirm this.[63] The assumption seems reasonable; if it is accurate, then the

---

[61] *AvP* VIII.3, no. 6. The inscription reads: θεόν Ἀδριανόν φλ. Μελιτίνη.
[62] Petsalis-Diomidis, *'Truly Beyond Wonders'*, 194.
[63] Ibid., 196.

largest of the temples in the sanctuary contained cult images of Asklepios and at least six other gods. Thus, the Hadrianic expansion of the sanctuary included not only innovative architectural features and additions, but also expansion of the group of gods present in the complex.

The identity of these gods is unknown, but we might be able to surmise something of their identity from an inscription of a *lex sacra* found in two places in and near the sanctuary. The inscription probably dates to the turn of the first and second centuries and was found in a ditch next to the Via Tecta, a partially colonnaded walkway that connected the Asklepieion to the city of Pergamon. The walkway followed an old Hellenistic road and approached the sanctuary at an angle. Smaller fragments of an inscription that repeats parts of the one found in the ditch indicate that there were two copies in the sanctuary. Wörrle believes that the inscription could have been displayed either at the monumental entrance to the sanctuary or somewhere inside. The second copy might have been displayed somewhere else inside the sanctuary.[64]

The inscription itself details some of the rituals that were required of the suppliants visiting the sanctuary who wished to practise incubation (ritualized sleeping overnight in a sanctuary). The appendix (pp. 217–19) has the text of the inscription in full, but what is most important here is the ritual life detailed by the inscription, and its inclusion of several gods alongside Asklepios. Zeus Apotropaios, Zeus Meilichios, Artemis Prothyraia, a second Artemis whose epithet is lost to fragmentation of the inscription, Ge, Tyche, Mnemosyne, Themis and Apollo constitute the collection of gods mentioned in the inscription. Since the inscription predates the Hadrianic expansion of the sanctuary, the rituals could be traditional rather than a Hadrianic innovation. Although the precise logic of the rituals is subject to interpretation, it is clear that there *is* a logic, and so the inclusion of these particular gods is not accidental or random. At the very least, the ritual invocation enables the suppliants to ensure protection and a proper frame of mind before entering the incubation chamber. But I also think that, in the logic of the rituals, the invocation of these particular gods works to bring a community of gods together for the mutual benefit of the suppliant, the sanctuary and the main god, Asklepios. If everything works as planned, the suppliant receives a cure for or some relief from what ails them; Asklepios receives the proper honour due to him; and the sanctuary gains the fame of being a major sacred space that can contribute to the health and well-being of Pergamon and those pilgrims who visit the sanctuary. The gods who are invoked all work together with the suppliant to these ends.[65]

---

[64] M. Wörrle, 'Die Lex sacra von der Hallenstraße (Inv. 1965, 20)', in *AvP* VIII.3, 167–8.
[65] See Stephen P. Ahearne-Kroll, 'Mnēmosynē at the Asklepieia', *CP* 109 (2014): 99–118, for an extended treatment of this idea with a focus on Mnēmosynē.

In the Pergamon Asklepieion of the first century we therefore have a fairly large but defined group of gods working together with suppliants to enact some sort of healing experience that involved honouring the gods and preparing the suppliant for encounter with Asklepios. At a minimum, this group includes Asklepios, Hygeia, Telesphoros, Apollo, Zeus Apotropaios, Zeus Meilichios, Artemis Prothyraia (and a second Artemis), Ge, Tyche, Mnemosyne and Themis. All but Asklepios, Hygeia, Telesphoros and Apollo are invoked as gods that contribute to the preparation of the suppliant for incubation. Asklepios, Hygeia, Telesphoros and Apollo are the core members of the sanctuary, who have some other purpose beyond ritual preparation for incubation. In fact, these divinities are all part of the mythological family of Asklepios: Apollo is the father of Asklepios, Hygeia his daughter,[66] and Telesphoros his son. We see this pattern in other Asklepieia also – namely a core group of family members, supplemented with additional gods who ensure the success of the ritual life of the sanctuary.

### Phrygia

I would like to expand the scope of inquiry here to talk about a region, Phrygia, while focusing on a particular local set of gods, namely the gods of justice, *Hosion kai Dikaion*, 'Holy and Just'.[67] These gods were widespread in the villages and countryside of Phrygia and beyond,[68] so it is worth seeing how they function and what other gods might be brought together with them.

Because the evidence largely comes from rural contexts where sanctuaries do not survive as well as in urban contexts, we need to consider mainly inscriptional evidence in painting a picture of these gods. A large majority of inscriptional evidence for Hosios and Dikaios as a pairing comes from Phrygia – especially north-western Phrygia and bordering Lydia – so scholars think that this cult

---

[66] Orphic Hymn 67 calls her Asklepios's wife, rather than his daughter.
[67] Marijana Ricl, 'Newly Published and Unpublished Inscriptions for Hosios and Dikaios and Their Contribution to the Study of the Cult', in *Vom Euphrat bis zum Bosporus. Kleinasien in der Antike. Festschrift für Elmar Schwertheim zum 65. Gebürtstag*, ed. Engelbert Winter (Bonn: Habelt, 2008), 564, calls them a 'divine couple'.
[68] Ibid., 563, mentions Lydia, Mysia, Bithynia, the Kibyratis and Macedonia all showing increasing attestation of these two gods, but Phrygia contains by far the most evidence for them as configured in various ways with other gods. The latest count of inscriptions that mention one or both of Hosias and Dikaios is 185, if we maintain Ricl's practice of including dedications to Theoi Dikaioi. See also A. Coşkun, 'Dionysiac Associations among the Dedicants of Ho-sios kai Dikaios. Revisiting Recently Published Inscriptions from the Mihalıççık District in North-West Galatia', *Gephyra* 19 (2020): 111.

originated in central Anatolia.⁶⁹ Much of the epigraphic evidence for Hosios and Dikaios comes either from funerary inscriptions or from votive inscriptions. The votive inscriptions generally mark a vow fulfilled by those who commissioned it, but it is usually not specified if the vow was for a specific act or simply a vow to express adherence to and honour of the gods. Sometimes the inscription does not include the καί between the deities:

Ἀγαθῇ τύχῃ· Κταηνοῖ Βαχιον τὸ περὶ Τύραννο- Ὁσίῳ Δικέῳ ὑπὲ[ρ] ἑατῶν κὲ τῶν ἰδ[ίων] εὐχήν, ἐπιμ[ελο]- υμένου Ἀππ[. .] [. .]θου κὲ Κλ[. .] [. . . .]τυρ[. . . .] - - - - - - - - - - - - -

For good fortune; The Ktaenoi Bachion around Tyrannos fulfilled a vow to Hosios (and?) Dikeos on behalf of themselves and their own (families); App(as?) son of (Anthos?) and Cl(audius) son of Tyrranos? attended to it.⁷⁰

This inscription appears on an altar; the altar also has a fragmentary pediment that shows a figure holding the bridles of four horses. The figure can be identified as either Helios or Apollo – the iconography of both includes driving a quadriga. Comparative regional evidence leads Hale Güney to Helios rather than Apollo, but Apollo makes sense as a god of justice in this region.⁷¹

Another inscription is clearly dedicated to Apollo, along with Hosios and Dikaios. This time it was both dedicated and set up by a 'slave of the emperors':

Χυρυσέρως αὐτοκρατόρων δοῦλος. vac Ἀπολλώνι Ὁσίῳ κὲ Δεικέῳ Χρυσέρως κὲ κώμη[τ]αι ὑπὲρ τῆς ἑαυτῶν σωτηρίας ἀνέστ[η]σαν εὐχάς.

---

⁶⁹ Hale Güney, 'New Inscriptions from Northeast Phrygia: The Cult of Hosios and Dikaios', *Gephyra* 15 (2018): 107.
⁷⁰ Ibid., 103, cat. no. 1 (translation modified). The lack of the καί could be practical or local custom when referring to the deities.
⁷¹ See Mitchell, *Anatolia*, 1:191: 'Apollo and the all-seeing sun Helios cast a baleful glare over man's [sic] affairs and no malefactor could escape their notice … Two Phrygian inscriptions, evidently from the same sanctuary, well illustrate the range and character of this pantheon. One invokes the saviour gods, and depicts a bust of Zeus, Dionysus, a mounted god with a double axe, and a god carrying a whip in a quadriga. The latter are identified as Apollo and as Mēn Dikaios, described as the "Eye of Justice and Moderation", Ὀφθαλμός Δικαιοσύνης καὶ Σωφροσύνης.' An inscription from the first century (*RECAM* II, 47) shows Helios as the object of honour, as ordered by Apollo: ΝΑΟΙΙΤΙΚΗ Ἡλίῳ Ἀπόλλωνος κατὰ κέλευσιν ('ΝΑΟΙΙΤΙΚĒ to Helios according to the command of Apollo').

Ch(y)ryserōs, a slave of the emperors. Chryseros and the villagers fulfill vows to Apollo, Hosios, and Deikeos [alternative spelling for Dikaios] for their own deliverance.[72]

This matches well with other inscriptions that have Apollo paired with one or both of these gods:

Γάιος κὲ Απφια ὑπὲρ τῶν ἰδίων κὲ Λαουας Ὁσίῳ Ἀπόλλωνι, θεοῖς ἐπηκόοις, εὐχήν.

Gaios and Apphia on behalf of their own (family) along with Laouas, fulfills a vow to Hosios (and) Apollo, attentive gods.[73]

The inscription was found on an altar with a bust of a woman on a pediment. Apollo is holding Marsyas the satyr by the neck in one hand and a lyre in the other. The story of Marsyas is, in part, about the hubris of the satyr and Apollo's just act of punishment for it.[74] So the theme of justice is emphasised in the inscription, even if Dikaios is not mentioned as an individual god along with Hosios. But this next inscription features Hosios and Dikaios alone as a pair:

[Ἀ]γαθῇ τύχῃ· [Ὁσί]ῳ καὶ Δικέῳ Παρ[. . .]διατε ὑπὲρ ἑαυ[τ]ῶν κὲ τῶν ἰδίων παντῶν εὐχήν.

For good fortune. N.N. fulfills a vow to Hosios and Dikeos on behalf of themselves and all their own (family).[75]

In all these inscriptions, we have a group effort, at both the human and divine levels. A person sets up the inscription, the vow, on behalf of themself and a group ('their own' or 'their family'), to a pair or group of gods for something unspecified. In the case of Apollo and Hosios and Dikaios, the theme of justice

---

[72] Güney, 'New Inscriptions from Northeast Phrygia', 104, cat. no. 2. Güney's third and fourth inscriptions (105, cat. no. 3; 106, cat. no. 4) seem to be along the same lines at this one, but they are too fragmentary, in my opinion, to reconstruct with any certainty. She translates αὐτοκρατόρων with the singular 'emperor' but the possibility exists that the slave served two emperors in succession or at the same time.
[73] *RECAM* II, 44.
[74] There are several versions of the story. One stream, going back to the fifth century BCE, has Marsyas picking up an *aulos* that had been cast away and cursed by Athena and then being killed by Apollo for his hubris. Another stream has him challenging Apollo to a music contest, *aulos* versus lyre, again with the satyr losing and being punished for the hubris of challenging a god.
[75] Güney, 'New Inscriptions from Northeast Phrygia', 107, cat. no. 5.

is present, and this theme is expressed both iconographically (scales of justice)[76] and mythologically (for example, the story of Marsyas). Although it is difficult to determine the details of the cultic life involving Hosios and Dikaios, mainly because their sanctuaries do not survive, we can say that these votive offerings are not simply for show. Many of them are found on altars, which implies cultic offerings, and others express a fealty by humans to honour these gods, either by praying in the hopes of receiving certain things (safety, justice) or for fulfilling a vow in thanksgiving for receiving something important.

### Across Anatolia

These examples – a major urban sanctuary in Pergamon and rural evidence across Phrygia – form only a small slice of the pattern that is ubiquitous across Anatolia. It is worth quoting Stephen Mitchell at length:

> One would find dedications or offerings to a range of deities not only in a single city, but in any given sanctuary. At Didyma there was a circle of altars in the sanctuary of Apollo, set up for his immortal colleagues. Two oracles of the early third century prescribed that an altar of Fortune and an altar of Kore should be added to the group with appropriate ceremony and ritual. In the sanctuary of Zeus at Panamara in Caria . . . the inscriptions refer not only to the principal temple of Zeus Panamaros, but to temples of Hera, Zeus Karios and Hera, a chapel and altar of Sarapis, and an altar of Artemis. Multiple invocations were common on a single monument, for instance the relief set up as a dedication to the gods of Motelleis, a small community in the territory of Phrygian Hierapolis, which depicts a bust of Zeus presiding over a group made up from Artemis, Mēn, and a rider god with a double axe, probably Apollo.[77]

What we have seen in Egypt and Palestine holds true for Anatolia also.

## Greece

### Athens and Its Environs

The religious landscape of Athens is vast, and so I am only able to give a snapshot of some of the highlights of the many examples of 'chords of gods' present in the city and its surroundings. Nonetheless, there are many prominent

---

[76] See Marijana Ricl, 'Hosios kai Dikaios. Première partie: catalogue des inscriptions', *Epigraphica Anatolica* 18 (1991): nos. 21, 26, 47, 48, 52, as typical examples.

[77] Mitchell, *Anatolia*, 2:15.

examples of the worship of small groups of gods, and some not so prominent. I will start with the most prominent (the Acropolis) and conclude with a very minor sanctuary (Kephisos).

## The Acropolis

The most famous religious and cultural site in Athens (if not all of Greece) is the Acropolis (Figure 1.7), which has as its centrepiece the Periclean Parthenon dedicated to the city's patron deity, Athena.[78] The Parthenon dominates the landscape and describes pictorially many founding moments of Athena's ascent as the city's patron — including her birth (depicted on the east pediment), her victory over Poseidon to secure her leadership of Athens (on the west pediment), and her role in the gigantomachy (on the east metopes). The landscape of the Acropolis contains other sanctuaries, however, which contribute to this story of Athens's greatness and prominence in classical times. When taken together, these sanctuaries do not simply focus all attention on Athena in the Parthenon, but provided the possibility for Athenian worshippers to experience the fullness of the divine community assembled with Athena that, together, established the

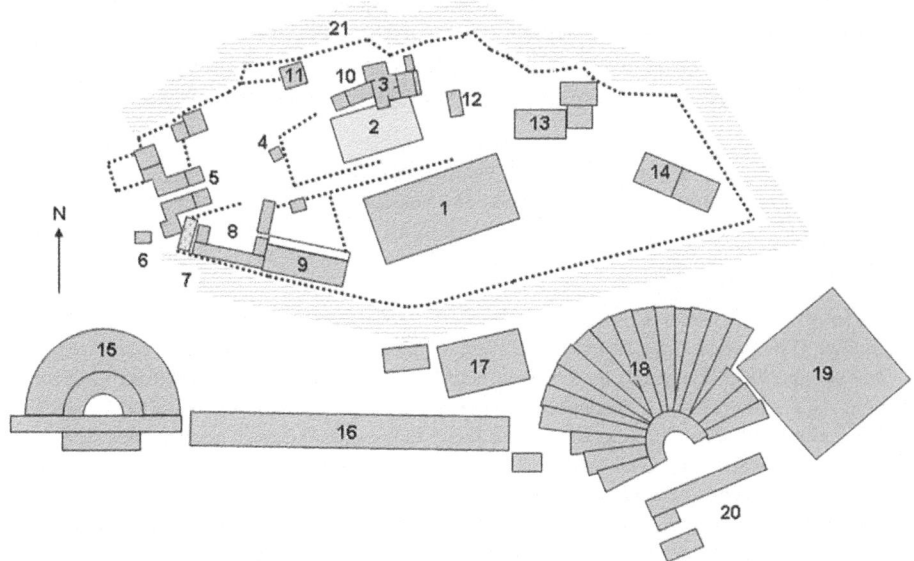

**Figure 1.7** Plan of the Acropolis. Madmedea. CC-A-SA-2.0 (https://creativecommons.org/licenses/by-sa/2.0/deed.en). Enhanced resolution.

---

[78] For an excellent treatment of the Acropolis in different periods of Greek history, see Jeffrey M. Hurwit, *The Athenian Acropolis: History, Myth, and Archaeology from the Neolithic Era to the Present* (Cambridge: Cambridge University Press, 1999).

greatness of Athens, protected the city and its inhabitants, and made Athenians the great people that they were. Acting together for the benefit of Athens, the divine community deserved proper honour, and what better place to show this than the Acropolis?

As one approaches the Acropolis up the western slope to enter the Propylaia (Figure 1.7, Building 5), to the right is the temple of Athena Nike (Building 6), which 'from the middle years of the sixth century . . . had occupied the projecting western bastion of the Acropolis'.[79] At the time of the construction of the Propylaia, the sanctuary contained a small *naiskos* that was probably constructed after the Persian wars, but sometime during the construction of the Propylaia the precinct of Athena Nike was expanded by some 8 square metres.[80] Understandably, the temple's north and south friezes showed several scenes of Athenians victorious in battle;[81] the east frieze showed Athena, Zeus and Poseidon assembled together. It is unclear in this case whether Athenians thought of this version of Athena as significantly different from the other depictions of her on the Acropolis.[82] Is it possible that they were honouring the partnership of Athena and Nike in bringing victory to Athens? Robin Francis Rhodes comments:

> In spite of her scale, in many ways Nike is the most immediately noticeable, the most striking element of the great entranceway to the Acropolis. She is an essential part of that entranceway: Her bastion and terrace are visually one with the Propylaia, and it is in this specific

---

[79] T. Leslie Shear, *Trophies of Victory: Public Building in Periklean Athens* (Princeton: Princeton University Press, 2016), 341. See Ira S. Mark, *The Sanctuary of Athena Nike in Athens: Architectural Stages and Chronology* (Princeton: American School of Classical Studies in Athens, 1993), for a treatment of the sanctuary as of 1988.

[80] Shear, *Trophies of Victory*, 341.

[81] The south frieze shows a decisive victory over the Persians at the battle of Plataea. See Michael Jameson, 'The Ritual of the Athena Nike Parapet', in *Ritual, Finance, Politics: Democratic Accounts Presented to David Lewis*, ed. R. Osborne and S. Hornblower (Oxford: Oxford University Press, 1994), 307–24, for a description of the rituals depicted on the parapet sculpture and an argument that they show a compressed scene of a *sphagia* (a pre-battle sacrifice to ensure victory) and its resulting celebration.

[82] 'The cultic double name allowed juxtapositions not just between a Greek and non-Greek god's name [Zeus Thebaieus referring to Amun-Re] but also between a major Greek god and a lesser: Apollo Paion, Artemis Eileithyia, Athena Nike. How the Greeks understood such compounds is not always clear, but it is plausible that in many cases the second element was taken as an epithet of the first: Artemis Eileithyia is Artemis in her relation to childbirth as Athena Hippia is Athena in her relation to horses . . . A parallel case in a slightly different way is that of Zeus Chthonios, Zeus of the earth and of the underworld. Is Zeus Chthonios to be understood as "Zeus in his aspect as god of the earth and the underworld", or is he rather "the underworld equivalent of Zeus"? . . . Even to pose the question is perhaps to seek a precision that the Greeks knew to be unattainable.' Parker, *On Greek Religion*, 69–70.

context, not in a general context of 'temples of the Acropolis', that her meaning and significance are to be found.[83]

Michael H. Jameson describes the rituals depicted on the parapet of the temple (a *sphagia* and its resultant celebration) as follows: 'The message is blunt, even brutal: Victory and Athena guarantee the success of the Athenian people, committed to battle. Nike, under Athena's eye, ensures by the violent act of killing that the Athenians will win.'[84] Although the cult statue of Athena in this temple evoked some sort of combination of Athena and Nike (famously called Apteros Nike, wingless victory), one wonders if the Athenians might have conceived of Nike present alongside Athena as they offered their worship. Certainly, the cult statue of Athena in the Parthenon, with Athena holding a miniature Nike in an upraised hand, would have reinforced this concept. More simply, it was certainly possible that the focus on victory that Athena Nike embodied was one major way in which Athena led the city and formed its civic identity, and the Athenians thought it proper to honour her in particular with cultic worship at this small temple.[85] However we make sense of the temple, with its reconstruction and expansion, 'the bastion became an integral part of the Acropolis'.[86]

The Propylaia itself offers some evidence for worship of a group of gods, which is not unusual for gates and gateways to sanctuaries.[87] In some form, the entrance to the Acropolis goes back to the earliest evidence of human activity on the site,[88] but there is no way to tell how far back cultic activity existed because of the several rebuilds of the Propylaia and the constant human activity that happened there from very early times. However, there is evidence

---

[83] Robin Francis Rhodes, *Architecture and Meaning on the Athenian Acropolis* (Cambridge: Cambridge University Press, 1995), 115.

[84] Jameson, 'The Ritual of the Athena Nike Parapet', 138. The parapet of the temple shows Nike adjusting her sandals, and there are multiple representations of Nike on the surviving sculpture of the temple, including the akroteria statues, which are the first seen by visitors as they approach the Acropolis up the west slope. For a thorough treatment of the reconstruction of the akroteria, see Peter Schultz, 'The Akroteria of the Temple of Athena Nike', *Hesperia* 70 (2001): 1–47.

[85] Robert Parker, *Greek Gods Abroad: Names, Natures, and Transformations* (Berkeley: University of California Press, 2017), 16. Parker argues for two main functions of epithets for Greek gods: 'One is to distinguish the god worshipped in one place from the same god worshipped in another ... The second broad function of the epithet was to provide focus, to pick out one aspect or power amid the many of a god of broad powers' (14–15).

[86] Shear, *Trophies of Victory*, 342.

[87] Constanze Graml, 'Wandering Maidens in the Acropolis Propylaia: Some Considerations on the Spatial Setting of the Cults of the Charites, Artemis and Hermes, Their Administration and Related Cult Images', *JHS* 142 (2022), 274–97.

[88] Ibid., p. 274.

for cultic practice before the Mnesiklean Propylaia was built.[89] Through a combination of material, epigraphic and literary evidence, Constanze Graml argues for the presences of Athena Nike, Artemis Brauronia, Athena Hygieia, Artemis Hekate (called Epipyrgidia [on the bastion] by Pausanias and located by him near the Temple of Athena Nike[90]), Hermes and the Charites, grouped in different ways depending on the time period being considered.[91] Pausanias is the main literary evidence, but *IG* I³ 383, lines 125–30, shows evidence for property belonging to both Hermes and Artemis Hekate (429/428 BCE),[92] and *IG* II² 5050 indicates that the priest of Artemis Epipyrgidia and the Charites had a marble throne in the front row of the Theatre of Dionysos in the first century BCE.[93]

Having passed through the Propylaia, immediately on the right is the sanctuary of Artemis Brauronia or 'Artemis of the Bear' (Building 8). This was clearly modelled after the famous pi-shaped temple at the Artemis sanctuary at Brauron, which was a regional sanctuary on the east coast of Attica (that is, more wide-ranging than a strictly local sanctuary, but not as widely famous as one like the oracle at Delphi). It is unclear when the sanctuary was built, but the latest date would be sometime before 416/415 BCE, when there is the earliest record of the removal of treasures from Brauron to the Acropolis.[94] The earliest evidence of dedicatory offerings to Artemis Brauronia on the Acropolis dates from between 402 and 400 BCE, but evidence for regular ritual practice can be found in *IG* I³ 369, which dates to approximately 426/425 BCE.[95] The sanctuary of Artemis Brauronia on the Acropolis linked Athens with Brauron by a procession that took place every four years during the Arkteia festival.[96] Aside from this quadrennial festival, 'everybody walking through the Propylaea up to the Parthenon passed it on their right-hand side'.[97] On the

---

[89] Ibid., p. 291. See Jos de Waele, *The Propylaia of the Akropolis in Athens: The Project of Mnesikles* (Amsterdam: J. C. Gieben, 1990), for an argument regarding the dimensions and layout of the Mnisiklean stage of the Propylaia.

[90] Paus. 1.30.2.

[91] Graml, 'Wandering Maidens', p. 291.

[92] See Shear, *Trophies of Victory*, 281.

[93] See ibid., 281n23.

[94] See ibid., 282–3.

[95] *IG* I³ 369 is a very long inscription that shows evidence of cultic ritual to a number of gods, including Artemis Brauronia.

[96] For a good treatment of the way that Artemis was urbanised, see Ivana Petrovic, 'Transforming Artemis: From the Goddess of the Outdoors to City Goddess', in *The Gods of Ancient Greece: Identities and Transformations*, ed. Jan N. Bremmer and Andrew Erskine (Edinburgh: Edinburgh University Press, 2010), 209–27.

[97] Pär Ola Sandin, 'Life and Death on the East Frieze of the Parthenon', *Symbolai Osloenses* 96 (2022), accessed 23 January 2024, https://doi.org/10.1080/00397679.2023.2175502. See the whole article for an interpretation of the depictions of the gods on the east frieze and their relation to imperial cultural dynamics.

east frieze of the Parthenon, Artemis appears with Aphrodite and Eros, the significance of which has been debated. But her importance to the Acropolis and the Parthenon is solidified by the east frieze, and by her presence in the sanctuary next to the Parthenon. This sanctuary also served to heighten the prominence of Athena on the Acropolis, and Athens in turn, because of the importance of Brauron's sanctuary in the region of Attica.

Along with Artemis's temple, we have the Erectheion (Building 3), which marked some of the most sacred ground in all of Athens. While the original location of the temple has been debated, J. Z. van Rookhuijzen has recently convincingly argued that the location remained consistent in its so-called 'Dörpfeld foundation' in the middle of the Acropolis from archaic Greece through to late antiquity, rather than having been relocated to the Karyatid Temple following the archaic temple's destruction by the Persians in 480 BCE.[98] It is the purported site of Erectheus's death and burial, either at the hands of Poseidon, who drove him into an opening in the earth with his trident,[99] or at the hands of Zeus (at Poseidon's request), who struck him down with his bolt of lightning.[100] All the major gods and important figures of Athens's origins were honoured in this temple: Athena, Poseidon and Hephaestus,[101] along with Kekrops, Boutis and Erechtheus. Zeus also was honoured, in the form of Zeus Kataibates, to reflect the killing of Erechtheus by Zeus's thunderbolt.[102]

Athena and Poseidon were, of course, the two gods who battled for the right to protect Athens, and the remains of their battle of gifts were housed at the Erectheion (the trident marks where Poseidon's salt water spring was created and the olive tree given by Athena, which won the day). Kekrops was the founding king of Athens; Boutis was the priest of Athena and Poseidon; and Erectheus was Boutis's brother, from whom all Athenians supposedly traced their ancestry. He was reared by Athena and was the product of Hephaestus's semen (emitted in an interruption of his and Athena's tryst) falling to the ground and impregnating Gaia. The original, mythically old wooden cult statue of Athena resided in the Erechtheion, and the sacred serpent of the Acropolis also lived there.[103] Mary B. Hollinshead has argued that the Temple of Athena Polias was built as part of the Erechtheion and was the likely setting for the ceremonies of the Plynteria and Kallynteria, during which the ancient olivewood statue of Athena was taken out of the temple, bathed and

---

[98] J. Z. van Rookhuijzen, 'The Erechtheion on the Acropolis of Athens', *Kernos* 34 (2021): 69–121.
[99] See Eur. *Ion* 281.
[100] See Hyg. *Fab.* 46.
[101] Homer has Hephaestus and Athena training master craftsmen (*Od.* 6.233 and 23.160), and they were seen as a complementary pair in providing healing gifts to humans.
[102] See G. W. Elderkin, 'The Cults of the Erechtheion', *Hesperia* 10 (1941): 114.
[103] There was apparently a sacred snake that lived on the Acropolis to which Athenians would offer a honey cake monthly.

adorned.[104] In some key ways, this temple marked the cultural and historical beginnings of Athens, at least in the traditions of the Athenians.

Two other temples are worthy of note: the sanctuary of Zeus Polieus (Building 13), where Pausanias describes the performance of the traditional sacrifice of bulls (Zeus, of course, being the father of Athena and brother of Poseidon);[105] and the sanctuary of Pandion (Building 14), the mythical son of Kekrops (or Erechtheus in some traditions). As Sylvain Lebreton has demonstrated in a careful study of the evidence for Zeus Polieus in Athens from the sixth century BCE to the beginning of the third century CE, the god was rooted on the Acropolis, which symbolised the highness of his location in Athenian culture. According to Lebreton, his political role in Athens did not include being an active protector of Athens; that was Athena Polias's role. Instead, his focus was on ensuring the political unity of Athenians and on supporting the protective role of Athena Polias.[106] The sanctuary of Pandion was specifically reserved for the eponymous tribe to offer their honours to Pandion, who was either one of the two legendary Athenian kings or the hero of the Attic tribe Pandionis.[107] Pausanias reports seeing a cult statue of Pandion in the sanctuary, but there is no other evidence for it.[108] Both of these sanctuaries are on the east side of the Acropolis.

Finally, we have the various manifestations of Athena on the Acropolis. We have already seen the temple of Athena Nike, the first temple visible as one approaches the Acropolis, and that of Athena Polias, superior to and supported by Zeus Polieus as the political leader and unifier of the Athenian community. Once through the Propylaia, visitors were greeted by the colossal bronze statue of Athena Promachos (Number 4), if Pausanias is to be believed.[109] This version of Athena showed her protection and leadership of Athenian soldiers as they headed into battle to protect Athens from all foreign threats, and was probably made by Pheidias and erected sometime after 490 BCE.[110] This form of Athena seems to have been 'the most popular

---

[104] Mary B. Hollinshead, 'The North Court of the Erechtheion and the Ritual of the Plynteria', *American Journal of Archaeology* 119 (2015): 117–90. See also Henrik Gerding, 'The Erechtheion and the Panathenaic Procession', *American Journal of Archaeology* 110 (2006): 389–401.

[105] Paus. 1.24.4.

[106] Sylvain Lebreton, 'Zeus Polieus à Athènes: les Bouphonies et au-delà', *Kernos* 28 (2015): 85–110.

[107] Paus. 1.5.3–5.

[108] Paus. 1.5.4.

[109] Paus. 1.28.2, where he mentions that the point of her spear and the crest of her helmet could be seen by sailors as they passed Sounion. Birte Lundgreen, A Methodological Enquiry: The Great Bronze Athena by Pheidias', *JHS* 117 (1997): 192–4, agrees that it was likely a colossus, based on non-literary evidence such as coinage.

[110] Lundgreen, 'A Methodological Enquiry', 190. If Pheidias made the statue, then his career likely did not start until after 470 (ibid., 191).

depiction of Athena on the Acropolis' on dedicatory plates, cups and other pottery.[111] Last, we have Athena Parthenos, whose statue was the focal point of the Parthenon (Building 1), itself the focal point of the Acropolis. The cult statue was famously crafted by the master sculptor Pheidias, who also made the statue of Zeus at the sanctuary of Olympia. Pausanias describes the statue as being made of ivory and gold, with a helmet depicting a sphinx flanked by griffins on either side, a full-length tunic, and an ivory breastplate with the head of Medusa. Athena held a statue of Nike in one hand and a spear in the other. There was a shield at her feet with scenes from the gigantomachy carved into it, and a serpent near the bottom of the spear.

Although the Acropolis was a complex religio-cultural centre, it had a tight historical and mythological logic to it. All the parts reflected some aspect of Athens's history or mythological beginnings, not just to relay the facts of Athens's origins but to interweave its origins with its identity and greatness in the present, and, in turn, with the identity and greatness of Athenians. The gods present on the Acropolis were not randomly chosen but carefully grouped and honoured in a host of ways throughout the course of a year. As a group of gods and as individual deities, Athenians would honour them, perpetuate Athenian greatness and ensure the enduring protection of Athena (in all her Acropolis manifestations) and her partners, both major (Poseidon, Hephaestus, Zeus) and minor (Kekrops, Erechtheus, Boutis, Pandion).

The Panathenaea demonstrates the importance of Athena to the Athenians, with its procession ending at the Acropolis, and its offerings to Athena Nike, Athena Polias and Athena Hygieia.[112] Athena Polias alone had about fifty cows sacrificed to her during the festival,[113] with the meat from the sacrifices distributed among the citizenry, whether to be consumed publicly or privately is unknown.[114] In addition, the famed but rare *peplos* was a central part of the

---

[111] Claudia Wagner, 'The Worship of Athena on the Athenian Acropolis: Dedications of Plaques and Plates', in *Athena in the Classical World*, ed. Susan Deecy and Alexandra Villing (Leiden: Brill, 2001), 91. See also Catherine M. Keesling, *The Votive Statues of the Athenian Acropolis* (Cambridge: Cambridge University Press, 2003), for an extensive treatment of votive *korai*, their iconography and identity. These statues were not Athena statues but generic figures dedicated to Athena, mostly from the archaic and early classical periods.

[112] 'The *Panathenaea*, one might say, summed up the goddess.' Robert Parker, *Polytheism and Society at Athens* (Oxford: Oxford University Press, 2005), 266. See Julia L. Shear, *Serving Athena: The Festival of the Panathenaia and the Construction of Athenian Identities* (Cambridge: Cambridge University Press, 2021), 116–70, for a recent and compelling analysis of the ways in which identity was constructed for Athenians in relation to Athena and other celebrants through the dynamic of reciprocity.

[113] Parker, *Polytheism and Society at Athens*, 265–6.

[114] Ibid., 267. See also M. H. Jameson, 'The Spectacular and the Obscure in Athenian Religion', in *Performance Culture and Athenian Democracy*, ed. S. Goldhill and R. Osborne (Cambridge: Cambridge University Press, 1999), 326.

procession, supposedly woven by over a hundred Athenian girls (by Hellenistic times) over the four years leading up to the festival.[115] The imagery woven into it was that of the gigantomachy, a key event in the creation of humankind and an event that highlighted Athena's prominence among the gods.[116] As Parker says, in reflecting on the meaning of the festival:

> As an emblem to set over the *Panathenaea*, the myth of Athena's victory in the gigantomachy is doubtless the best, because it brings out the triumphant self-assertion that marks the festival, the absence of discord or of concern with Dionysiac depths . . . That single myth sheds no more light on much of what the Athenians felt and thought at, and about, the *Panathenaea* than does any other summation of a complex experience in a few words.[117]

The Acropolis, at the centre of it all, shows the importance of a group of gods surrounding a main god to both a local population and a regional and wider population.

### *Asklepieia at Athens and Piraeus*

At Piraeus there is substantial evidence of an active and expansive Asklepieion functioning into the Roman imperial period.[118] In the late nineteenth century, a construction project uncovered a Hellenistic dedicatory inscription of a priest of Asklepios and Hygieia, found with the remains of a fifth-century BCE boundary stone.[119] In the subsequent excavation of the site (its first), a wealth of fragmentary evidence was found, all associated with Askplepios and Hygieia.[120] A much more recent excavation uncovered evidence that

---

[115] Parker, *Polytheism and Society at Athens*, 264.
[116] See Emma Stafford, 'Visualizing Creation in Ancient Greece', *Religion and the Arts* 13 (2009): 428–30, for a discussion of the gigantomachy as part of the creation myths depicted visually in ancient Greece. Zoe Stamatopoulou, 'Weaving Titans for Athena: Euripides and the Panathenaic *Peplos* (*Hec.* 466–74 and *IT* 218–24),' *CQ* 62 (2012): 72, calls the evidence for the depiction of the gigantomachy in the *peplos* 'unanimous'.
[117] Parker, *Polytheism and Society at Athens*, 268.
[118] Dimitris Grigoropoulos, 'The Piraeus from 86 BC to Late Antiquity: Continuity and Change in the Landscape, Function and Economy of the Port of Roman Athens', *Annual of the British School at Athens* 111 (2016): 253.
[119] Jessica Lamont, 'Asklepios in the Piraeus and the Mechanisms of Cult Appropriation', in *Autopsy in Athens: Recent Archaeological Research on Athens and Attica*, ed. Margaret M. Miles (Oxford: Oxbow, 2015), 38. The inscription is *IG* II² 4453, and it reads: [ἱε]ρεὺς Φορμ[ίω]ν Ἡδύλου | [Ἐ]λευσίνιος Ἀσκληπιῶι | [καί] Ὑγιείαι ἀνέθηκε.
[120] Ibid., 38: 'In a very short period, the excavations yielded fragments of statues, statuettes, votive reliefs, and anatomical votives – all associated with Asklepios and Hygieia.'

points to a far more extensive complex included in the Asklepieion than was previously thought. Several buildings and an open area extend south and east from the main temple into an area long associated with Zeus Meilichios and Zeus Philios.[121]

A complex *lex sacra* survives that was probably inscribed at several different points over the life of the sanctuary, showing the way in which the rituals there became more complex over time.[122] The inscription is fairly straightforward, in that it describes which offerings must be made to various gods and divine figures. Among them are Maleatas, Apollo, Hermes, Iaso, Akeso, Panakeia, the dogs, the huntsmen, Helios and Mnemosyne. Other than Helios and Mnemosyne, all the other divine figures are part of Asklepios's family or figure in the traditional stories of Asklepios's death and subsequent transformation into a god. It is debated as to what role Helios plays, but his popularity in the area seems part of the reason for his inclusion. And Mnemosyne shows up at many Asklepieia, probably to ensure good memory of the dream encounter with Asklepios and to articulate it well afterwards.[123] All the gods were important to honour, most likely before one entered the incubation chamber.

The Asklepieion in Athens proper was related geographically to the one in Piraeus, to the extent that Piraeus was related to Athens. Otherwise, there does not seem to be any formal relationship between the two sanctuaries. The Athenian sanctuary was located on the south slope of the Acropolis next to the Theatre of Dionysos. Pausanias has a brief description of it, most of which describes the lore around the spring located within it and the Sauromatic breastplate found among its votive offerings. But he starts his description by saying, 'The sanctuary of Asklepios is worth seeing both for the statues made of the god and his children and for the paintings' (τοῦ δὲ Ἀσκληπιοῦ τὸ ἱερὸν ἔς τε τὰ ἀγάλματά ἐστιν, ὁπόσα τοῦ θεοῦ πεποίηται καὶ τῶν παίδων, καὶ ἐς τὰς γραφὰς θέας ἄξιον; Paus. 1.21.4). The statues of Asklepios and at least part of his family give the sense that Asklepios had a defined group of divine figures around him in his sanctuaries supporting his beneficial work – a typical feature of Asklepieia that we have also seen at Pergamon and Piraeus.

The presence of other figures in the sanctuary was not a late phenomenon but dated from the founding of the sanctuary in c. 420 BCE, when Asklepios was brought from a debated location outside Athens (either Zea or Epidauros) through Piraeus to the Athenian Eleusinion (at which he stayed for several days)

---

[121] See references in ibid., no. 13.
[122] *IG* II² 4962.
[123] See Ahearne-Kroll, 'Mnēmosynē at the Asklepieia', for a more complete analysis of Mnemosyne's role in the ritual life of Asklepios sanctuaries and for a discussion of the Piraeus *lex sacra*.

and then to the south slope of the Acropolis.[124] The famous but fragmentary Telemachos monument marks the founding of the sanctuary and its subsequent development during successive archons through the course of at least ten years (where the surviving inscription cuts off).[125] It begins: 'Telemachos first set up the sanctuary and altar to Asklepios, and to Hygieia, and the Asklepiadae and the daughters of Asklepios . . .' ([Τ]ηλέμαχος ἱδ[ρύσατο τὸ ἱ]- | [ερ]ὸν καὶ τὸν βω[μὸν τῶι Ἀσ]- | [σκλ]ηπιῶι πρῶτ[ος καὶ Ὑγι]- | [είαι], τοῖς Ἀσς[κληπιάδαι]- | [ς καὶ τ]αῖς ᾿Ασσκ[ληπιὸ θυγ]- | [ατράσιν] καὶ - - - - - - - - - -]).[126] Although the inscription is heavily reconstructed, it does indicate a multiplicity of gods and figures associated with Asklepios as the original figures to which the sanctuary was dedicated. This falls in line with the traditional grouping of gods and divine figures found with Asklepios at other sanctuaries in principle if not in detail – a group of family members or other figures associated with him mythologically. In this case, the Asklepiades are those physicians (either living or not) who trace their lineage back to Asklepios.

## Healing at the Areopagos

On the south slope of the Areopagos, between the Areopagos and the Pnyx, there was a sanctuary to the healing god/hero Amynos, containing an open-air shrine and a well.[127] The sanctuary itself goes back to the sixth century BCE, but the earliest private dedications that have been found are from the

---

[124] A festival marking this occasion (the Epidauria) contained a procession that likely marked Asklepios's original route into the city from Piraeus to the sanctuary on the south slope. See Bronwen L. Wickkiser, *Asklepios, Medicine, and the Politics of Healing in Fifth-Century Athens: Between Craft and Cult* (Baltimore: Johns Hopkins University Press, 2008), 74, and Parker, *Polytheism and Society at Athens*, 462, for a description of the festival.

[125] The text of the inscription (SEG 25.226, with a new version of lines 1–26 found at SEG 47.232) is reconstructed by Kevin Clinton in 'The Epidauria and the Arrival of Asclepius in Athens', in *Ancient Greek Cult Practice from the Epigraphical Evidence*, ed. R. Hägg (Stockholm: Swedish Institute at Athens, 1994), 17–34; it is treated thoroughly by Wickkiser, *Asklepios*, 62, and discussed throughout the rest of her book since the monument is the central piece of evidence for the founding of the sanctuary in Athens.

[126] Text and translation from Wickkiser, *Asklepios*, 67–70.

[127] John S. Kloppenborg and Richard S. Ascough, *Greco-Roman Associations: Texts, Translations, and Commentary*, vol. 1, *Attica, Central Greece, Macedonia, Thrace* (Berlin: Walter de Gruyter, 2011), 46, call Amynos a god, but Emily Kearns, *The Heroes of Attica* (London: University of London, Institute of Classical Studies, 1989), 17, 147, includes him among the healing heroes of Athens. The line between gods and heroes in Greek religion is often drawn pretty clearly by modern scholars (for example, William Scott Ferguson, 'The Attic Orgeones and the Cult of Heroes', *HTR* 37 (1944): 61–140, who distinguishes *orgeōnes* who are devoted to heroes from those devoted to gods or goddesses). But I am not sure that, to ancient Greeks, the distinction was all that important functionally.

fourth century BCE.[128] The dedications are from both men and women,[129] indicating a mixed-gender sanctuary, and some dedications mention Amynos alone. However, an inscription related to an association of citizens (therefore male) refers to 'the common affairs of the *orgeōnes*[130] of Amynos and Asklepios and Dexion'.[131] The inscription goes on to instruct that the decree (regarding honouring two brothers who were members of the association and who acted in a particularly praiseworthy manner with respect to the association and to the association's gods) be inscribed on two stelae and be set up in 'the sanctuary of Dexios' and 'in the sanctuary of Amynos and Asklepios'.[132] Although these were two distinct sanctuaries, the pairing of them seems to indicated that their locations were near enough to each other to be associated.[133] Clearly, the sanctuary of Amynos and Asklepios indicates a small chord of gods – both were divine healing figures located in a sanctuary and supported by an association of Athenian citizen *orgeōnes*, but there is evidence that links Amynos, Asklepios and Dexios together through this association, even though the two sanctuaries were distinct. *IG* II² 1253 (c. 263 BCE); *IG* II² 1259 (c. 313/312 BCE; found in the same location as *IG* II² 1252); and *IG* II² 4487 (second century BCE) are all honorary decrees from the same association connected to Amynos, Asklepios and Dexios.

There is nothing known about Amynos's mythology, but his sphere of influence (healing) gives a clear connection to Asklepios. There were several Athenian places of worship in Athens and nearby Piraeus that made Asklepios a prominent healing presence in the city. Amynos's sanctuary predates by a century that of the main sanctuary on the south slope of the Acropolis, which was established in the late fifth century. It makes sense, then, for adherents to a healing hero/deity to establish a connection with a more famous and prominent healing deity like Asklepios, in order to bolster the sanctuary's standing in Athens. Dexios was the 'heroised Sophocles' associated with the arrival of Asklepios in Athens, who purportedly received the god into his home and set up an altar upon his arrival.[134] Although Dexios's place of worship is unknown, it makes perfect sense that this deity would be associated by the *orgeōnes* with Amynos and Asklepios. This chord of three healers both supported and was supported by the association linked with it. Whether or not

---

[128] Kearns, *The Heroes of Attica*, 147.
[129] Ibid., 20.
[130] *Orgeōnes* is one of the many terms that refer to associations, in Greek evidence. LSJ defines it as the members of a religious association.
[131] *IG* II² 1252+999, 3–4; translation Kloppenborg and Ascough, *Greco-Roman Associations*, 44.
[132] *IG* II² 1252+999, 16–17; translation Kloppenborg and Ascough, *Greco-Roman Associations*, 44.
[133] The location of the sanctuary of Dexios is unknown.
[134] See Wickkiser, *Asklepios*, 62–76, for a discussion of the arrival and establishment of the Asklepios cult in Athens.

the association members that are known from the inscriptions were people of prominence or not is disputed.[135]

### Athenian Agora

A long inscription found in the Athenian Agora from the early third century BCE contains a decree from an *orgeōnes* regarding two associations, one near the property of Kalliphanes and the '*koinon* . . . of the hero Echelos'.[136] (Echelos was known from the district Echelidai near Neon Phaleron, an Athenian port 5 kilometres south-west of the Acropolis of Athens on the coast of the Sardonic Gulf.[137]) The dedication was posted to maintain the stability of the ritual life of the temple where offerings were made to Echelos, by declaring the names of those who owed anything to the *koinonia* and setting them by the altar (lines 5–12). The inscription goes on to describe some particular offerings that should be made on the seventeenth and eighteenth of the month of Hekatombaion. These offerings include a young pig to 'the Heroines' (ταῖς ἡρωίναις) and an adult animal (ἱερεῖον τέλεον) to the hero (that is, Echelos), and then the same offering to Echelos on the last day of the month (lines 12–16).

John Kloppenborg and Richard Ascough separate the two associations by location, one being near the property of Kalliphanes in Athens and one being in Neon Phaleron.[138] But the inscription indicates a common ritual life and place of worship in the Agora, or at least a single temple where offerings to Echelos and the Heroines were made, and where the stele was posted to publicly shame those who owed something to the partnership. It is clear from the inscription that, although there were two associations, the first probably

---

[135] See Kloppenborg and Ascough, *Greco-Roman Associations*, 47, for a summary of the scholarly disagreements over the status of the association members.

[136] *Agora* 16:161. The Greek of the quoted phrase is [τῶι κοιν]ῶι . . . τῶ[ι τοῦ ἥρωος Ἐ]χέλου (lines 3–5).

[137] A two-sided relief found near Phaleron with inscriptions on each side from the late fifth century BCE contains on one side a depiction of the capture of the nymph Basile by Echelon, with the two riding a three-horse chariot, seemingly led by Hermes with whip in hand ahead of the chariot. The inscription above the relief reads Ἑρμῆς Ἔχελος [Β]ασίλη ('Hermes Echelos Basile'), with a very fragmentary part that seems to indicate the dedicant as Kephisodotos. On the back of the marble is a depiction of six figures of debatable identification, but the inscription reads Ἑρμῆι καὶ Νύμπαισιν Ἀ<λ>εξὸ [τήνδ᾽ἀνέθηκεν] ('Alexo [dedicates this] to Hermes and the Nymphs'). For the inscription, see *IG* II² 4546. For a discussion of the relief, along with photographs of both sides, see Nicholas E. Crosby, 'A Basrelief from Phaleron (Plate XII)', *American Journal of Archaeology* 9, no. 2 (1894): 202–5. Basile herself was worshipped in Athens as part of a trio of gods (Kodros, Neleus and Basile), in Erchia (alone) and in Eitea (alone, but in a temple 'that would have occupied an important position in the deme': Kearns, *The Heroes of Attica*, 151). See also H. A. Shapiro, 'The Attic Deity Basile', *ZPE* 63 (1986): 134–6.

[138] Kloppenborg and Ascough, *Greco-Roman Associations*, 81.

linked to the Heroines and the second to Echelos, the offerings were made in one temple to these deities (heroes), thus connecting them by their sanctuary.

While there is some speculation about the mythology of Echelos, according to Kearns nothing is known for certain.[139] The marble relief found in Phaleron (with the inscription *IG* II² 4546) seems to indicate some tradition or mythology around Echelos abducting Basile (or Iasile as Kearns has it), perhaps as his bride. But his connection with the unnamed Heroines is not mentioned anywhere in extant mythology.

*Kephisos*

On or near the River Kephisos, at Echelidai a few miles from Athens, where the Kephisos empties into the Aegean, there was a minor shrine, of which two marble reliefs and an inscribed stele are the only remains (see Figure 1.8). The reliefs describe a scene where a mother presents her son to someone who is likely Kephisos the river god, probably for divine protection. The first part of the inscription reads:

Ξενοκράτεια Κηφισο ἱερὸν ἱδρύσατο και ἀνέθηκεν ξυνβώμοις τε θεοῖς διδασκαλίας τόδε δῶρον ('Xenocrateia dedicates and sets up this holy gift to Kephisos and the altar sharing gods').[140]

These altar-sharing gods or another closely related group are inscribed on the surviving stele: Hestia, Kephisos, Apollo Pythios, Leto, Artemis Lochia, Iliethuia, Achelous, Kallirhoe, Geraistan Nymphs of Birth and Rhapso.[141] It seems that all these gods had a role to play in birthing and raising Xenokrateia's son, as symbolised by her presentation of him to Kephisos with the other gods surrounding them. Only together would this group ensure the health and vitality of the son. In the words of Robert Parker, 'No clearer expression is found anywhere in Greek art or literature of the idea of putting a child under divine protection than this little group.'[142]

We find here a group of gods working together, even sharing the altar of the sanctuary, to ensure the well-being of a mother and her son.[143] And

---

[139] Kearns, *The Heroes of Attica*, 165.
[140] *IG* II² 4548, 1–4.
[141] *IG* II² 4547. The two gods that can be identified in the relief (Apollo Pythios and Achelous) both show up on the list from the stele, so it is probable that the rest of the gods in the relief can be identified as such.
[142] Parker, *Polytheism and Society at Athens*, 430.
[143] Violaine Sebillotte Cuchet, 'Families et société à Athènes à l'époque classique: un éclairage par les études de genre', in *Pallas. Famille et société dans le monde grec, en Italie et à Rome du Ve au IIe siècle avant J.-C.* (Toulouse: Presses universitaires du Midi, 2017), 80.

**Figure 1.8** Relief of Xenocrateia and Kephisos, c. 400 BCE, at Kephisos. National Archaeological Museum of Athens. Photo by Jerónimo Roure Pérez. Licence CC by 4.0 IT (https://creativecommons.org/licenses/by-sa/4.0/deed.en)

the mother and son properly honour Kephisos and his altar-sharing gods, all of whom have connections to childbirth and child rearing, with the proper performance of the necessary rituals and the dedication of plaque and stele. The configuration and worship of this group is particular to this local sanctuary not far from Athens, a configuration that combines panhellenic concerns (such as Leto giving birth to the twins Apollo and Artemis, the quintessential 'fair birth' in Greek myth) with very local ones (honouring the local river god Kephisos).

**Olympia (Sanctuary of Zeus)**

The great sanctuary of Zeus at Olympia offers another fine example of the grouping of gods at a major sanctuary in Greece. It dates back to the archaic period and remained functional and active through the Roman period. Pausanias says that the earliest deity worshipped there was not Zeus but Ge, who had an oracle there (Paus. 5.14.10), and Eileithyia (Paus. 6.20.1–6).[144] Zeus followed shortly thereafter, probably as a weather deity, based on the votive figures found from the early years of the site.[145] U. Sinn has argued for Zeus as a warrior god, based on about forty terracotta votive figurines from the late tenth century to the late seventh century BCE, many of which were armed.[146] The sanctuary contains multiple manifestations of Zeus that address his major concerns (adjudication, oaths and warfare).[147] It would be too much to offer a thorough analysis of the sanctuary and its gods for our purposes, but I would like to focus on one passage from Pausanias that helps illustrate the overall point of this chapter: the functioning of a chord of gods within a local sanctuary alongside the main god – in this case, during Pausanias's time.

In 5.13–14, Pausanias gives a lengthy description of the ritual life of the sanctuary in the second century CE. He writes in some detail of the altar of Zeus, sacrificed upon at all festivals but also daily by the local Eleans. Then he proceeds to discuss the other altars and does so 'in the order for them according to which the Eleans are accustomed to sacrificing on the altars' (τῇ ἐς αὐτοὺς τάξει, καθ' ἥντινα Ἠλεῖοι θύειν ἐπὶ τῶν βωμῶν νομίζουσι, 5.14.4). He mentions a large group of gods, but he intersperses his comments with mythological justification or local custom. Included are Hestia, Olympic Zeus, Zeus Laoetas and Poseidon Laoetas (on one altar), Artemis, Athena (Goddess

---

[144] See N. Kreutz, *Zeus und die griechischen Poleis* (Tübingen: Marie Leidorf, 2007), 154.
[145] Judith M. Barringer, 'Zeus at Olympia', in *The Gods of Ancient Greece*, ed. Bremmer and Erskine, 158.
[146] U. Sinn, 'Die Stellung der Wettkämpfe im Kult des Zeus Olympios,' *Nikephoros* 4 (1991): 43.
[147] Barringer, 'Zeus at Olympia', 155.

of Booty), Ergane, Alpheius and Athena (on one altar), Hephaestus (some call this altar the altar of Zeus Ares), Herakles Perastates, Herakles's brothers Epimedes, Idas, Paionaios and Iasos, Zeus of the Courtyard, Zeus of the Thunderbolt, the Unknown Gods, Zeus Katharisios, Nike, Zeus Chthonios, 'all the gods', Hera Olympias, Apollo and Hermes (on one altar), Homonoia (Concord), Athena, Mother of the gods, Hermes Enagonios, Kairos, Heracles (either one of the Curetes or the son of Alcmena), Ge, Themis, Zeus Kataibatos, Dionysos and the Graces (on the same altar), the Muses and the Nymphs. These are the gods inside the sacred precinct (Ἄλτις), and the number is quite high. But even within this large group there are smaller groupings that are linked together by a common altar or by mythological episode. The description gives the effect that there is some logic to the grouping of gods, even if the group is fairly large and universalistic (for example, the inclusion of altars to unknown gods and all the gods). At the end of this long list, Pausanias reminds the reader that the order in which he is describing the altars is not random but according to the order that the Eleans perform their ritual offerings (μεμνήσθω δέ τις οὐ κατὰ στοῖχον τῆς ἱδρύσεως ἀριθμοθμένους τοὺς βωμοὺς, τῇ δὲ τάξει τῇ Ἠλείων ἐς τὰς θυσίας συμπερινοστοῦντα ἡμῖν τὸν λόγον, 5.14.10).

The multiplicity of these gods does not take away from the centrality of Zeus, but instead complement his worship and prominence. The hundreds of dedicatory objects found at the sanctuary – statues, weaponry, armour, plaques, sculpture – brought by worshippers from far and near testify to the importance of Zeus as the central figure of the sanctuary, and to the importance of the sanctuary itself as bringing glory and fame to Zeus from all around Greece.[148] But Zeus was not alone; instead he was accompanied by numerous gods, perhaps also present to bring glory and fame to him, though in their case it was in the divine world.

## Rome and Latium

Finally, we come to Rome and its surroundings, whose religious culture is no less complex than that of the other regions we have covered. But similar patterns emerge with regard to the interaction of humans and small groups of gods. As John Scheid has put it, 'a "divine court" always surrounded the main patron

---

[148] See Julia Kindt, *Rethinking Greek Religion* (Cambridge: Cambridge University Press, 2012), 123–54, for a good recent treatment of the dedications at the sanctuary of Zeus at Olympia. Her treatment aims to problematise the separation of 'panhellenic' and 'local' that she sees in scholars of Greek religion, and uses the myriad of dedications as the foundation of her argument.

deity of a sanctuary', in a manner similar to what we have seen in numerous other examples above.[149] A few Roman examples will show the similarities.

**Augustan Forum/Temple of Mars Ultor**

The Augustan Forum with its massive Temple of Mars Ultor was, by all accounts, one of Augustus's major contributions to Rome. Roman tradition holds that he vowed its erection even before he was emperor, in 42 BCE in Philippi when he defeated Brutus and Cassius, the conspirators of the murder of his adoptive father, Julius Caesar. Augustus dedicated the temple to Mars the Avenger to commemorate the revenge he was able to visit upon Brutus and Cassius and his 'vengeance on the Parthians' by the recovery of 'the standards lost by Crassus in his defeat at the hands of the Parthians', which were placed in the innermost shrine of the temple.[150] His choice to put the temple in this forum marked a first in Roman history: a temple of the god of war inside the Roman pomerium.

The structure of the complex was remarkable in its symmetry, intertwining divine presence, familial relations and mythology relating its inhabitants. The plan of the forum and temple in Figure 1.9 shows the basic layout; two pairs of semicircular *exedrae* (or 'hemicycles'), one pair near the temple of Mars Ultor and one further away, although the exact location and contents of the latter pair is unknown to date.[151] The statuary in the forum was extensive, with more than a hundred larger-than-life-size statues inscribed with the great deeds of each of these important Roman heroes along the stoa of the boundary of the forum,[152] together with the statuary of each *exedra*.[153] The display of these statues throughout the forum 'was not artistic, [but] . . . was well in line with Augustus' intentions' to display statuary more publicly rather than in the houses of the wealthy.[154] In this case, statues honoured the men who 'built Rome'.[155] The effects of this massive display of Roman heroes and gods were

---

[149] John Scheid, *An Introduction to Roman Religion*, trans. Janet Lloyd (Bloomington: Indiana University Press, 2003), 159.

[150] Mary Beard, John North and Simon Price, *Religions of Rome*, 2 vols (Cambridge: Cambridge University Press, 1998), 1:199.

[151] The second pair of hemicycles were unknown until the excavations under the Via dei Fori Imperiali; see E. La Rocca, 'La nuova imagine dei Fori Imperiali: appunti in margine degli scavi;, *RM* 108 (2001), 184–95, cited in Josephine Shaya, 'The Public Life of Monuments: The *Summi Viri* of the Forum of Augustus', *AJA* 117 (2013): 85.

[152] Shaya, 'The Public Life of Monuments', 85.

[153] For a thorough study of the gallery of heroes of the Augustan Forum, see Joseph Geiger, *The First Hall of Fame: A Study of the Statues in the Forum Augustum* (Leiden: Brill, 2008).

[154] Ibid., 180.

[155] Shaya, 'The Public Life of Monuments', 88.

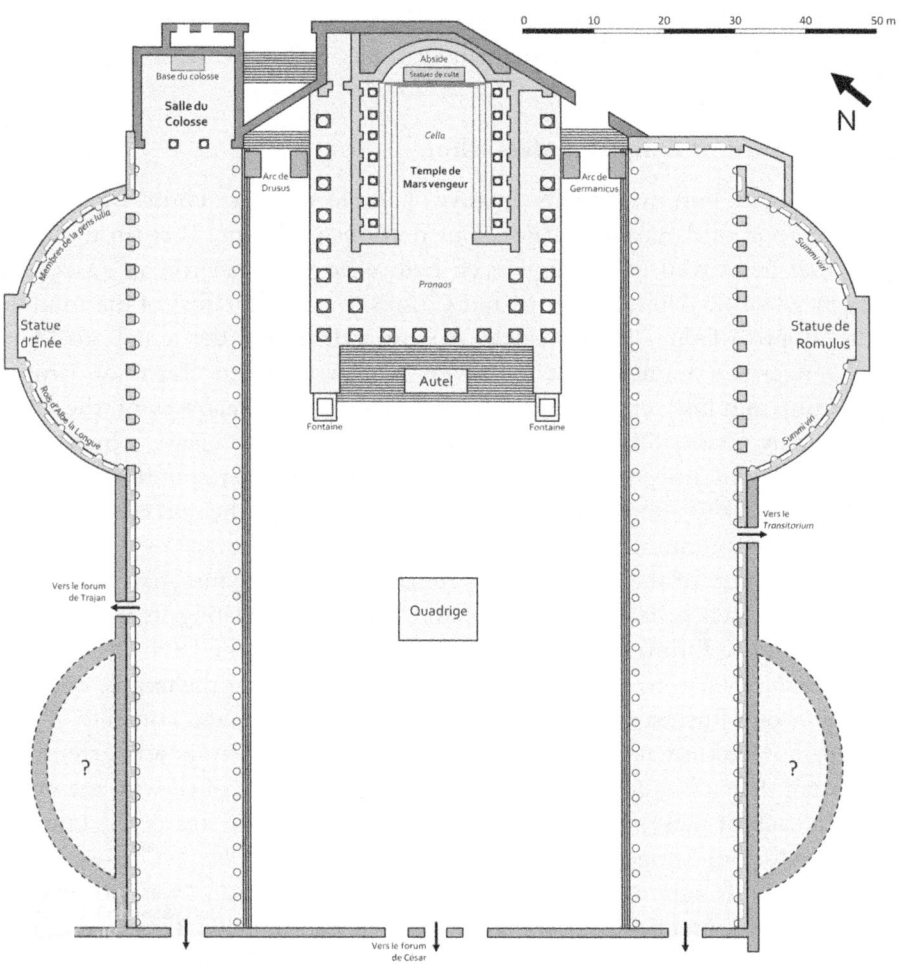

**Figure 1.9** Plan of the Forum of Augustus. Plan by Cassius Ahenobarbus. Licence by 3.0 IT (https://creativecommons.org/licenses/by-sa/3.0/deed.en). Enhanced resolution.

likely greater than the effects of representing the achievements or characteristics in the individual statues themselves.[156] As de Angelis puts it,

> From the parallel stress on the origins of Roma and the Julian family (embodied by Romulus and Aeneas, respectively) to the celebration of Roman history in its exemplary fullness; from the many allusions to

[156] Geiger, *The First Hall of Fame*, 181, recalls Ovid's description of the forum in the *Fasti*, which mentions the statuary in groups rather than individually. Geiger goes on: 'One may not be wide off the mark in supposing that with this perspective the main intention of the Princeps was achieved: the sum total, the long procession of the men who had made the Republic great, must have seemed to him more important than its constituents...The kind of impression left on the viewer must have been intentional.'

piety to its combination with the sphere of war, the forum functions as a perfect showcase for the ideals and values upheld by the first *princeps*.[157]

The forum was also a fluid space to continue honouring Roman heroes well after Augustus's death. For example, a wax tablet among the Sulpicii archive has an Alexandrian, Trupho, son of Potamo, promise to appear 'in Rome in the Forum Augustus, in front of the triumphal statue of Gnaeus Sentius Saturninus' in March and September of 45 CE. Saturninus's statue was erected in 44 CE to honour his role in the conquest of Britain the previous year.[158] In other words, the forum was not just a monument to the Roman past,[159] but an active and changing space where the best of Rome were honoured as everyday legal business and religious ritual were performed.

The north exedra had as its centrepiece a statue of Aeneas depicted escaping Troy; he holds his son in his right hand, and his father Anchises is seated on his right shoulder, carrying a box containing the penates. Alongside Aeneas were statues of the kings of Alba Longa (Aeneas's descendants) and the Julian descendants of Augustus. In the south exedra, directly opposite Aeneas along an axis of the forum, was a statue of Romulus carrying a tropaion, 'signifying his status as the first commander to win the arms of a defeated enemy in single combat'.[160] Around Romulus were other republican military heroes celebrating their prowess in battle.[161] The centre point of the axis connecting the statue of Aeneas and Romulus was the inscription dedicated to Caesar Augustus displayed prominently on the Temple of Mars's architrave (the crossbeam under the temple's pediment).

Perpendicular to the Aeneas/Augustus inscription/Romulus axis, a second axis passed through the only other overt representation of Augustus in the forum, a statue of his quadriga.[162] On the same axis, the centre of the pediment

[157] Francesco de Angelis, 'Decoration and Attention in the Forum of Augustus: The Agency of Ancient Imagery between Ritual and Routine', in *Principles of Decoration in the Roman World*, ed. Annette Haug and M. Taylor Lauritsen (Berlin: De Gruyter, 2021), 18.

[158] See TPSulp 14 for the details of the bail appearance (*vadimonium*). See de Angelis, 'Decoration and Attention', 20, for a discussion of this and other *vadimonia* that reference the Augustan Forum.

[159] See Shaya, 'The Public Life of Monuments', 84–7.

[160] Arthur J. Droge, 'Finding His Niche: On the "Autoapotheiosis" of Augustus', *Memoirs of the American Academy in Rome* 56/57 (2011/2012), 92; see also Beard, North and Price, *Religions of Rome*, 1:200.

[161] Beard, North, and Price, *Religions of Rome*, 1:200.

[162] It is ambiguous as to whether Augustus is represented in the chariot sculpture: 'The entire people of Rome gave me the title "Father of the Country", and had it inscribed in the vestibule of my residence, in the Senate House, and in the Forum of Augustus beneath the chariot sculpture placed there in my honor by decree of the Senate' (Populusque Romanus universus appellavit me patrem patriae, idque in vestibulo aedium mearum inscribendum et in curia Iulia et in foro Aug. sub quadrigis quae mihi ex s.c. positae sunt censuit; *RG* 35). Translation from Peter Aicher, *Rome Alive: A Source Guide to the Ancient City*, vol. 1 (Mundelein, IL: Bolchazy-Carducci, 2004), 198.

of the Temple of Mars Ultor likely depicted a sculpture of Mars holding a spear and dressed naked from the waste up, with what seems to be a radiant crown, indicating both his military prowess and his divine status.[163] On Mars's left side was Venus, mother of Aeneas and founder of the Julian line, and therefore Augustus's divine ancestor. Next to her was Romulus, founder of Rome, followed by the personification of the Palatine, where the city was founded. On Mars's right was Fortuna, followed by Roma and the personification of the River Tiber.

Following the axis further leads directly to a large apse at the back of the temple. Most scholars think that the cult statue of Mars was located in this apse, which was elevated about 2 metres above the floor of the *cella*, with five steps along its entire width. The question of what was located in the apse has generally been answered by cult statues of at least Mars and Venus, but sometimes including Julius Caesar.[164] The answer to this question hinges on the size of the statue(s) because Droge has pointed out (following Ganzert) that recent analysis of the apse substructure shows that it could not have held a large marble cult statue of Mars nor several marble statues:

> Put simply, it appears that the apse was never designed to display a cult statue (or statues) of any kind. If this is indeed the case, we have something very novel here: not just a raised apse at the back of the temple's *cella* but a Roman temple without a cult statue.[165]

While Droge makes a persuasive argument about the apse, it is not necessary to argue for the lack of a cult statue in the temple as a whole, especially since

---

[163] Although the pediment sculptures no longer exist, a relief depicting the temple survives from an altar relief from the Villa Medici. Droge, 'Finding His Niche', 98, argues that the figure in the centre is not necessarily Mars since the iconography with him naked from the waste up, holding a spear and placing one foot on a globe, is very different from surviving statuary and iconography of Mars: 'The central figure does not wear the typical crested helmet and cuirass of Mars, nor does he hold a shield ... In his left hand he holds a scepter, symbol of imperium.' By comparing the figure with a clear representation of Augustus from the Ravenna relief (of Claudian date) which looks almost identical, Droge claims that the ambiguity of the figure on the temple pediment was intentional, and so 'The spectator is being invited, I submit, to see this figure as Augustus, the deus Invictus (that is, as one of the "unconquered gods" in Ovid's description)' (99). Droge refers here to Ovid *Fasti* 5.559–60: prospicit armipotens operis fastigial summi et probat invictos summa tenere. ('Warlike [Mars] looks upon the pediment of the lofty edifice and approves that unconquered gods [invictos deos] occupy the places of honor'; translation from Droge, 'Finding His Niche', 99).

[164] See Beard, North and Price, *Religions of Rome*, 1:200. See also Paul Zanker, *The Power of Images in the Age of Augustus* (Ann Arbor: University of Michigan Press, 1998); Duncan Fishwick, 'The Statue of Julius Caesar in the Pantheon', *Latomus* 51 (1992): 329–36; and many others.

[165] Droge, 'Finding His Niche', 105; see also J. Ganzert, *Im Allerheiligsten des Augustusforums. Fokus 'oikoumenischer Akkulturation'* (Mainz: Verlag Philipp von Zabern, 2000).

Ovid seems to comment on the statue by saying, 'The god is enormous' (*deus ingens*). But if the apse was not designed to hold an enormous marble statue, then it does seem likely that the statue of Mars was not located on the platform of the apse.[166] In any case, whether Mars was present iconically or through some other means, the god was thought to be present. And if Mars was made present through a cult statue, most scholars do not doubt that a cult statue of Venus stood beside it.[167]

The design of the Forum of Augustus and the Temple of Mars Ultor within it was very purposeful with respect to what it communicated about Augustus. As a whole the Augustan Forum 'was an architectural and artistic declaration of the restored Republic'.[168] More specifically, the divine and semi-divine figures represented there – at minimum, Mars, Venus, Romulus and Aeneas – were chosen to be honoured in this place to build a mythology of Augustus as the proper leader of this restored Rome. The design of the forum places the inscription naming Augustus at the centre of the shorter axis, equidistant between Aeneas and his story and Romulus and his story, linking Augustus to the two mythic storylines of these founding figures of Rome. Newland articulates this well: 'The version of Roman history offered here represents a clear line of symbolic succession from Aeneas and Romulus to Augustus, from glorious beginnings to triumphant culmination.'[169]

But the location of the temple itself and the way that Mars is depicted tells us something about the mythic world being constructed and asserted by Augustus. As I mentioned above, Augustus's decision to build his forum and put the Temple of Mars Ultor inside it was the first time in Roman history that a temple of Mars was brought within the pomerium, signalling the

---

[166] Droge argues for a different function, namely as a place where Augustus would sit when holding senatorial sessions or performing other imperial duties as emperor. This plays into his overall argument that Augustus was representing himself as a god in various ways in the forum and temple complex.

[167] See Beard, North and Price, *Religions of Rome*, 1:200. Trevor Luke, *Ushering in a New Republic: Theologies of Arrival at Rome in the First Century BCE* (Ann Arbor: University of Michigan Press, 2014), 270, assumes that Mars, Venus and Julius Caesar resided in the temple in his argument for a certain Augustan theology that joins together the two narrative chains of Aeneas and Romulus: 'These two narrative chains, represented by statues in opposing hemicycles, were brought together in the Temple of Mars Ultor, where a trinity of heavenly gods – Mars, Venus, and the divine Caesar – resided ... The path from the entrance of the Forum to the Temple of Mars Ultor may therefore be viewed as a linear journey in status to ever-loftier honorands that ends in the celestial deities Mars, Venus, and Caesar.'

[168] Alain M. Gowing, *Empire and Memory: The Representation of the Roman Republic in Imperial Culture* (Cambridge: Cambridge University Press, 2005), 138.

[169] Carole E. Newlands, *Playing with Time: Ovid and the Fasti* (Ithaca: Cornell University Press, 1995), 98.

emperor's desire to place Mars at the centre of his imperial identity.[170] The specific name he gave Mars – Avenger – certainly emphasises Mars's military character, but specifically as avenger of Julius Caesar's death and of any incursion of a foreign power on the ruling might of Rome. Therefore, at the same time that Augustus claimed direct genealogical line to Mars through Romulus and an indirect relation via Aeneas and his mother Venus, consort of Mars, he also defined Mars in a particular way, which, in turn, defined the foundation of his own rule.

Ovid captures this myth of Augustus in his poetic rendering of the structure seen through the eyes of Mars as he descends to observe the Augustan Forum and Temple of Mars Ultor:

> The Avenger himself descends from the sky to his own honors and to the temple to be seen in the Forum Augustum. The god is huge, like the building; Mars should not live in the city of his son in any other way. This is a shrine worthy of giants' trophies: from here it is fitting for the Marching God to initiate wild war, whether we are provoked from the East by some impious enemy, or whether we must conquer an enemy from the West. The powerful god of arms surveys the gable at the building's top and he approves of the unconquered divinities possessing the summit; he surveys the weapons of diverse form on the doors, and arms of lands conquered by his soldiers. On one side he sees Aeneas weighed down with his beloved burden and so many ancestors of noble Julian lineage; on the other side he sees Ilia's son bearing on his shoulders a leader's weapons, and the fair deeds of men inscribed under them. He sees too the temple adorned with the name of Augustus, and the work seemed greater when he had read the name of Caesar. (*Fasti* 5.551–68)[171]

The last line indicates that Mars's vision culminates when he sees the name Augustus and deems the work as seeming greater because of it.

Further, if Droge's argument is even partially persuasive, Augustus is not grounding his authority and rule solely in the history and mythology of descent and cooperation with Mars, Venus, Aeneas, Romulus and the divine Julius,

---

[170] Ibid., 92–3: 'In Republican times temples to Mars were placed outside the pomerium. Vitruvius explains that Mars was kept outside the city walls so that he could repel foreign invaders rather than foster dissension among Rome's citizens. Augustus broke dramatically with tradition, therefore, when he brought Mars within the city walls and enshrined him in the heart of the city. By this time Mars had become assimilated with the Greek god Ares and had lost his ancient agricultural function.'

[171] Translated in Newlands, *Playing with Time*, 97.

but he is also inserting himself into this family as the latest divine instantiation of the greatness embodied in it.[172] Key to Droge's argument is the aniconic worship of Mars, with the understanding that Augustus takes his rightful place on the apse where Romans would expect a cult statue of Mars, alongside Venus and perhaps Julius Caesar. As I mentioned above, while Droge's argument that the apse was not designed to hold a cult statue or statues is persuasive, it does not necessarily mean that there were no statues anywhere in the temple. Ovid, indeed, indicates the presence of statuary: 'Should a matron enter your temple of mighty Mars, Augustus, there in armor by the door stands Venus beside the Avenger' (*Tristia* 2.295–6).[173] Augustus's possible placement on the apse in the execution of his imperial duties is both intriguing and imaginable; if statuary of at least Mars and Venus is likely, then Augustus's self-presentation is as one god among these other gods.[174]

The complex of the Forum of Augustus, then, exemplifies the pattern we have seen in our other locations. We have a small group of divine figures (Mars, Venus, Julius Caesar, Romulus, Aeneas and perhaps Augustus) historically and mythologically related to each other (through a combination of actual genealogical/historical connection – for example, Julius and Augustus – and constructed mythological/historical connection), working together cultically on behalf of a population (Augustan Rome).

---

[172] 'Now, however, in the period culminating in the dedication of the forum complex, we see Augustus treading a bit more heavily, as we witness a renewed experiment in "self-apotheosis" on his part, and this time through the fabrication of a myth more daring than anything that had preceded it and expressed on an equally unprecedented scale architecturally.' Droge, 'Finding His Niche', 91. Droge rightly points to the uncritical acceptance given to the characterisation of Augustus as supposedly not wanting to be thought of as divine during his lifetime.

[173] Venerit in magni templum, tua munera, Martis, stat Venus Ultorie iuncta, vir ante fores (translated in Aicher, *Rome Alive*, 200).

[174] 'Suetonius claims that the forum was built out of necessity to provide yet another space for law courts, just as Caesar had constructed his own forum ostensibly to relieve the congestion of the old Roman Forum. But there is no mention in Dio's list of activities that took place there, which emphasises instead the forum and the temple's ceremonial functions ... If Dio is reliable here [Dio 55.10.2–4], his description goes far beyond the "practical" functions mentioned by Suetonius and suggests something much more ambitious: namely, that the forum complex would serve as a kind of mythic "war room" for the imperium Romanum (which is to say, the imperium Augustum), as well as usurp some of the ceremonies previously conducted at the Temple of Jupiter Optimus Maximus.' Droge, 'Finding His Niche', 90. See also Darryl A. Phillips, 'The Temple of Divus Iulius and the Restoration of Legislative Assemblies under Augustus', *Phoenix* 65, nos. 3–4 (2011): 372: 'Here generals would make sacrifices before leaving Rome to take up their commands, the Senate would meet to award triumphs, the triumphant general would dedicate his regalia to Mars, and statues of new triumphatores would be set up for public view.'

### Temple of Fortuna Primigenia

Developed in the second century BCE at Praeneste, 40km south-east of Rome, the sanctuary of the goddess Fortuna was one of the grand building projects that resulted from the wealth pouring into Rome and its surroundings from the many successful conquests during this time.[175] It was the largest-known complex of the cult of Venus Fortuna, and it received significant numbers of pilgrims during the festival in her honour.[176] Before the site of the newer temple complex was developed in the first century CE,[177] it was the site of an earlier temple for Fortuna and a well-known oracle.[178] Cicero discusses 'the traditional origin of the most famous lots' when naming the oracle at Praeneste.[179] In the midst of his description of the oracle, he mentions that the site where a rock sacred to the oracle from which ancient lots sprang forth was near the statue of infant Jupiter, who sat in the lap of Fortuna along with Juno, together wanting to suckle from Fortuna (*Div.* 2.85). He goes on to mention that the site of the newer temple of Fortuna was built on the spot where honey flowed from an olive tree (*Div.* 2.86). But he soon dismisses the oracle by claiming that, although the sanctuary preserves the ancient lots, it is only the commoners who continue to consult them; no magistrate or reputable man does so any longer.[180]

The sanctuary complex is quite impressive, as it is built in a terrace design on several levels.[181] Figure 1.10 shows a three-dimensional rendering of the complex, with the Temple of Fortuna Primigenia standing on the highest level, marking the spot of the sacred honey-bearing olive tree, behind the theatre. Down a few levels, we find the oracular shrine, which was a small circular structure covering a pit into which a child would be lowered to the lots (*sortes*), retrieving one which would then be interpreted by a *sortilegus* for the

---

[175] Beard, Price and North, *Religions of Rome*, 2:97.

[176] Marina Prusac, 'Personifications of *Eudaimonia, Felicitas* and *Fortuna* in Greek and Roman Art,' *Symbolae Osloenses* 85 (2011), accessed 5 July 2023, https://doi.org/10.1080/00397679.20 11.631365

[177] Ibid.

[178] Beard, Price and North, *Religions of Rome*, 2:97; Prusac, 'Personifications'.

[179] Atque ut in haruspicina fecimus, sic videamus, clarissimarum sortium quae tradatur inventio (Cic. *Div.* 2.85; trans. W. A. Falconer, *Cicero*, vol. 20, *De senectute; De amicitia; De divinatione* (Cambridge, MA: Harvard University Press, 1923)).

[180] Quis enim magistratus aut quis vir illustrior utitur sortibus (*Div.* 2.87; trans. Falconer). Scheid, *An Introduction to Roman Religion*, 124, asserts that after Rome had conquered the Mediterranean, 'most of the great oracles of Italy (such as Praeneste) and the Mediterranean (Delphi, for example) lost their renown and their power'.

[181] In the midst of a discussion of motifs of 'Augustan propaganda', Colin Wells says, 'No Augustan building is so radical, so outrageous for its day, as the Sanctuary of Fortuna Primigenia at Praeneste, now dated to the 2nd century BC, restored by Sulla.' Colin Wells, *The Roman Empire*, 2nd ed. (Cambridge, MA: Harvard University Press, 1993), 81.

**Figure 1.10** 3-D rendering of the Sanctuary of Fortuna Praenestae. (Purchased from Deposit Photos 26 October 2023)

one seeking guidance. Just behind the structure was an apse where the statues of Fortuna, Jupiter and Juno probably stood, as Cicero indicated.

The mythological connection between the three figures is unclear, but there definitely is a connection. This particular manifestation of Fortuna – Fortuna Primigenia – seems pretty stable as 'a primordial mother-goddess' whose main power was 'to encourage fecundity'.[182] Jupiter and Juno are depicted in this apse statue as twin children of Fortuna, and two other inscriptions call Jupiter the child of Fortuna.[183] But in a different inscription, Fortuna Primigenia is described as the firstborn child of Jupiter.[184] While this seems to muddy the depiction of her as the mother of Juno and Jupiter, R. Joy Littlewood insightfully argues,

> Fortuna's dual role as mother and daughter represents not only the perpetual cycle of women in which daughters become mothers, but also the continuous cycle of agrarian growth, represented by Demeter and Persephone in the Greek mystery cult at Eleusis.[185]

[182] R. Joy Littlewood, 'Fortune', *The Oxford Encyclopedia of Ancient Greece and Rome*. Online edition, ed. Michael Gagarin (Oxford University Press, 2010).
[183] *CIL* 14.2862 (Fortunae Iovis puero) and 14.2868 (Fortunae Iovi puero).
[184] *CIL* 1.60.
[185] Littlewood, 'Fortune'.

Juno and Jupiter's connection was ancient and they were also widely known as a couple and associated with marriage. Aside from the assumed cultic activity in the temple, the oracle's functioning evoked this connection among the three gods, given the statuary and the focus on Fortuna's role as female progenitor. As with our many other examples in this chapter, we have here a sanctuary that houses a small group of gods that are connected through a local mythology and cultic activity that is grounded in the particular history of that location and working together for the benefit of local communities (in this case, those who consulted the oracle).

**Domestic Contexts**

Religion in Roman dwellings also shows the familiar pattern I have been arguing for throughout the chapter. Petronius witnesses to the common presence of various household gods (at least in dwellings of a wealthier class) when he comments upon what Encolpius and Ascyltos saw upon entry into Trimalchio's house: 'a large cupboard containing silver *Lares* and a marble image of Venus'.[186] Although the combination of gods varied from household to household, statuettes and depictions of the Lares have been found in many places; the finds have been especially fruitful in those houses buried by the eruption of Vesuvius.[187] Generally speaking, common people among the ancients seemed to view the Lares as gods of the streets and paths, at least according to Arnobius.[188] Arnobius also refers to several other ancient authors who had varying opinions about the Lares: Nigidius (Figulus) states that they are guardians of the house and home, which is notable for our purposes.[189]

The Lares were not individually named but were particular to each family,[190] apparently functioning to protect the land on which the family lived,

---

[186] Petron. 29.8; translation in Annemarie Kaufmann-Heinimann, 'Religion in the House', *A Companion to Roman Religion*, ed. Jörg Rüpke (Chichester: Wiley-Blackwell, 2011), 197.

[187] The most recent and most extensive treatment of the Lares is Harriet I. Flower, *The Dancing Lares and the Serpent in the Garden: Religion at the Roman Street Corner* (Princeton: Princeton University Press, 2017).

[188] Arn. *Adv. gentiles* 3.41.

[189] Ibid. See Flower, *The Dancing Lares*, 7–10, for a discussion of these perspectives and others from Varro. Flower spends a fair amount of space arguing against the ancient intellectual view of the *lares* being primarily gods related to the dead: 'It leads to a curious picture of *lares* shrines throughout the Roman city as if these were all set up either to commemorate or to appease the dead on every street corner and even more implausibly in every kitchen' (10).

[190] John Bodel, Cicero's Minerva, *Penates*, and the Mother of the *Lares*: An Outline of Roman Domestic Religion', in *Household and Family Religion in Antiquity*, ed. John Bodel and Saul M. Olyan (Oxford: Blackwell, 2008), 249, calls them 'generic and collective'.

and so therefore not mobile.¹⁹¹ Typical lararia were either a three-dimensional sculpted shrine or altar (Figure 1.11) or a two-dimensional painted shrine (Figures 1.12 and 1.13). The iconography is similar – especially in the imperial period under the influence of Augustan reforms¹⁹² – with a depiction of the *genius* of the *paterfamilias* (usually a man dressed in a toga) between two dancing youths (the Lares) with long hair, dressed in short tunics and in the act of pouring wine for a feast.¹⁹³ There are variations to this pattern, but the *lares* and *genius* are consistently present in different configurations. Below this depiction is usually a large snake (representing either the *genius* or protection of the family). The *genius* was honoured by swearing by it and by celebrating its birthday, which coincided with the birth of the *paterfamilias*.¹⁹⁴

**Figure 1.11** Lararium, House of the Red Walls VIII 5, 37 Pompeii Prowalk, first century CE. Photo by Mary Harrsch. Licensed under the Creative Commons Attribution-Share Alike 4.0 International licence (https://creativecommons.org/licenses/by-sa/4.0/deed.en). Enhanced resolution.

---

¹⁹¹ Scheid, *An Introduction to Roman Religion*, 165; Ken Dowden, 'Religious Practices of the Individual and Family: Rome', in *Religions of the Ancient World: A Guide*, ed. Sarah Iles Johnston (Cambridge, MA: Belknap Press of Harvard University Press, 2004), 435.
¹⁹² These reforms regularised domestic religious activity to reflect and connect more with Augustus and official religious practice. See Kaufmann-Heinimann, 'Religion in the House', 199, 201; Scheid, *An Introduction to Roman Religion*, 165.
¹⁹³ Flower, *The Dancing Lares*, 11.
¹⁹⁴ See Chapter Three for a description of the *genius* in more detail.

**Figure 1.12** Fresco of lararium with a niche and altar, mid-first century BCE. Located in kitchen of Villa 6, Terzigno. Photo by Tyler Bell. Licensed under the Creative Commons Attribution 2.0 Generic licence (https://creativecommons.org/licenses/by/2.0/deed.en). Enhanced resolution.

**Figure 1.13** Painted Roman lararium, House of the Vettii, Pompeii, first century CE. Photo by Patricio Lorente. Licensed under the Creative Commons Attribution-Share Alike 2.5 Generic licence (https://creativecommons.org/licenses/by-sa/2.5/deed.en). Enhanced resolution.

As the empire became established, a custom developed of honouring the Juno of the *materfamilias*, which was 'the feminine equivalent of a genius'.[195] Additional gods were present, in particular the Penates, which were 'pluralistic and individualized in orientation'[196] and 'were in some senses vague deities lodged in the innermost part of a house, but they could be separated out into a number of individual deities particularly revered by the family'.[197] It is unclear whether any named god was numbered among the Penates.[198] They were also moveable, so when the family relocated, the Penates went along with them.[199] It seems possible that Vesta, as the household hearth goddess, could be considered part of the group of Penates and so she would also be relocatable.[200] Among these household gods can also be found other gods, such as Venus in the Propertius example above, or Isis-Fortuna depicted variously with a cornucopia and/or a rudder.[201] Cicero describes the conveyance of a Minerva statue from his house to his father's before his house was destroyed.[202]

Along with these gods, cultic activity, although varied, was consistently present in the household. The Lares and Penates, like all other gods, needed respect and honour, so regular food and drink offerings were made. The Lares received a libation during the regular Roman evening meal, between the two main courses.[203] Sometimes scraps of leftover food or food that has been dropped on the floor would be burned and offered to them.[204] The hearth fire, central to the practical workings of the house (heat and food preparation, in particular) was 'a place of communication' with the divine world, in particular with Vesta, as were the household shrines that depicted the Lares, *genius* and Penates,[205] which were found most often in kitchens, 'but also in *atria* and the small rooms opening off them (*alae*), peristyles, and gardens'.[206] The Lares, in particular, were honoured in various ways and so were manifested with various epithets, all having to do with 'moments of transition': for example, return from a journey (highways – Lares viales, sea crossings – Lares permarini), being a soldier (Lares militares), marriage (offerings to the Lares compitales at the

---

[195] Scheid, *An Introduction to Roman Religion*, 166.
[196] Bodel, 'Cicero's Minerva', 249.
[197] Scheid, *An Introduction to Roman Religion*, 166.
[198] Dowden, 'Religious Practices', 435.
[199] Depicted most vividly in the Aeneas sculpture in the south exedra of the Augustan Forum in Rome.
[200] Dowden, 'Religious Practices', 435.
[201] Ibid., 435.
[202] Cic. *Leg.* 2.42, as cited in Bodel, 'Cicero's Minerva', 252.
[203] Flower, *The Dancing Lares*, 10.
[204] Ibid., 15–16.
[205] Dowden, 'Religious Practices', 435.
[206] Bodel, 'Cicero's Minerva', 255.

crossroads, among offerings to others) and maturity to adulthood for boys (dedication of the childhood *bulla* (locket) to the Lares).[207]

So, while there could be a great deal of variation in the configuration of deities from house to house, a general pattern across households can be identified: one of a defined group of gods present in the family. How they are connected to each family is not always clear; in other words, what kind of mythological connection a particular family might have with each of the gods would have varied and unfortunately was not commented upon much by ancient writers. However, the connection was concretised through the history of the family, even if we cannot explain the particulars. Each family had its own Lares connected to the land on which they dwelt, remarkably represented with very consistent iconography across Roman culture, despite this local context. Each family also had the Penates, which were more permanent and mobile. And each family was animated and protected by the *genius* of the *paterfamilias* and/or the Juno of the *materfamilias*. The space in which families worshipped these gods varied depending on the wealth of the family,[208] but the history and generational traditions of the family were what connected the gods to the family and to each other. Each set of traditions was very localised, even if some of the additional gods were well known across regions (Venus, Hestia, Isis-Fortuna and so on). The locality of the family determined the configuration of particular gods, but the pattern matches what we have seen in other more public contexts: small groups of gods, connected by history/genealogy/mythology, honoured cultically in locally specific ways and working together for the human community of adherents.

**Capitoline Triad**

The Capitolium Hill in Rome included 'the most significant temple of Roman state religion, that of the *trias capitolina*', the Capitoline Triad – Jupiter, Juno and Minerva.[209] The temple supposedly originated in the first year of the Republic, according to Livy and Tacitus, but, regardless of its origins, it was the centre of the political life of Rome.[210] It housed new consuls and their first Senate sessions, sacrifices by military commanders as they headed off to

---

[207] Dowden, 'Religious Practices', 435–6.
[208] 'Not all houses ran to a built-up or wooden lararium in the atrium or extra rooms devoted to a cult as did grand aristocratic residences. In poorer houses, without an atrium or specially decorated rooms, the earthenware statuettes of the family "pantheon" would be kept in cupboards, and sacrifices would generally be made on the ground or, when banquets were held, in the flames of a portable altar.' Scheid, *An Introduction to Roman Religion*, 73.
[209] Reinhard Förtsch and Walter Eder, 'Capitolium', in *Brill's New Pauly*, https://doi.org/10.1163/1574-9347_bnp_e12220600.
[210] Liv. 1.38.7, 2.8.6; Tac. *Hist.* 3.72.2.

their campaigns, and the culmination of triumphal processions.[211] Sanctuaries of the triad (Capitolia) were built across the empire – but mainly in the western provinces[212] – normally in the forum of the city, raised up (naturally or artificially) to imitate the Roman temple complex, and oftentimes with triple *cellae* to house all three gods.[213] Beard, North and Price helpfully point out that Capitolia built in the colonies 'provided a very clear link with the capital'.[214]

The triad was invoked in mainly political contexts.[215] Figure 1.14 shows the only surviving statue group representing the three gods, in contrast to the Capitoline temple in Rome, where each of the three were represented with their own statues.[216] In this statue group, there is no mention of their relationship but, mythologically, Jupiter was the king, Juno was his wife/queen and Minerva was his daughter (born to Metis, following the Greek succession myth of Zeus and the birth of Athena). Cultically, aside from the offerings made in the sanctuary, the Roman Games (*Ludi Romani*) of 13 September and the Plebian Games (*Ludi Plebei*) of 13 November were celebrated partially in honour of the Capitoline triad, where a great sacrifice was offered and feasted upon by the senators on the Capitol.[217] It was also a scene of ongoing offerings and forms of entertainment, if we can trust Seneca's description of the goings-on at the Capitoline:

> One servant informs Jupiter of the name of those who visit him, another tells him the time; one is his bather, another his anointer . . . An expert mime-actor . . . used to act a mime each day in the Capitol, as if the gods would enjoy watching a player when men had ceased to.[218]

A few other examples that I will only briefly mention point to the pattern of worship of small groups of gods in Roman culture that parallels similar patterns

---

[211] Förtsch and Eder, 'Capitolium'.
[212] Ibid.
[213] See Tacitus 4.53, where he mentions a temple dedication ritual in which the praetor, Helvidius Priscus, prays to Jupiter, Juno, Minerva and the 'gods who protect the empire'. See also Eder, 'Capitolium'; and Beard, North and Price, *Religions of Rome*, 2:244–5, for a pictorial description of both a Capitolium in an Italian colony (Cosa, north of Rome) and one in Africa (Sufetula) and 1:334–6, for a number of examples across the empire.
[214] Beard, North and Price, *Religions of Rome*, 1:334.
[215] Jörg Rüpke, *Religion of the Romans*, trans. and ed. Richard Gordon (Cambridge: Polity Press, 2007), 77. See also Maria-Corina Nicholae, 'The Capitoline Triad in Roman Dacia', *Peuce*, vol. 9, *Volum Dedicate Liu Florin Topoleanu la a 60-A Aniverare* (Tulcea: Institutul de Cercetari Eco-Muzeale, 2011), 291–304.
[216] Rüpke, *Religion of the Romans*, 77.
[217] Scheid, *An Introduction to Roman Religion*, 52, 90.
[218] Seneca, fr. 36 (Haase), translated and quoted in Beard, North and Price, *Religions of Rome*, 1:218. See ibid., 2:234, for the full fragment found in Augustine's *The City of God*, which details the activities in the sanctuary.

**Figure 1.14** The Capitoline Triad (left to right: Juno, Jupiter and Minerva). 160–80 CE. Rodolfo Lanciani Archaeological Museum, Montecelio. Photo by Sailko. Licence CC by 3.0 IT (https://creativecommons.org/licenses/by/3.0/). Enhanced resolution.

in other places around the Mediterranean. There are the many places across the Roman and Greek worlds where the Dioscuri/Gemini – the twins Castor and Pollux – were worshipped, including in the Roman Forum in the Temple of Castor and Pollux, going back to the fifth century BCE. Worship of this pair existed 'in thoroughly Greek form ... at Lavinium',[219] but the connection between southern Italian religion and plebeian religion in Rome may have affected the form of the worship in Rome itself.[220] The Temple of Aesculapius on Rome's Tiber Island had its own manifestation of the god Asklepios, presumably with some of the other divine figures regularly associated with him found across the Mediterranean Asklepieia. And the Temple of Isis at Pompeii included niches, probably for cult statues of various deities; there is evidence for Bacchus and Venus (both 'staple[s] of the local pantheon'[221]), Harpocrates and Osiris.[222] In addition, John Scheid describes a phenomenon where the typical Roman temple included the '"master altar", which belonged to the

---

[219] Beard, North and Price, *Religions of Rome*, 1:66.
[220] See Liv. 2.42.5, which indicates that the temple of Castor was dedicated without the presence of Pollux.
[221] Molly Swetnam-Burland, *Egypt in Italy: Visions of Egypt in Roman Imperial Culture* (Cambridge: Cambridge University Press, 2015), 122.
[222] For a good discussion of the sanctuary of Isis in Pompeii, see ibid., ch. 3.

deity who owned the temple' and temporary altars (*temporales*) 'erected for "guest" deities'.[223] All of these examples match the pattern shown in disparate locations and cultures around the ancient Mediterranean, as we have seen throughout this chapter.

This brief trip around the Mediterranean has brought forth an abundance of evidence of a pattern of worship of small (and not so small) groups of gods in particular sanctuaries and other settings. These sanctuaries might be located anywhere: city centres, 'suburban' outskirts of cities, rural locations available to several villages, or domestic settings. The gods were usually linked historically, mythologically or genealogically based on local traditions and were usually all involved in the cultic life of worshippers. So, if one were to visit a shrine or sanctuary of a particular god, one would need to attend also to the other gods present. The other gods' presences seem to have been understood as integral to the honouring of the main god, oftentimes having complementary roles to play in the logic of the sanctuary that was necessary for the proper relationship being built and maintained between human and divine communities. This clearly fits into Schatzki's notion of social practice that we discussed in Chapter One. And the same practice is evident in Corinth, to which we now turn.

---

[223] Scheid, *An Introduction to Roman Religion*, 70–1.

CHAPTER TWO

# Chords of Gods in Corinth

Since Roman Corinth in Paul's time was a part of the larger Roman world – colonised and ruled by Rome but culturally mixed and still very much steeped in its Greek traditions – we can expect to find a continuity with the chord of gods pattern I sketched in the previous chapter, and indeed we do. In Paul's Corinth, we have a landscape of Greek religious practice dating back to the classical period or beyond, updated and transformed for the first century, combined with Roman religious practice established over the previous hundred or so years of Roman colonisation. Although there were many options for worship and interaction in densely populated Corinth and the surrounding area (Isthmia and Cenchreae), the nature of these options did not simply mean one could worship many individual gods at their sanctuaries. In many, if not most, cases, sanctuaries housed several gods together, even if the sanctuary was known by the name of one god, just as happened across the Mediterranean world. Much as I did in the previous chapter, I will give some representative examples of the pattern of worship of small groups of gods, but this time only in the Corinthian region. This worship of small groups of gods in Corinth very clearly fits the notion of social practice that grounds this study.

As an orientation to the ancient city of Corinth, please see the maps in Figures 2.1 and 2.2.

## The Acrocorinthian Aphrodite

The Acrocorinth, high above the main settlement, housed the important sanctuary of Aphrodite, the patron goddess of Corinth. Figure 2.3 shows the view from the Acrocorinth looking north (present day), and Figure 2.4 provides a map of the ancient Acrocorinth. Unfortunately, little remains of the sanctuary of Aphrodite, so no detailed maps or reconstructions of the sanctuary are available. We learn from Pausanias a bit about the sanctuaries present on the Acrocorinth:

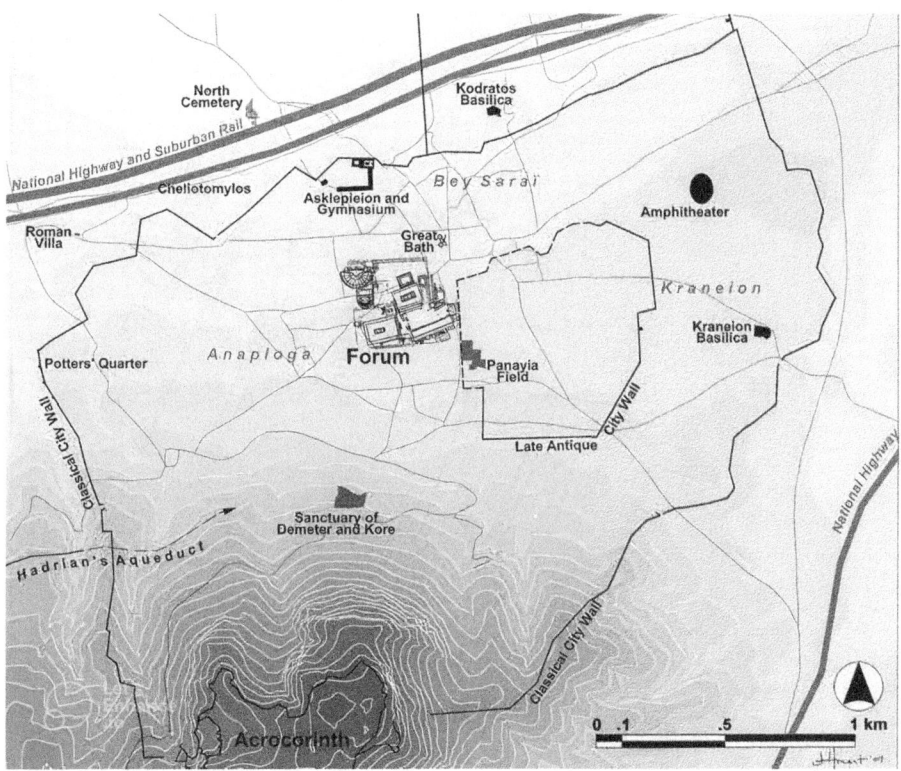

**Figure 2.1** Map of ancient Corinth. (From Steven J. Friesen, Daniel N. Schowalter and James C. Walters, eds, *Corinth in Context: Comparative Studies on Religion and Society* [Leiden: Brill, 2010], 516.) Used with permission.

As one goes up to Acrocorinth – this is the summit of a mountain above the city which Briareus, as arbitrator, gave to Helios, but Helios, according to the Corinthians, ceded to Aphrodite – now as one goes up to this Acrocorinth there are sacred enclosures of Isis, one of which they designate Isis Pelagia, the other, Egyptian Isis; and two of Sarapis, the second of which is called 'in Kanopos'. After them, altars of Helios have been constructed, and there is a sanctuary of Ananke and Bia, which they are not in the custom of entering. Above this there is a temple of the Mother of the Gods with a stele and throne; the goddess herself and the throne are both of stone. The temple of the Morai and that of Demeter and Kore have statues that are not on public view. Here also is the sanctuary of Hera Bounaia founded by Bounos, son of Hermes, and for this reason the goddess is called Bounaia. (Paus. 2.4.6–7)[1]

---

[1] Translation from Nancy Bookidis and Ronald S. Stroud, *The Sanctuary of Demeter and Kore: Topography and Architecture* (Princeton: ASCSA, 1997), 3. All other translations from Pausanias are my own.

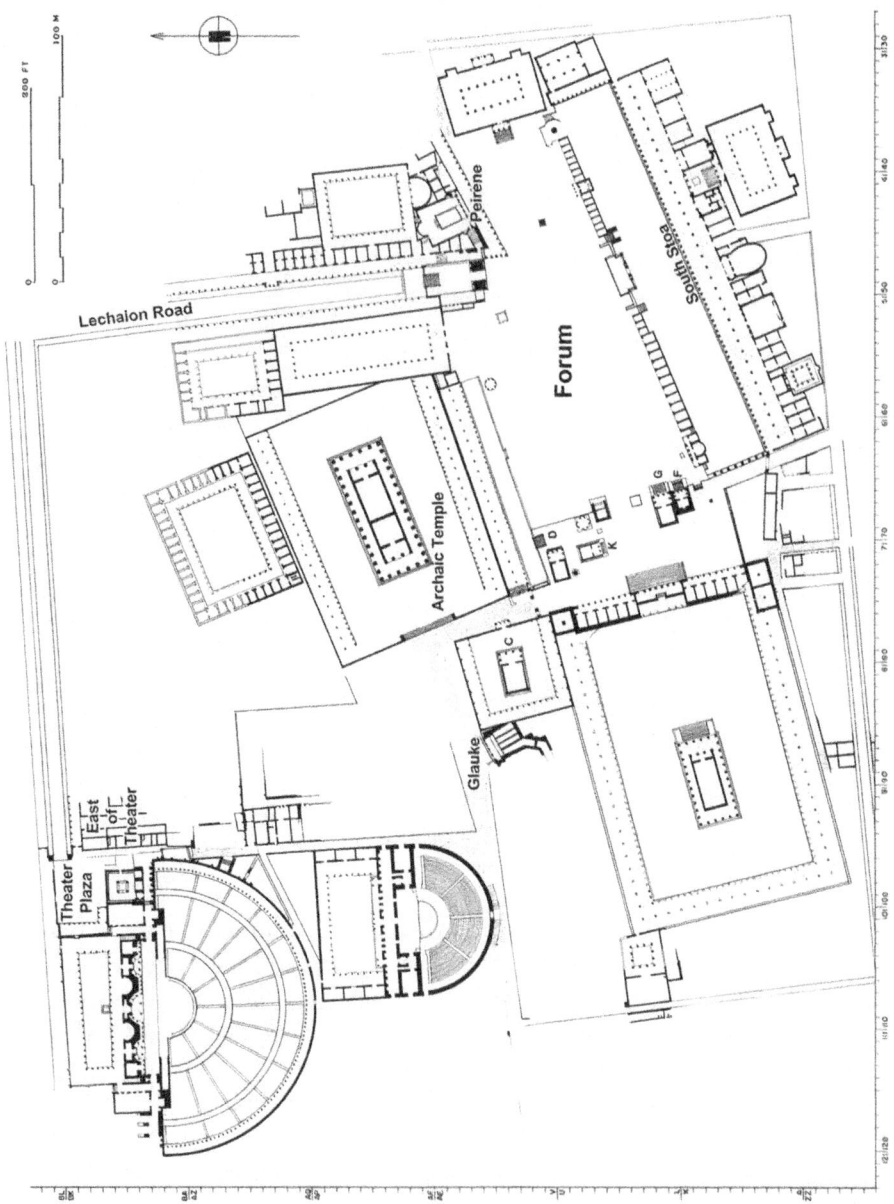

**Figure 2.2** Map of central Corinth (From Friesen, Schowalter Walters, *Corinth in Context*, 517.) Used with permission.

# CHORDS OF GODS IN CORINTH 85

**Figure 2.3** The Acrocorinth looking north. (Public domain)

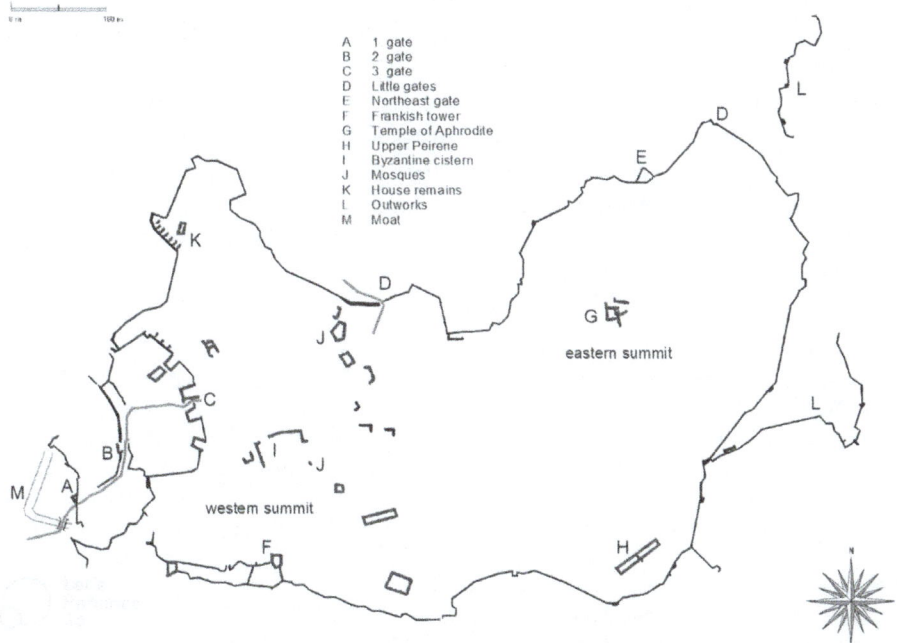

**Figure 2.4** Plan of the Acrocorinth. (Public domain)

Pausanias was writing in the second century CE, but most of the sanctuaries he mentions go back to classical times and some are even older. The archaeological record for some sort of cultic site related to Aphrodite on the Acrocorinth might extend as far as the late eleventh century or early tenth century BCE, although worship of the goddess as a patroness of the city probably began sometime in the eighth century BCE with the *synoikismos* of Corinth.[2] Strabo, visiting Corinth in 29 BCE, mentions the sanctuary, which means that the cult of Aphrodite must have been revived shortly after the founding of the Roman colony in 44 BCE.[3] Pausanias's description of the role of Aphrodite in Corinth shows that the Corinthians of the second century CE thought of her as having a long connection to the city.

In another passage, Pausanius describes the sanctuary as having other gods represented therein: 'On the summit of the Acrocorinth is a temple of Aphrodite. The images are Aphrodite armed, Helios, and Eros holding a bow' (Ἀνελθοῦσι δὲ ἐς τὸν Ἀκροκόρινθον ναός ἐστιν Ἀφροδίτης· ἀγάλματα δὲ αὐτή τε ὡπλισμένη καὶ Ἥλιος καὶ Ἔρως ἔχων τόξον; 2.5.1). Numismatic evidence from the imperial period shows the association of Eros with the statue of Aphrodite at Corinth.[4] While this does not prove that Eros was in the temple with Aphrodite, it does show a long-standing tradition of Eros and Aphrodite being associated with each other, which fits with widespread iconography of the two together.[5] Pausanias claims that the Corinthians thought that Helios was the original occupant of the Acrocorinth but then ceded it to Aphrodite, and yet Helios remained important enough to be represented in Aphrodite's sanctuary in the second century and to have an altar on the Acrocorinth (2.4.6). So we have a long history of cultic activity associated with both Helios and Aphrodite that extends into the first and second centuries CE. The historical connections also go back to the traditions surrounding the founding of Corinth, with Helios ceding the city to Aphrodite.

---

[2] Nancy Bookidis, 'The Sanctuaries of Corinth', in *Corinth: The Centenary*, ed. C. K. Williams II and N. Bookidis (Princeton: ASCSA, 2003), 248. There is some debate about the date of the unification of Corinth: J. B. Salmon, *Wealthy Corinth: A History of the City to 338 B.C.* (Oxford: Oxford University Press, 1984), 57–9 argues for a seventh-century date.

[3] Nancy Bookidis, 'Religion in Corinth: 146 BCE to 100 CE', in *Urban Religion in Roman Corinth*, ed. D. N. Schowalter and S. J. Friesen (Cambridge, MA: Harvard University Press, 2005), 160.

[4] See Friedrich Imhoof-Blumer and Percy Gardner, *A Numismatic Commentary on Pausanias* (1885; repr., Charleston, SC: Nabu Press, 2012), 25–7, for evidence from Marcus Aurelius, L. Verus, Commodus, and Plautilla. Pausanias also locates Aphrodite in the Isthmian Poseidon sanctuary; in the middle of the base of the cult statue of Poseidon and Amphitrite, Thalassa was depicted holding up the baby Aphrodite, representing her mythic origins from sea foam (Paus. 2.1.7).

[5] See Erika Simon, *The Gods of the Greeks*, trans. Alan Shapiro, 4th ed. (Madison: University of Wisconsin Press, 2021), 165–98.

Mythologically, Hesiod has Eros as one of the primordial gods, being the fourth god to come into existence,[6] whereas Parmenides gives Eros as the first to come into existence.[7] As we move forward in time, Eros becomes a child of various gods, eventually being linked with Aphrodite as her son in the Hellenistic epic *Argonautica* and then again as the son of the Roman Venus in Ovid's *Metamorphoses*.[8] If the Acrocorinthian sanctuary of Aphrodite was not configured out of whole cloth in Pausianias's time, then we have a collection of three gods linked mythologically and genealogically: Aphrodite linked with Helios by at least one local Corinthian origin story; and Aphrodite linked with Eros mythologically by the Hellenistic and early imperial Roman period as mother and son. Since we have no material or detailed literary evidence for the rituals associated with the sanctuary is it hard to say what exactly happened cultically there with respect to these three gods.[9] The fact that Pausanias talks about sanctuaries with altars, means that we have to assume that the sanctuaries were cultically active during his time, and most likely many years before his time, too. It seems reasonable, then, to posit a group of three gods (Aphrodite, Helios and Eros), connected through traditions and local history, who were cultically active in the sanctuary during the first century CE.

## The Sanctuary of Demeter and Kore

We now turn to the mother–daughter divine pair most famous from the Homeric *Hymn to Demeter* and its associated traditions, Demeter and Persephone – the latter here, as in many other places, named Kore. The site of the sanctuary of Demeter and Kore on the north slope of the Acrocorinth shows evidence of cultic worship extending as far back as the ninth century BCE, but the late eighth century BCE has the first secure evidence for worship of

---

[6] Hes. *Theog.* 116–22.
[7] Parmenides, frag. 13.
[8] Ap. Rhod. *Argon.* 3.25ff; OAp. Rhod. *Argon.*
[9] 3.25ff; description of cultic prostitution associated with Aphrodite has been roundly and convincingly rejected as Roman propaganda by several recent scholars. The traditional view was that sacred prostitution was an aspect of Near Eastern religion associated with the cults of Ishtar and Astarte. Aphrodite's origins are often associated with Astarte, hence the connection with sacred prostitution: see Stephanie L. Budin, 'Sacred Prostitution in the First Person', in *Prostitutes and Courtesans in the Ancient World*, ed. C. Faraone and L. McLure (Madison: University of Wisconsin Press, 2006), 83. But S. M. Hooks, 'Sacred Prostitution in Israel and the Ancient Near East' (PhD diss., Hebrew Union College, 1985), convincingly argued that sacred prostitution never existed in the Ancient Near East, which means that there is a need for a re-evaluation of the classical evidence. See Stephanie L. Budin, 'A Reconstruction of the Aphrodite-Ashtart Syncretism', *Numen* 51 (2004): 102–3, for a brief summary of the evidence, and Budin, 'Sacred Prostitution', for a thorough treatment of the evidence and the scholarship around this topic.

Demeter. The construction of the earliest temple is dated to the early seventh century, although the cultic worship likely preceded its construction.[10] The plan in Figure 2.5 shows the sanctuary in the Roman period. It was already quite complex and developed before the Roman colonisation of Corinth. After colonisation, the sanctuary was renovated and changed, but remained a vibrant and important sacred site for the city. Diodorus (mid-first century BCE) mentions an episode from the fourth century BCE in which Timoleon hears a prediction received in a dream from two Corinthian priestesses of Demeter and Kore that the goddesses would accompany Timoleon on an upcoming voyage to their sacred island. When he realises that Demeter and Kore are supporting him and his companions, Timoleon dedicates the ship to the goddesses, using ναός to describe the newly dedicated vessel (16.66.4–5). Note that the goddesses act together.[11]

There is some evidence for the presence of two other gods in the sanctuary, Dionysos and Artemis. A clay *pinax* from the fourth or third century BCE with

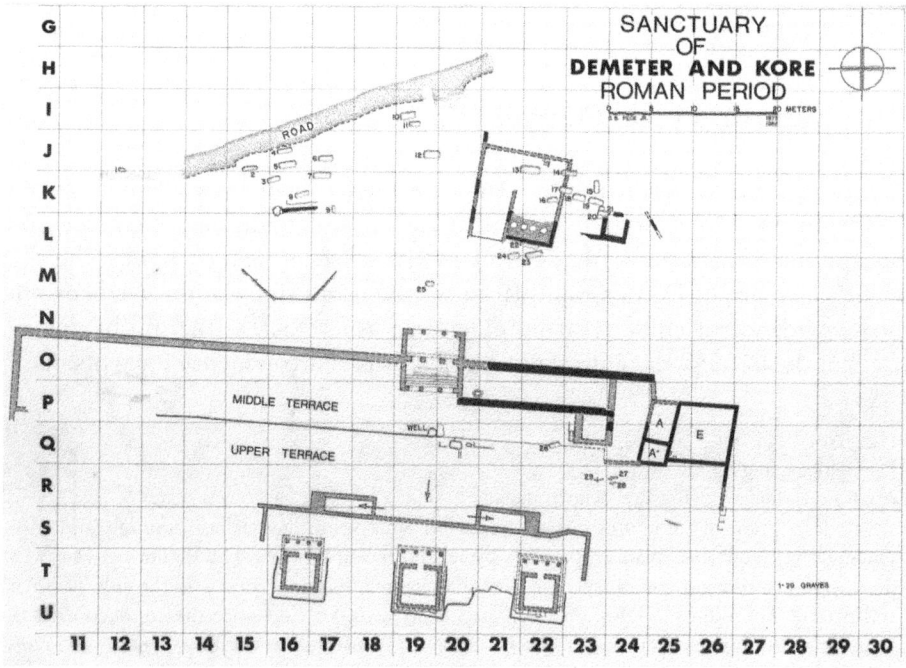

**Figure 2.5** Plan of the Sanctuary of Demeter and Kore on the Acrocorinth in the Roman period. Used with permission from the American Academy of Classical Studies in Athens.

---

[10] Bookidis, 'The Sanctuaries of Corinth', 248–9.
[11] Plut. *Vit. Tim.* 8 has a similar reference to the event that Diodorus describes.

the inscription ΔΙΟΝΥΣΟΥ was found intact in the sanctuary (Figure 2.6a).[12] The association of Dionysos with Demeter and Kore in Eleusis provides precedence for a relationship here. The procession from Athens to Eleusis during the Eleusinian mysteries was envisioned to be led by the mysterious figure Iacchos, which is likely a variant name of Dionysos. In addition, there are versions of the Dionysian myth that make Persephone his mother (and Zeus his father) found in the Orphic tradition and witnessed in the Derveni Papyrus.[13] And fragment 70c of Pindar (*POxy.* XIII 1604, fr. 2) might refer to a dithyramb performed at the sanctuary of Demeter and Kore on the Acrocorinth, for which this *pinax* could lend some additional evidence.[14] Another intact

**Figure 2.6** Intact *pinakes* from the Acrocorinth Sanctuary of Demeter and Kore, both found on the upper terrace, from the late Roman period: (a) ΔΙΟΝΥΣΟΥ (Dionysou); (b) ΑΛΦΙΑΙΑΣ (Alphiaias). Used with permission from the American Academy of Classical Studies in Athens.

---

[12] Ronald S. Stroud, *The Sanctuary of Demeter and Kore: The Inscriptions* (Princeton: ASCSA, 2013), 72, inscription 98.

[13] See Fritz Graf and Sarah Iles Johnston, *Ritual Texts for the Afterlife: Orpheus and the Bacchic Gold Tablets*, 2nd ed. (London: Routledge, 2013), especially ch. 3, for a discussion of the various threads of this mythological relationship between Persephone and Dionysos.

[14] See P. Wilson, 'The Politics of Dance: Dithyrambic Contest and Social Order', in *Sport and Festival in the Ancient Greek World*, ed. D. J. Phillips and D. Pritchard (Swansea: Classical Press of Wales, 2003), 163–96, for a detailed argument for this connection. See also Michalis Tiverios, 'Artemis, Dionysos und Eleusinische Gottheiten', *Mitteilungen* 119 (2004): 148, for a discussion of the connection between Dionysos and Demeter through Egyptian origins and at Eleusis.

*pinax* was found in the sanctuary during the same period with the inscription ΑΛΦΙΑΙΑΣ (see Figure 2.6b),[15] which is an epithet associated with Artemis in Elis, a statue of whom Pausianias mentions as existing in his day at the temple of Artemis Alphiaias in Lentrini in Elis (6.22.8–11).

After the sacking of Corinth and its re-founding a century later, the sanctuary was one of the earliest ones reinstituted, but with some changes due to the Roman colonisation of the city. There is no evidence for the continued presence of Dionysos or Artemis, but there is continued evidence of both Demeter and Kore in the sanctuary, along with at least one other god. The Roman remains show evidence of three temples on the upper terrace of the sanctuary at the time of Pausanias (see Figure 2.7): one to Demeter, one to Kore and the third one probably to the Moirai – the three divine Fates who determined and monitored humans' destinies.[16] The upper terrace seems to be where the centre of the sanctuary's focus shifted in the Roman period, and the

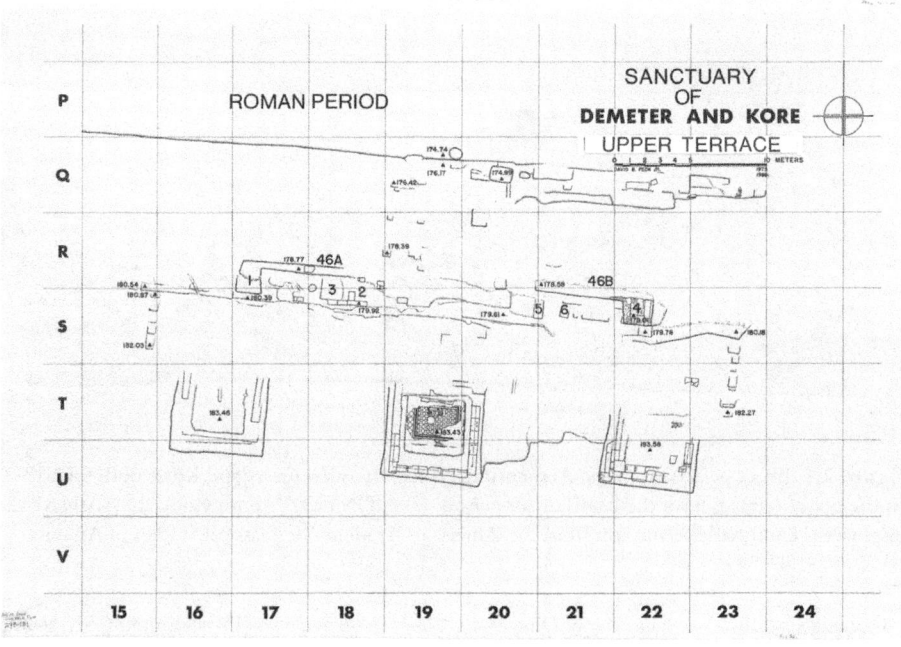

**Figure 2.7** Plan of the Roman upper terrace of the Sanctuary of Demeter and Kore, where three temples are located: one to Demeter, one to Kore and one to an unknown god/gods. Used with permission from the American Academy of Classical Studies in Athens.

---

[15] Stroud, *The Sanctuary of Demeter and Kore*, 74, inscription 99.
[16] See Bookidis and Stroud, *Sanctuary of Demeter and Kore*, 362–71, for an analysis of the identities of the three temples.

three temples were probably constructed sometime in the second half of the first century.[17] Regardless of the precise identification of these three temples, it appears that the worship of more deities along with Demeter and Kore predated the construction of the temples.

In the body of her work on Corinth, much of it unpublished or in process, Barbette Spaeth has argued strongly for a more extensive Roman character to Corinth, especially in the years of early colonisation. Most foundationally, she 'has shown that votive inscriptions, dedications, and priesthoods during the Roman imperial period overwhelmingly name Roman gods and Roman priesthoods despite the common assumption that Greek culture re-emerged as the dominant force by the 2nd century CE'.[18] In a 2017 article, Spaeth argues for a reinterpretation of the reliefs on archaistic blocks found in the forum, writing:

> From a conceptual point of view, this new interpretation of the divinities on the Corinthian reliefs indicates the importance of recognizing that Corinth in the Roman era was a *Roman* city. Therefore, its public cults should be considered Roman, and not Greek, unless proven otherwise.[19]

With regard to the sanctuary of Demeter and Kore, Spaeth contends that the three temples that were built in the Roman period were not temples to Demeter, Kore and the Morai, but ones to Ceres, Liber and Libera, the Roman equivalents of Demeter, Dionysos and Kore. These were not just Roman veneers placed over Greek gods, 'but rather divinities with their own cultic associations and forms of worship, and their cults were promoted as a matter of state policy by the ruling elite of the city'.[20]

Bookidis argues against the three Roman deities being associated with the sanctuary, for four reasons: (1) lack of evidence of the triad in the rest of Greece and the eastern Mediterranean; (2) the presence of a first- or second-century CE curse tablet in the sanctuary invoking 'Lady Demeter' (see below); (3) a mosaic inscription from the third or fourth century CE that contains the name 'Neotera', which is an epithet for Persephone at Eleusis; and (4) the

---

[17] Ibid., 435–6.
[18] Christine M. Thomas, 'Greek Heritage in Roman Corinth and Ephesos: Hybrid Identities and Strategies of Display in the Material Record of Traditional Mediterranean Religions', in *Corinth in Context: Comparative Studies on Religion and Society*, ed. Steven J. Friesen, Daniel N. Schowalter and James C. Walters (Leiden: Brill, 2010), 119n9. Barbette Spaeth's work on this topic comes from papers read at the Annual Meeting of the Society of Biblical Literature, which are not publicly available.
[19] Barbette Stanley Spaeth, 'Greek Gods or Roman? The Corinthian Archaistic Blocks and Religion in Roman Corinth', *AJA* 121 (2017): 421 (emphasis original).
[20] Ibid.

presence of the cult of Demeter and Kore together with Dionysos, Eueteria, Artemis and Kore in the Sacred Glen at Isthmia.[21] So, although Spaeth's argument is suggestive, to make sense of all the evidence within her argument would mean that the three temples were built within the rededicated sanctuary to honour the Roman state gods. The result was a sanctuary that remained identified with Demeter and Kore but incorporated the Roman gods as part of the Roman cultural shift that happened during the early imperial period of Corinth. This is certainly possible, but it raises some questions about Spaeth's conclusions and makes the sanctuary unnecessarily complicated.

Later evidence for prayer tablets left at the sanctuary shows that it was a place where other gods were invoked for special purposes, termed 'magic' by some scholars but not by any ancient witness.[22] These tablets do not necessarily locate particular gods at the sanctuary, but they do invoke gods that make sense within a Demeter/Kore sanctuary. Eighteen lead tablets were found in the sanctuary, all dated to the Roman period (first century BCE to fifth century CE) and all but one in Greek. Most of them were curse tablets similar to those found across the Roman world, and at least six had women as their targets, with one or two possibly written or commissioned by women.[23] Stroud describes the find of ten of the tablets in one area of one building as:

> an unusual stratified context suggestive of rituals that were performed in the Sanctuary over a period of more than two centuries, beginning at the latest about the middle of the 1st century A.D. These rituals required not only lamps, incense burners, altars, and other items described in the *Greek Magical Papyri* (*PGM*), but also the deposition of inscribed lead tablets.[24]

A find of this sort in a sanctuary of Demeter and Kore is not unprecedented; there were similar deposits in Demeter/Kore sanctuaries in Knidos, Morgantina, Mytilene, Selinous and Rhodes.[25] Following Faraone's argument about the connection between depositing of lead tablets in Demeter sanctuaries and

---

[21] Bookidis, 'Religion in Corinth', 162.

[22] See Stroud, *Sanctuary of Demeter and Kore*, 81–157, for a description and discussion of the eighteen lead tablets found in the sanctuary. Stroud is aware of the problems with the term magic: 'This rarely paralleled archaeological context for at least 10 of the tablets has led me intentionally to use the controversial and loaded adjective "magical" in the title of this chapter, because I believe that most, though not all, scholars would agree in describing the activities in the Building of the Tablets as "magic"' (82). See also Joseph L. Rife, 'Religion and Society at Roman Kenchreai', in *Corinth in Context*, ed. Friesen, Schowalter and Walters, 422–3.

[23] Stroud, *Sanctuary of Demeter and Kore*, 81.

[24] Ibid.

[25] See ibid., 83 and the references there for information about these sanctuary finds.

the Thesmophoria,²⁶ Stroud argues that at least two of the tablets might have been connected with this festival in the Corinthian sanctuary. The tablets (125 and 126) were found fastened together, and they involve a curse of a certain Karpime Babbia. In the curse, several deities are invoked – the Moirai, Hermes of the Underworld, Ge, the children of Ge and Ananke.²⁷ In Tablet 127, 'the gods of the underworld' are evoked (θεοὶ κατ[α]χθόνιοι).²⁸ And in Tablet 133, Demeter herself is evoked as Κυρία Δήμητρα, 'Lady Demeter'.²⁹ These gods are all gods related to the Underworld and to issues of justice, which makes sense in a sanctuary of Demeter and Kore.

Therefore, at the sanctuary of Demeter and Kore, we have a sanctuary with a consistent presence of a mother–daughter pair of gods from the early classical period through to the second century CE and beyond. We also have classical evidence for Artemis and maybe Dionysos, and then later into the Roman period for the Moirai (probably), and gods evoked in *defixiones* that relate to justice and the Underworld. There are only loose mythological connections between Artemis and Demeter, but Dionysos and Persephone were seen as having connections both to each other and to the Underworld.³⁰ Dionysos was the son of Persephone in some traditions associated with Orpheus, where Persephone (like her mother Demeter) goes through a grieving process over the loss of her son Dionysos, dismembered by the Titans.³¹ Given the role that they play in determining the fate of individuals, it is reasonable to associate the Moirai with Demeter and Kore; they are fittingly found together in this sanctuary.

As mentioned, Spaeth raises the possibility that Ceres, Liber and Libera were incorporated into the sanctuary at some point to reflect and promote the Roman culture dominant in Corinth after its colonisation in 44 BCE. But this does not necessarily affect the wider conclusion that there was a defined group of gods present in the sanctuary at any given time, even if the grouping was fluid at different cultural moments in the history of Corinth.

---

²⁶ Christopher A. Faraone, 'Curses, Crime Detection, and Conflict Resolution at the Festival of Demeter Thesmophoria', *JHS* 131 (2011): 25–44.
²⁷ Stroud, *Sanctuary of Demeter and Kore*, 105.
²⁸ Ibid., 115.
²⁹ Ibid., 125.
³⁰ 'Hades and Dionysos are the same' (Heraclitus, *DK* 22 B 15). A festival of Dionysos, the Anthesteria, was celebrated across Greece; one of its elements consisted of rituals to ensure a happy afterlife. See Graf and Johnston, *Ritual Texts*, 73; Sarah Iles Johnston, *Restless Dead: Encounters between the Living and the Dead in Ancient Greece* (Berkeley: University of California Press, 1999), 63–6.
³¹ See Graf and Johnston *Ritual Texts*, 66–93, for an extended discussion of the various myths of Dionysos's origins.

## Isis and Sarapis

The evidence for Isis and Sarapis in the Corinthian area shows up both in the archaeological findings and in literature. An inscription on the base of a small marble tripod found at the base of the north side of the Acrocorinth reads: 'Philotis, daughter of Philonidas, to Sarapis (and) Isis' (Φιλωτίς | Φιλωνίδα | Σαράπι, Ἴσ[ι]).[32] The inscription dates to the third or second century BCE, and its find location could indicate that it is from the temple described by Pausanias (2.4.6–7).[33] A Latin inscription from about the first century CE found on the fragment of a green marble column in the theatre on the side of the forum opposite the Acrocorinth reads: 'To Isis and Sarapis, Caius Iulius Syrus devoted (this)' (Isi et Sarapi | v(ovit) | C. Iulius [S]yr[us]).[34] Aside from the references in Pausanias, Apuleius in *Metamorphosis* 11.7–18 describes the festival of Isis Pelagia at Kenchreai, the details of which we cannot be sure are historically accurate. While the evidence is fragmentary, and it is hard to determine the exact nature of the sanctuaries present in Corinth and its environs, it is clear that Isis and Sarapis were strong presences in this area. As Bookidis says,

> Whether his [Apuleius's] account is fact or fiction, the popularity of Sarapis and Isis at Corinth is manifested in four sanctuaries to the two deities at the base of the Acrocorinth, in a fifth to the Sarapis in the South Stoa, on a column from the theater, dedicated to both deities by C. Iulius Syros in the 1st century, and possibly in two more heads identified as Sarapis.[35]

The basic mythology around Isis was imported into the Greek world from Egypt, and thus underwent some transformation. In the original, Osiris, Isis's brother and husband, is murdered and then resurrected through the mourning of Isis and her sister. Isis becomes pregnant by Osiris after his resurrection and she gives birth to Horus, who then attacks, or even kills, Isis and ascends to his father's throne. Isis's popularity in Egypt was widespread and she later became known as μυριώνυμος ('invoked by innumerable names'; Plut *De Is. et Os.* 53.372f).[36] She was also connected through Osiris with Apis, the oracular sacred bull worshipped at Memphis as far back as the Old Kingdom in Egypt. The embalmed bull entombed at Saqqara was termed Osiris-Apis (Diod. Sic. 1.85.4);

---

[32] *RICIS* 102/0101.
[33] Stroud, *Sanctuary of Demeter and Kore*, 6.
[34] *RICIS* 102/0102.
[35] Bookidis, 'Sanctuaries of Corinth', 257.
[36] Richard L. Gordon, 'Isis', in *Oxford Classical Dictionary*, 4th ed. (Oxford: Oxford University Press, 2012).

in Ptolemaic times, this name was combined at the creation of the Sarapis cult in Alexandria.[37] Sarapis and Osiris are so closely aligned that the pairing of Sarapis with Isis makes sense. He later became thought of as the consort of Isis, as witnessed in the Maroneia aretology (c. 100 BCE).[38]

The continuous historical presence of Isis and Sarapis in the Corinthian region extends from at least the third century BCE through to the second century CE. They sometimes appear separately but mostly together; given their mythological connection, it is not unreasonable to think that both were invoked even during the worship of only one. Other than literary evidence, it is hard to determine the precise nature of Isis and Osiris worship in the region, but it seems fairly certain that they were present and honoured together in the city of Corinth proper, and in Kenchreai.

## Sanctuary of Poseidon at Isthmia

Isthmia was the location of the famed Isthmian Games, the founding of which is traditionally dated at 584 BCE.[39] The games were created and celebrated in honour of Melikertes-Palaimon,[40] and by the Roman period his temple was located within the bounds of the great Poseidon sanctuary. The Poseidon complex has a long history that goes back to the archaic age, but by the time of the Roman period it had reached the height of its importance and complexity. Figure 2.8 shows a plan of the sanctuary of Poseidon within the wider civic landscape; Figure 2.9 provides a composite close-up plan of the sanctuary, including the sanctuary of Palaimon as part of the complex. The Isthmian Games' connection with this sanctuary elevated it to what scholars categorise as one of four panhellenic sanctuaries.[41] Alongside this, we have a great example of how a group of gods could be present and honoured at a local sanctuary, even one with widespread (that is, panhellenic) fame.

Again, we start with Pausanias, who describes the sanctuary in this way:

> On the temple (τῷ ναῷ) . . . stand bronze Tritons. In the fore-temple (ἐν τῷ προνάῳ) are two images of Poseidon, a third of Amphitrite, and

---

[37] Richard L. Gordon, 'Apis', in *Oxford Classical Dictionary*.
[38] Richard L. Gordon, 'Sarapis', in *Oxford Classical Dictionary*.
[39] See 'The Michigan State University Excavations at Isthmia', https://msuisthmia.org.
[40] Paus. 1.44.7–8 tells the story of the body of Melikertes being carried by a dolphin to the Corinthian isthmus, where after being renamed Palaimon, he received honours including the Isthmian Games.
[41] The other three being Olympia, Delphi, and Nemea. All four are identified as panhellenic mainly because of the games that were held at each sanctuary, which drew people from across the Greek world.

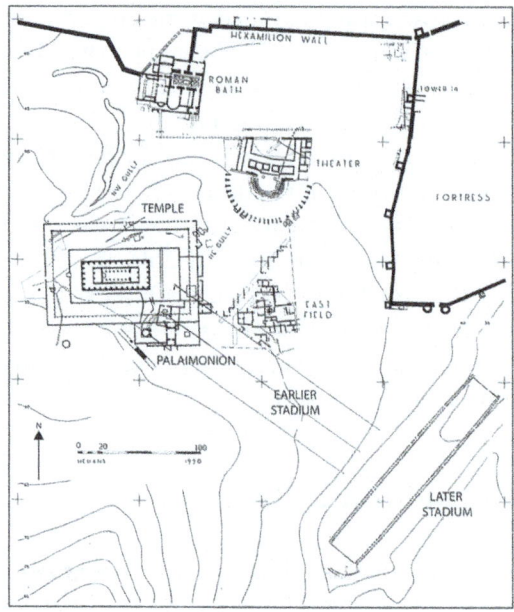

**Figure 2.8** Plan of the Sanctuary of Poseidon at Isthmia. (Public domain; https://lucian.uchicago.edu/blogs/isthmia/files/2010/06/genplan.gif)

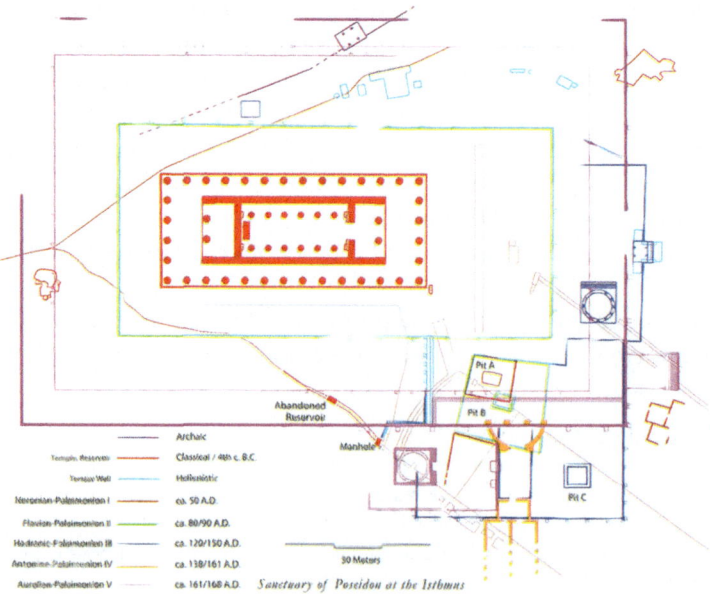

**Figure 2.9** Close-up plan of the Sanctuary of Poseidon and Palaimon. (Public domain; https://lucian.uchicago.edu/blogs/isthmia/files/2012/03/composite.gif)

Sea, which is also bronze ... On the chariot Amphitrite and Poseidon stand and the boy Palaimon is upright on a dolphin ... On the base, upon which is the chariot in the middle, Sea is sculpted as holding up the girl Aphrodite, and on either side are those called the Nereides (2.1.7–8).

He later goes into more detail:

Within the precinct on the left is a temple of Palaimon, and in it are statues of Poseidon, Leukothea, and Palaimon himself. There is further what is called an aduton and a chamber underground in it where they say that [the body of] Palaimon remains concealed (2.2.1).

He also describes another sanctuary (ἱερόν) with an altar to Cyclopes and the graves of Sisyphus (ruler of ancient Corinth and founder of the Isthmian Games) and Neleus (son of Poseidon and Tyro). However, it is unclear what relation this sanctuary and the graves have to the sanctuary of Poseidon.

According to Oscar Broneer, what Pausanias saw as he approached the sanctuary were cult statues, meaning that they were not simply art or honorary monuments to the gods.[42] Their placement within the sanctuary makes sense of them as having this significance. The sanctuary and statues seem to have survived as they were for at least another century because Philostratus describes something very similar.[43] Unfortunately, nothing is known about the statues in the classical period, but there is evidence for both an archaic building and a classical temple on the site. Broneer thinks it likely that Poseidon and Amphitrite 'had always shared worship both in the Archaic building and in the Classical Temple'.[44] He goes on: 'In Roman Imperial times, prior to Pausanias' visit, the cult statues appear to have consisted of a standing figure of Poseidon and a seated Amphitrite.'[45]

---

[42] Oscar Broneer, *Isthmia*, vol. 1, *Temple of Poseidon* (Princeton: ASCSA, 1971), 88. See also Mary C. Sturgeon, 'New Sculptures from the Isthmian Palaimonion', in *Bridge of the Untiring Sea: The Corinthian Isthmus from Prehistory to Late Antiquity*, ed. Elizabeth R. Gebhard and Timothy E. Gregory (Athens: American School of Classical Studies, 2015), 159–92, who reconstructs several statue fragments from the sanctuary of Palaimon with various identifications (Roman officials or priests of the sanctuary), indicating that the cult statues were not the only statuary present in the temple.

[43] Philostr. *VS* 2.551: 'and there are the Isthmian statues, which are both of the colossus of the Isthmia [Poseidon] and the one of Amphitrites, which he placed in the temple, and I do not pass over the dolphin of Melikertes' (καὶ τὰ Ἰσθμοῖ ἀγάλματα ὅ τε τοῦ Ἰσθμίου κολοσσὸς καὶ ὁ τῆς Ἀμφιτρίτης καὶ τὰ ἄλλα, ὧν τὸ ἱερὸν ἐνέπλησεν, οὐδὲ τὸν τοῦ Μελικέρτου παρελθὼν δελφῖνα). See Broneer, *Isthmia: Temple of Poseidon*, 89–90.

[44] Ibid., 103.

[45] Ibid.

Herodes Atticus gave the temple a new set of statues, which Pausanias also describes (Poseidon, Amphitrite, the Tritons and Palaimon/Melikertes). Pseudo-Lucian mentions that Nero purportedly sang a hymn to the gods in his visit to begin the Isthmian canal construction:

> The games may have been celebrated again in the fall of 67 CE when Nero inaugurated the Isthmian canal, since he is reported to have sung a hymn to Poseidon and Amphitrite and a short song to Melikertes and Leucothea to celebrate the event. (Ps.-Lucian, *Nero* 3)[46]

While the presence of Melikertes (later renamed Palaimon) in the sanctuary seems to go back to the archaic period in Corinth, along with Pausanias, there is second-century CE Corinthian numismatic evidence showing the boy, his dolphin and his temple (see Figure 2.10).[47] Broneer concludes:

> For more than a millennium the Temple had been the religious center on the Corinthian Isthmus, the largest and most famous of the many cult houses dedicated to Poseidon and Amphitrite, divine rulers of the sea and patrons of the Isthmian Games.[48]

The presence of multiple gods at Poseidon's sanctuary for centuries before and during Paul's time is therefore well established.

**Figure 2.10** Temple of Melikertes on obverse of Marcus Aurelius coin. (Public domain)

---

[46] προελθὼν δὲ τῆς σκηνῆς ὕμνον μὲν Ἀμφιτρίτης τε καὶ Ποσειδῶνος ᾖσε καὶ ᾆσμα οὐ μέγα Μελικέρτῃ τε καὶ Λευκοθέᾳ.
[47] Elizabeth R. Gebhard, 'Rites for Melikertes-Palaimon in the Early Roman Corinthia', in *Urban Religion in Roman Corinth*, ed. Schowalter and Friesen, 167–8.
[48] Broneer, *Isthmia: Temple of Poseidon*, 103.

Mythologically, the sea and its dangers hold all these gods together. The maritime roles of Poseidon and his wife Amphitrite are widely known, so there is no need to go into detail describing them. Melikertes and his mother Leukothea (both found with Poseidon in the temple of Palaimon) were widely appealed to in Roman imperial times for protection from the sea.[49] Their story has many variations, but the basic plot is that Hermes took the infant Dionysos to Ino and Athamas to be reared as a girl. Hera (or Jove in later traditions) became angry and drove Ino and Athamas mad, causing both to kill their sons, with Ino plunging Melikertes into a basin of boiling water (or simply jumping into the sea with him). She then jumped into the sea with Melikertes, after which they were deified (by Neptune or Poseidon at the request of Venus), a process which granted them a wide range of powers.[50] It was through the deification process that Palaimon gained his connection with Poseidon and the Nereids.

Palaimon's principal cult site was in the sanctuary of Poseidon in Isthmia. So, while what Pausanias describes in the sanctuary might not have been precisely configured as such in the mid-first century CE of Paul's Corinthians, the mythological connection among these gods certainly goes back many centuries before Pausanias. We have present and functioning in the most prominent sanctuary of Poseidon a husband–wife pair (Poseidon and Amphitrite) along with their children (the Tritons) and a mother–son pair (Leukothea and Palaimon) who are also linked with Poseidon, along with some supporting figures (the Nereids). This is a distinct group that is related in cult, in myth/history and in genealogy. The prominence of the site with respect to the Isthmian Games and the cultic activity associated with Palaimon related to the games at the panhellenic site reinforces the idea that the pattern of worship of small groups of gods in one sanctuary was part of the normal cultic activity in the Corinthian region, as much as across the Mediterranean world.

## Sanctuary of Asklepios

The life of the sanctuary of Asklepios (see Figure 2.11), located north of the forum along the city wall of the classical period (see Figure 2.1), is difficult to describe in detail because virtually all the evidence for the complex is archaeological. There is only one literary reference – a brief comment from Pausanias – which clearly shows that he did not linger in the sanctuary. But the archaeological record is fascinating, so a brief discussion of its history is worthwhile.

---

[49] See the references in John G. Hawthorne, 'The Myth of Palaemon', *TAPA* 89 (1958): 92–8.
[50] Aeschylus's lost play *Athamas* told the story; the fullest extant version can be found in Ov. *Met.* 4.542. See Gebhard, 'Rites for Melikertes-Palaimon', 169–70 and the references there, for further detail.

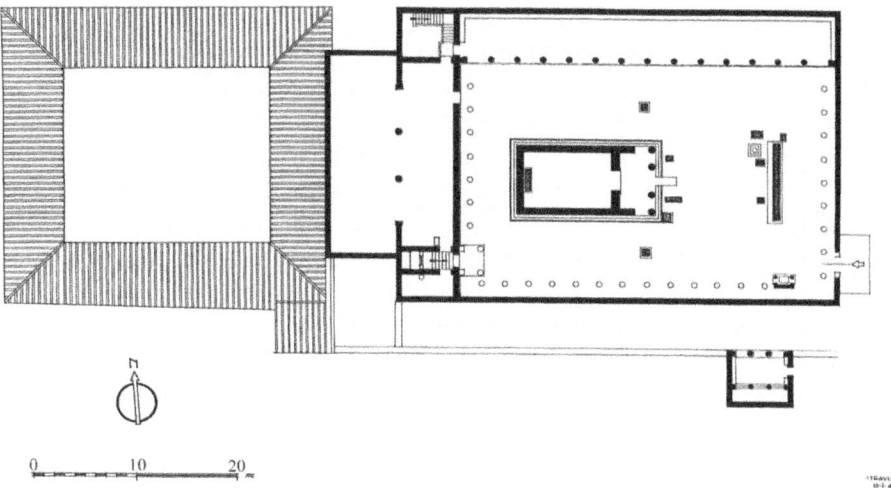

**Figure 2.11** Plan of the Hellenistic Corinthian Asklepieion. (Modified from Bronwen L. Wickkiser, 'Asklepios in Greek and Roman Corinth', in *Corinth in Context: Comparative Studies on Religion and Society*, edited by Steven J. Friesen, Daniel N. Schowalter, and James C. Walters [Leiden: Brill, 2010], 48.) Used with permission.

There are three distinct periods in the life of the Asklepieion: the archaic to Hellenistic period up to 146 BCE, when the city was sacked by the Roman general Mummius; the 102-year pre-colonisation period following; and the Roman period, which began in 44 BCE, when the city was officially colonised.[51] This sanctuary goes back as far as the earliest Asklepieia in Greece, so its significance should not be underestimated, even if there is relatively little information we can glean about its daily life from the archaeological record. Like many major Asklepieia across the Mediterranean, the one in Corinth started small and not associated with Asklepios, but in the fifth century, coinciding with the growth in popularity of medicine,[52] the sanctuary started to expand and by the fourth century had reached its zenith in terms of prominence. The original archaic buildings were razed and a new temple complex was built in its place. At some point in this period, more than a hundred terracotta anatomical votive offerings – the sanctuary's most notable feature from a popular modern perspective – were buried in the grounds, probably either to make room for more or to preserve them during the process of constructing the new temple.

---

[51] For an excellent treatment of the history of the sanctuary, see Bronwen L. Wickkiser, 'Asklepios in Greek and Roman Corinth', in *Corinth in Context*, ed. Friesen, Schowalter and Walters, 37–66, which I follow throughout this paragraph.

[52] See Wickkiser, 'Asklepios in Greek and Roman Corinth', 46–7; and Bronwen L. Wickkiser, *Asklepios, Medicine, and the Politics of Healing in Fifth-Century Athens: Between Craft and Cult* (Baltimore: Johns Hopkins University Press, 2008), ch. 3.

After the sacking of the city in 146 BCE, the sanctuary was partially damaged, but it seems to have still been active between that time and the Roman colonisation, if at a much reduced level than previously. At the time of the colonisation of the city, the Asklepieion was one of the first sanctuaries to witness cultic activity and be rebuilt.[53] It seems that there was not a dedicated incubation building, which was a hallmark of Asklepieia in Greece and Anatolia. There is some thought among scholars that the 'Roman' style of worshipping Asklepios was imported to Corinth after the colonisation, which might account for this lack of dedicated incubation space.[54] By the time of Pausanias's reference, the sanctuary had been re-established for almost two centuries and would last another three before fading away in the fifth and sixth centuries CE with the rise of Christianity.

The earliest evidence for activity at the site of the Asklepieion is tied to Apollo rather than to Asklepios. A krater with an inscription to Apollo on its rim, dated to the early sixth century BCE, is the earliest attestation of a deity on the site.[55] The origin of the site as an Apollo sanctuary fits well with other Asklepieia, such as those at Epidauros, Delphi, Kos and Pergamon. The link to Apollo might have lasted several centuries past the point when Asklepios became associated with the site and eventually became dominant in the fifth and fourth centuries BCE. Several male figurines that likely depict Apollo have been found and dated to this era, so it is possible that Apollo and Asklepios were linked in the earlier stages of the Asklepieion,[56] perhaps the highest point in popularity during its thousand years of existence. Apollo and Asklepios certainly remained partners in healing and cultic activity in other Asklepieia right through to late antiquity. Pergamon is an excellent example where an early second-century CE inscription documents that the fees due at the end of the sanctuary rituals and incubation were paid to both Asklepios and Apollo.[57] As mentioned, the classical and early Hellenistic periods of the Corinthian sanctuary featured the famous terracotta anatomical votive offerings, but there is no indication to whom they were dedicated. They could very well have been offered in thanksgiving to Apollo, Asklepios or both.[58] There is no evidence

---

[53] Wickkiser, 'Asklepios in Greek and Roman Corinth', 56: 'At least four sanctuaries within the walls of Greek Corinth were renewed by Roman Corinth: the Archaic Temple of Apollo in the forum area, the Sanctuary of Demeter and Kore on the north slope of Acrocorinth, the Sanctuary of Aphrodite atop Acrocorinth, and the Asklepieion.'

[54] See Gil H. Renberg, 'Was Incubation Practiced in the Latin West?', *Archiv für Religionsgeschichte* 8 (2006): 105–47, for the lack of incubation evidence in the Latin West.

[55] Carl Roebuck, *The Asklepieion and Lerna* (Athens: American School of Classical Studies, 1951), 16, fig. 1.

[56] Ibid., 153.

[57] See Stephen P. Ahearne-Kroll, 'Mnēmosynē at the Asklepieia', *CP* 109 (2014): 115–17, for the inscription.

[58] Wickkiser, 'Asklepios in Greek and Roman Corinth', 55, says, 'Can we be sure the 100-plus anatomical votives were dedicated to Asklepios rather than to Apollo?'

in the Roman period that Apollo was included in the sanctuary, which might reflect the rebuilding of the sanctuary after Roman colonisation.

Hygieia, one of Asklepios's mythical daughters, was possibly also part of the sanctuary in this early period and certainly was so in the Roman period. Roebuck says:

> There are some indications, too, of the existence of a statue base in the cuttings in the bedrock along the rear wall of the cella. The base was apparently long and narrow and designed to hold two statues – probably Asklepios and Hygieia, if both deities were honored in this early period.[59]

There is no archaeological evidence for her presence in the later Roman sanctuary.[60] However, Pausanias's short statement about the sanctuary includes a reference to the statues of Asklepios and Hygieia (2.4.5). And we have some coinage from second-century Corinth that feature Asklepios and Hygieia alone and together.[61] Coins are not definitive evidence of the presence of these deities, but when paired with the literary evidence from Pausanias, the probability of Asklepios and Hygieia being present together in the sanctuary certainly increases. If we can understand the archaeological evidence that Roebuck describes as indicative of Hygieia's presence in the classical period, then it appears that she was continuously present in the sanctuary for most of its life.

Finally, Telesphoros – son of Asklepios, who is found in other Asklepieia and perhaps developed a cult of his own at some point in the first or second century CE – might also have been present in the Corinthian Asklepieion. Roebuck writes that a particular figurine 'may represent a youthful deity associated with the cult of Asklepios. The type resembles the figures identified as Telesphoros.'[62] This figurine is from the pre-Roman period; otherwise, there is no evidence of his presence in the sanctuary at any point during the Roman era.

As we saw in the previous chapter, Asklepios and Apollo are mythologically son and father, and Apollo's role in establishing Asklepios as a deified healer runs throughout several strands of the mythological tradition. It would be surprising if there were no evidence for Apollo in the sanctuary's early years, especially with a sanctuary this old. Hygieia is one of Asklepios's daughters and

---

[59] Roebuck, *The Asklepieion and Lerna*, 34.
[60] Ibid., 153.
[61] Examples are from the reign of Lucius Verus (together, and Hygieia alone) and Commodus (Asklepios). See Imhoof-Bloomer and Gardner, *Numismatic Commentary*, 25n30.
[62] Roebuck, *The Asklepieion and Lerna*, 138.

**Figure 2.12** Medical box from Herculaneum, with image of Asklepios and Hygieia, first century CE. (Public domain)

Telesphoros one of his sons. In many other sanctuaries, Hygieia works alongside Asklepios and is appropriately honoured. Take, for example, the relief from Piraeus or the medical box from Herculaneum (Figure 2.12), separated by four centuries. She is ubiquitously present with him across the Mediterranean world and across time. Telesphoros also often appears, but more as sort of a sidekick to Asklepios. However, in the second century CE, there seems to have been some elevation of Telesphoros's status in Pergamon and Epidauros, where he received his own honours, even if they were in the context of the Asklepieia there. So we have every reason to think that Asklepios was not alone in the Corinthian sanctuary and likely had his traditionally closest family members with him – father Apollo, daughter Hygieia and son Telesphoros.

## Colonial/State Protective Divinities

As discussed above, Barbette Spaeth argues for the presence of Ceres, Liber and Libera in the sanctuary of Demeter and Kore on the north slope of Acrocorinth. But in another aspect of her greater body of work on Corinth, she examines reliefs on two large blocks found near the south-west corner of the forum. The blocks have lost their original archaeological context, having been reused in other applications, so it is hard to determine how and where they were originally used.[63] However, given their size and the quality of the reliefs (a single image on each of the three sides of the blocks), Spaeth surmises that they could have been used as 'pillars . . . or bases for freestanding statues'.[64] The figures are carved in an archaistic style, and there are attributes of all of the depictions that indicate that they show divinities. The figures have traditionally been identified as Greek gods – initially by Williams and then more or less followed by subsequent scholars. But Spaeth points to the fact that Corinth was a Roman colony by the time that these stone blocks were produced, and therefore the gods should be identified as Roman rather than Greek. She provides a lengthy analysis of the images in the context of similar imagery on coins and other sculptures and statuary. She also notes that the inscriptional and votive evidence of Corinth up until Hadrian is mostly Latin rather than Greek, and the content of the inscriptions depict a Corinth that was politically and religiously predominantly Roman.[65] Spaeth further notes that the size and likely location of the blocks (the forum) could indicate a relationship to the state cult of Rome.[66] She suggests that there could have been an open-air sanctuary built in the forum where the Roman gods of the new colony could receive cult and be honoured properly.[67] After a long and detailed analysis, she concludes that the gods should be identified as the Genius of Roman Corinth, Fortuna, Athena/Minerva, Ceres, Libera (or Prosperina) and Liber.

What held these six gods together was their role in protecting the new Roman colony. Ceres, Liber and Libera were the members of a long-standing triadic cult located in the temple on the Aventine Hill in Rome. That cult was born out of the 'struggle of the orders', a long political and power struggle between the plebians and patricians. Eventually, or so the prevailing historical theory goes, the plebians created a state within a state, with institutions that mirrored those of the patricians, including the establishment of the triad of Ceres, Liber and Libera as a counter to the primary state Capitoline triad of Jupiter, Juno and Minerva.[68] Gregory Pellam acknowledges the widespread acceptance of this theory but offers a challenge that reorients the purpose of

---

[63] Spaeth, 'Greek Gods or Roman?', 397.
[64] Ibid., 398.
[65] Ibid., 400–1.
[66] Ibid., 399.
[67] Ibid., 417. Part of Spaeth's argument is the fact that money was not abundantly available for the construction of large new temples during the founding years of the colony, so an open-air sanctuary would have been an inexpensive solution to properly honour the Roman tutelary gods.
[68] See Gregory Pellam, 'Ceres, the Plebs, and "Libertas" in the Roman Republic', *Historia: Zeitschrift für Alte Geschichte* 63 (2014): 74–5 and the references there, for a summary of the 'struggle of the orders' theory of Republican Rome.

the triad Ceres, Liber and Libera to be focused more on *libertas* than on the plebs per se.⁶⁹ If his argument holds against the prevailing view, the reorientation of the triad's focus towards *libertas* would mean that it would have appealed widely to all Romans in all social and political classes, since *libertas* was extremely important overall to Roman culture and identity.⁷⁰ It is easy to see how this triad, if representing, expressing and protecting Roman *libertas*, would have been important for a colonial Corinth, too. As protectors of the new colony, the triad would have worked together to ensure *libertas* for all its citizens as they built the institutions and population into a new and thriving Roman city. Spaeth's conjecture of an open-air sanctuary with the triad as an important part of its cultic life in the new colony's forum would make sense, especially in the early years, when the character of the city was established. The addition of the Genius of Corinth and Fortuna fits well with the traditional protective nature of the triad.

Whether or not Spaeth's and Pellam's theories are fully convincing, they at least raise the strong possibility of the incorporation of this small group of Roman gods into the colony's early life to protect the developing city and advance the *libertas* of its citizens and institutions. Such a fundamental civic and cultural virtue would have been apparent to all Corinthians, and the expression of the virtue through the cultic activity of a small group of gods in a central, open-air sanctuary would have prominently displayed the pattern we have seen so far in Corinth and its surroundings.

## Worship of Gens Iulia and Other Imperial Worship

Although one would expect imperial worship to be one of the cultural foundations in a colony like Corinth, Mary E. Hoskins Walbank was one of the first to examine the evidence for such worship, and certainly the first to study it extensively.⁷¹ She argues that the first stage of development in the worship of the imperial family was the worship of Julius Caesar, which is indicated by

---

⁶⁹ One example from John Scheid, *The Gods, the State, and the Individual: Reflections on Civic Religion in Rome*, trans. Clifford Ando (Philadelphia: University of Pennsylvania Press, 2016), 93, shows the unquestioned acceptance of the characterisation of the triad as focused on the plebs: 'On the one hand, the priestesses of Ceres were not attached to the cult of Ceres, Liber, and Libera: that was the cult tied to the plebs, and it was celebrated by the flamen of Ceres. The priestesses of Ceres rather concerned themselves with the cult of Ceres-Demeter and Proserpina-Kore, which was not the same thing as the plebeian triad Ceres, Liber, and Libera.'
⁷⁰ Pellam, 'Ceres'.
⁷¹ Mary E. Hoskins Walbank, 'Evidence for the Imperial Cult in Julio-Claudian Corinth', in *Subject and Rule: The Cult of the Ruling Power in Classical Antiquity*, ed. A. Small (Ann Arbor: Journal of Roman Archaeology, 1996), 201–14.

only one fragmentary inscription: DIVO IUL[io] CAESARI [sacrum].[72] The inscription is dated to the late Republic or very early empire, based on the letter forms.[73] Although this scant piece of evidence does not give us much to go on, it would fit with the pattern of encouragement by the triumvirs to establish and operate the cult of Divus Iulius in the provinces.[74] As Augustus rose to power, one of the first Corinthian coins issued under his rule combines the heads of Augustus and Julius Caesar, celebrating the founder of the colony but also implying the close link of Augustus to his deified father, making him *divi filius* in image if not in name.[75]

The establishment of the cult to the imperial family was thus underway and its 'lasting importance in Corinth comes from an inscription honouring the first high-priest of the provincial imperial cult of Achaia, which is dated to early in the reign of Nero. It includes ... [honours to the] *flamen divi Iulii*.'[76] This, along with worship of the *Domus Augusta*, firmly indicates a clear presence of imperial worship for the first 100 years of Corinth's existence as a Roman colony. Walbank further argues that worship implies an altar and probably a temple, which she thinks is shown on an issue of Tiberian coins,

> all of which have on the reverse a hexastyle temple usually, but not always, inscribed with the words GENT(i) or (is) IVLI(ae) on the architrave ... This inscription to the Gens Iulia is unique among the provincial coinages, including other Julian colonies.[77]

The series of coins have various representations of members of the *Domus Augustus* – Tiberius, Augustus and Livia in two forms – all arguably dated to 32/33 or 33/34 CE, the latter half of Tiberius's rule (see Figure 2.13 for one example).[78]

The location of the temple represented on the reverse of the coins is very difficult to determine. Walbank offers some suggestions for various extant but unidentified buildings. Her most interesting suggestion for our purposes is that the refurbished archaic temple to Apollo was used for worship of the Gens Iulia. The problem with identifying it with the temple depicted on the coins is that Pausanias's description of the temple and statue of Apollo (Paus. 2.3.6) matches

---

[72] J. H. Kent, *Corinth*, vol. VIII.3, *The Inscriptions (1926–1950)* (Princeton: ASCSA, 1966), no. 50.
[73] Walbank 'Evidence for the Imperial Cult', 201.
[74] Ibid., 202.
[75] Ibid.
[76] Ibid.
[77] Ibid.
[78] M. Amandry, *Le monnayage des duovirs corinthiens*. BHS supplément 15. (Paris: École française d'Athènes, 1988), 66. C. J. Howgego, 'After the Colt Has Bolted: A Review of Amandry on Roman Corinth', *NC* 149 (1989): 199–208, critiques the dating, preferring an earlier date for the issue, but he does not dispute the characterisation of the temple on the reverse of the coins.

**Figure 2.13** Typical Tiberian coin from Corinth: (a) obverse with image of Tiberius; (b) reverse with six-columned temple carrying inscription GE[NT] IVLI. Used with permission from the Ashmolean Museum of Art and Archaeology.

the remains of the archaic temple exactly. So there seems to be no doubt that the remains of the archaic temple continued to be used for Apollo worship after its refurbishment at the founding of the colony. However, Pausanias's descriptions were not akin to ancient videography but a select description by a philhellenic author not really interested in depicting the Roman aspects of the landscapes he visited. One plausible possibility that Walbank raises is that the refurbished Apollo temple continued to be the location of Apollo worship but also served as the location for worship of the Gens Iulia.[79]

Nancy Bookidis raises the question briefly of 'whether Apollo, Roma and Tyche/Fortuna might not make more sense on a temple dedicated to Augustus rather than one dedicated to the Capitoline Triad'.[80] This would fit Augustus's connection to and adoption of Apollo as his patron deity, and an inscription that mentions a statue of Apollo Augustus.[81] There was also the widespread practice of placing deified imperial figures within existing temples to other gods with whom the imperial figure wished to be associated. We have seen this already in the previous chapter, with Augustus's order to build his new temples in Palestine to house himself and Roma, at minimum, and at the Pergamon Asklepieion's new Temple of Zeus Asklepios Soter, which housed a statue of Hadrian depicted as a god.[82]

---

[79] Walbank, 'Evidence for the Imperial Cult', 205–6, where she bases part of her argument on the dual *cellae* that are found in the remains of the Roman-era temple.

[80] Bookidis, 'Religion in Corinth', 157.

[81] CIL 3.534.

[82] See Simon R. F. Price, *Rituals and Power: The Roman Imperial Cult in Asia Minor* (Cambridge: Cambridge University Press, 1984), 146–56, for temple-sharing between traditional god and emperor.

A further piece of evidence for the presence of imperial worship is the Base of the *Augustales* found in the Corinthian forum, which was the base of a statue of Augustus dedicated by the *Augustales* sometime in the first century CE. The inscription on it reads: [divo a]VGVS[to] | [sacrum] | [au]GVSTALES ('sacred to the deified Augustus, the *Augustales* [made it]').[83] The base was likely part of a statue that complemented a tall circular monument with a colossal statue of Augustus sitting atop it, elevating him well above the forum. While this was probably not a cult statue, according to Walbank, it is 'important evidence of the cult of Divus Augustus at Corinth'.[84] Laird describes its dedication as locating 'it within the empire-wide system of the imperial cult'.[85] The *Augustales* were a municipal group that existed in the first three centuries CE and whose main function was to promote the empire at the local level: '*Augustales* are traditionally identified as municipal organizers of the imperial cult although emperor worship was just one of several public activities undertaken by the organization and its members.'[86] Interestingly, the group was mainly found in the West, with Corinth and Patrae as the only two Achaian colonies where inscriptional evidence for the *Augustales* survive,[87] perhaps raising still further the importance of imperial worship in Corinth, relative to the rest of Greece.

Along with this evidence, Bookidis points out that 'at least sixty-two inscriptions make reference to the imperial cult', including references to the Lares Augusti, the Genius Augusti, Saturnus Augustus, several subsidiary cults, the *flamen divi Iulii* and the *flamen Augusti*.[88] It seems pretty secure, then, that we have the active presence of, and cultic activity around, many of the deities associated with imperial worship. Putting aside the question of whether or not the various figures would be considered humans or deities or both, the honours that were accorded them indicates an ongoing cultic life aimed at their worship. Since we do not have clear evidence where this cultic life happened, it is hard to determine the precise configuration of these divine figures, but they are all held together by the mythology surrounding Julius Caesar and Augustus and their royal descendants. As we saw in the last chapter, Augustus's mythology tied him to several strands of Roman history and divine authority, and linked him to other divine figures. In Corinth, we can posit with some certainty this same dynamic of presence and worship.

---

[83] Allen Brown West, *Corinth*, vol. VIII.2, *The Latin Inscriptions* (Cambridge, MA: Harvard University Press for ASCSA, 1931), nos. 13 and 86–90. Translation from Margaret L. Laird, 'The Emperor in a Roman Town: The Base of the Augustales in the Forum at Corinth', in *Corinth in Context*, ed. Friesen, Schowalter and Walters, 78.

[84] Walbank, 'Evidence for the Imperial Cult', 210.

[85] Laird, 'The Emperor in a Roman Town', 70.

[86] Ibid., 72, and the references in n. 14 for further information on the *Augustales*.

[87] Ibid., 73.

[88] Bookidis, 'Religion in Corinth', 156.

## Corinthian Domestic Religion

I would like to finish this chapter with a few words about Corinthian domestic religion. The material evidence for domestic religion is most prevalent in the best-preserved dwellings across the Roman world. Corinth is not a major location for these sorts of remains, unlike the cities buried in the eruption of Vesuvius, for instance. So, we must assume that the basics of Roman domestic religious practice described in the previous chapter would hold for Roman Corinth as well. But there is some evidence from the Corinthian context which allows us to fill out the picture in a bit more detail for this region.

First, with regard to the *domus*, there is an active archaeological site at the Panayia Field just south-east of the Corinthian forum that contains a 'large, well-appointed dwelling' of 'considerable affluence'.[89] In one of the central but small rooms, a group of statuettes was found in remarkable condition, strewn on the floor. The statuette group, ranging in date from the late first to the mid-third or early fourth century CE, numbered nine and included Artemis (twice), Asklepios (twice), Roma, Dionysos, Herakles, Europa/Sosandra and Pan. The statues were finely sculpted, which would match the setting in a very wealthy dwelling, and the remains included paint and gilding on some. The location of the find, in a small, somewhat nondescript room in the dwelling, raises the question of their function in the house. Were they decorative or religious in significance? If they were purely decorative, then their location likely would have been in a more prominent and lavishly decorated room. Lea M. Stirling contends, despite the lack of explicit evidence of cultic activity (remains of offerings, for example), that 'the centrality of the room, the faintly sacral air of its painted decoration (in the form of a garland), and the presence of the exquisite miniature statuary itself all combine to suggest that this room housed a domestic shrine'.[90] Close to the forum in other locations were found cult statuettes of Asklepios and Dionysos in one house and a Europa-type statuette in another, both sites dated to the fourth century CE.

Some of these gods overlapped with the civic or local gods who had sanctuaries of their own or with other gods in Corinth (for example, Asklepios, Dionysos, Artemis – the last perhaps at the Demeter/Kore sanctuary), and most of them also appear in numismatic imagery, 'often depicted in the same configurations'.[91] But the presence of Roma is unattested anywhere in Corinth

---

[89] Lea M. Stirling, 'Pagan Statuettes in Late Antique Corinth: Sculpture from the Panayia Domus', *Hesperia* 77, no. 1 (2008): 127, which describes the dwelling as having at least two peristyles, and outdoor space with a decorative pool, geometric mosaic floors, marble paving in some rooms, two fountains and painted walls (both figural and non-figural). In my discussion here, I follow Stirling for the description of the statuettes, their context and their meaning.
[90] Ibid., 130.
[91] Ibid., 136.

with any certainty,[92] and Stirling says, 'it is unique to find a marble statuette of Roma in a domestic context; this is the only example known to me'.[93] So, while this Roma statuette seems to be unusual in a domestic setting in Corinth and beyond, the statuette group as a phenomenon matches other finds outside of Corinth. The Roma statuette might be a local late antique variant on the common pattern of domestic piety.

Second, we have evidence of a number of stele shrines across the city. While these are not located within houses, some of them are related to a domestic setting, and are 'particularly Corinthian', according to Bookidis.[94] She describes some of the finds as follows: 'A number of these, including the shrine excavated in 1977 beneath the west end of the South Stoa ... and six shrines in the Potters' Quarter ... were built on top of ruined houses.'[95] This caught the attention of Williams, who has studied these shrines as part of the domestic religion particular to Corinth.[96] The Erosa shrine, for example, (fifth–fourth century BCE) was found to be:

> a single-roomed structure erected over the ruins of the southeast corner of an earlier, larger building. The shrine was constructed upon the walls of what may have been a storeroom divided by a partition wall. The larger building, almost certainly a house, had a central court that was paved in crushed limestone, a typical flooring material for such open spaces.[97]

Williams asserts that the room was not originally constructed as part of the larger building but erected over the remains of that building, thus marking it out.[98] Another example contains a hearth found under a crossroads, which Williams and Zervos argue was probably temporarily constructed in the Hellenistic period.[99] Statuettes of two seated women with miniature votive offerings were found with the hearth. Because there were no cultic remains discovered there, Williams and Zervos reject the possibility that this hearth

---

[92] There is a visual parallel to a public statue on the pediment of Temple E in the forum, but there is some disagreement about the identity of that statue (Roma, Enyo and Nike have all been suggested). See ibid., 131 and the literature cited there.
[93] Ibid.
[94] Bookidis, 'Sanctuaries of Corinth', 253.
[95] Ibid., 252–3.
[96] Kaufman Williams and O. H. Zervos, 'Corinth, 1982: East of the Theater', *Hesperia* 52 (1983): 1–17; Kaufman Williams, 'The City of Corinth and Its Domestic Religion', *Hesperia* 50 (1981): 408–21.
[97] Williams, 'The City of Corinth', 413.
[98] Ibid., 413.
[99] Williams and Zervos, 'Corinth, 1982', 7.

was originally part of a house and that the figures were household gods being utilised to honour the abandoned house. Instead they assert that this was, less piously, a pair of 'heroines, not goddesses, partaking of a ritual meal'.[100] I am not sure what basis Williams and Zervos have for claiming that the depiction of heroines engaged in a ritual meal is any less pious than the use of figurines to worship a pair of goddesses. The ritual meal depiction might represent a different kind of piety, but the devaluation of the depiction as less pious is unwarranted, since heroes and heroines were worshipped throughout the Greek and Roman world by humans in ways similar to the worship of gods and goddesses.[101]

After surveying the evidence of all the stele shrines, Williams finds that there is a pattern that emerges with many of them that indicates that they tend to be built on the ruins of houses. At most of these sites, there is evidence of heroes and/or gods being honoured in some way, so he posits that these Corinthians maintained a connection to the houses they were forced to abandon for some reason, and the shrines marked their ancestral connections to the household gods that they once worshipped in the house. The activity continued this honouring of the gods even beyond the existence of the house itself.

With one exception, the practice did not seem to last very long after the destruction of the house, perhaps only a few generations. The exception was a shrine found at the west end of the South Stoa, which 'survived from its inception in the 6th century down to the destruction of Corinth in 146 B.C.'[102] This pattern would seem to fit in a more general way with the purported connection between the Lares and the land on which the houses were built, as discussed in the previous chapter. While the unnamed Lares were present in the domestic evidence, there were often also other household gods that could also be considered Lares, except that, in these cases, we know the identity of the gods. The complex of evidence points to a rich world of divine connection between household (that is, family), household structure, and location of the household structure, as defined by a small group of gods for any given family.

Although there is little direct evidence from the first century for domestic religion in Corinth, the evidence both from the classical and Hellenistic periods and from the fourth century CE gives us no reason to doubt the worship of small groups of gods in domestic settings, all connected by family traditions that were both historical and mythological in the sense described in the Introduction.

---

[100] Ibid., 8.
[101] See Gunnel Ekroth, *The Sacrificial Rituals of Greek Hero-Cults* (Liège: Centre international d'étude de la religion grecque antique, 2002), for a thorough treatment of the worship practices in hero cults, including blood rituals, *theoxenia* and *thysia* rituals.
[102] Williams, 'The City of Corinth', 418.

## Conclusion

There is other fragmentary evidence for the possible presence of groups of gods in Corinth: the Capitoline Triad;[103] worship of Demeter, Kore, Dionysos, Euteria and Artemis together in Isthmia (mentioned briefly above); the cult of the Nymphs in classical and Hellenistic Corinth;[104] and the gods worshipped along the harbour at Kenchreai.[105] And, of course, the descriptions of Pausanias, which I have referenced intermittently above, show a plethora of possibilities but oftentimes no corroborating evidence. While I have not performed a comprehensive analysis of the religious culture at Corinth, I have shown a consistent pattern of worship of small groups of gods from the archaic period through to the imperial Roman era. This fits the general pattern of worship across the ancient Mediterranean discussed in the previous chapter. The details of worship are very interesting but less important for our purposes. What matters is that there is a consistent pattern, and this pattern indicates that the Corinthians during Paul's time were accustomed to thinking of and actively worshipping gods in small groups in various settings. These small groups were not random but instead had a logic to them in most cases: a mythological connection or historical connection, a common genealogy, or a political reason for being together. Sometimes the evidence does not make it clear what the precise connections were, but it is clear that they included cultic activity within sanctuaries, domestic contexts, roadside shrines, and civic contexts. Like all cultic activity, that involved chords of gods working to build and reinforce human–divine reciprocal relationships and for the mutual benefit of humans and gods alike. The pattern indicates the kind of social practice that Schatzki defined: the nexus of sayings and doings for Corinthian religious activity.

We enter into the Pauline section of this study with the practice of the worship of small groups of gods firmly established, and with the likelihood that Paul's Corinthian audience(s) would have heard his preaching through a certain religio-cultural lens. Their gods were arranged not as individuals and not as an indefinite plethora, but as chords of gods connected and working together in small groups to interact reciprocally with the Corinthians for the benefit of both human and divine communities.

---

[103] Paus. 2.4.5 mentions Zeus Capitolinus.
[104] See Theodora Kopestonsky, 'The Greek Cult of the Nymphs at Corinth', *Hesperia* 85 (2016): 711–77.
[105] See Rife, 'Religion and Society at Roman Kenchreai'.

CHAPTER THREE

# The *Pneuma* in Corinth

It is fairly self-explanatory how Paul's (father) god and (lord Jesus) Christ language would represent personified divine figures. It is not so clear whether his *pneuma* language would have similarly represented a personified divine figure to the Corinthians. What follows is a focus on the language of *pneuma* in the Corinthian correspondence to see whether it would fit with the general expectations of Paul's audience when they heard such a term. Next, we need to get a sense of the constitution of Paul's initial Corinthian audience to see how the range of possible understandings of *pneuma* might match up with the constituents of his group. Finally, I will address some of the language of *pneuma* in 1 and 2 Corinthians, assuming that Paul's use of this language in the letters has some basic continuity with his unrecoverable initial conversations with the Corinthians.

## Scholarly Approaches to *Pneuma* in Paul's Writings

Greeks and Romans consistently personified their gods and depicted them in human, or partially human, form regardless of the nature of the god. While gentiles could easily imagine Paul's (father) god and (lord Jesus) Christ as personified, anthropomorphised divine beings, it is unclear whether this was the case for the *pneuma*.[1] Scholars who have studied Paul's pneumatology as a theological concept tend to approach the topic from one of two points of view: (1) questions of origins, which lead them to the Hebrew Bible and

---

[1] I will usually leave this term untranslated, since its precise meaning in Paul can be perceived in various ways, unlike those of father and son.

Second Temple Jewish writings;[2] or (2) questions of the relationship of the *pneuma* to Jesus and god (the father) or the function of the *pneuma* in Paul's theology.[3] Both of these approaches try to make sense of Paul's construction of the 'Holy Spirit' (as biblical theologians usually refer to the πνεῦμα) as the basis for understanding theological truths expressed in his writings and as the basis for understanding later trinitarian formulations by the church fathers. And both of these approaches are concerned with Paul's intention in writing about the *pneuma* as he does, which means that they do not speak to gentile reception of Paul's language.

A third, much more compelling line of inquiry is one that looks at Stoic understandings of *pneuma* as a way of approaching Paul's use of the term and concept. While not quite focused on gentile reception, this approach does lean heavily towards contextualisation of Paul, or at least comparison between Stoic philosophical constructs and Paul's writings. A fourth approach looks at Paul's understanding of *pneuma* under the rubric of spirit possession in cross-cultural comparison, the latest treatment of which is by Giovanni Bazzana. But we will begin with the Stoics.

---

[2] Finny Philip, *The Origins of Pauline Pneumatology* (Tübingen: Mohr Siebeck, 2005); Gordon D. Fee, *God's Empowering Presence: The Holy Spirit in the Letters of Paul* (Peabody, MA: Hendrickson, 1994), 904–16; Friedrich Wilhelm Horn, *Das Angeld des Geistes. Studien zur paulinischen Pneumatologie* (Göttingen: Vandenhoeck & Ruprecht, 1992); John W. Yates, *The Spirit and Creation in Paul* (Tübingen: Mohr Siebeck, 2008); John R. Levison, *Filled with the Spirit* (Grand Rapids, MI: Eerdmans, 2009); James B. Shelton, 'Delphi and Jerusalem: Two Spirits or Holy Spirit?', *Pneuma* 33 (2011): 47–58; George T. Montague, *The Holy Spirit: Growth of a Biblical Tradition* (New York: Paulist Press, 1976); C. Tibbs, *Religious Experience of Pneuma: Communication with the Spirit World in 1 Corinthians 12 and 14* (Tübingen: Mohr Siebeck, 2007).

[3] Hermann Gunkel, *The Influence of the Holy Spirit: The Popular View of the Apostolic Age and the Teaching of the Apostle Paul*, trans. Roy A. Harrisville and Philip A. Quanbeck II (Philadelphia: Fortress, 1979; German original 1888); Ingo Hermann, *Kyrios und Pneuma. Studien zur Christologie der paulinischen Hauptbriefe* (Munich: Kösel, 1961); Max Turner, *The Holy Spirit and Spiritual Gifts, Then and Now* (Carlisle: Paternoster, 1996); Craig S. Keener, *The Mind of the Spirit: Paul's Approach to Transformed Thinking* (Grand Rapids, MI: Baker Academic, 2016); Fee, *God's Empowering Presence*; Volker Rabens, *The Holy Spirit and Ethics in Paul: Transforming and Empowering for Religious-Ethical Life*, 2nd ed. (Minneapolis: Fortress, 2013); Volker Rabens, 'Power from In Between: The Relational Experience of the Holy Spirit and Spiritual Gifts in Paul's Churches', in *The Spirit and Christ in the New Testament and Christian Theology: Essays in Honor of Max Turner*, ed. I. Howard Marshall, Volker Rabens and Cornelis Bennema (Grand Rapids, MI: Eerdmans, 2012), 138–55; James D. G. Dunn, *Jesus and the Spirit: A Study of the Religious and Charismatic Experience of Jesus and the First Christians as Reflected in the New Testament* (London: SCM Press, 1975); James D. G. Dunn, *The Theology of Paul the Apostle* (Edinburgh: T & T Clark, 1998); Mehrdad Fatehi, *The Spirit's Relation to the Risen Lord in Paul: An Examination of Its Christological Implications* (Tübingen: Mohr Siebeck, 2000); Kurt Stalder, *Das Werk des Geistes in der Heilgung bei Paulus* (Zurich: EVZ-Verlag, 1962).

## Comparative Approaches

In *Paul and the Stoics*, Troels Engberg-Pedersen constructs a framework to explain Paul's dynamic ethics as expressed mainly in Romans and Galatians, although he also discusses Philippians in some detail. This framework, which he calls the I-X-S model, is an interpretive grid that he constructs in order to demonstrate 'that very much of what appeared problematic and incoherent in Paul's letters falls into place and makes coherent sense once it is seen in the light of certain central ideas in Stoic ethics'.[4] He uses the model to bridge Stoic and Pauline conceptions of identity: 'I' represents self-oriented identity, 'X' represents membership in a group with a higher cause and 'S' represents the wholesale adoption of the group's identity and its correlative collective morality.[5] Engberg-Pedersen is careful not to argue for direct influence of the Stoics on Paul, but with the I-X-S model he is able to make clear comparisons between the two 'systems' of ethical thought. His main goal is to elucidate the ethical exhortations of Paul in comparison with the Stoic ethical framework (as he sees it), so the nature of the *pneuma* is not a major concern of his. However, he does discuss where the *pneuma* fits into his I-X-S model, and in the midst of that discussion we get a sense of what he thinks of the *pneuma* in Paul.

> *Pistis* is primarily a term for the basic grasp and conviction that goes into the initial call and conversion to the Christ gospel . . . The *pneuma* by contrast is an entity that is primarily connected with being in the group. It highlights a certain stable state of the believer . . . The upshot is that *pistis* and the *pneuma* may after all be distinguished in the way I have suggested: that *pistis* has its primary role in connection with the occurrent event of entering the group and the *pneuma* in connection with the stable state of being in it. But they are also so closely connected by Paul that it would be totally false to see the one as 'theological' and the other as 'ethical'.[6]

Engberg-Pedersen goes on to argue that the *pneuma* functions to be 'responsible for a set of mental attitudes, which are, moreover, genuinely other-directed: the virtues'.[7] Clearly, for him, the *pneuma* has a major cognitive role to play in Paul's ethical framework.

It is not until Engberg-Pedersen's later work ('The Material Spirit: Cosmology and Ethics in Paul' and *Cosmology and Self in the Apostle Paul: The Material Spirit*) that he reflects more extensively on the nature of the *pneuma*

---

[4] Troels Engberg-Pedersen, *Paul and the Stoics* (Louisville, KY: Westminster John Knox, 2000), 4.
[5] Kathy L. Gaca, review of Troels Engberg-Pedersen, *Paul and the Stoics*, RBL (2002), https://www.sblcentral.org/API/Reviews/2893_2913.pdf, provides a helpful summary of the I-X-S model.
[6] Engberg-Pedersen, *Paul and the Stoics*, 158–9.
[7] Ibid., 160.

in Paul.⁸ As the titles of both works indicate, he sees the *pneuma* in Paul as a material substance very much akin to how Stoics thought of *pneuma* and related to the body in Paul in a way that is inseparable from Paul's cosmology. He argues that Paul's worldview is bound together with his notion of self by his 'constant focus on body and bodiliness',⁹ which is similar to that of the Stoics. 'In both Paul and the Stoics, a material, bodily notion of *pneuma* ("spirit") plays a central role' in philosophical cosmology.¹⁰ Engberg-Pedersen is certainly right in saying, 'The importance of the *pneuma* in Paul's thought can be hardly overstated. In fact, once one has become attuned to it, one will find the *pneuma* everywhere in Paul, even where it is not actually mentioned.'¹¹

The most important passage for Engberg-Pedersen's argument is Paul's discussion of resurrection in 1 Corinthians 15, which holds together the dynamic work already started by the *pneuma* to transform Paul and the other believers into beings with pneumatic bodies, which will only be complete at the resurrection. This transformation is a literal, material transformation due to the *pneuma*'s material substance, the same stuff as that of heavenly bodies such as stars and the moon. The transformation expresses Paul's cosmological worldview because the end result is a heavenly existence with god in contrast to a '"psychic" and mortal body of flesh and blood'.¹² Engberg-Pedersen's reading of 1 Corinthians 15 sees that

> the *pneuma* is specifically tied to heaven and that it is a physical element (like heaven itself) that may enter into and transform an earthly, physical body of flesh and blood so that it will obtain the same form as a heavenly, physical body like the sun, the moon and the stars (15:41).¹³

Hence the cosmological dimension of the *pneuma*. He extends his reading of this chapter to other important passages in Paul where the *pneuma* features heavily (2 Cor. 1–7, Phil. 3–4, Gal. 5 and Rom. 7–8).

While Engberg-Pedersen's take on *pneuma* in Paul goes a long way in explaining some of the ethical and cosmological claims that Paul makes about the way in which the material *pneuma* affects members of the Pauline assemblies and the assembly as a whole, his take has been critiqued. Emma Wasserman points out that 'virtually all ancient thought held a materialist

---

⁸ Troels Engberg-Pedersen, 'The Material Spirit: Cosmology and Ethics in Paul', *NTS* 55 (2009): 179–97; Troels Engberg-Pedersen, *Cosmology and Self in the Apostle Paul: The Material Spirit* (Oxford: Oxford University Press, 2010).
⁹ Ibid., vii.
¹⁰ Ibid.
¹¹ Engberg-Pedersen, 'The Material Spirit', 175.
¹² Ibid., 185.
¹³ Ibid., 186.

cosmology, so the argument for the unique contribution of Stoic materialism needs defense'.[14] Further, he 'seems to assume that Paul must be consistently Stoic ... and not an intellectual synthesizer of any number of traditions'.[15] For our purposes, Engberg-Pedersen does not consider whether most gentiles in Paul's audiences – except for Stoic philosophers or those familiar with Stoic understandings of *pneuma* – would have understood him in the ways Engberg-Pedersen argues Paul intended. Giovanni Bazzana raises a similar doubt: 'In all likelihood not many of [the Corinthians] were steeped in the subtleties of Stoic doctrines to the degree needed to follow Paul's reasoning.'[16]

In other words, Engberg-Pederson's approach is still driven by Pauline intention rather than gentile reception. Perhaps some of the more well-educated members of Paul's assembly might have understood Paul mapping out his cosmology and its effects on believers in Stoic, materialistic terms, at least initially. Stanley Stowers's schema of Paul preaching first to elites and then enlisting them in his effort to spread his *paideia* to the rest of the assembly, which I will discuss in Chapter Five, could work with Engberg-Pedersen's presentation of Paul's understanding of *pneuma* in Stoic cosmological terms.[17] But even with Stowers's schema, those whom Paul might have enlisted were of higher status relative to the majority of assembly members. Yet Paul's concern seemed not just for the elite few among the assembly.

Caroline Johnson Hodge discusses the function of the *pneuma* with respect to Paul's framework of ethnicity and how gentiles fit or not into 'Paul's ethnic map'.[18] She argues that Paul's configuration of identity is theological: ethnicity is determined by one's relationship with the god of Israel, which is the ethnic dividing line that lumps gentiles together on one side of that line (and not the correct side). Since Paul's initial audiences were gentile by intention, this dividing line is a theological crisis for gentiles and, according to Johnson Hodge, is expressed in ethnic and ancestral terms. Gentiles have the wrong ancestry (not the god of Israel) and therefore can have no part in the inheritance of promises and blessings of the god of Israel. Paul likewise formulates the solution to this problem in ethnic terms, namely by asserting a pathway for gentiles to become Israelite heirs by undergoing baptism into Christ (see Gal. 3:29). Once one is

---

[14] Emma Wasserman, review of Troels Engberg-Pedersen, *Cosmology and Self in the Apostle Paul: The Material Spirit*, CBQ 77 (2015): 370.

[15] Ibid.

[16] Giovanni B. Bazzana, *Having the Spirit of Christ: Spirit Possession and Exorcism in the Early Christ Groups* (New Haven: Yale University Press, 2020), 120.

[17] See Stanley K. Stowers, 'Kinds of Myth, Meals, and Power: Paul and the Corinthians', in *Redescribing Paul and the Corinthians*, ed. Ron Cameron and Merrill P. Miller (Atlanta: SBL, 2011), 105–50.

[18] Caroline Johnson Hodge, *If Sons, Then Heirs: A Study of Kinship and Ethnicity in the Letters of Paul* (Oxford: Oxford University Press, 2007), 67.

baptised into Christ, one becomes part of Israel. Johnson Hodge puts this quite succinctly: 'If oppositional ethnic construction (Jews/non-Jews) defines the problem, aggregative ethnic construction (gentiles-in-Christ linked to Israel) defines the solution.'[19] Galatians and Romans set down in most depth what this process entails, and there Paul describes it as an adoption process as sons, resulting in membership of a household as a free person (Gal. 4:1–7 and Rom. 8:14–17). This adoption is effected by the process of god sending the *pneuma* of god's son into the hearts of the baptised, enabling them to be called sons, and therefore heirs (Gal. 4:6–7). So, according to Johnson Hodge's reading of Paul, the *pneuma* of Christ is the means by which gentiles are transformed into sons[20] and incorporated into Israel as family members, thus becoming part of the *ethnos*, with all the rights, responsibilities and blessings therein.[21]

Johnson Hodge's reasoning is compelling and, I think, accurately articulates Paul's argument in Galatians and Romans. With Engberg-Pedersen, Johnson Hodge appeals to Stoic ideas of *pneuma* and the process by which it blends with entities to effect change in them.[22] And just like Engberg-Pedersen does, she talks about the issue of the *pneuma* from Paul's point of view and not his audience's. The Corinthians were neither the Galatians nor the Romans, and the issues were potentially quite different in those contexts. And Paul's intention in his argument might have been quite different from what the Corinthians understood when they heard these statements about the *pneuma*. Whether or not Paul explained his understanding of adoption via the *pneuma* into Christ – and therefore Israel – in the same way to the Corinthians as he did in Galatians and Romans is difficult to know. He certainly defined the Corinthians as *pneumatikos*: as having the *pneuma* of Christ, and being a collective entity in which the *pneuma* of god dwells, as we see in the first few chapters of 1 Corinthians. But it seems that the reason he wrote this was because the Corinthians did not see themselves this way, and perhaps had a different understanding of *pneuma* from the one that Paul was trying to clarify. So, while the Corinthians shared a common framework of the importance of ethnicity, which was widespread in the ancient Mediterranean world, we cannot assume that they also shared Paul's understanding of how the *pneuma* functioned in that framework.

Giovanni Bazzana's recent work on spirit possession among Christ followers takes a different approach that intersects with Engberg-Pedersen's work but is also distinct from it.[23] Like Engberg-Pedersen, Bazzana argues

---

[19] Ibid., 67.
[20] Ibid., 72.
[21] Ibid., 67–77, for the full argument.
[22] See especially ibid., 75.
[23] Bazzana, *Having the Spirit of Christ*.

that Paul's understanding of *pneuma* is as a physical substance akin to a Stoic understanding of *pneuma*. He recognises the complexity and ambiguity of usage of *pneuma* in Paul, but his way through it is by examining this language through the lens of spirit possession, both in cross-cultural anthropological studies and in early Christ groups. He argues that Paul's *pneuma* is actually the risen and transformed Christ, even when Paul refers to the *pneuma* without any direct qualifier or modifier, or where the reference is ambiguous. The *pneuma* is a physical substance, like that of the Stoic *pneuma*, but it is the substance of Christ, rather than a distinct divine entity, and the assembly – individuals and the whole – are possessed by it.

The ambiguity of usage, Bazzana argues, reflects Paul's ambiguity of religious experience, which was similar to that in cultures that experience spirit possession. There is a simultaneous presence and absence of the *pneuma*, and not a complete erasure of the one being possessed. Basing his work on Michael Lambek and other anthropologists, Bazzana says, 'far from being problematic for possession cults, a dialectic between presence and absence is fundamental for the phenomenon itself and even constitutive of the "truth" of the experience'.[24] Further, 'far from being an indication that Paul (and his fellow Christ believers) did not conceive of Christ as a πνεῦμα, that Christ is at times experienced as *present* and at times as *absent* is what constitutes the experience of Christ's "reality" as a "spirit"'.[25] So, although one is believed to be possessed in an ongoing way, the experience is not steady or even, in terms of the sense of presence. But the possessed state for Paul is consistently described as being 'in Christ':

> Being 'in Christ' is the idiom through which Paul expresses the experience of possession by a πνεῦμα, which is identified with the risen Christ and which, through its presence in them, grants to believers salvation from the eschatological wrath and the expectation of eternal life.[26]

There is also a desire or longing to be in deeper contact with the possessing *pneuma*,[27] and the effect of being possessed is not just ecstasy but motivation to moral activity, both individually and socially. When viewed through this cultural pattern of religious experience, Bazzana argues, Paul's language of *pneuma* makes sense if it is the *pneuma* of Christ that is the possessing entity.

Bazzana's work makes sense of much of Paul's *pneuma* language. His overall construct of the importance of the *pneuma* – not just in Paul's theology but

---

[24] Ibid., 117.
[25] Ibid.
[26] Ibid., 22.
[27] Ibid., 117.

in his whole presentation of the social and moral ramifications of Christ's death and resurrection – is compelling too. What I do not think he does well enough is to distinguish between what Paul is explaining to his assemblies and what is actually being perceived by them. Bazzana conflates Paul and his assemblies to the point that what Paul says about possession by Christ's *pneuma* is not in dispute by his assemblies.[28] I do not think that is quite accurate, at least in Corinth. The whole of 1 Corinthians is rhetorically structured to advocate for unity of the assembly in the face of divisions and factions. Paul's argument relies a great deal on the unifying effect of the *pneuma*, which insinuates that the assembly does not perceive themselves as possessed by the *pneuma* in the same way that Paul does, or at least with the same effects. There seems to be a perception gap between Paul and his assemblies in Corinth with regard to the *pneuma*. It is therefore important to discuss some ways that *pneuma* was understood among ancient gentiles, to get a sense of the possible expectations that Paul's Corinthian audience might have had when they heard him talking about the *pneuma*.

### Genetic approaches

H. Liesegang's classic study argues that *pneuma* could indicate a sentient being in Greek prior to Paul's time, finding its origins in what he calls 'Greek mysticism'.[29] This mysticism dealt with the possession by a god to the extent that the human faculties were displaced by those of a divine *pneuma*, which resulted in wisdom, ecstatic possession and oracular activity.[30] The purview of this sort of possession and activity of *pneuma* was primarily in popular circles, Liesegang argues, but he goes on to note that Plato picked up this notion to a certain extent.[31] Philo and then later Christianity's concept of the *pneuma* did not evolve mainly from Septuagint or Jewish literary circles but from this mystical heritage from the Greek tradition.[32] Leisegang's influence shows itself

---

[28] The quote cited above in the paragraph critiquing Engberg-Petersen is typical of the extent of Bazzana's argument regarding the agreement of Paul and his assemblies: a parenthetical remark such as '(and his fellow Christ believers)', as if to assume complete assent to Paul's view of the *pneuma* and its possession of the assembly.

[29] H. Leisegang, *Der heilige Geist. Das Wesen und Werden der mystisch-intuitiven Erkenntnis in der Philosophie und Religion der Griechen* (1919; repr., Darmstadt: Wissenschaftliche Buchgestellschaft, 1967), 1–12.

[30] Ibid., especially 113–36.

[31] Ibid., 124, 129–32.

[32] Ibid., 1–3, 11–13. See also H. Leisegang, *Pneuma Hagion. Der Ursprung des Geistbegriffs der synoptischen Evangelien aus der griechischen Mystik* (1922; repr., Hildesheim: Georg Olms, 1970), 1–4.

in later studies of πνεῦμα in *The Theological Dictionary of the New Testament* and *The New International Dictionary of New Testament Theology*.[33]

Leisegang and his scholarly heirs have been heavily critiqued by Terence Paige, who offers a thorough study of the term *pneuma* in Greek literature in the centuries before Paul.[34] Paige finds significant methodological flaws in Leisegang's inquiry, among which are: (1) beginning with Philo, who was not pagan, and using Jewish, Christian and Gnostic texts as evidence for pre-Christian views; (2) failing to adequately account for the literary context, religious activity and perspective of the writers, and for the genre of many of the passages examined to build the characteristic usage of *pneuma*; and (3) confusing lexicography with 'a History-of-Religions', resulting in

> certain conceptions which are in evidence in pre-Christian times becom[ing] attached to the term πνεῦμα more as a result of that word's significance to later Christianity than of its actually ever having been used in connection with any of these prior religious conceptions.[35]

Paige argues convincingly that 'the semantic range of πνεῦμα did not encroach upon that of δαιμόνια [daimons] until the second century C.E. in pagan writings; earlier this meaning ("spirit") occurs only in Jewish and Christian documents'.[36] He starts by analysing philosophical writers, focusing on Plato's theory of inspiration and the role of *pneuma* in Stoic writers. Plato does not extensively discuss divine inspiration in terms of πνεῦμα or its verbal cognates (such as those derived from πνέω, 'blow'), only mentioning it four times in his writings. His most extensive discussion of inspiration appears in the *Phaedrus*, where Socrates declares the best kind of inspiration (ἐπίπνοια) is actually the insanity (μανία) of a lover (*Phdr.* 265b.5). Paige continues

> The most one can say is that within Plato one finds, borrowed from the stock imagery of the language of his day, the term ἐπίπνοια only rarely

---

[33] H. Kleinknecht, 'πνεῦμα', in *TDNT*, 6:357–8, where he employs much of the same language that Leisegang uses to describe πνεῦμα in pre-Christian usage, bypassing possible Jewish origins in favour of pagan ones. E. Kamlah, 'πνεῦμα', in *NIDNTT*, 3:690: 'In obvious dependence upon Plato, they [Roman era writers] used πνεῦμα to denote inspiration, regarding it as a material substance which filled a man and enabled him to prophesy. This prophetic πνεῦμα was considered in turn to be "enthusiastic," visionary, demonic, holy (*hieron*), even divine. Papyrus finds reveal the active part it played in popular religion (always given to magic and soothsaying), and in the so-called Mithras Liturgy ... it appears among the four elements, being described as "holy" and "immortal" and as elevating its recipients above mortal nature, probably by analogy with prophetic ecstasy.'

[34] Terence Paige, 'Who Believes in "Spirit"? Πνεῦμα in Pagan Usage and Implications for the Gentile Christian Mission', *HTR* 95 (2002): 417–36.

[35] Ibid., 420.

[36] Ibid., 427.

used to indicate divine influence. And he never uses πνεῦμα in relation to inspiration.[37]

So this, in Paige's mind, debunks the long-held notion of a Platonic πνεῦμα-mysticism.

Rick Strelan, however, has a different reading of the *Phaedrus* in reference to 'madness' (μανία) by appealing to Socrates's statement about prophecy at Delphi and Dodona:[38]

> If madness were simply bad, all would be fine. But as it is, the greatest of all good things come to us through madness, provided that the madness is divinely given (θείᾳ). First, the prophetess at Delphi and priestesses at Dodona do many good things for Greece, in private and public matters, when they are mad, but when they are of sound mind and self-controlled they do next to nothing for our country. (*Phdr.* 244a–b)[39]

Beyond the sections that relate to Strelan's comments, the rest of the passage goes on to discuss the superiority of the mantic arts over the oinomastic arts, primarily because of the divine nature of the mania (literally 'mania coming from a god'; μανίαν ... τὴν ἐκ θεοῦ; *Phdr.* 244d) which is necessary for mantic arts to occur, even calling μανία 'beautiful' when 'mixed with a divine portion' (ἀλλ' ὡς καλοῦ ὄντος, ὅταν θείᾳ μοίρᾳ γίγνηται; 244c). Furthermore, Socrates describes a third form of μανία and 'possession' (κατοκωχή) which comes from a particular group of gods, the Muses, and 'takes hold of ... a soul' (λαβοῦσα ... ψυχήν), raising the soul up with 'Dionysiac frenzy' (ἐκβακχεύουσα) to produce various forms of poetry. This μανία is crucial to Plato for the production of superior quality poetry: 'Whoever comes to the doors of poetry without the madness of the Muses ... will fall short of his aim; the poetry of those who are mad will obliterate the poetry of a sound and self-controlled mind' (245c).

While Paige is right to point out that πνεῦμα and its cognates are not used by Plato in this passage, it is clear that something of the gods, if not a god or gods themselves, mingles with the human to elevate their abilities and transform them (temporarily) into producing divine things for the benefit of

---

[37] Ibid., 424.
[38] Rick Strelan, 'What Might a Pagan Have Understood by "Holy Spirit"?', *Colloquium* 42 (2010): 155.
[39] Unless otherwise noted, translations of the *Phaedrus* are from Stephen Scully, *Plato's Phaedrus: A Translation with Notes, Glossary, Appendices, Interpretive Essay and Introduction* (Newburyport, MA: Focus, 2003).

humanity. Paige claims not to be doing a lexical study of πνεῦμα but rather a history-of-religions study, but he fails to account for this basic notion of possession and mania in the *Phaedrus* simply because it does not contain πνεῦμα or its cognates.

As Paige goes on to discuss Stoic writers, it is worth spending some time on Stoic notions of *pneuma* in dialogue with his argument.[40] The notion of *pneuma* plays a large role in Stoic metaphysics and cosmology, as we have already seen from Engberg-Pedersen's work, being one of the basic material elements of the universe. Starting with Zeno, or at least with what later authors depict as Zeno's teachings, *pneuma* is what causes life in humans and what is generated from the body as breath. Because it is of the body's generation, *pneuma* is a corporeal substance.[41] Further, the *pneuma* and the soul become intertwined conceptually for Zeno because, when a person dies, the soul is undoubtedly the thing that departs; since the breath also departs upon death, soul and *pneuma* are intimately connected.[42] These notions do not necessarily lend themselves to *pneuma* being a material substance, but when the question of how *pneuma* enters a person is raised, Zeno attributes it to its presence within the *sperma* of the parents as a microcosm of the material of the cosmos. Thus, *pneuma* of an individual is the mixture of parental *sperma* each containing the *pneuma* of the parent.[43] Zeno's thought was developed by Chrysippus, but it is difficult to get a clear picture of that development as so very little evidence of Chrysippus's understanding of *pneuma* survives.

Hellenistic and Roman era Stoics and commentators on the Stoics talk about *pneuma* in clearly materialist ways and relate it to the four elements of the universe (fire, air, water and earth). *Pneuma* comes from the mixture of fire and air, the two active elements of the four.[44] Along these lines, Galen claims that the Stoics, along with other like-minded thinkers, hold that there is a distinction between what sustains and what is sustained, and he places the *pneumatikē* on the sustaining end of that distinction.[45] Further, *pneuma* holds together all reality and contributes to the interconnectedness of the entire universe through its tensile movement (simultaneously inwards and outwards),

---

[40] For a more thorough treatment of the development of Stoic notions of *pneuma*, see Robert Heller, 'Pneuma in Early Stoicism' (PhD diss., Royal Holloway, University of London, 2018).

[41] Tertullian, *De anim.* 5 (*SVF* 1.137).

[42] Calchidius, *In Tim.* 220 (*SVF* 1.138).

[43] Heller, 'Pneuma in Early Stoicism', 56.

[44] On the active and passive elements, see Nemesius 164.15–18 (*SVF* 2.418). References to *SVF* in this paragraph come from A. A. Long and D. N. Sedley, *The Hellenistic Philosophers*, 2 vols (Cambridge: Cambridge University Press, 1987).

[45] Galen, *Nat. Fac.* 7.524.9–14 (*SVF* 2.439). See also Plutarch, *Comm. not.* 1085C-D (*SVF* 2.444).

so that a change in one thing will affect other things and other parts of the world.[46] Samuel Sambursky puts it this way:

> Although [*pneuma*] was supposed to be corporeal, a very tenuous matter filling the whole universe and interpenetrating all bodies, it fulfilled the functions of a physical field by its tensional qualities and by its capacity to give bodies a coherent structure with well-defined physical properties.[47]

What is also important is that *pneuma* 'is the vehicle for divine intelligence'.[48] As Stowers explains, 'In Paul's world *pneuma* (wind, air, breath, spirit) ... is a refined, qualitative higher substance with its own power of movement and intelligence.'[49] This intelligence is what makes anticipating the response of Paul's Corinthian audiences tricky because intelligence is also what can be attributed to an autonomous, personified deity. More on this later.

According to Paige, some thought that there was a connection between *pneuma* and prophecy, because of the traces and aftereffects of actions left behind by the interconnectedness caused by *pneuma*. Stoics believed that prophetic figures could detect and interpret these signs, hence the link between *pneuma* and prophecy. But Paige argues that this is not the same as later Christian understandings of prophecy being the result of a divinely sent *pneuma*.[50] Further, Stoics sometimes described god as *pneuma*, or at least the essence of god, but it connotes that the reality of god has a material substance like everything else in the universe. *Pneuma* was not a sentient being separate from god for Stoics, and Origen pointed this out in his refutation of Celsus, who claimed an identity of the Christian and Stoic understanding of *pneuma*.[51] At the end of his discussion of philosophical writers, Paige notes that *daimons*

> served as divine intermediaries, communicating messages from the gods to humans and carrying prayers from humans to the gods ... [But] the

---

[46] See Alexander, *On mixture*, 224.14–17, 23–6 (*SVF* 2.442); Nemesius 70.6–71.4; and Galen, *Motu Musc.* 4.402.12–4.403.10 (*SVF* 2.450). Long and Sedley, *The Hellenistic Philosophers*, 1:289, say that *pneuma* 'is the principle of internal coherence for individual bodies; and because it permeates everything without corruption, it makes the world as a whole a single coherent body'.

[47] Samuel Sambursky, *The Physical World of Late Antiquity* (Princeton: Princeton University Press, 1962), 3.

[48] Long and Sedley, *The Hellenistic Philosophers*, 289.

[49] Stanley K. Stowers, 'Matter and Spirit, or What is Pauline Participation in Christ?', in *The Holy Spirit: Classic and Contemporary Readings*, ed. Eugene F. Rogers, Jr (Chichester: Wiley-Blackwell, 2009), 94.

[50] Paige, 'Who Believes in "Spirit"?', 425.

[51] See Origen, *C. Cels.* 6.70–1, for Origen's description of Celsus's identification of Stoic and Christian notions of πνεῦμα, and see *C. Cels.* 4.70.6–7 for Origen's description of the Christian πνεῦμα as both 'intelligent' and incorporeal.

semantic range of πνεῦμα did not encroach upon that of δαιμόνιον until the second century C.E. in pagan writings.[52]

Paige does not account for the widespread understanding of *pneuma* in materialist terms beyond that of the Stoics, however. Dale B. Martin takes a much wider view in his efforts to describe ancient ideologies of the body in which to read the Corinthian letters. He says, 'For most ancient theorists, pneuma is a kind of "stuff" that is the agent of perception, motion, and life itself; it pervades other forms of stuff and, together with those other forms, constitutes the self.'[53] While the notion of materialist *pneuma* originally goes back to the early theorists of Stoicism,[54] by the first century, *pneuma* as a substance – even as the substance of life – was accepted by a variety of theorists.[55] But Martin also claims that there was a widespread belief in the materialist notion of *pneuma*, even beyond that of philosophical and medical thinkers (who interacted with and even followed philosophical thinkers and schools in developing their medical theories[56]): 'Artemidorus shows that the connection between internal and external pneuma was presupposed in popular thought as well; his *Dream Handbook* mentions in passing that "our spirit [*pneuma*] has something in common with the atmosphere and the outer air" (2.60).'[57] Martin's point here is erroneous, however. Although he is using the standard critical edition of Artemidorus's handbook,[58] he seems to misread the text at this point. Where he reads πνεῦμα, the text actually reads ψυχή. Artemidorus does use πνεῦμα several times, but each time it means either the life-breath of a person (1.14; 1.44; 1.74) or simply a person's

---

[52] Paige, 'Who Believes in "Spirit"?', 427.

[53] Dale B. Martin, *The Corinthian Body* (New Haven: Yale University Press, 1995), 21.

[54] Chrysippus (according to Galen) construed it as a mixture of fire and air: 'This *pneuma* holds two parts, both elements and states, which are blended with each other thoroughly, the cold and the hot ... air and fire' (τοῦτ' οὖν τὸ πνεῦμα δύο μὲν κέκτηται μόριά τε καὶ στοιχεῖα καὶ καταστάσεις, δι' ὅλων ἀλλήλοις κεκραμ[μ]ένα, τὸ ψυχρὸν καὶ θερμόν ... ἀέρα τε καὶ πῦρ) (Galen, *Plac.* 5.3.8; *SVF* 2.841). For a similar definition of *pneuma* according to Chrysippus, see also Stobaeus, *Eclogae* 1.153.24 (*SVF* 2. 471). See also Alexander, *On mixture*, 224.14–17, 23–6 (*SVF* 2.444).

[55] See Martin, *Corinthian Body*, 21–2.

[56] See ibid., 22–5. See also Vivian Nutton, *Ancient Medicine*, 2nd ed. (London: Routledge, 2012), 207–21, who describes one influential rival to humoral theory and the successful Methodist and Empiricist schools of the first and second centuries, namely, the Pneumatists, 'so called because they placed a great deal of emphasis on *pneuma*, or spirit, as the controlling factor in health and disease' (207). The opinions of the Pneumatist thinkers that can be reconstructed seem to rely heavily on a mixture of Stoicism and Hippocratic medicine, with the core belief not only that *pneuma* held together the universe, but that a balance of the properties of *pneuma* (which governed the heat and cold of the body) was the underlying principle of good health. See Nutton, *Ancient Medicine*, 208–11.

[57] Martin, *The Corinthian Body*, 22.

[58] Roger Pack, ed., *Artimidori Daldiani Onirocriticon Libri V* (Leipzig: Teubner, 1963).

breath (1.56). His understanding, then, does not really match the materialist notions that Martin claims, but he does have a sense that *pneuma* means something linked to a human's ability to live.

Paige continues his critique of Leisegang and his successors by considering the Delphic oracle, because of several uses of πνεῦμα by late Hellenistic and early imperial era writers on the oracle.[59] A closer look at the usage of πνεῦμα and similar terminology in these writings, according to Paige, shows that they refer not to a sentient being or god but are associated with the 'vapours' that are inhaled by the Pythia during her divination process. In *De divinatione*, Cicero mentions a theory of 'vapours' that arise from the crevice upon which the Pythia sits on her tripod when giving her oracles.[60] The vapours 'inspire' the Pythia in her divination, but they do not 'possess' her in a way that they take over her personality with that of another entity. Strabo seems also to be aware of this 'holy gas' explanation for the Pythia's abilities,[61] as does Plutarch, who discusses the μαντικὸν πνεῦμα of the oracle as a kind of 'holy gas' that facilitates prophecy, the most important local substance influencing the Pythia at Delphi.[62] But this 'holy gas' does not put the Pythia into an ecstatic condition or lead her to speak in a language not her own, akin to glossolalia described in 1 Corinthians. Instead, the Pythia speaks her oracles in poetic Greek hexameter in the classical period, and usually gives 'yes' or 'no' answers in later periods. Everything that happens at Delphi with respect to the Pythia indicates that the *pneuma* described by ancient writers is nothing more than the local substance that facilitates her work of speaking for Apollo, and it is not a sentient being. In this, it resembles other Greek oracles, which have local processes and substances involved in the ritual production of oracular activity.[63]

---

[59] I only briefly summarise here Paige, 'Who Believes in "Spirit"?', 427–30.
[60] See Cic. *Div.* 1.79. See also 1.114: 'I believe, too, that there were certain subterranean vapours which had the effect of inspiring persons to utter oracles' (trans. W. A. Falconer, *Cicero*, vol. 20, *De senectute; De amicitia; De divinatione* (Cambridge, MA: Harvard University Press, 1923)).
[61] Strabo 9.3.5.
[62] Plutarch, *De def. or.* 432D.
[63] See Paige, 'Who Believes in "Spirit"?', 429, for some examples from Claros, Didyma, Argos, Aegira and Ephyra. One could add the oracle of Trophonius at Lebadaea, where sacrifices were offered and consumed, ritual bathing occurred, and supplicants drank from two springs and prayed to the statue of Trophonius before entering into an oven-like shaft to encounter the god. However, the local nature of an oracle does not preclude possession by a divine being; it only indicates a particular way in which the god works based on the particular location of the oracle. So, Apollo works at Delphi in a particular way through the Pythia, but he is also the principal god at other oracles such as at Claros, Delos and Didyma. While there are differences in local procedures of divination, there is also continuity of Apollo's presence. The combination of the universal and local is a key component of Greek religion and it defies systemisation. See Julia Kindt, *Rethinking Greek Religion* (Cambridge: Cambridge University Press, 2012), 123–54, for a good discussion of the intricacies of the debate between the local and the universal in Greek religious practice.

However, Plato talks about the oracles at both Delphi and Dodona as producing a positive kind of μανία for their practitioners.⁶⁴ And Strabo says that an opening from the earth emits the *pneuma*, particularly a πνεῦμα ἐνθουσιαστικόν – an inspiring vapour or breath.⁶⁵ This is similar to Plutarch's μαντικὸν πνεῦμα, which does not indicate that the *pneuma* is a divine being but that it causes something to happen to allow a 'madness' or inspiration. This inspiration, while not the *pneuma* itself, does have something of the god involved. Lucan describes the priestesses of Delphi as experiencing the detrimental effect of repeatedly being cast into an ecstatic frenzy.⁶⁶ Finally, Aristides also speaks of the Pythia as being in an ecstatic state (ἐκστωσιν ἑαυτῶν) during their divinatory work.⁶⁷ So, it is not as clear cut as Paige indicates when it comes to the ecstatic state of the Pythia or other oracular officials. As Strelan writes,

> This raises serious questions against the argument that the *pneumata* at Delphi were believed to be mere vapours and not indicative of the god's *pneuma*. No matter if the vapours were in fact 'natural' (from a modern Western perspective anyway), they were consistently interpreted as indicative of the divine presence within the body of the prophetess.⁶⁸

There are also places where gentile notions of *pneuma/spiritus* indicate some sort of agency and personal nature like that of a *daimon* and not just as a material substance or breath/vapour. Again, we return to the Stoics, in this case Seneca, who claims that 'God is near you, he is with you, he is within you. This is what I mean, Lucilius: a holy spirit indwells within us, one who marks our good and bad deeds, and is our guardian.'⁶⁹ This holy spirit's moral actions and guardianship, in particular, seem like personified actions rather than an effect of being under the influence of a foreign substance that simply changes a state of mind or emotion. Similarly, poets talk of being filled with a god or a *pneuma* of a god and it determining their poetic activity, not as something that simply allows them to write better poetry but as something that controls their activity.⁷⁰

---

⁶⁴ Pl. *Phdr.* 244a–b.
⁶⁵ Strabo 9.3.5.
⁶⁶ Lucan, *Pharsalia* 5.116–19.
⁶⁷ Aristid. *Or.* 34.
⁶⁸ Strelan, 'What Might a Pagan Have Understood?', 165.
⁶⁹ Prope est a te deus, tecum est, intus est. Ita dico, Lucili: sacer intra nos spiritus sedet, malorum bonorumque nostrorum observator et custos (Seneca, *Ep. Moral.* 41.1–2; trans. Richard M. Gummere in *Seneca: Epistles*, vol. 1, *Epistles 1–65* (Cambridge, MA: Harvard University Press, 1917).
⁷⁰ See Strelan, 'What Might a Pagan Have Understood?' 167, for a list of references.

Some of this language that the poets use could be understood metaphorically or as a statement of the status of their discourse as intellectually superior to other forms of discourse,[71] but metaphor only works if it refers to something that is indicative of reality. And Plutarch does use *pneuma* with overtones of a divine being in another writing about oracles, *De defectu oraculorum*. In part, this work is about the question of why oracles in Plutarch's day are either less important or fading from the religious landscape. Late in the work, there is a description of the death of the Pythia when a group of foreigners came to consult the oracle. The initial libations had no effect, but then the priests pushed things a little too far in their efforts to elicit a prophecy. They forced the Pythia to go to the oracle against her will and everything went awry. Her strange voice was the first indication, which Plutarch describes as coming from someone 'filled with a speechless and evil *pneuma*'; she then became hysterical, ran out of the building and threw herself down. She lived only a few more days.[72] Plutarch's other usages of *pneuma* in this work border on a personified being, but they are more ambiguous.

It is not until the second century CE, with Celsus's reference to *pneuma* and Origen's rebuttal of it, that Paige finds the earliest non-Christian, non-Jewish reference to *pneuma* as referring to a divine being. Origen quotes Celsus's attempt to discredit prophets and their activity in Phoenicia and Palestine in the late second century. Amidst Celsus's disparaging, he says,

> It is common and customary for each of them to say, 'I am God or a son of God or a divine spirit (πνεῦμα θεῖον). And I have come; for the cosmos is being destroyed, and you, O people, are ruined because of [your] offences.'[73]

Here, πνεῦμα seems to be used in a sense much more akin to δαίμων or δαιμόνιον as a supernatural being. But this postdates Paul by a century and so does not lend itself to a usage familiar to Paul's audiences. 'The circumstances of this writing and the uniqueness of this usage should lead us to conclude this is not a native Greek usage, but a clear borrowing from Christian (and Jewish) religious vocabulary.'[74] Therefore, in Paige's view, Paul's gentile audiences would not have recognised his use of πνεῦμα because there was a 'semantic differential' between Christian and Jewish usage of the term, on the one hand, and gentile understandings of it, on the other.[75] Paige concludes his analysis:

---

[71] See Bruce Lincoln, *Theorizing Myth* (Chicago: University of Chicago Press, 1999), 3–46, for a discussion of the power of certain forms of discourse among ancient Greek elites.

[72] See Plutarch, *De def. or.* 438A–C (quote at 438B).

[73] Origen, *C. Cels.* 7.9.

[74] Paige, 'Who Believes in "Spirit"?', 431.

[75] Ibid., 434.

'We can say with confidence then that the meaning of "spirit" for πνεῦμα is a distinctly Jewish-Christian religious-technical use.'⁷⁶ Nevertheless, as Strelan has argued, if not completely persuasively, there is the possibility that Jewish and gentile understandings of πνεῦμα and ἅγιος ('holy') overlap more than Paige realises, so that when a gentile hears the regular use of ἅγιος πνεῦμα by Paul, they may hear resonances of their own experience of the cultic lives of gods.⁷⁷

Paige asks some important questions that anticipate the topic of my work in this book. It is worth quoting him at length:

> A further question for historians of early Christianity and the history of missions is this: how successful were Christians in communicating this very distinct meaning of πνεῦμα to a pagan audience? Given the fact that this Jewish-Christian meaning for πνεῦμα represents a kind of specialized religious dialect unfamiliar to most Greek speakers, how did this semantic differential affect Gentile evangelism and Gentile Christian understanding of theology and worship? How quickly did Gentiles grasp that πνεῦμα was being used for what they would normally call θεός, δαίμων or δαιμόνιον? How easily did they move from a worldview in which a multiplicity of gods, δαίμονες and other demigods operated – for good and for evil – to a conception of a single overarching good Spirit of God? How far did various opinions on the functions of δαίμονες as intermediary beings interfere with or alter their understandings of the Spirit's function? Did Stoicism help or hinder? Did they ever confuse the Holy Spirit with the 'good *daimōn*' (ἀγαθὸς δαίμων), the familiar guardian of the household cult?⁷⁸

Before ending his article, Paige suggests that the Corinthians' issues with understanding the Spirit and spiritual gifts 'may well be the result of understanding the πνεῦμα θεοῦ as similar to a δαίμων in Greek'.⁷⁹ Finally, in his last two sentences, he claims that Paul's letters address gentile believers' attempts at assimilating 'significant changes in their conception of deity and divine intermediaries'.⁸⁰ Here is where I part with Paige because, as I will argue below, it is the familiarity of

---

⁷⁶ Ibid., 433.
⁷⁷ 'If the predominant sense of ἅγιος for both Jews and pagans is that of a site or a set of rituals set apart and not to be polluted or profaned, then it seems reasonable to suggest they all adopted that same sense when it was used in conjunction with *pneuma*. If pagans heard a Christian talk of "holy spirit" they might well have understood them to be talking in cultic terms. When the holy spirit comes into or upon a person or fills a person, their body becomes a ritually pure cultic site, a site in which a god was present, and that holiness is manifested by behavior that is peculiar to the holy' (Strelan, 'What Might a Pagan Have Understood?', 168).
⁷⁸ Paige, 'Who Believes in "Spirit"?', 434.
⁷⁹ Ibid., 435.
⁸⁰ Ibid., 436.

Paul's chord of gods that could have drawn the gentile believers to the assembly. The conceptual differences are what commentators often zero in on, but I think the conceptual differences are less important precisely because of the familiarity of the concept of a group of divine figures working together for the benefit of their adherents.

## Ranges of Meaning of *Pneuma*

The range of meaning for *pneuma* in gentile circles of the first century that we have explored covers a wide span of evidence and perspectives, but the vast majority have something to do with the life force of a human and/or a material substance pervasive throughout the universe that holds the universe together through tension, with a few scattered references to *pneuma* as a seemingly independent, personified divine agent. The biggest question is whether or not marginally educated or non-educated Corinthians would have been familiar with the dominant meaning of *pneuma*, because the evidence we have for this understanding of *pneuma* comes from philosophers and medical theorists primarily, with the occasional reference in more 'popular'-level writing such as that of Artemidorus.

We will see below that even those with very little formal education were introduced to philosophical maxims and gnomic sayings at the basic stages of learning to read and write. It is certainly possible that they would have come across *pneuma* in their early education, even though, to my knowledge, there are no extant examples of *pneuma* in the surviving school exercises. Some enslaved individuals were part of the education process and so would have had a fairly high level of education themselves to be effective in their roles as *pedagogues* or readers for their masters.[81] And, of course, we have the example of Epictetus, who studied with Musonius Rufus while he was enslaved (*Diatr.* 1.7) and then went on to be a philosopher himself after he was freed.

There are other avenues of exposure where marginally educated and even uneducated individuals might have come across philosophy, and possibly philosophical notions of *pneuma*, namely in public speeches by philosophers, since many of them were public figures and orators (for example, Dio Chrysostom and Cicero). Ramsay MacMullen points to casual public lectures at temples and less casual ones for festivals,[82] and Elizabeth Rawson talks of the

---

[81] Elizabeth Rawson, *Intellectual Life in the Late Roman Republic* (Baltimore: Johns Hopkins University Press, 1985), 51.

[82] Philostr. *V A* 7f, 8.18; Plut. *Mor.* 410, 412D; Aristid. *Or.* 25.2; Dio Chrys. *Or.* 27.5–6. See Ramsay MacMullen, *Paganism in the Roman Empire* (New Haven: Yale University Press, 1981), 11. See also Rawson, *Intellectual Life*, 51: 'Lectures on a larger scale, perhaps open to the public in general, were a feature of the Hellenistic world.'

reference from Cicero to a public lecture in Rome by the doctor Asclepiades that Cicero regarded as show rhetoric.[83] There is also epigraphical evidence for summaries of philosophical doctrines: an Epicurean treatise described by Diogenes of Oenoanda, placed on the wall of a portico in Lycia.[84] Public theatre often dealt with philosophy and philosophical figures, which could be an avenue for a wider swath of the population beyond the more elite and educated.[85] Medical thinkers widely based their theories on some notion of *pneuma* as a substance, and the general public would have interacted with physicians who practised their craft with this in mind.[86] Finally, Elizabeth Rawson discusses the lower-end literary works, especially on Epicureanism, that might have been produced for public consumption.[87]

This range of possible encounters with Stoic, medical and other philosophical understandings of *pneuma* shows that, in Rawson's terms, 'Even illiteracy would be no bar to some sorts of quasi-intellectual activity.'[88] But all this evidence is fairly circumstantial. Yes, we have many avenues for less-elite, less-educated and non-educated people to encounter philosophy. But we have no direct evidence of encountering *pneuma* as a technical term with any specific meaning attached to it. And if a marginally educated or non-educated person came across *pneuma* through a school exercise or gnomic saying, or through an encounter with a physician, would there be anything but a superficial understanding of this term communicated? This makes our speculation about Paul's initial Corinthian audiences complicated, even speculative. Would the less-educated or non-educated Corinthians have understood Paul's use of *pneuma* in only the simplest of terms, as merely 'breath' or 'wind'? Would Paul have explained the nature of *pneuma* as a technical term? Or when he mentioned *pneuma* alongside father and son, god

---

[83] Rawson, *Intellectual Life*, 52, pointing to Cic. *De or.* 1.62: 'Since Cicero says that Asclepiades was more eloquent than others of his calling, perhaps there were rival speakers on medicine in Rome, and certainly *akroaseis* [public lectures] by doctors were not rare in the East, though some severe members of the profession despised them.'

[84] William V. Harris, *Ancient Literacy* (Cambridge, MA: Harvard University Press, 1989), 219–20; Harris does not give the inscriptional reference.

[85] Rawson, *Intellectual Life*, 52: 'Drama ... apart from familiarizing its audience with Greek mythology and occasionally Roman history had ... always had contacts with popular philosophy.' She goes on to describe the use of philosophy and philosophic characters by street mimes, a medium readily available to all who had time to watch.

[86] I thank Joshua Reno for helping me think of ways in which Corinthians would have had some knowledge of *pneuma* via philosophy, even if never being formally educated in the concept.

[87] Rawson, *Intellectual Life*, 48–9.

[88] Ibid., 53. One reviewer of this chapter claimed Rawson's work as describing 'illiterate' Stoics, especially in rural areas. The closest that Rawson comes to this notion is to refer to a letter from Cassius to Cicero, somewhat sarcastically referring to *rustici Stoici* to deride someone in their circles (ibid., 48–9; see Cic. *Fam.* 15.16).

and Christ, would his audiences assume something more specific than simply 'breath' or 'wind' or maybe even 'cause of life'?

Hints of personification or an anthropomorphised entity in Paul's speech and teaching may have led less philosophically knowledgeable Corinthians to think of *pneuma* as a divine entity along the lines of a *daimōn*, as Paige admits[89] – a lesser, mediating divine figure that is definitely not human but also is not of the status of a major god such as Zeus or Athena. Paige acknowledges that Jews and early 'Christians' had this notion of *pneuma* in their traditions, but he draws a clear cultural distinction between Jews and 'Christians', on the one hand, and pagans, on the other.[90] As has been argued for decades now, this clear cultural divide did not exist, and to separate out or ignore this usage because it comes from Jewish or 'Christian' sources tilts the evidence in favour of Paige's argument when it should problematise it.

The Septuagint's range of meaning of πνεῦμα intersects significantly with what we find in common usages in other Greek literature: wind, breath, animating principle or life force, and something (perhaps the material) of the divinity or of humans.[91] But there is another set of uses that indicate a rational being, a divine personification. The Wisdom of Solomon personifies wisdom in several ways throughout the work, but right from the early verses, wisdom is metaphorically compared to a '*holy pneuma* of *paideia*' (1:5; ἅγιον γὰρ πνεῦμα παιδείας). Less metaphorically, we have Numbers 16:22, in which Moses and Aaron try to calm god's anger when god commands them to separate themselves from the congregation so that god might destroy them for their insolence. They refer to god as 'god of *pneumatōn* and all flesh' (θεὸς τῶν πνευμάτων καὶ πάσης σαρκός). Numbers 26:16 has the same moniker for god. Judges 9:23 narrates that 'God sent out an evil *pneuma* (πνεῦμα πονηρόν) in midst of Abimalech and Shechem.' In 3 Kingdoms 22:19–23 we hear of Micaiah's vision of god sitting on his throne and asking for someone to offer to entice King Ahab to act. Verse 21 has a *pneuma* step forward, stand before the throne and speak to god, describing how it will corrupt the prophets of Ahab. And Ben Sira 39:28 uses *pneuma* to describe beings created for vengeance (ἔστιν πνεύματα, ἃ εἰς ἐκδίκησιν ἔκτισται) who will visit the wrath of the one who created them.

Other Jewish texts of the Second Temple period witness to this divine, autonomous, personified being usage. Fragment A of the Book of Jubilees has two instances, which are found in the retelling of the creation of the world:

---

[89] Paige, 'Who Believes in "Spirit"?', 434.

[90] I use quotation marks here to indicate that I think it is erroneous to use the term 'Christian' to describe followers of Jesus/Christ so soon after Jesus's death.

[91] See Hos. 4:19; Ez. 13:11; and Is. 25:4 for wind or air in movement. See Ps. 145:4; Jer. 10:14; Ez. 37:14; Sir. 38:23; Gen. 6:17, 7:15; and Bar. 2:17 for breath or animating life force. See Gen. 1:2; Mic. 2:7, 3:8; Hag. 2:5; Zech. 1:6; Ps. 50:13; Wis. 9:17; and many other places for πνεῦμα θεοῦ, πνεῦμα κυρίου or πνεῦμα with a possessive pronoun referring to god or the lord.

on the first day, among the things that god created were 'the *pneumata* who minister before him' (fr. a, ln 28; τὰ πνεύματα τὰ λειτοθργοῦντα ἐνώπιον αὐτοῦ) and 'all his created *pneumata* which are in the heavens and on earth' (fr. a, ln 39; πάντων τῶν πνευμάτων τῶν κτισμάτων αὐτοῦ τῶν ἐν οὐρανοῖς καὶ ἐν τῇ γῇ). In the Book of Enoch, Enoch speaks to Raphael and asks him about the identity of a certain *pneuma* that he encountered whose voice went up to heaven. Raphael identifies it as the *pneuma* that went out from Abel, whom his brother Cain murdered (Enoch 22:6–7). Although this usage of *pneuma* is linked with a human, it seems to now be separate from, or at least a different form of, Abel. This is not an exhaustive list of occurrences of this usage in the Septuagint and Second Temple Jewish literature, but all of them clearly indicate a divine, autonomous, personified being with no link to god or humans, virtue or vice.

The canonical gospels also show abundant evidence for embodiment and personification of *pneuma*. A clear example of this from the Gospel of Mark (the earliest of the gospels) would be the baptism scene of the *pneuma* descending from the heavens like a dove and entering into Jesus at 1:10. At 3:22 Jesus is accused of having Beezeboul and then casts out *daimonia* (3:22; ἐν τῷ ἄρχοντι τῶν δαιμονίων). Jesus in turn accuses the scribes of blasphemy because they have blasphemed against the holy spirit (3:29; τὸ πνεῦμα τὸ ἅγιον). Jesus's purported possession by either Beelzeboul or the holy spirit does not use the traditional vocabulary of possession in Greek sources that Paige points to (ἐπίπνοια, ἔνθεος, ἐνθοθσιάζω, ἐνθουσιασμός, μανία, μαίνομαι). Paige claims that this vocabulary is never used by the gospel writers but instead they always use δαιμονίζομαι.[92] This is simply not true. In the case of Mark's baptism scene, the dove-like *pneuma* comes down from heaven and goes into Jesus (1:10; εἰς αὐτόν).[93] The bodily manifestation of *pneuma* here might speak to its materiality, but it also speaks to its integrity as a separate being from god.[94] Similarly, Mark 3 does not use δαιμονίζομαι to describe the accusation against Jesus that he is possessed by Beelzeboul. Beelzeboul is identified as a *daimonion*, but when the scribes of Jerusalem make their accusation, they say Jesus 'has Beelzeboul' (Βεελζεβοὺλ ἔχει). The issue is one of hierarchy of beings, because they accuse Jesus of casting out *daimonia* by the leader of *daimonia*. When Jesus later refutes their accusation by clearly implying that he casts out *daimonia* by the holy *pneuma* and not Beelzeboul, there is no insinuation that the *pneuma* is anything but the being from 1:10. The comparison is now

---

[92] Paige, 'Who Believes in "Spirit"?', 428.
[93] Later manuscripts have ἐπ' in place of εἰς, but this is clearly a harmonisation with Matthew and Luke, which both have ἐπ'.
[94] Unless, of course, one reads this as the stuff of god sent by god that temporarily takes a bodily form before stoically mixing with Jesus, as *pneuma* was understood to do.

Beelzeboul – leader of the *daimonia* – versus the holy *pneuma* – autonomous being versus autonomous being. The contrast between Beelzeboul and the holy *pneuma* here clearly indicates equivalence: these are not philosophical materialist understandings of these two figures but personifications of divine beings on either side of the good and evil divide.

Other examples can be found in Mark; three will suffice. First, the unclean spirit (τὸ πνεῦμα τὸ ἀκάθαρτον, repeated three times) that Jesus exorcises in 1:21–8 not only possess the man but also speaks and physically moves him (1:26). There is no usage of δαιμόνιον or δαιμονίζω. Second, in 3:11 unclean *pneumata* bow down to Jesus upon seeing him and shout out his identity. Again, Mark describes the *pneuma* as the one physically moving and speaking, not the ones who have the *pneuma*, and there is no usage of δαιμόνιον or δαιμονίζω. Third, in 5:1–20, a man with an unclean *pneuma* who lives in the tombs comes to meet Jesus upon his arrival in Geraza. The story quickly turns to describing the spirits (now plural) begging Jesus and acting on Jesus's orders. Again, there is no usage of δαιμόνιον or δαιμονίζω.[95]

While Mark might be categorised as 'Christian' by some like Paige and so wholly separate from gentile culture, that assumes an artificial cultural divide. First, there are no such thing as non-Jewish followers of Jesus in the gospels, neither the writers nor the characters that are based on the actual people they depict. And if the episodes in Mark's gospel go back to traditions that predate it, which is certainly possible, then there is an equivalence in the divine categories of *daimōn/daimonion* and *pneuma* in terms of personification and autonomy that is contemporary with Paul's Corinthian letters, since Mark's gospel was likely written between fifteen and twenty years after the Corinthian correspondence. Plutarch's use of *pneuma* in *De defectu oraculorum* that we discussed above confirms a non-Jewish personified and autonomous use of *pneuma* that we find in Mark and the other canonical gospels. Neither usage required explanation from the authors, indicating that their usage was not novel. Whether or not the Corinthians would have heard these stories or know of similar usages to what we see in them and Plutarch is impossible to know, but there were certainly Jews in Corinth in the first century, some of whom became part of the Corinthian assembly (1 Cor. 7:18–19).[96] The

---

[95] See also Mark 6:7, 7:25, 9:14–27 and 13:11, for similar usage of *pneuma* as a supernatural being with power to cause physical movement and speech.

[96] Because of the likely late date of Acts, I hesitate to rely on it for historical information in the first century. But Acts 18 does portray Paul coming to Corinth and meeting Priscilla and Aquila, two Jews who left Rome after the expulsion of Jews by Claudius. While in Corinth, he would 'dispute' (διελέγετο) in the synagogue and try to persuade Jews and Greeks. If Acts is at all accurate, there was a Jewish population in first-century Corinth, but the pattern of Paul preaching in and being rejected in the synagogue is consistent in Acts, so it is difficult to tell what is literary construction and what reflects actual events.

cultural interaction of Jews and non-Jews in Corinth would have been real, and perhaps resulted in a wider notion of *pneuma* that included Jewish notions of a personified *pneuma*. This is at least as likely as marginally or non-educated Corinthians having a materialist understanding of *pneuma* similar to what philosophers taught.

Given the (at least partially) Roman context of Corinth, we have to consider the Roman *genius* and *numen* in our discussion of *pneuma*. This is not to say that *genius* and *numen* were seen as equivalent to *pneuma* in any of the senses I have described above. It is a matter of trying to anticipate the ways in which a Corinthian audience might have interpreted Paul's *pneuma* language through the lens of their Roman traditions regarding *genius* and *numen*. Further problematising the comparison is that, according to Duncan Fishwick, 'There seems to be no definitive exposition of the fundamental distinction between *genius* and *numen*.'[97]

Ancient sources generally present the *genius* as a divine being 'closely associated with each individual person, appearing at a birth and leaving the world at death'.[98] Censorinus in his *Birthday Book* explains that *genius est deus* (the *genius* is a god) whose main responsibility is to protect the one with whom it is associated, and that protection starts at birth (3.1) and 'never goes away from us even for a second ... to the last day of our life' (3.5).[99] Other ancient authors conceive of the *genius* as the 'life-force of all things yet to be born' (*vim omnium rerum gignendarum*).[100] In at least one ancient author, it is linked to both men and women (Serv. Auct. Aen. 2.351), but often the Juno is referred to with the overtone of the counterpart to the male *genius*. Although the basic idea of the *genius* was a deity linked to the head of the household, this concept was extended to apply to various special people or groups of people: Genius Augusti (imperial *genius*); *genius populi Romani* (*genius* of the Roman people); *genius senatus* (of the senate); *genius hominum mortuorum* (of the deceased) and *genius funerarius* (of the funeral procession); *genius legionis/ militaris* (of the legions or of war); *genius urbis Romae* (of the city of Rome); *genius oppidi* (of the town); *genius theatri*; *genius coloniae/provinciae*; and even *genii* of the gods (generally and particular gods).[101]

---

[97] Duncan Fishwick, 'Genius and Numen', in *Studies in the Ruler Cult of the Western Provinces of the Roman Empire, Part 2.1* (Leiden: Brill, 1990), 377n11, https://doi.org/10.1163/9789004295759_002.

[98] Harriet I. Flower, *The Dancing Lares and the Serpent in the Garden: Religion at the Roman Street Corner* (Princeton: Princeton University Press, 2017), 6.

[99] Translation by Holt N. Parker, *The Birthday Book: Censorinus* (Chicago: University of Chicago Press, 2007).

[100] Isid. Orig. 8.11.88. Translation by Wolfram-Aslan Maharam in 'Genius', in *Brill's New Pauly*, https://doi.org/10.1163/1574-9347_bnp_e421560. See also Apul. *De deo Socratis* 15.151; Fest. 84.3–7; Mart. Cp. 2.152).

[101] See Maharam, 'Genius', for details of the iconography of each of these figures.

Typical iconography of the *genius* from Pompeiian remains shows it flanked by two Lares (Roman domestic and crossroads deity), oftentimes making an offering at an altar. A good example of this iconography is found in the top portion of the painting in Figure 3.1: a *genius* is in the centre of the scene, holding a cornucopia with his left arm and making an offering with his right hand.[102] The cornucopia is another common feature of the iconography of the *genius*. Although the *genius* is dressed in a toga with the head covered by its hem – a typical human Roman dress for ritual action – the cornucopia 'identifies him as a deity: he cannot be human'.[103] Flower argues that the attire closely resembles that of the paterfamilias, indicating the protective power of the *genius* and connection with the head of the household. The *genius* is depicted as smaller than the two Lares on either side of him, indicating the relative status of the deities; it may also indicate that the Lares are the recipients of the libation offering that the *genius* is making. The scene shows a remarkable depiction of the interaction of typical human ritual action towards the gods and intra-divine ritual action, with the libation offering by the *genius* and the pig, which is seemingly up next in the ritual but is brought forth by a human slave as the human flute player provides the accompanying ritual music.[104]

Obviously, iconography varies depending on the location and nature of the particular *genius* being depicted.[105] But the *genius* is clearly a personification, an independent divine entity related only to the person, group of people, or other god to whom it is attached. The key is the protective nature of the deity, which clearly runs through all of the various manifestations or kinds of *genii*. The *pneuma* is never referred to as a god in any of the extant ancient literary sources, to my knowledge. And the personification of the *pneuma* is not as common in its varying conceptualisations. As far as I can tell, the *genius* is always personified iconographically and conceptually. The connection of the *genius* with a god, however, is suggestive and may have some resemblance for the Corinthians to Paul's use of phrases like τὸ πνεῦμα τοῦ θεοῦ (1 Cor. 2:11) throughout the Corinthian correspondence.

As mentioned, Fishwick notes that there is no clear distinction between *genius* and *numen*.[106] Before the Augustan period, *numen* connotes the will of

---

[102] The provenance of the painting is unclear, even though it is attributed to a Pompeiian room outside of a domestic context (VII.2 or 3, possibly). It was found on 6 June 1761, but the findspot is unknown, according to Thomas Frölich, *Lararien- und Fassadenbilder in den Vesuvstädten. Untersuchungen sur 'volkstümlichen' pompejanischen Malerei* (Mainz: P. von Zabern, 1991), L98. See Flower, *The Dancing Lares*, 54n4, for a fuller discussion of the provenance.

[103] Flower, *The Dancing Lares*, 55.

[104] See ibid., 56, for Flower's reading of the painting.

[105] See Flower's collection of illustrations at the back of ibid. (no page number given) to get a sense of the range of iconography of the Lares and *genii* in Pompeii and beyond.

[106] Fishwick, 'Genius and Numen', 377n11.

**Figure 3.1** Pompeiian painting with *genius* at the centre of the top portion. Photo by ArchaiOptix. Licence CC by 4.0 IT (https://creativecommons.org/licenses/by-sa/4.0/deed.en)

a specific deity, and not necessarily the deity itself.[107] *Inscr. Ital.* 13.2.115 indicates that a cult of Numen Augusti was started in 6 CE in Rome, but it is hard to determine what this actually consisted of or what its relationship with the Genius Augusti might have been because there is so little surviving evidence with which to cross-reference it. The little evidence comes from outside of Rome (*IRT* 324; *RIT* 48; Pl. LXXIV a–c). An inscription from 11 CE from Narbo references an altar to the Numen Augusti which also records details about what should be offered to the emperor's *numen* and when (*CIL* 12.4333 = *ILSI* 112). A bit later, in Rome, in 18 CE, *CIL* 11.3303 (= *ILS* 154) attests to rites associated with an altar to Numen Augustum (likely a variant of Numen Augusti). In the inscription, the *genii* of Augustus and Tiberius are invited to the feast at the altar, indicating the distinction between the Genius Augusti and the Numen Augusti, which seems also to indicate a distinction between *numen* and *genius* more generally.[108] According to Francesca Prescendi, the evidence shows that 'Neither [the emperor's] person nor his *genius* was meant, but the divine power inherent in the emperor, and the force of the gods that manifested itself in and through the emperor.'[109]

In the post-Augustan period, a broader meaning of the concept developed to include a meaning synonymous to 'deity', something Fishwick calls 'standard practice' by the time of Commodus.[110] More suggestive is the usage of the *numen* in Roman sources, where

> *numen* appears in pre-Augustan as well as later texts in connection with the genitive of a god's name (oldest evidence: Accius in Non. 173,27: *nomen et numen Iovis*), with the genitive of the words *deus* and *divus* (e.g. Cic. Div. 1,120) or in adjectival connection with *divinus* (e.g. Cic. Nat. D. 1,22).[111]

This overlaps somewhat with the use of *pneuma* discussed above in 1 Cor. 2:11 and other places. Given the range of meanings of *numen* both as a divine power or force of the gods that manifested itself 'in and through' a person

---

[107] W. Pötscher, '"Numen" und "numen Augusti"', *ANRW* II 16.1 (Berlin: De Gruyter, 1978), 371–3.

[108] See Fishwick, 'Genius and Numen', 378–81. Further, *ILTG* 160 and *CIL* 3.3487 give evidence of offerings to both the *numen* and the *genius* of Lucius Caesar and Hadrian, respectively, indicating a non-identity of the *numen* and *genius*. See also Pötscher, '"Numen" und "Numen Augusti"', 387–92, for a good treatment of the *numen Augusti*.

[109] Francesca Prescendi, 'Numen', in *Brill's New Pauly*, https://doi.org/10.1163/1574-9347_bnp_e826240.

[110] See Duncan Fishwick, '"Sanctissimum numen": Emperor or God?', *ZPE* 89 (1991): 196–200 (quote at 198), for a discussion of the use of *numen* to refer to the emperor as a god in *CIL* 8.16417.

[111] Prescendi, 'Numen'.

(that is, the emperor), and as a deity, there is more similarity with the range of meaning of *pneuma* we saw from the evidence – both an ethereal substance and a divine being – than there is for *genius*.

## Personification of the Gods of the Greeks and Romans

Greeks and Romans had a long history of personifying the objects of their worship, even if what was personified was quite abstract or non-personal. A very brief treatment of this phenomenon follows, to give a sense of the Corinthians' everyday experience of the gods. Major gods or mythological figures are pretty obviously anthropomorphic entities: Zeus, Apollo, Artemis, Asklepios, Athena, Demeter, Mars, Jupiter, Juno and the like are all human-like. They look and often act like humans, at least in part, even if their appearance sometimes changes to match their divine status.[112]

Other gods that are less overtly 'people' are still consistently represented in anthropomorphic terms. Nature gods, such as Helios and Kephisos, are good examples, where, both iconographically and cultically, they appear anthropomorphic. Helios is found throughout the Greek world in cultic settings, usually with a sun-ray nimbus, often riding his chariot, drawn by either two or four horses (see Figure 3.2) His nimbus and chariot symbolise his nature as the sun god; however, he is not depicted as the sun but as a person with symbolic elements related to the sun. Other nature gods follow the same pattern. In Chapter One, I discussed a stele found in Kephisos, which represented the river god anthropomorphically as the main figure receiving the child dedicated by the supplicant. The image is not that of a river but of a person at the head of the group of gods, indicating the local prominence of Kephisos.

There are some gods who are not completely anthropomorphic in their iconography and statuary, such as Pan and Triton, both of whom have mixed animal and human parts. Pan – most likely associated with shepherding and flocks as his earliest manifestation in his homeland of Arcadia – is part goat and part human. His realms of influence range from shepherding and hunting of small game to military patrol of solitary rocky regions where he lives and oracular/prophetic powers, in addition to the association of his name with the

---

[112] Demeter comes to mind, as depicted in the Homeric *Hymn to Demeter*. She disguises herself as a human (as do many gods in many stories) as she grieves the loss of her daughter, Persephone. But once her identity is discovered, her divine glory shines forth in an overwhelming way, and her human-like characteristics are dwarfed and obscured (*Hom. Hymn Dem.* 275–80). Demeter's cult statues in her sanctuaries, however, and various representations of her as a goddess show her in anthropomorphic form.

**Figure 3.2** Helios in a chariot drawn by four horses, from the Temple of Athena, Ilion, fourth century BCE. (Purchased from Alamy 26 October 2023)

Greek *pan*, giving him the characteristic of a universal god in later Roman times.[113] Despite this large range of qualities, powers and realms of responsibility, he is consistently depicted as half goat and half human: not fully anthropomorphised but enough to be considered a personified god.

Triton is the son of Poseidon and Amphitrite and functions mainly in concert with his father.[114] He usually carries a trident, but is often depicted as holding a conch shell that would make an extremely loud noise when he blew it. Unlike his father, who is depicted as fully anthropomorphic,[115] Triton is usually depicted as a man with a fish torso and tail – what we would call a merman (see Figure 3.3). Pausanias describes the famous temple of Poseidon in Isthmia as having Tritons (that is, Triton statues) standing 'on the temple' (τῷ ναῷ), clearly involving Triton in the cultic life of his father.[116] Like Pan, Triton is not fully anthropomorphic, but he is clearly a personified god.

Romans had analogous anthropomorphic images for many of their gods. The gods that parallel the major Olympian deities are obviously still anthropomorphic figures, even if particular gods and goddesses take on different

---

[113] See M. Jost, 'Pan', in *Oxford Classical Dictionary*, 4th ed. (Oxford: Oxford University Press, 2012).
[114] Hes. *Theog.* 930; cf. Hom. *Il.* 13.20; Hom. *Od.* 5.
[115] See the west pediment of the Parthenon for a classic example of Poseidon's anthropomorphic form.
[116] Paus. 2.1.7.

**Figure 3.3** Right side panel from 'Statue Base of Marcus Antonius', second half of second century BCE, showing sea thiasos for the wedding of Poseidon and Amphitrite. Detail: Nereids riding a sea dragon, and a Triton. (Public domain)

roles or nuances of influence in their Roman contexts. Diana, for example – although the parallel of Artemis who retains some of the same mythological history (for example, being the sibling of Apollo) and appropriates traditional iconographic features of Artemis[117] – becomes a

> powerful deity whose authority could guarantee hegemony and whose ritual practice could be manipulated to provide divine support for a federal cult led by Rome. This is not a nymphlike goddess of women and children. She is a patron of warriors and leaders and a divine guarantor of hegemony among the Latins.[118]

Carin Green characterises Diana through the lens of her cult in Aricia, but Diana is still a female, a fully anthropomorphised goddess represented as such in Aricia and elsewhere.

Luna, the Roman goddess of the moon (although Diana and Juno are also associated with the moon[119]), is similar to Helios in the sense that she represents a natural phenomenon in a personified form. She is often referred to in literature along with her counterpart Sol, the sun god, but she is listed among some of the most important deities in Rome by Varro and Vergil.[120]

---

[117] Carin M. C. Green, *Roman Religion and the Cult of Diana at Aricia* (Cambridge: Cambridge University Press, 2007), 77.
[118] Ibid., 131.
[119] Ibid., 73.
[120] Varro, *Rust.* 1.1.4–6;Varro *Ling.* 5.74;Verg. *G.* 1.5–25. See John Scheid,'Luna', in *Oxford Classical Dictionary*, 4th ed (Oxford: Oxford University Press, 2012).

**Figure 3.4** Altar with the goddess Luna, second or third century CE, Mithraeum, Mundelsheim. Licence CC by 4.0 IT (https://creativecommons.org/licenses/by-sa/4.0/deed.en)

Her iconography sometimes has her with a crescent on her head and a torch in her right hand (see Figure 3.4), but she also is depicted, like her Greek solar counterpart, driving a chariot (*biga*); in her case it is pulled by two horses or oxen rather than the four horses that are common for Helios. Just as Helios's features are symbolic of the sun,[121] Luna is shown with features that link her to the moon, but she is still anthropomorphic.

Romans also had an abundance of gods that personified virtues or forces that protected their society. Gods such as Fortuna (good fortune), Honos (honour), Justitia (justice), Libertas (freedom) and Virtus (manliness) were just as important as any of the gods associated with the Greek Olympian gods. These values and actions personified in gods 'were supposed to characterize the actions of the élite', so it made some sense for Romans to worship them as gods.[122] And where they were imagined iconographically, they were personified and imagined anthropomorphically.

---

[121] In 2016, divers off Caesarea Maritima found, among other treasures, an oil lamp with a figuring of Sol depicted much like Helios, along with the bust of a statue of Luna. The collection of artifacts were dated to the early fifth century.

[122] Jörg Rüpke, *Religion of the Romans*, trans. and ed. Richard Gordon (Cambridge: Polity Press, 2007), 78.

## The Social Constitution of Paul's Corinthians

As with most things Pauline, the social makeup of Paul's communities has been a long-standing issue that has received a lot of attention over the last hundred or more years.[123] Deissmann's 1910 take on the issue influenced the conversation significantly, particularly his statement that there was a 'close inward connection between the gospel and the lower classes'.[124] From that point on, the lower classes had to be taken into account for any treatment of the issue of who made up early groups of Jesus followers. But the question was far from settled, and scholars have swung from arguing that the early movement was made up of and geared towards the poor and non-elites to arguing that it was controlled and shaped by elites, even if the assemblies were of mixed status.

In the 1970s and 1980s, Wayne Meeks and Gert Theissen both argued for a mixed social makeup with regard to status in early Christian groups, and this formed the basis of a widely held consensus that still carries significant sway with many present-day scholars. But as Cavan Concannon helpfully points out – following Steven Friesen's challenge of Meeks's and Theissen's analyses – the focus of those analyses is on social status, which is a difficult category to quantify and therefore a difficult category to rely on for a clear and stable picture of the composition of the early Jesus movement:

> This is because social status has come to carry too many dimensions for the concept to be analytically useful; the dimensions have no relationship with one another, and we lack most of the information necessary to carry out an analysis of social status in Pauline collectives, given the paucity of our evidence.[125]

---

[123] The bibliography is extensive, but some of the influential works are G. Adolf Deissmann, *Light from the Ancient East: The New Testament Illustrated by Recently Discovered Texts of the Greco-Roman World* (London: Hodder & Stoughton, 1910); W. H. Wuellner 'The Sociological Implications of I Corinthians 1:26–28 Reconsidered', in *Studia Evangelica VI*, ed. Elizabeth A. Livingstone (Berlin: Akademie Verlag, 1973), 666–72; Abraham Malherbe, *Social Aspects of Early Christianity* (Philadelphia: Fortress, 1977); Gerd Theissen, *The Social Setting of Pauline Christianity*, trans. John H. Schütz (Edinburgh: T & T Clark, 1982); Wayne A. Meeks, *The First Urban Christians: The Social World of the Apostle Paul* (New Haven: Yale University Press, 1983); Jürgen Becker, *Christian Beginnings* (Louisville, KY: Westminster/John Knox, 1993). See Bruce W. Longenecker, 'Socio-Economic Profiling of the First Urban Christians', in *After the First Urban Christians: The Social-Scientific Study of Pauline Christianity Twenty-Five Years Later*, ed. Todd D. Still and David G. Horrell (London: T & T Clark, 2009), 36–59, for a useful review of the issue.

[124] Deissmann, *Light from the Ancient East*, 403.

[125] Cavin W. Concannon, 'The Matter of Class: Assemblages, Networks, and the Shape of the Pauline Collectives', in *The Struggle over Class: Socioeconomic Analysis of Ancient Christian Texts*, ed. G. Anthony Keddie, Michael Flexsenhar III and Steven J. Friesen (Atlanta: SBL Press, 2021), 63.

Friesen changed the focus of the analysis to consider wealth instead of social status, in an effort to be more precise and data-driven about the possible composition of the groups of early Jesus followers.[126] He and Walter Scheidel refined and expanded Friesen's initial scale, as did Bruce W. Longenecker.[127] Most recently, Thomas R. Blanton IV has modified the scale and called it the Friesen–Longenecker Economic Scale (see Table 3.1).[128] These scales represent sub-levels of those living in the first-century Roman empire based on their wealth relevant to subsistence-level living.

Some have critiqued the almost exclusive emphasis on wealth in these models. In particular, L. L. Welborn has pointed to the 'missing category,

**Table 3.1** Thomas R. Blanton IV's version of the Friesen–Longenecker Economic Scale. Used with permission from Oxford University Press.

| Scale | Description | Includes |
| --- | --- | --- |
| ES 1 | Imperial elites | Imperial dynasty, Roman senatorial families, a few retainers, local royalty, a few freed persons |
| ES 2 | Regional or provincial elites | Equestrian families, provincial officials, some retainers, some decurial families, some freed persons, some retired military officers |
| ES 3 | Municipal elites | Most decurial families, wealthy men and women who do not hold office, some freed persons, some retainers, some veterans, some merchants |
| ES 4 | Moderate surplus | Some merchants, some traders, some freed persons, some artisans (especially those who employ others), military veterans |
| ES 5 | Stable near subsistence level (with reasonable hope of remaining above the minimum level to sustain life) | Many merchants and traders, regular wage earners, artisans, large shop owners, freed persons, some farm families |
| ES 6 | At subsistence level (and often below minimum level to sustain life) | Small farm families, laborers (skilled and unskilled), artisans (especially those employed by others), wage earners, most merchants and traders, small shop/tavern owners |
| ES 7 | Below subsistence level | Some farm families, unattached widows, orphans, beggars, disabled, unskilled day laborers, prisoners |

[126] Steven Friesen, 'Poverty in Pauline Studies: Beyond the So-Called New Consensus', *JSNT* 26 (2004): 323–61.
[127] Bruce W. Longenecker, *Remember the Poor: Paul, Poverty, and the Greco-Roman World* (Grand Rapids, MI: Eerdmans, 2010), 36–49.
[128] Thomas R. Blanton IV, 'Wealth, Poverty, Economy', in *The Oxford Handbook of the Synoptic Gospels*, ed. Stephen P. Ahearne-Kroll (Oxford: Oxford University Press, 2023), 298.

"class'", in Longenecker's *Remember the Poor*. For Welborn, the analytical absence of the category of class obfuscates Paul's efforts to 'actively *transform* the class system of Roman society from within, through a revolution in social values'.[129] Meanwhile, Peter Oakes critiques Friesen's model as overly focused on resources, or lack thereof, as a way of understanding the social makeup of early Jesus groups. Oakes says:

> By thinking of these [resources] in income-equivalent terms, this gives him a one-dimensional, and very concrete, variable to use – as opposed to problematically multi-dimensional variables such as status. However, ancient sources (and certainly the New Testament) hardly ever tell us the resources of a particular poor person or group. They tell us behaviour ... We cannot map this behaviour directly onto resources ... But if, as I would hope, we are to take Friesen's project further, into more specific analysis of poverty, the form of the New Testament data will drive us towards constructing a behaviourally based poverty scale, rather than a resource-based one.[130]

One major problem for my project is that the ES scale, even the most revised and expanded one, is a generalised picture of life in the Roman empire which pays no attention to localised variations. The scale may or may not represent life in Corinth very accurately, for instance, so we need to proceed with caution when utilising it on the local level. Concannon, again, helpfully reminds us of the complexity of social life among ancient Christ groups – indeed, among any social group. Whatever category of analysis one chooses to use – class, status, wealth and so on – it is only one aspect of the everyday social realities of a person living in a particular place and time. Concannon follows the work of Jacques Rancière and Giles Deleuze to begin to build an appreciation of the complexities of what individuals experienced as part of a shifting network of assemblages. Leatherworkers, like Paul might have been, each had multiple networks to negotiate on a daily basis to perform their trade, each of which was 'conditioned by a series of local and constantly shifting set of relations': for example, cattle production, including the agricultural economy where they were raised; tanners; tools makers; raw material production and acquisition to make the tools; various levels of legal status of individuals (freeborn, freedman or slave); commercial or domestic space

---

[129] L. L. Welborn, review of Bruce W. Longenecker, *Remember the Poor: Paul, Poverty, and the Greco-Roman World* in *RBL* (July 2012), https://www.sblcentral.org/API/Reviews/7899_9350.pdf (emphasis original).
[130] Peter Oakes, 'Constructing Poverty Scales for Graeco-Roman Society: A Response to Steven Friesen's "Poverty in Pauline Studies"', *JSNT* 26 (2004): 367–8.

to perform their trade, which itself had a certain place within the local civic landscape; and so on:

> For each actant, we cannot explain the economic level, the social standing, or the ways in which these shape the affective states or dispositions without immersing ourselves in a seemingly endless web of relations within a swarming assemblage of people and things.[131]

While I agree with this assessment, it is a daunting and virtually impossible task to attend to all these details, especially when the data for the ancient world is so sparse relative to modern contexts. What I think we can do is to be humble and measured about our goals in analysing and understanding ancient Christ groups, and we can be transparent that whatever we conclude only scratches the surface of ancient realities, and even that scratch is likely to be flawed. I propose to pick at one thread of the ancient world to see where it might lead in imagining the beginnings of the Christ group at Corinth: the thread of the practice of worshipping small groups of gods.

One important aspect of the group in Corinth is how they might have heard and understood Paul's preaching about *pneuma*. Because this term had a materialist meaning in philosophical and medical circles, we need to examine the question of the levels of education of group members to see if it is reasonable to assume that members of the Corinthian group would have been able to understand the materialist philosophical and medical notion of *pneuma*. Since we do not have a roster of the members of Paul's initial audience with their educational history, one correlation that will help us understand this dynamic is that of wealth, which circles us back to the ES scale in Table 3.1. While personal wealth is not the only factor in determining one's level of education, interaction with wealthier individuals and groups increases the likelihood of more extended and sophisticated education. Let us take a brief look at how education worked in ancient Rome, so that we can make an informed, albeit imperfect, assessment of the range of possibilities for how members of the Corinthian group might have understood *pneuma*.

Ian Phillip Brown argued in his 2020 doctoral dissertation for a more complex understanding of the educational activity of ancients during the late Republic and early empire.[132] Instead of focusing on a simplistic model of education that begins with letters, progresses through rhetoric and then finally reaches philosophy, with each stage winnowing down the number of students

---

[131] Concannon, 'The Matter of Class', especially 67–70 (quotes from 67–8).

[132] Ian Phillip Brown, 'The *Pepaideumenoi* and Jesus: Ancient Education and Marginal Intellectuals in Paul's Corinth and the Gospel of Thomas', (PhD diss., University of Toronto, 2020). I follow his work throughout this section.

and increasing the proportion of those of high social status who continue, Brown follows a number of recent scholars of ancient Roman and Greek education who focus the purpose of education on the teaching and learning of *paideia*. *Paideia* is not a curriculum or body of knowledge, but a term that indicates a cultured life. Those who possessed *paideia*, the *pepaideumenoi*, could do so at varying levels, and its acquisition was one element in claiming a part in its cultural significance. While only the best and most fully educated could stake a claim to be someone who was truly among the *pepaideumenoi*, even those with the most basic formal education could claim to have acquired some level of *paideia*, which 'was constructed at the earliest levels of ancient education'.[133]

The initial stages of formal education were concerned with attaining reading and writing skills by copying and reciting, among other things, philosophical maxims and excerpts from Homer; in doing so, these students could claim some participation in 'a culture that valued *paideia*'.[134] But it was not only the students who benefited from this sort of education. *Didaskaloi*, grammarians and pedagogues, many of whom were enslaved or freedmen (especially pedagogues), also participated in 'achieving some measure of social capital through their role as teachers of *paideia*', even though they possessed 'little to no economic status'.[135] Suetonius identified some grammarians who even wrote books.[136] This segment of the formal educational world not only were instructors of the rudimentary skills of their students, but also provided a small foothold in the elite culture of *paideia*, something that instructors could claim for themselves, even if they had not achieved the highest levels of philosophical education.

Brown goes on to argue that, 'of the small number of people who had any education, the vast majority possessed a "marginal" education, at least insofar as the educated elite understood it'. Further, 'in spite of the various holes in their training, students at almost all levels of *encyclia paideia* were taught the cultural significance of their education, and the cultural capital available to one who could perform their education'.[137] He picks up on Theresa Morgan's model of Roman education, which focuses on the evidence of school texts rather than secondary ancient literary evidence to construct her 'core and periphery' model. For Morgan, the core was equivalent to 'what most people learned, what they learned first and, in the case of reading, what they went on practicing longest'.[138] Peripheral education is so termed by Morgan

---

[133] Ibid., 40–1.
[134] Ibid., 41.
[135] Ibid., 29.
[136] Ibid., 41; see Suet. *Gram et rhet*.
[137] Brown, 'The *Pepaideumenoi* and Jesus', 73.
[138] Theresa Morgan, *Literate Education in the Hellenistic and Roman Worlds* (New York: Cambridge University Press, 1998), 71.

because this is the type of education that only the few who went on to formal rhetorical and philosophical education received. The content of core education included philosophy and rhetoric but not at the depth or sophistication that the peripherally educated enjoyed. In other words, all of those who received some amount of formal education also received some philosophical education by 'exercises such as gnomic sayings and copying Homer', namely, 'the most popular *paideic* content'.[139]

Brown's group of 'marginally educated' are those who had some core education and thus some basic exposure and understanding of *paideia* that helped create a shared sense of Greekness or Romanness. It is important to stress here that even the marginally educated were part of the small but diverse minority of those educated in ancient Greek and Roman societies, perhaps somewhere slightly more than the 5–10 per cent range that Paul Veyne claims would have been aware of Stoic preaching and societal ideals in vogue in the early empire.[140] So it is likely that, if there were some among the Corinthians with formal education of some sort – and these individuals could be included among the more elite or enslaved or freedmen – they would have been able to understand Paul's usage of *pneuma* in materialist philosophical terms.

Demographically speaking, it is impossible to determine with any detail who was part of Paul's group of Corinthians but, before the group was formed, his audiences could have included anyone from Corinth. Having a sense of the cultural demography of Corinth might give us a slightly clearer picture of Paul's potential initial audiences. Benjamin W. Millis offers an excellent examination of the literary, epigraphical and numismatic evidence for the ethnic makeup of the original colonists and the effect of Roman culture on their descendants. The colonists were most likely not Roman military veterans, as many think, but primarily Greek freedmen, their descendants and their families.[141] Corinth's inscriptional evidence is usually taken as an indication that the city's culture was mostly Roman since the number of inscriptions in Latin far outweighs the number in Greek. But Willis's conclusion is more nuanced and helpful because he argues that

> the more an inscription was meant for public display and public consumption in a Roman context, the more likely it was to have been

---

[139] Brown, 'The *Pepaideumenoi* and Jesus', 76.

[140] Paul Veyne, 'The Roman Empire', in *A History of Private Life*, vol. 1, *From Pagan Rome to Byzantium*, ed. Paul Veyne (Cambridge, MA: Belknap Press of Harvard University Press, 1987), 36.

[141] See Benjamin W. Millis, 'The Social and Ethnic Origins of the Colonists in Early Roman Corinth,' in *Corinth in Context: Comparative Studies on Religion and Society*, ed. Steven J. Friesen, Daniel N. Schowalter and James C. Walters (Leiden: Brill, 2011), 17–21, for the argument against the colonists being military veterans, and 21–3, for the argument for the colonists being freedmen or their descendants.

written in Latin. The more an inscription was used for private communication, the more likely it was to have been written in Greek. The quasi-public, quasi-private world of funerary monuments is one area in which these two languages meet and overlap.[142]

Millis goes on to describe a complex hybrid Corinthian society made up of Hellenised Roman elites and Greek freedmen who could engage with both Greek and Roman culture. The elite seemed 'the most capable, or willing, to straddle the cultural divide, while the lower strata seemed more solidly Greek in outlook'.[143] He points to the probability of different ethnic origins for this cultural divide, with the elite (mostly freedmen with a long familiarity with Roman culture) being more comfortable with Roman language and culture, whereas the lower strata comprised local populations or populations not as familiar with Roman culture. Millis's analysis lends itself to a picture of Paul's audience as a group living in a culture that was both Greek and Roman, with varying levels of comfort and access to each.

With this information about economic state, education and demography, we can circle back to what Friesen and Scheidel, on the one hand, and Longenecker, on the other, have said about the likely makeup of the population of the empire, and then make an educated guess about the makeup of the population of Paul's initial Corinthian audiences. Scheidel and Friesen's study of the overall size of the Roman economy at its second-century peak is an attempt not only to describe the economic production of the Roman empire but also to get a better sense of the demographic breakdown with respect to what economic levels the population as a whole occupied. They argue, in part,

> that the top 1.5 per cent of households controlled around one-fifth of the total income; that economically 'middling' non-élite groups accounted for a modest share of the population (around 10 per cent) but perhaps another fifth of total income; and that the vast majority of the population lived close to subsistence but cumulatively generated more than half of overall output.[144]

Further, Scheidel and Friesen claim that their findings are based on a conservative assessment of Roman economic history, 'but serve to qualify both dichotomous visions of a Roman society divided into élites and subsistence workers on the one hand and overly optimistic assessments of income growth and the

---

[142] Ibid., 31.
[143] Ibid.
[144] Walter Scheidel and Steven J. Friesen, 'The Size of the Economy and the Distribution of Income in the Roman Empire', *JRS* 99 (2009): 62.

role of "middling" elements on the other'.[145] They number the population of the elite groups (senatorial order, equestrian order, decurional order and other wealthy) at approximately 1.2–1.7 per cent.[146] They break down the civilian non-elite population relative to subsistence-level income; the total population for these groups is approximately 97 per cent. The eight levels range from 0.25–0.49 times the subsistence level at the low end to 5 times the subsistence level at the high end.

For their optimistic scenario, the largest group of this 97 per cent of the population is 0.50–0.74 times subsistence (55 per cent of the population). The second largest group is 0.75–0.99 times subsistence (19 per cent of the population). The third largest group is 0.25–0.49 times subsistence (10 per cent of the population).[147] This means that, optimistically, 84 per cent of the population had an income below subsistence level, leaving about 13 per cent at or above subsistence, not including the elite.[148] From this 13 per cent, Schiedel and Friesen consider the 'middling' group as those at 2.4 times 'bare bones' subsistence, which, for their economic scale, means that between 6 and 12 per cent of the population would fall into the 'middling' group.[149] Since education was not free in the ancient Roman world, those in the middling group would be the most likely to have some formal education (other than the elite 1.5 per cent) and therefore some connection to the *paideia* of their particular locality, perhaps even including some basic knowledge of medical and philosophical concepts of *pneuma*.

Blanton's revised economic scale shown in Table 3.1 roughly corresponds with Scheidel and Friesen's work, as well as with Longenecker's scale. Longenecker takes this scale and tries to map it onto what we know about particular people associated with Christ groups in the first century. Although there are potential problems with using status as a category, as we have seen, legal status can be used carefully as a nuance to the economic scale we have been discussing, because legal status and income do not always match each other. An enslaved person, for instance, might have a low legal status but a high income if enslaved as a household manager to a wealthy individual. And the education

---

[145] Ibid., 63.
[146] Ibid., 71, table 6.
[147] Ibid., 84, table 9.
[148] In the midst of his review of Friesen's earlier work on the makeup of early Jesus groups in relation to wealth in the ancient economy, Concannon comments, 'I am convinced that, given the massive disparities in wealth inequality in antiquity, it is likely that the earliest Christians were much poorer than the average mainline or evangelical Protestant churchgoer in the contemporary United States' ('The Matter of Class', 63). Scheidel and Friesen's analysis would certainly support this, assuming that the makeup of the early Jesus groups roughly corresponded to a cross-section of the Roman population.
[149] Scheidel and Friesen, 'The Size of the Economy', 84.

level of an enslaved person could also be quite high. So, when more nuance and care with categories and technical terms is employed, a picture might emerge of Pauline assemblies as mixed with regard to status and power (economic, social, political and so on). The distribution of status and power within any particular Pauline assembly is very difficult to determine with any precision. What seems clear is that the most elite members of Corinthian society seem to be absent in Paul's Corinthian assembly, as Meeks has pointed out: 'It is hardly surprising that we meet no landed aristocrats, no senators, equites, nor . . . decurions.'[150] The social portrait of the Corinthian assembly should not be one of a binary mixture of elite/non-elite, but more like a spectrum of non-elite, reflecting the spectrum presented in Blanton's chart and resembling the relative spectrum of wealth for which Scheidel and Friesen have convincingly argued.

One of the key elements of Stanley Stowers's argument about the beginnings of Paul's assemblies and the slow spread of members is that Paul first appealed to elite individuals with his alternative *paideia*. These elite would have been the leaders of their houses (Stephanas, for example), and these household leaders would then have been the conduits for the spread of the *paideia* to other non-elite members of the household and to the social networks of the household leader.[151] While this is not unreasonable, we have to condition this argument to reflect Stowers's characterisation of a local householder like Stephanas as elite. He was probably among the most elite in the group but, relative to the truly elite classes, he was probably in the middling group, the upper 5–10 per cent of the non-elite. Someone like Stephanus probably had some formal education that, coupled with his excess income, gained him cultural status that was not available to those group members lower down the scale.

Longenecker discusses some scholars who have been rethinking the social organisational centre of these assemblies; in their analysis, 'the influence of the householder is greatly reduced or altogether absent'.[152] At the basis of this scholarship is a focus on the variety of possible locations where the assemblies might have met. David Horrell comments, 'NT studies should pay more attention to the varieties of domestic space in the urban setting of Corinth and other cities of the Roman empire, and consider these as possible settings for early Christian meetings.'[153] Edward Adams's monograph takes a thorough

---

[150] Meeks, *The First Urban Christians*, 73.
[151] Stowers, 'Kinds of Myth', and Stanley K. Stowers, 'Does Pauline Christianity Resemble a Hellenistic Philosophy?', in *Redescribing Paul and the Corinthians*, ed. Cameron and Miller, especially 219–44, which both make extended arguments for Paul's success in Corinth.
[152] Longenecker, 'Socio-Economic Profiling', 42.
[153] David Horrell, 'Domestic Space and Christian Meetings at Corinth: Imagining New Contexts and the Buidlings East of the Theatre', *NTS* 50 (2004): 369, cited in Longenecker, 'Socio-Economic Profiling', 42.

look at the possibilities and concludes that households are only one among many options for early meeting places for the Jesus movement.[154] While the findings of these scholars do not negate Stowers's schema – Paul's preaching an alternative *paideia* to Stephanas and his house – it does open up the possibility that Paul had initial conversations with other less elite Corinthians who were not necessarily connected with Stephanas's house and who had little or no formal education.

The difficulty of pinpointing the makeup of the Corinthian assembly is that all the evidence we have is from Paul, and his letters are not unmodified snapshots of life in Corinth but rhetorically sophisticated epistles that try to shape audience opinion through various rhetorical constructions. Separating out Paul's rhetorical purposes from what is actually happening on the ground is difficult. Longenecker concludes:

> Paul seems to address his communities as if they were comprised primarily of people belonging to ES5. At times the rhetorical target is broad enough to incorporate both ES5 and ES6 . . . At times Paul moved the level of economic characterization up or down from that point, for rhetorical effect, or when addressing particular people or groups. But in general, ES5 seems to be where his own mental averaging of his communities seems to gravitate most naturally.[155]

Longenecker characterises ES5 as stable near subsistence level and ES6 as subsistence level. I am not convinced that ES5 would necessarily represent the rhetorical target, however. Paul's language is sophisticated enough to expect that target to have a high enough level of education to understand what he is saying. Those near subsistence level might be freed persons who were educated while enslaved, but the average person at the ES5 level would seem not to have had the income to engage in the kind of formal education necessary to fully grasp Paul's rhetorically sophisticated arguments; perhaps those at the upper end of this level might. So, some from ES4 and ES5 might have had enough core education and perhaps some peripheral education (in Morgan's terms) to pick up on some of the philosophical overtones of Paul's rhetoric, at least recognising that Paul's language participates in the greater world of *paideia* that the well educated and socially elite occupied. It makes no sense that Paul would have written to an audience none of whom could understand what he

---

[154] Edward Adams, *The Earliest Christian Meeting Places: Almost Exclusively Houses?*, rev. ed. (London: T & T Clark, 2016). Adams's analysis continues well beyond the time of Paul, but it is a good example of the way that a wider lens can help imagine a more variegated landscape in the early years of the Jesus movement.

[155] Longenecker, 'Socio-Economic Profiling', 51–2.

was talking about; it is more likely that there might have been some from the lower ES4 and upper ES5 levels among its members.

One of Meeks's main contributions to the study of the origins of the Christ movement is that he posited socioeconomic motivations for joining the movement. Longenecker argues that socioeconomic benefits would have been a factor in taking part in Paul's assemblies because,

> If Paul's communities took initiatives to care for the poor, and if they gathered to share food and drink in corporate dinners and other occasions, it is relatively easy to see what economic attraction such communities would have held for people in ES6 and ES7 who fell beyond the structures of a household.[156]

Drawing on John Patterson's work on the nature of *collegia* in Italy, Longenecker says that this characteristic of early assemblies would have been different from that of most *collegia*, which were interested in members of higher socioeconomic status.[157] This difference could reasonably have generated at least one motivation for people on the lower end of the socioeconomic scale to join the movement – increased economic security. However, those higher up the scale, who did not need the extra economic security, would not necessarily have been attracted to this group. What would have been the incentive for them, since the main motivation for joining a *collegium* or *collegium*-like group would be to increase social standing and honour, either through affiliation in the group or through sponsoring it as a patron? But if the group were populated largely with those lower down the economic scale and/or low-status individuals, there would be little or no social incentive for higher-status individuals to join the group as members, and little social gain from sponsoring it.[158] While this does not eliminate the possibility of the presence of more elite members of Paul's initial Corinthian audience, it would seem to limit the widespread appeal among the more elite.

This raises a potential problem for Stowers's schema of Paul initially attracting higher-status individuals like Stephanas or Gaius through the presentation of an alternative *paideia*. While the reasons for attraction to this *paideia* make some sense as Stowers presents them (as an esoteric alternative apocalyptic *paideia* compared to the prevailing groups teaching traditional *paideia*), the

---

[156] Ibid., 52. ES6 and ES7 are those at and below subsistence level, respectively.
[157] Ibid., 53–5; John Patterson, *Landscapes and Cities: Rural Settlement and Civic Transformation in Early Imperial Italy* (Oxford: Oxford University Press, 2006).
[158] See Longenecker, 'Socio-Economic Profiling', 55–7, for a more detailed discussion of these points, although he focuses on the later stages of this early period, when the movement was possibly beginning to be perceived as somewhat counter to pro-Roman culture. This later stage is beyond the scope of my inquiry.

social and economic factors might have negatively affected the prospect of Paul attracting an adequate number of more elite sponsors and leaders. So we are left with those individuals on the lower end of the economic scale with at most a core education, if any at all. How would one go about attracting these people? I do not think that Longenecker's analysis fits for the initial period of Paul's missionary activity because there is no developed assembly of Corinthians to 'sell' to potential new members. Without the infrastructure of care and economic security already functioning, what would attract these individuals? This is one reason why I have turned to the familiarity of Paul's god language as a possible hook for both lower- and higher-status individuals. The pattern of practice I have described in the previous two chapters represents the practice of individuals across the socioeconomic spectrum of Corinth, so we do not have to choose which rhetorical or actual target Paul is aiming for. And by trying to imagine how Paul's grouping of gods might have been familiar to the Corinthians, his intended target becomes less of a concern.

To sum up, it seems reasonable to think that Paul's group in Corinth consisted mostly of those living around subsistence level or lower with little formal education. These would likely not have understood Paul's use of *pneuma* in materialist philosophical terms because of their lack of formal education. Instead, they would have been more likely to understand *pneuma* as a personified supernatural/divine being, somewhat along the lines of how *daimōn* or *daimonia* were understood. But there were also likely some members of the Corinthian group who were more elite and had some formal education, which means that they had had some exposure to materialist philosophical notions of *pneuma*. These members of the group would have been more likely to understand *pneuma* as such, and so would likely not have thought of it as a personified supernatural/divine being.

## *Pneuma* in Paul

As I have noted already, many scholars have discussed Paul's likely meaning in the use of *pneuma* in his letters. I think it makes most sense that he thought of the *pneuma* in materialist philosophical terms. As Emma Wasserman points out, most ancient philosophical systems, except Platonism, had materialist cosmologies, though *pneuma* fitted in different ways into each overall cosmology.[159] Given Paul's sophistication of thought and rhetoric, it would make sense that he would draw upon philosophical notions of the materialist *pneuma*

---

[159] Wasserman, review of *Cosmology and Self*, 370. See also Martin, *The Corinthian Body*, 21, who says, 'For most ancient theorists, pneuma is a kind of "stuff" that is the agent of perception, motion, and life itself; it pervades other forms of stuff and, together with those other forms, constitutes the self.'

and maybe even upon the basic schema of how *pneuma* works as a material. For Paul to have had a materialist understanding of *pneuma* would therefore have put him in the company of many ancient philosophers, however consistent or sophisticated his thinking was on the topic.

Unfortunately, we do not have access to Paul's initial interactions with the Corinthians. All we have are his letters. We need to make the important assumption that his language about his god(s) in the Corinthian correspondence has some fundamental continuity with his interactions before he wrote these letters. In other words, we should assume he talked about the *pneuma*, (lord Jesus) Christ and (father) god in those initial conversations with the Corinthians. The philosophical traditions around *pneuma* as a material substance might not have been a stumbling block to recognising *pneuma* as such for those more elite or more educated Corinthians familiar enough with those traditions. As I discussed above, the majority of Corinthian assemblies were likely below the economically middling group, with little or no formal education, and so these characteristics of *pneuma* might not have been the first thing that came to mind when they heard Paul talking about it.

The majority of instances when Paul uses πνεῦμα or its cognates are easiest to understand with materialist notions of *pneuma* in mind. For Paul, the material is the stuff of his god and/or Christ,[160] and so those Corinthians who had these notions as part of their cultural vocabulary would have had no trouble seeing *pneuma* as the substance of Paul's god and not as a separate divine entity. These same instances would have been confusing to those who do not have this understanding, who perhaps had a cursory exposure to philosophy or medicine and therefore a basic idea of what *pneuma* is and how it works as a material substance – that is, the majority of the Corinthians. And the instances that do not clearly fit into a materialist view of *pneuma* would have been even more confusing, but in these cases for everyone, not just the marginally educated or non-educated. In these cases, I would point to the traditions around *pneuma* as a personified and autonomous divine/supernatural being that we saw in the Septuagint, Mark and Plutarch. I also think that there are several examples of *pneuma* in 1 and 2 Corinthians that are easy to imagine being understood as an autonomous, personified supernatural being by marginally educated or non-educated Corinthians.

1 Corinthians 3:16 is somewhat ambiguous, but I believe there is good reason to number it among the examples that show individual identity for the *pneuma*, especially when paired with 6:19. The verse follows a fairly long metaphor of the assembly as a building built by Paul with a foundation of 'Jesus Christ'. The building metaphor flows into the metaphor of the assembly

---

[160] See Stowers, 'Matter and Spirit', and Martin, *The Corinthian Body*, especially 104–36, in addition to the scholars mentioned above who hold this view.

being 'the temple of god' (ναὸς θεοῦ). The NRSV translates 3:16 as: 'Do you not know that you are God's temple and that God's Spirit dwells in you?', which indicates individuation of the *pneuma* but in a way that seems as if the main nuance and purpose of the image are to show that *pneuma* personally possesses the individual. Although a footnote in the translation indicates that 'you' is plural, the translation seems more modern and Christian than the context warrants. I think a better translation would be to emphasise the building imagery carried over from the previous metaphor, since a ναός is a building and a very common structure encountered by the Corinthians on a daily basis. So I suggest 'Do you not know that you are the temple of god (ναὸς θεοῦ) and the *pneuma* of god dwells among you (οἰκεῖ ἐν ὑμῖν)?' Translating οἰκεῖ ἐν ὑμῖν as 'dwells among you' de-emphasises the individualism of the NRSV translation.[161] When the building metaphor is carried over to this verse, we have to remember that the ναὸς θεοῦ would evoke any temple in Corinth, each of which would have the image or images of the god or gods that occupied that space.[162] The image would indicate the presence of the divinity in that building. In Paul's metaphor, the building is the collective, the assembly, which is also the location of his god. The metaphor limps because there is no image of Paul's god. Instead, the image is replaced with

---

[161] See Margaret M. Mitchell, *Paul and the Rhetoric of Reconciliation: An Exegetical Investigation of the Language and Composition of 1 Corinthians* (Tübingen: Mohr Siebeck, 1992); and John R. Lanci, *A New Temple for Corinth: Rhetorical and Archaeological Approaches to Pauline Imagery* (New York: Peter Lang, 1997), who both emphasise the metaphor of 'building' as central to Paul's argument about the community. For both, Paul is emphasising a concern not for the individual but for that of the life of the community that is central to his metaphor here and throughout the letter. See also Anthony C. Thiselton, *The First Epistle to the Corinthians: A Commentary on the Greek Text*. (Grand Rapids, MI: Eerdmans, 2000), 307: 'The very image of a *building* ... applied to the church, excludes individualism; it is not a single object but a corporate structure, a community'; and 316: 'Paul is not saying that each individual Christian is a temple within which God's Spirit dwells, but rather that the Spirit of God dwells in the Christian community *corporately as community*.' And see Wolfgang Schrage, *Der erste Brief an die Korinther*, 4 vols (Zurich: Benziger, 1991–2001), 1:295; Hans Conzelmann, *1 Corinthians: A Commentary on the First Epistle to the Corinthians* (Philadelphia: Fortress, 1975), 75; Raymond F. Collins, *First Corinthians* (Collegeville, MN: Liturgical Press, 1999), 160.

[162] Many commentators go right to the Jerusalem temple as the main referent for Paul's use of ναὸς θεοῦ (Joseph A. Fitzmyer, *First Corinthians* (New Haven: Yale University Press, 2008), 202–3; Collins, *First Corinthians*, 161), but with Horsley, I argue that the Corinthians would have thought first of their own context of Corinthian civic life, rife with sanctuaries, to unpack this image (Richard A. Horsley, *1 Corinthians* (Nashville: Abingdon, 1998), 66). Gordon D. Fee, *The First Epistle to the Corinthians*, rev. ed. (Grand Rapids, MI: Eerdmans, 2014), 159, says, 'The imagery of the church as temple would have been easily understood by the Corinthians as well, although perhaps not with all of its rich OT overtone.' It is a bit condescending and presumptive that Paul's meaning would not have included the 'rich' overtones of cultic life in Corinth.

πνεῦμα τοῦ θεοῦ, perhaps just the 'stuff' or manifestation of Paul's god, but perhaps a separate entity.

The individuation of *pneuma* becomes clearer when considering the similar statement in 6:19: 'Do you not know that your [pl.] body[163] is a temple of the holy *pneuma* in you (ναὸς τοῦ ἐν ὑμῖν ἁγίου πνεύματός ἐστιν), which you have from god (οὗ ἔχετε ἀπὸ θεοῦ)?' In this verse, the temple imagery is repeated, but the 'deity' dwelling within it is τοῦ ... ἁγίου πνεύματός, definite article and modifier included. While the connection with god is maintained, this time god is more specifically the origin of the holy spirit (ἀπὸ θεοῦ), rather than the spirit ambiguously being τοῦ θεοῦ. The building metaphor of temple and deity dwelling within maps onto the daily cultic reality of the Corinthians much more precisely in this verse than in 3:16, giving both verses the nuance of individuation for the *pneuma*, analogous to the personified god or gods found in sanctuaries across Corinth. I will discuss this image more in Chapter Four.

1 Corinthians 12 contains several references to *pneuma*, but one stands out as having the most potential for being understood by the Corinthians as a distinct divine entity. Famously, this is the chapter that describes the variety of spiritual gifts bestowed upon the assembly. Paul spends a long time describing them and ranking their importance, with an end in mind that he articulates in Chapter 14 – the relegation of disruptive tongue-speakers to a lower status in the assembly, anticipated by the hierarchical ranking of spiritual gifts in 12:28, with tongue-speakers last on the list of eight gifts.[164] Verse 3 has the first relevant reference to πνεῦμα θεοῦ, where Paul claims that those who speak ἐν πνεύματι θεοῦ are limited in their speech – they cannot curse Jesus. Conversely, those who say 'Jesus is lord' (Κύριος Ἰησοῦς) must be doing so ἐν πνεύματι ἁγίῳ. These datives can be understood instrumentally,[165] which fits well with materialist usage of *pneuma*.

---

[163] Some later manuscripts 'correct' or change τὸ σῶμα to τὰ σώματα (A<sup>c</sup> L Ψ 33. 81. 104. 365. 1175. 1505. 1881. 2464 *pm* lat sy<sup>p</sup>; Cl Cyp Lcf Ambst). Regardless of the singular or plural form of 'body', most commentators treat this statement as directed towards individuals rather than the assembly as a whole, almost ignoring the second person plural pronouns in the sentence. Fee, *First Epistle to the Corinthians*, 291: 'In referring to the body as the temple of the Spirit, Paul has taken the imagery that properly belongs to the church as a whole (cf. 3:16; 2 Cor. 6:16; Eph. 2:21–22) and in this single instance applied it to the individual believer.' See also Fitzmyer, *First Corinthians*, 216–17.

[164] Fitzmyer agrees: 'The numbering undoubtedly is meant to indicate an order of importance', but then hedges: 'but it could be simply an indication of historical time when such functions emerged in the church' (*First Corinthians*, 482).

[165] As do Timothy A. Brookins and Bruce W. Longenecker, *I Corinthians 10–16: A Handbook on the Greek Text* (Waco, TX: Baylor University Press, 2016), for the first one only (curiously), and as the NRSV translates both of them.

The next eleven verses are rife with references to *pneuma*, with verses 4–6 starting off a tricolon of sorts that seems to distinguish between the πνεῦμα, Jesus (as κύριος) and θεός, each described as responsible for three parallel activities in the life of the Corinthian assembly.[166] The *pneuma* is linked to a variety of χαρίσματα, the *kyrios* to a variety of διακονίαι and *theos* to a variety of ἐνεργήματα – distinct but overlapping qualities. Πνεῦμα, κύριος and θεός all appear with the attributive αὐτος, which hammers home the claims of the unifying nature of their activity – the same *pneuma*, the same *kyrios*, the same *theos*, whom the Corinthians all encounter in their collective lives together and who all act as the basis of this collective life. The *pneuma* stands alongside the *kyrios* and *theos*, which are both indisputably individual, personified divine actors responsible for important assembly characteristics, giving the clear impression of the same individuation and personification for the *pneuma*.

While there are clear references to *pneuma* in 2 Corinthians, Chapter 3 is both confusing in its use of *pneuma* and also clear in its personification. The first reference to πνεῦμα in this chapter (3:3) is located in a metaphor of letters of reference. The assembly, so Paul says, is 'a letter of Christ supplied by us, written not with ink but with the *pneuma* of the living god'. Here we have the three figures in one metaphor – Christ, the *pneuma* and god – seemingly distinct but with the *pneuma* qualified as πνεῦμα τοῦ θεοῦ ζῶντος. The dative πνεύματι used here is in parallel to μέλανι (ink), which clearly has no agency. So, μέλανι is a dative of instrument, which means that πνεύματι would be too. In the metaphor, *pneuma* is the instrument with which the assembly is 'written', like ink would be used in writing a letter. We have a distinction of *pneuma* from Christ and god, but we have a lack of agency, muddying the presentation of *pneuma* as the personification of a divine entity.

Verses 4–6 extend the imagery of the metaphor, talking about 'their' (Paul and his co-workers') source (god) of being competent (ἱκανός) in their ministry of the new covenant. Paul uses similar imagery of letter – with the term γράμματος instead of ἐπιστολή (v. 2) – contrasted with πνεύματος to describe the nature of their work ('of a written character' versus 'of a *pneuma*'), and then he specifies: 'For the letter kills, but the *pneuma* gives life.'[167] With the definite articles on both 'letter' and '*pneuma*', it becomes easier to argue for a personification of *pneuma* because there is individuation and agency (the *pneuma* gives

---

[166] Ibid., 66. Although not poetry in the strict sense, this parallelism evokes Hebrew poetic parallelism.

[167] This image of a life-giving *pneuma* is very similar to the image used to describe Christ as the last Adam in 1 Cor. 15:45: 'The last Adam [turned] into a life-giving *pneuma*' (ὁ ἔσχατος Ἀδὰμ εἰς πνεῦμα ζῳοποιοῦν), muddying the personification of πνεῦμα presented in 2 Cor. 3:6.

life).¹⁶⁸ But it is still not entirely clear. The next reference, in verse 8, confirms and extends the personification, where *pneuma* is the descriptor for the new ministry (ἡ διακονία τοῦ πνεύματος), the genitive perhaps even indicating the source or origin of the ministry. Again, if we are talking about Paul's intention, it is easier to argue a Stoic-like understanding of *pneuma*'s agency, since *pneuma* animates the universe and ties it together. But we are assuming relative ignorance of developed Stoic philosophical categories by most of Paul's assembly members.

Towards the end of 2 Corinthians 3, we have one of the more difficult passages in the letter with respect to the use of πνεῦμα. In the conclusion of Paul's convoluted argument about the new ministry, he brings in the image of Moses needing to wear a veil over his face to enable the people of Israel to view him without being affected by the residual divine glow he received during his encounter with god on Sinai.¹⁶⁹ Paul uses the veil as a metaphor for misunderstanding and says in verse 16, 'But whenever someone would turn to the lord (πρὸς κύριον), the veil is removed.' In the Septuagint, κύριος refers to god, whereas the normal usage of the term in Paul refers to Jesus (Christ), as in 'lord Jesus [Christ]'.¹⁷⁰ But Paul pivots in verse 17 and says, 'And the lord is the *pneuma*' (ὁ δὲ κύριος τὸ πνεῦμά ἐστιν) and follows this with 'and where the *pneuma* of the lord is, there is freedom' (οὗ δὲ τὸ πνεῦμα κυρίου, ἐλευθερία). The confusion is self-evident: is the lord the *pneuma* or is the usual designation – the *pneuma* of the lord – what is meant? At the end of verse 18, a somewhat ambiguous construction appears: καθάπερ ἀπὸ κυρίου πνεύματος. Although Greek word order allows for varying translation, it should probably be translated as 'just as from the lord *pneuma*'.¹⁷¹ The use of the predicate nominative in the first part of verse 17 blurs the distinction between κύριος of the Septuagint, κύριος of Paul (that is, Jesus (Christ)) and the *pneuma*, but by the end of verse 18 we have a fairly clear identification and personification of *pneuma* as κύριος. This reference could also be 2 Corinthians' version of 1 Corinthians 15:45, where 'the last Adam [i.e. Christ] [turned] into a life-endowing *pneuma*' (ἐγένετο . . . ὁ ἔσχατος Ἀδὰμ εἰς πνεῦμα ζῳοποιοῦν). If this is the case, then τὸ πνεῦμα κυρίου (2 Cor. 3:17) would be indicating that the lord Jesus is τὸ πνεῦμα, erasing the distinction between Jesus and τὸ πνεῦμα.

---

¹⁶⁸ Hans Heinrich Wendt, *Die Begriffe Fleisch und Geist im biblischen Sprachgebrauch* (Gotha: Berthes, 1878), 142–5, argued that its life-giving power determines the πνεῦμα's supernatural existence. See Rabens, *The Holy Spirit and Ethics in Paul*, 262–3, for a discussion about Wendt in the history of scholarship on the materialist notion of *pneuma*.

¹⁶⁹ See Exod. 34:33–5.

¹⁷⁰ In 1 Corinthians, every chapter except chapter 13 has at least one instance of κύριος in reference to Jesus.

¹⁷¹ See Margaret E. Thrall, *2 Corinthians: A Critical and Exegetical Commentary*, 2 vols (London: T & T Clark, 2004), 1:287, for the options for translating κυρίου πνεύματος.

Finally, 2 Corinthians ends with what commentators commonly think of as a 'Trinitarian form',[172] a 'triadic expression',[173] or at least 'proto-trinitarian':[174] 'The favour (ἡ χάρις) of the lord Jesus Christ and the love of god and the partnership of the holy *pneuma* (ἡ κοινωνία τοῦ ἁγίου πνεύματος) be with you all' (13:13).[175] Much as in 1 Corinthians 12:4–6, the three figures stand side by side, with no indication that *pneuma* is the stuff of the other two. God and Lord Jesus Christ are clearly divine personifications; when *pneuma* is put alongside them, it is very easy to imagine a Corinthian thinking the same of the *pneuma* as of god and (lord Jesus) Christ. This is the clearest grouping of these three where there is apparently a clear distinction among the three figures, and it seems like a well-established formulation of the grouping of divine figures by this time in Paul's interaction with the Corinthians.

While there are many places in the Corinthian correspondence where *pneuma* is used to describe something other than a personified deity, there are enough instances where there is seemingly individual personification of *pneuma* to warrant thinking that the marginally educated or non-educated members of Corinthian assembly (that is, the majority) might have understood it as a distinct divinity like (father) god and (lord Jesus) Christ. The Corinthian letters do not necessarily get us to Paul's original preaching, but I think we can assume that most of the major concepts that he writes about are not new to the Corinthians, even if their particular instantiation in the life of the assembly might have been by the time Paul wrote to them. In other words, I assume that the presentation of the *pneuma* is not created from scratch in 1 and 2 Corinthians. At the very least, it would have been familiar to the Corinthians from previous conversations and the extensive time Paul spent with them.

---

[172] Fee, *God's Empowering Presence*, 362. He even goes as far as to say, 'It needs to be noted, finally, how thoroughly and unmistakably Trinitarian this prayer is. That Paul would include the Holy Spirit as an equal member of this triadic formula, and that he would pray to the Spirit on their behalf, says as much about his understanding of the Spirit both as person and as deity as any direct statement of this kind ever could' (364–5).

[173] Larry W. Hurtado, 'The Binitarian Shape of Early Christian Worship', in *The Jewish Roots of Christological Monotheism: Papers from the St. Andrews Conference on the Historical Origins on the Worship of Jesus*, ed. Carey C. Newman, James R. Davila and Gladys S. Lewis (Leiden: Brill, 1999), 195.

[174] Craig S. Keener, *1–2 Corinthians* (Cambridge: Cambridge University Press, 2005), 246. Thrall comments, 'It would be possible to see in the Pauline formula one of the starting points of trinitarian development' (Thrall, *2 Corinthians*, 2:920). C. K. Barrett, *A Commentary on the Second Epistle to the Corinthians*, (London: Black, 1973), 345, opts for a proto-trinitarian view of the phrase: 'Christ, God, the Spirit, appearing in balanced clauses in one sentence, must stand on one divine level.'

[175] I translate the verse somewhat unconventionally because 'grace' (translating χάρις) is now a technical theological term with certain connotations that I do not think were clearly present among early Christians. Similarly with 'communion' or 'fellowship' for κοινωνία.

We can also posit a situation where 1 Corinthians in particular is Paul's attempt to clarify earlier discussions about the unfolding of the end times and the roles that (father) god, (lord Jesus) Christ and *pneuma* play in that unfolding. By the time of 1 Corinthians, Paul might, among other things, be trying to explain the role of these three figures to the better-educated members of the assembly by drawing upon philosophical concepts of *pneuma* that would be understandable to them. The initial conversations might or might not have included this sort of in-depth, philosophical talk. While he most likely included *pneuma* in his initial preaching, without the developed, philosophical clarifications of *pneuma* that we find in 1 Corinthians, the majority of Corinthians with whom Paul might have talked who later joined the movement (that is, the marginally educated or non-educated) would plausibly have heard *pneuma* in personified terms and not in materialist philosophical terms.

At the very least, we have two clear divine personifications, (father) god and (lord Jesus) Christ, and one possibly understood as a personified supernatural/divine being, *pneuma*, that form the centre of Paul's preaching. If we leave behind modern ideas of monotheism and polytheism when thinking about Paul, it is much easier to compare his language about these two or three figures with the cultural context in which he lived and worked.

CHAPTER FOUR

# Genealogy, History, Mythology and Cult of Paul's God(s)

In Chapters One and Two, I demonstrated a clear pattern in ancient Mediterranean (including Corinthian) religious practice of interacting with small groups of gods – chords of gods – that were connected by local or regional traditions (mythologies, histories, genealogies and cultic activity). This pattern did not just extend to a wide range of geographical locations, but it also encompassed various modes of religiosity,[1] a range of sacred settings (sanctuaries, temples, groves, civic institutions, voluntary associations and domestic settings) and extended periods of time (from the pre-classical era through to late antiquity). First-century Corinthians would have experienced and lived this pattern of religious practice, so we would have every reason to expect Paul's language about his god(s) to be received by the Corinthians within the categories of this social milieu. In Chapter Three, we looked at the variety of ways in which *pneuma* could have been understood by ancients, depending on their level of education and social location, and we investigated *pneuma* in Paul to see how his usage might have been understood by the heterogeneous assembly of Corinthians. We now turn to Paul's writings to discover whether his presentation of his three divine figures fits within the general pattern we saw in Chapters One and Two.

---

[1] Of Stanley Stowers's modes of religiosity, the three that are relevant to this study are the religion of everyday social exchange, civic religion and the religion of literary cultural producers. All of these modes centre around the kind of practices that the adherents undertake and in the contexts in which these practices happen. See Stanley K. Stowers, 'The Religion of Plant and Animal Offerings Versus the Religion of Meanings, Essences, and Textual Mysteries', in *Ancient Mediterranean Sacrifice*, ed. Jennifer Wright Knust and Zsuzsanna Várhelyi (Oxford: Oxford University Press, 2011), 35–6; and Stanley K. Stowers, 'Religion as a Social Kind' (unpublished manuscript, December 2020), presented to the Redescribing Christian Origins group at the 2020 SBL Annual Meeting. Many thanks to Prof. Stowers for allowing me to use this paper in preparing my book.

As I mentioned earlier, the only evidence we have for Paul's interaction with the Corinthians is the Corinthian correspondence. To reiterate, the two major problems are that the evidence is told from Paul's perspective and not the Corinthians' perspective, and that the letters are not the earliest interaction that Paul had with the Corinthians. The only thing we can do with this evidence is to assume that there was some fundamental continuity between the early days of the Paul–Corinthians interaction and the letters that he wrote them several years later.[2] Because Paul was a product of his culture in all its complexity, I will assume that his presentation of his god(s) was not something that he developed from scratch in the letters but instead reflected his Jewish traditions, albeit interpreted through the lens of what he believed was an experience of the risen Christ. Although Paul's unpacking of his understanding of god, Christ and *pneuma* certainly developed to a certain extent by the time he wrote his letters, as his interaction with the Corinthians happened after his purported experience of Christ, there does not seem to be any indication that there was a presentation of his god(s) in the letters that was either new or contradictory to a previous presentation.[3]

Two or three distinct figures working together comprised Paul's presentation of his god(s), and his appeals to the Corinthians to join the movement and to remain within it relied on this depiction of the divine realm. We have to imagine what that would have sounded like to the Corinthians, whose regular religious practice involved small groups of gods. One thing to keep in mind is the heterogeneity of the Corinthians in terms of education and economic security. Different Corinthians likely understood Paul's references to *pneuma* differently, regardless of how Paul intended. Those who were more economically secure, and certain people affiliated with them, likely had more formal education and therefore were more likely to have understood *pneuma* in materialist philosophical terms; whereas those with less economic security – and who were therefore less likely to have formal education – probably would have understood *pneuma* as a divine being distinct from the other two.[4] As I go

---

[2] Joseph Fitzmyer has a particularly detailed treatment of Pauline chronology, especially as it relates to Corinth. The extant correspondence (1 and 2 Corinthians) omits at least one and maybe two letters that Paul wrote to the Corinthians (one before the writing of 1 Corinthians and one in between 1 and 2 Corinthians). This complex collection of letters and perhaps some information from Acts witness to Paul's interaction with the Corinthians during the better part of the 50s CE. See Joseph A. Fitzmyer, *First Corinthians* (New Haven: Yale University Press, 2008), 37–45.

[3] Even the somewhat ill-fitting 2 Cor. 6:14–7:1 – possibly a fragment from an early letter of Paul inserted between 6:13 and 7:2, or some other extra-mural fragment by Paul or someone else – still invokes Christ as a divine entity distinct from god. Taken with the temple imagery from the passages from 1 Cor. 3:16 and 6:19, we might also be able to understand the *pneuma* as being involved in an oblique way in that fragment. I will discuss this passage below in more detail.

[4] See Chapter Three for a more detailed treatment of this topic.

through my analysis below, I will try to preserve these varying understandings of *pneuma* among the Corinthians. Whether it is two (plus a related materialist *pneuma*) or three divine beings that constituted Paul's god(s) matters less in what follows than the idea of there being more than one divine being in his presentation.

We turn now to a more detailed examination of 1 and 2 Corinthians to see if and how these figures are related genealogically, historically, mythologically and cultically. If there is enough evidence of these kinds of relationships between the divine figures – and I think there is – then we can posit a fundamental similarity between the basic categories of Paul's presentation of his god(s) and the Corinthians' experience of small groups of gods in Corinth and beyond. I do not intend to provide a comprehensive treatment of all aspects of Paul's mythology or the theological ramifications of Jesus's death and resurrection. Rather, I will identify and describe in these two letters the elements of the pattern we argued for in Chapters One and Two, which will allow me to posit a reasonable scenario of reception by Paul's Corinthians.

## Genealogy, History, Mythology

It is difficult to separate out history and myth when talking about the way in which Israel's past is described in Paul's writings. He quotes or refers to Israel's scriptures extensively, which he considers history, but he does not simply repeat the events depicted there. 'Rewriting' of scripture only partially matches scribal comparands from his era and before, but Paul is his own person and I do not think that 'rewritten scripture' best characterises what he is doing in his writings.[5] He more fundamentally re-envisions Israel's past, present and future in light of his purported experience of the risen Christ, so he fits well under the concept of 'mythmaker', as described in the Introduction. Paul's reinterpretation of Israel's past in light of his current circumstances also fits well with what Bruce Lincoln says regarding narratives about beginnings told by groups or institutions:

> Sometimes such narratives style themselves 'origin myths'; sometimes 'histories of foundation'. Sometimes they advance no generic claims and defy easy categorization, blurring – indeed defying – the distinction

---

[5] See József Zsengellér, *Rewritten Bible after Fifty Years: Texts, Terms, or Techniques? A Last Dialogue with Geza Vermes* (Leiden: Brill, 2014), for a series of essays assessing the state of the field in Second Temple Judaism. Curiously, while there are essays on Philo, Josephus, Midrash, Samaritan literature and even Nag Hammadi, there are no essays on Paul, as if he were not a Jew and did not contribute to the literary production of the Second Temple period.

between history and myth. This interstitial status may produce confusion for analysts and others, but it adds to the stories' fascination.[6]

Paul certainly blurs or even defies the distinction between myth and history, especially since much of how Israel's past, present and future unfold for him is fundamentally tied to the three divine figures he presents, two of which were not envisioned as part of Israel's past prior to Paul's writings.[7] So, in Paul's case, and in the case of the Corinthians who heard him, history and mythology go hand in hand.

**God**

Genealogy and history/mythology are interconnected for Paul's three divine figures, just as they are for local groups of divine figures in Corinth. 'God' is the main figure of this triad, and Paul uses this designator most frequently in the Corinthian letters for this figure – more than a hundred times in 1 Corinthians and over seventy times in 2 Corinthians. God is clearly the architect of the events of Israel's unfolding history; god is active in Paul's present,[8] in Israel's past[9] and in the cosmos's future.[10] But god is also a father god, and is so in three ways: simply 'the father'; the father of Christ; and the father of Paul and the Corinthians.

---

[6] Bruce Lincoln, *Between History and Myth: Stories of Harald Fairhair and the Founding of the State* (Chicago: University of Chicago Press, 2014), 1.

[7] While the 'spirit' was an animating force for prophets, it was not depicted as a divine entity distinct from Israel's god.

[8] Among god's actions in Paul's present: calling (Paul: 1 Cor. 1:1; Jews and Greeks: 1 Cor. 1:24; 'us' and 'them': 1 Cor. 7:15–17); saving those who believe (1 Cor. 1:21); choosing the weak to nullify the powerful (1 Cor. 1:28); making grow (1 Cor. 3:7); giving his *pneuma* (1 Cor. 2:12–14); revealing mysteries (1 Cor. 4:1); being faithful (1 Cor. 10:13; 2 Cor. 1:18); arranging the parts of the 'body' (1 Cor. 12:18–31); being the head of Christ (1 Cor. 11:3); sending Paul and his co-workers (2 Cor. 2:17); shining the light of knowledge (2 Cor. 4:6); making Christ to be sin 'for us' (2 Cor. 5:21); comforting/consoling (2 Cor. 1:4; 7:6); giving *charis* (1 Cor. 1:4; 2 Cor. 8:1; 9:14); activating charisms among the Corinthians (1 Cor. 12:6); giving victory to the assembly (1 Cor. 15:57); appealing to Corinthians through Paul and co-workers (2 Cor. 5:20).

[9] Among god's past actions: making foolish the world's wisdom (1 Cor. 1:20, 27–9); decreeing wisdom 'before the ages' (1 Cor. 2:7); raising Christ (1 Cor. 6:14; 15:15); appointing various gifts (1 Cor. 12:28); subjecting all things to himself (1 Cor. 15:27); making Paul and his co-workers apostles (2 Cor. 1:1; 2:17); speaking through scripture (2 Cor. 4:6; 6:16); giving the *pneuma* (2 Cor. 5:5); reconciling the world to himself (2 Cor. 5:18–19).

[10] Among god's future actions: destroying food and stomach (1 Cor. 6:13); raising 'us' or the dead (1 Cor. 6:14; 2 Cor. 1:9); striking down in the wilderness (1 Cor. 10:5); receiving the kingdom from Christ (1 Cor. 15:24); being all in all (1 Cor. 15:28); humbling Paul before the Corinthians (2 Cor. 12:21).

The first designator occurs only twice – god the father (εἷς θεὸς ὁ πατήρ, 1 Cor. 8:6; τῷ θεῷ καὶ πατρί, 1 Cor. 15:24) – but it has cosmic overtones both times. 1 Corinthians 8:6 refers to the one god of Israel's history, but the complex of stories and events around that god is not just a designator declared within a cultural vacuum. It is a political statement over and against the other competing gods that occupy the cultural spaces in which Israel lives. It is a declaration of superiority: of all the gods Israel encounters among its cultural interlocutors, the god of Israel is the one superior god.[11] Paul reinforces this idea with the qualifying phrase 'from whom are all things and we are [going] toward him' (ἐξ οὗ τὰ πάντα καὶ ἡμεῖς εἰς αὐτόν). His father god is the source of everything and the reason for the Corinthian assembly's existence. The second occurrence (15:24) is literally a cosmic reference because it marks the moment at the end times when the kingdom is handed over to god by Christ. This moment is the final stage of the eschatological process, in which the deity takes complete control of the universe after Christ defeats all enemies and hands over the kingdom, in order that 'god might be all in all' (ἵνα ᾖ ὁ θεὸς [τὰ] πάντα ἐν πᾶσιν; 15:28). At this moment of cosmic finality and superiority, god is called 'god and father', indicating royalty and universal patriarchy – the father of the universe, similar to other chief gods such as Greek Zeus or Roman Jupiter. In short, Paul's god controls everything in the cosmos. This is the basis for Paul's mythology about his god, and it is intertwined with the history of Israel – past, present and future – as it unfolds before Paul's eyes.

The second use of 'father' to describe Paul's god is father of Christ and, logically, Christ as son of the father god. Here we see the mingling of mythological and genealogical categories. Two simple and virtually identical references in 2 Corinthians 1:3 and 11:31 (ὁ θεὸς καὶ πατὴρ τοῦ κυρίου ἡμῶν Ἰησοῦ [Χριστοῦ in 1:3]) are both associated with a declaration of blessing

---

[11] See Raymond F. Collins, *First Corinthians* (Collegeville, MN: Liturgical Press, 1999), 315: 'In contrast to the so-called gods recognized by elements of the Corinthian population, their many gods and lords, Paul places the one God of his biblical tradition (cf. Deut. 6:4). The contrast functions on two levels. There is a contrast between the anonymous persons to whom allusion is made in Paul's "so-called" of verse 5 and the "us" of verse 6. There is also a contrast between the many gods and many lords of popular perception and the one God and one Lord of the Christian confession.' While Collins discusses the various gods present in Corinth according to several authors (Pausanias, in particular), he ignores the possibility of this context meaning anything other than a contrasting context to Paul's 'monotheistic confession of faith', as he labels this section of the letter (313). Collins relies on Hurtado to explain away any chance of Paul's statement being understood as anything other than monotheism – a 'Christian mutation of the Jewish monotheistic tradition' (315, citing Larry W. Hurtado, *One God, One Lord: Early Christian Devotion and Ancient Jewish Monotheism* (Philadelphia: Fortress, 1988), 97–9). To me, this smacks of modern Christian interpreters trying desperately to uphold later trinitarian doctrines rather than trying to make sense of Paul's comments in first-century Jewish, Greek and Roman contexts.

by Paul, but more importantly they establish the foundational relationship between the two divine figures. Jesus does not exist independent of the father god but in relation to him.[12] Because of this relationship, Jesus is called 'his son' (1 Cor. 1:9) or 'the son of god' (2 Cor. 1:19) or just 'the son' (1 Cor. 15:28).[13] The two references in 1 Corinthians are important for two different reasons. As we have already seen, 15:28 is part of Paul's description of the final moments of the eschaton, when the kingdom is handed over to god by Christ. The filial designation sets up a hierarchical process whereby the son works to subject all things to himself, but then the 'son himself is subjected to the one who subjects all things to himself, in order that god may be all in all' (αὐτὸς ὁ υἱὸς ὑποταγήσεται τῷ ὑποτάξαντι αὐτῷ τὰ πάντα, ἵνα ᾖ ὁ θεὸς [τὰ] πάντα ἐν πᾶσιν, 1 Cor. 15:28). The role of the son helps establishes the final order of the cosmos, with god at the top over all things and in all things.[14] Paul's cosmic myth relies on the filial relationship between father and son deities, showing the mythological importance of the son.

The reference in 1:9 reads, 'Faithful is god, through whom you were called into the association of his son Jesus Christ our lord' (πιστὸς ὁ θεός, δι' οὗ ἐκλήθητε εἰς κοινωνίαν τοῦ υἱοῦ αὐτοῦ Ἰησοῦ Χριστοῦ τοῦ κυρίου ἡμῶν). Paul asserts that his god is not just the god of the universe but also the one who directs the Corinthians to associate with Jesus, god's son. The association is expressed in filial terms. The Corinthians are called into association not only with Jesus but also with god's son, 'Jesus Christ our lord'. (I will unpack 'Christ our lord' below, when talking about the ramifications of these titles for the mythology of the Corinthian assembly.) The filial relationship grounds the association between the Corinthians, on the one hand, and Jesus and god, on the other.

The final use of 'father' to describe Paul's god is 'god our father', both times found in the opening greetings of the two letters: χάρις ὑμῖν καὶ εἰρήνη ἀπὸ θεοῦ πατρὸς ἡμῶν καὶ κυρίου Ἰησοῦ Χριστοῦ ('χάρις[15] to you and peace from god our father and the lord Jesus Christ', identical in 1 Corinthians 1:3 and 2 Corinthians 1:2[16]). While this seems like an innocuous blessing of the Corinthians to start off the letters in positive ways, I think there is an

---

[12] The later conciliar debates about the origins of Jesus are not applicable here, but Paul's language and assertions about Jesus certainly played a role in those debates.

[13] This last reference is the only time that Paul uses 'the son' in reference to Christ. As Fitzmyer, *First Corinthians*, 578, writes: 'Implicitly it is playing on the mutual relation of "son" and "father" that every human being instinctively knows; but it is also one of the NT springboards for the relation of two persons of the Trinity in later Christian theology.'

[14] Ibid., 575: 'Paul ends these five verses (24–28) with a purpose clause that affirms that God (the Father, 15:24) will be the goal or final cause of everything.'

[15] I choose to leave χάρις untranslated as I do not think that the Paul's usage of the term is reflected in the theological development that has accumulated over the centuries since that time.

[16] See also Phil. 1:2.

important feature that ties into the other two uses of 'father' as a designator for god.[17] 'Our father' indicates a filial relationship between the Corinthians and god, but it also indicates a familial relationship among the Corinthians themselves, hearkening to the use of κοινωνία in 1 Corinthians 1:9. By starting each letter this way, Paul is not just stating what he thinks is the identity of his god, but he is also asserting the familial relationship that he thinks exists – or should exist – among the Corinthians. Given his discussion of factionalism in 1 Corinthians and a rupture between him and the Corinthians described in 2 Corinthians, this opening blessing is not innocuous but a serious statement expressing the ideal status of the assembly in the face of real divisions. Further, since Jesus is already depicted as son to the father, then this would make the Corinthians siblings with each other and Jesus. What Paul is claiming and encouraging for the Corinthians through this imagery is that they be socially formed into a family with each other and with god. Since myth and mythic language facilitates social formation, the genealogical language that Paul uses can be thought of mythically as well.[18]

**Christ Jesus**

As I have discussed above, the filial relationship between god and Jesus grounds the cosmic mythology Paul presents in 1 Corinthians 15. There are also two other designators that speak to the historical/mythological role that Jesus plays for Paul and that affect his presentation of the divine figures to the Corinthians. The first is Χριστός, which is often used by Paul as part of a double name for Jesus, it seems,[19] but which is also used as a name/term independent of Ἰησοῦς. The term has clear royal overtones in the history of ancient Near Eastern and Mediterranean culture.[20] These overtones speak to Jesus's cosmic

---

[17] Frank J. Matera, *II Corinthians: A Commentary* (Louisville, KY: Westminster John Knox, 2003), 35, characterises 2 Cor. 1:1–11 as 'not insignificant; for, as he often does in his correspondence, Paul employs these introductory verses to signal important themes that he will develop in the body of the letter'.

[18] See the Introduction above; and see the essays in Ron Cameron and Merrill P. Miller, *Redescribing Paul and the Corinthians* (Atlanta: SBL, 2011), for an extended discussion of social formation and mythmaking in Paul's Corinthian letters.

[19] Fitzmyer, *First Corinthians*, 124, where he also notes that Paul is the only New Testament writer who uses 'Christ Jesus', other than several passages in Acts that Fitzmyer dismisses as being introduced by copyists 'familiar with Pauline usage'. See also Collins, *First Corinthians*, 48, for a brief discussion of Christ in relation to some other designators.

[20] See Adela Yarbro Collins and John J. Collins, *King and Messiah as Son of God: Divine, Human, and Angelic Figures in Biblical and Related Literature* (Grand Rapids, MI: Eerdmans, 2008), and Joseph A. Fitzmyer, *The One Who Is to Come* (Grand Rapids, MI: Eerdmans, 2007), for excellent treatments of the royal overtones of messianic language, including χριστός, in the ancient Near East.

royal role in 1 Corinthians 15:20–8, where Χριστός and υἱός both refer to the same figure – the one who subjugates all enemies and turns the kingdom over to the father – and they fit well with the long-standing and widespread royal ideology of kings being sons of gods and therefore divine figures. It is therefore worth giving a few examples of the royal overtones of divine sonship from Hellenistic Greek and Roman culture, since Corinth stood at the intersection of both.

We see a good example in Theokritos, Idyll 17, regarding Alexander the Great and Ptolemy I:

> Him [Herakles] the father made equal in honor even to the blessed immortals, and a golden throne is built for him in the house of Zeus; beside him ... sits Alexander ... who brought destruction to the Persians ... Both [Alexander and Ptolemy I] have as ancestor the mighty son of Herakles, and both trace their family back in the end to Herakles.[21]

What is important here for our purposes is that 'all three boasted divine parentage'.[22] Other stories like this one developed in many cities regarding other Hellenistic kings, especially the Diodokoi, resulting in divine honours being paid these kings. Ptolemy IV Philopator is a good example. He won a victory against Antiochus III at Raphia in 217 BCE and it was configured as a victory of Horus over Seth,[23] a myth that finds it fullest extant expression in 'The Contendings of Horus and Seth', a twentieth-dynasty (twelfth-century BCE) Egyptian literary work narrating the battles between Horus and Seth for the right to succeed Osiris as king of Egypt. Ptolemy IV's successor, Ptolemy V Epiphanes, is depicted in line 3 of the Rosetta stone as 'living image of Zeus' (εἰκόνος ζώσης τοῦ Διός) and 'son of Helios' (or 'the sun') (υἱοῦ τοῦ Ἡλίου). In a similar way, the divine origin of Alexander provides a model for

---

[21] τῆνον καὶ μακάρεσσι πατὴρ ὁμότιμον ἔθηκενἀθανάτοις, καί οἱ χρύσεος θρόνος ἐν Διὸς οἴκῳ δέδμηται· παρὰ δ' αὐτὸν Ἀλέξανδρος φίλα εἰδώςἑδριάει, Πέρσαισι βαρὺς θεὸς αἰολομίτρας. ἀντία δ' Ἡρακλῆος ἕδρα κενταυροφόνοιοἵδρυται στερεοῖο τετυγμένα ἐξ ἀδάμαντος· ἔνθα σὺν ἄλλοισιν θαλίας ἔχει Οὐρανίδῃσι, χαίρων υἱωνῶν περιώσιον υἱωνοῖσιν, ὅττι σφεων Κρονίδης μελέων ἐξείλετο γῆρας, ἀθάνατοι δὲ καλεῦνται ἑοὶ νέποδες γεγαῶτες. ἄμφω γὰρ πρόγονός σφιν ὁ καρτερὸς Ἡρακλείδας, ἀμφότεροι δ' ἀριθμεῦνται ἐς ἔσχατον Ἡρακλῆα (Theocritus, *Encomium of Ptolemy Philadelphus*, translated in Richard Hunter, ed. and trans., *Theocritus: Encomium of Ptolemy Philadelphus. Text and Translation with Introduction and Commentary* (Berkeley: University of California Press, 2003), 79).

[22] Ivana Petrovic, 'Deification: Gods or Men?', in *The Oxford Handbook of Ancient Greek Religion*, ed. Esther Eidinow and Julia Kindt (Oxford: Oxford University Press, 2015), 435.

[23] Yarbro Collins and Collins, *King and Messiah*, 50.

a story of Seleucus's mother saying that she had a dream where she learned of his conception by Apollo.[24]

The notion of a king as offspring of a divine figure also existed in Rome, with some elements in continuity with the history of notions and practices of divine kingship in Hellenistic times, and other elements novel to the Roman context. After the many great deeds attributed to Julius Caesar and his ascension to power over Rome, he was granted divine-like honours just before his assassination. This status meant that a priest was assigned to his cult, his house was fitted with a pediment like that of a temple, and his image was included along with those of the gods in formal processions. After his assassination, he was formally declared divinised in 42 BCE, thus making him *divus Iulius*.[25]

Especially in the eastern provinces of the empire, Augustus became the centre of a complex and extensive apparatus of divine honours offered '"to", "for" and "by" the Emperor', in the words of Bruce Winter.[26] Being the adopted son of Julius, he was de facto a son of a god, which thereby invested him with a certain divine status upon his ascent to the throne. However, this was not the only claim to his divine sonship. Suetonius tells us about the tradition surrounding Augustus's conception, in which his mother, Atia, fell asleep in the temple of Apollo and was visited by a serpent which permanently pigmented her skin. Augustus was born nine months later and was thus thought of as son of Apollo (Suet. *Aug.* 94.4). Clearly this story was fashioned in the manner of the traditions surrounding the miraculous conception of Alexander the Great, interweaving Alexander's and Augustus's public characterisations as having divine origins and thus being the offspring of the gods.

One of the best examples of the development of notions of Roman imperial divine sonship is an inscription from a statue base found at Lapethos in

---

[24] See ibid., *King and Messiah*, 52, and literature cited there. For more on Hellenistic kings and the divine honours given to them, and their possible apotheosis, see K. Buraselis and S. Aneziri, 'Die griechische und hellenistische Apotheose', *ThesCRA* (2004): 158–86; S. Caneva, 'Queens and Ruler Cults in Early Hellenism: Observations on Festivals, and on the Administration and Ideological Meaning of Cults', *Kernos* 25 (2012): 75–102; Angelos Chaniotis, 'The Divinity of Hellenistic Rulers', in *A Companion to the Hellenistic World*, ed. A. Erskine (Malden, MA: Blackwell, 2003), 431–46; and P. Iossif, A. S. Chankowski, and C. C. Lorber, eds., *More than Men, Less than Gods: Studies on Royal Cult and Imperial Worship* (Leuven: Peters, 2011).

[25] Mary Beard, John North and Simon Price, *Religions of Rome*, 2 vols (Cambridge: Cambridge University Press, 1998), 1:140, including quote.

[26] Bruce W. Winter, *Divine Honours for the Caesars: The First Christians' Responses* (Grand Rapids, MI: Eerdmans, 2015), 49. See also Michael Peppard, 'Brother against Brother: Controversiae about Inheritance Disputes and 1 Corinthians 6:1–11', *JBL* 133 (2014): 91: 'Modern scholars estimate that between 25,000 and 50,000 portraits of Augustus existed in the Roman Empire – about one portrait for every 1,000–2,000 people ... It does not seem an exaggeration to call the emperor – especially Augustus – the only Empire-wide god in the Roman pantheon.' See Simon Price, *Rituals and Power: The Roman Imperial Cult in Asia Minor* (Cambridge: Cambridge University Press, 1984), for the seminal and thorough treatment of imperial cultic activity in Asia Minor.

Cyprus, dated 29/30 CE.²⁷ The inscription is a dedication to Tiberius by the priest Adrastos. It is worth quoting in full:

> To the god Tiberius Augustus, son of the god Augustus, Emperor, greatest high priest, tribunicia potestas the 31st time, in the time of Lucius Axius Naso, proconsul, and Marcus Etrilius Lupercus, legatus, and Gaius Flavius Figulus, quaestor. Adrastos son of Adrastos, friend of Caesar, the hereditary priest of the sanctuary and statue of Tiberius Caesar Augustus established in the gymnasium by him from his own means, the patriot and model of virtue, the one serving free of charge and voluntarily as gymnasiarch and the priest of the gods in the gymnasium, established the sanctuary and the statue to his god at his own expense, while Dionysius son of Dionysius was ephebarch along with Apollodorus, friend of Caesar. Adrastos son of Adrastos, friend of Caesar dedicates this, co-dedicated with his son Adrastos, friend of Caesar, also free of charge and voluntarily as gymnasiarch for children, on the birthday of Tiberius. (Year) 16, Apogonikos 24.²⁸

Regardless of the possible nature of this inscription as a political dedication to the emperor by an underling, perhaps to win Tiberius's favour, there is no hesitation in the dedication of the statue to Tiberius as both a god (θεῶι) and a son of the god Augustus (θεοῦ Σεβαστοῦ υἱῶι). Adrastos also names himself as the priest of the sanctuary and the statue of Tiberius, which seems to be located within the gymnasium along with all the other gods present there,

---

²⁷ Thanks to Michael Peppard for bringing this inscription to my attention.
²⁸ My translation. The text of *IGR* III 933 is:

Τιβερίωι Καίσαρι Σεβαστῶι θεῶι θεοῦ Σεβαστοῦ υἱῶι,
Αὐτοκράτορι, ἀρχιερεῖ μεγίστωι, δημαρχικῆς ἐξουσίας
τὸ λα, ἐπὶ Λευκίου Ἀξίου Νάσονος ἀνθυπάτου καὶ Μάρκου
Ἐτρειλίου Λουπέρκου πρεσβευτοῦ καὶ Γαίου Φλαβίου Φίγλου ταμία {ι},
Ἄδραστος Ἀδράστου φιλόκαισαρ, ὁ ἐνγενικὸς ἱερεὺς τοῦ
ἐν τῷ γυμνασίωι κατεσκευασμένου ὑπὸ αὐτοῦ ἐκ τοῦ ἰδίου
Τιβερίου Καίσαρος Σεβαστοῦ ναοῦ καὶ ἀγάλματος, ὁ φιλόπατρις
καὶ πανάρετος, καὶ δωρεὰν καὶ αὐθαίρετος γυμνασίαρχος καὶ
ἱερεὺς τῶν ἐν γυμνασίωι θεῶν κατεσκεύασεν τὸν ναὸν καὶ
τὸ ἄγαλμα ἰδίοις ἀναλώμασιν τῶι α<ὑ>τοῦ θεῶι, ἐφηβαρχοῦντος
Διονυσίου τοῦ Διονυσίου τοῦ καὶ Ἀπολλοδότου φιλοκαίσαρος.
Ἄδραστος Ἀδράστου φιλόκαισαρ καθιέρωσεν συνκαθιεροῦντος
καὶ τοῦ υἱοῦ αὐτοῦ Ἀδράστου φιλοκαίσαρος, τοῦ καὶ αὐτοῦ δωρεὰν
καὶ αὐθαιρέτου γυμνασιάρχου τῶν παίδων, τῆι γενεσίωι
Τιβερίου,
                      (ἔτους) ις, Ἀπογονικοῦ κδ.

further indication of the nature of sanctuary life being constituted by small groups of gods.

Χριστός fits within this historical/cultural context, so when Paul uses this term as a name for Jesus, the Corinthians would likely have heard it as a royal term, even though Paul's use of it might also include Jewish messianic overtones. The royal role that Jesus plays is particularly manifest in 1 Corinthians 15:20–8, as discussed briefly above. Christ hands over the kingdom to god at the end times, after destroying all of god's enemies, putting them 'under his feet' (verses 24–7).[29] But this last role for Christ is predicated on and grounded in his resurrection from the dead, which is the main subject of the chapter. The resurrection of Christ is not a singular event but something that inaugurates a new cosmic era. Christ is the 'first fruits of those who have fallen asleep' (ἀπαρχὴ τῶν κεκοιμημένων; 15:20), and he is the undoing of death generally, which was brought into human existence by Adam: 'For just as all die by Adam, so also all will be made alive by Christ' (verse 22).[30] Towards the end of the chapter, Christ enables the final victory over death through his resurrection from death (verses 54–7). In other words, his royal role is played out beginning with his death and resurrection, and at the end of the process as god's king on earth who consolidates god's power.

The beginning of the process of Christ's kingship is also tied in with the local history/mythology of the Corinthian assembly, or at least this seems to be what Paul is asserting at the beginning of Chapter 15.[31] He prefaces his argument by reminding the Corinthians of the basis of their life together, the content of 'good news which I announced to you, which you also received, in which you also stand, and through which you are being rescued' (15:1–2).[32] His recitation of the tradition as it pertains to Christ begins with a divine passive in verse 2 (that is, the gospel is the means by which god is saving the Corinthians), but then Paul goes on to describe the definitive act of history, in his mind: 'that Christ died on behalf of our sins according to the scriptures, and that he was buried, and that he was raised on the third day according to the scriptures' (15:3–4).[33] Paul is reciting the history of Israel, or at least what he sees as the latest episode in it, but he is also rewriting and reinterpreting

---

[29] The quotation (from verse 27) draws on Ps. 8:6.
[30] ὥσπερ γὰρ ἐν τῷ Ἀδὰμ πάντες ἀποθνῄσκουσιν, οὕτως καὶ ἐν τῷ Χριστῷ πάντες ζῳοποιηθήσονται. I think both prepositional phrases that begin with ἐν τῷ make most sense as instrumental datives.
[31] This local history/mythology intersects significantly with the wider movement outside Corinth, but Paul formulates it specifically for the needs of the Corinthians at this moment.
[32] τὸ εὐαγγέλιον ὃ εὐηγγελισάμην ὑμῖν, ὃ καὶ παρελάβετε, ἐν ᾧ καὶ ἑστήκατε, δι' οὗ καὶ σῴζεσθε, τίνι λόγῳ εὐηγγελισάμην ὑμῖν εἰ κατέχετε, ἐκτὸς εἰ μὴ εἰκῇ ἐπιστεύσατε.
[33] ὅτι Χριστὸς ἀπέθανεν ὑπὲρ τῶν ἁμαρτιῶν ἡμῶν κατὰ τὰς γραφὰς καὶ ὅτι ἐτάφη καὶ ὅτι ἐγήγερται τῇ ἡμέρᾳ τῇ τρίτῃ κατὰ τὰς γραφάς.

this history to include Christ at the most foundational level. Although god is not mentioned directly, the events of Christ's death, burial and resurrection happen 'according to scripture', which is the story of Israel's interaction with their god and which is considered by Paul as god's authoritative witness to that history. So, for Paul, Christ's death and resurrection happening 'according to scripture' means that it is foretold – even if not explicitly – according to god's will, however that is defined.

Many have tried to find where in the Hebrew Bible or Septuagint these events are foretold, but these scholars misunderstand the purpose of 'according to the scriptures'. This search has been fruitless because Paul is not thinking canonically, in the way that so many modern Christians think, and so he is not referring to a passage of scripture but a general ethos of scripture. 'According to the scriptures' is therefore best understood as 'according to god's teachings and desire for human history'. Richard B. Hays's body of work on the interpretation of scripture by Paul discusses this idea at length, but he makes the salient point in 'Three Dramatic Roles: The Law in Romans 3–4':

> The Law (=Scripture) also bears witness more generally, in Paul's understanding, to the gospel . . . Indeed, elsewhere he asserts it as a matter of the first importance that the death and resurrection of Jesus occurred 'according to the Scriptures' (1 Cor 15:3–4), and in a passage such as Rom 15:3 he assumes that Christ is the speaker of Ps 69, without feeling the need to supply any supporting argument for this extraordinary assertion. The conclusion that follows from such observations is that the whole question of Paul's reading of Scripture as a witness to Jesus Christ demands careful attention.[34]

However, even Hays makes the error of trying to find a 'script' or particular passage in scripture from which Paul reads and interprets the impact of Christ's life, death and resurrection: he argues that the 'psalms of the Righteous Sufferer' may be 'the "Scripture" to which the confessional formula of 1 Cor 15:3–4 refers'.[35] As I have argued elsewhere, there are serious problems with characterising these lament psalms as 'psalms of the Righteous Sufferer' because they do not portray the psalmist as righteous or innocent but as complaining to god that the suffering seems out of place for the kind of relationship experienced in the past between god and the psalmist (imagined or referred to

---

[34] Richard B. Hays, 'Three Dramatic Roles: The Law in Romans 3–4', in *The Conversion of the Imagination: Paul as Interpreter of Israel's Scripture* (Grand Rapids, MI: Eerdmans, 2005), 95–6.

[35] Richard B. Hays, 'Christ Prays the Psalms', in *The Conversion of the Imagination*, 118.

as David, hardly a completely righteous or innocent figure by any measure).³⁶ Paul is not referring to a defined text or group of texts as a script for Jesus's life – the variety of scripture passages he uses throughout his writings clearly shows this – but instead he is reimagining the history of Israel in the light of Christ's life, death and resurrection.³⁷ In other words, he is creating a new Israelite mythology, written through the lens of Christ.³⁸

The creative retelling and weaving together of several stories from Israel's history in 1 Corinthians 10:1–5 again present Christ within this history, essentially rewriting the mythology of Israel to include Christ.

> Our forefathers all were under the cloud and all passed through the sea, and all were baptized into Moses in the cloud and in the sea, and all ate the same spiritual food, and all drank the same spiritual drink. For they drank from the spiritual rock that followed [them], and the rock was Christ. (10:1–4)³⁹

This is a remarkable reworking of the traditions of Israel. Not only are several episodes of the Exodus drama conflated into a single narrative, but the terminology used to tell the story betrays Paul's perspective as a follower of Christ. The Hebrews' journey out of Egypt – being led by the pillar of cloud by day and fire by night (Exod. 13:17–22), guiding them to the Red Sea, where they crossed with the miraculous help of god mediated through Moses (Exod. 14:1–31) – is described with baptismal language nowhere present in the story but taken from the baptismal practices of early Jesus followers.⁴⁰ The language

---

³⁶ Stephen P. Ahearne-Kroll, *The Psalms of Lament in Mark's Passion: Jesus' Davidic Suffering* (Cambridge: Cambridge University Press, 2007), 13–16, and throughout. If one defines 'righteous' as someone in right relationship with god (that is, a faithful relationship, loyal only to god), regardless of the person's moral life, then one might be able to make the argument for this characterisation of the psalms of individual lament. But attaching this to the life of Christ would raise all sorts of problems with regard to the moral life of Jesus that I imagine most commentators would not want to entertain.

³⁷ Collins, *First Corinthians*, 530, calls 'according to the scriptures' 'not a fulfillment formula … [but] an interpretive formula'. I think this is exactly right.

³⁸ One thinks of Bruce Lincoln's foundational insight in *Theorizing Myth* (Chicago: University of Chicago Press, 1999), 147, where he defines myth as 'ideology in narrative form'. Lincoln argues for a conscious authorial attempt in a wide range of literature in various contexts to advance particular ideologies in the foundational narratives of their cultures and historical moments. Paul is acting no differently in his own context of Jewish culture in the first century.

³⁹ οἱ πατέρες ἡμῶν πάντες ὑπὸ τὴν νεφέλην ἦσαν καὶ πάντες διὰ τῆς θαλάσσης διῆλθον καὶ πάντες εἰς τὸν Μωϋσῆν ἐβαπτίσθησαν ἐν τῇ νεφέλῃ καὶ ἐν τῇ θαλάσσῃ καὶ πάντες τὸ αὐτὸ πνευματικὸν βρῶμα ἔφαγον καὶ πάντες τὸ αὐτὸ πνευματικὸν ἔπιον πόμα· ἔπινον γὰρ ἐκ πνευματικῆς ἀκολουθούσης πέτρας, ἡ πέτρα δὲ ἦν ὁ Χριστός.

⁴⁰ Πάντες εἰς τὸν Μωϋσῆν ἐβαπτίθησαν clearly mimics the language in 1 Cor. 1:13, 15; and 12:13, all of which have some form of βαπτίζω modified by a prepositional phrase beginning with εἰς.

of the Hebrews eating the same spiritual food and drinking the same spiritual drink certainly anticipates the language in 1 Corinthians 12:4–13, with the repetition of αὐτός with a definite article (the same *pneuma*, the same lord, the same god), culminating in verse 13: 'For we were all baptized into one body by one *pneuma* . . . and we all drank of the one *pneuma*.' In addition, the story of god providing water from a rock at Moses's hand at Meribah (Exod. 17:1–7) becomes a story of the presence of Christ (the rock) that was the place from which the water came to quench the thirst of the Hebrews. Christ is now ensconced in the history and mythology of several key events of Israel's history right alongside god.

Along with the grounding of these events in the mythological history of Israel (their scriptures), there is another indicator of the mythological nature of this passage in the language in verse 3: 'I hand on to you in the first importance what I also received' (παρέδωκα γὰρ ὑμῖν ἐν πρώτοις, ὃ καὶ παρέλαβον).[41] Most commentators recognise that this sentence contains technical language of instruction.[42] Raymond Collins characterises the language as an assertion of a common gospel preached among others who preach the gospel of Christ.[43] But he also says, 'There is but one and the same gospel across time and space',[44] giving the insinuation of a universal gospel, one raised up to be the foundational narrative of Israel (in Paul's view) – a classic move of mythographers who try

---

[41] Fitzmyer, *First Corinthians*, 409, points to Wis. 14:15 as an example of handing on traditions created around honouring a dead son: 'For a father, consumed with grief at an untimely bereavement, made an image of his child, who had been suddenly taken from him; he now honored as a god what was once a dead human being, and handed on (παρέδωκεν) to his dependents secret rites and initiations (μυστήρια καὶ τελετάς).' Richard A. Horsley, *1 Corinthians* (Nashville: Abingdon, 1998), 160, says, 'Hellenistic philosophies used the same terms in transmitting their standard doctrines.' See also Wolfgang Schrage, *Der erste Brief an die Korinther* (Zurich: Benziger, 1999), 29–31. Dinarchus (a late fourth-century to early third-century BCE Corinthian orator) uses παραδίδωμι to describe the traditional gods, that is, the gods that had been handed down through long-standing traditions (*Against Demosthenes*, 1.94). Plato (and many others) talks about traditions handed down from the ancients (*Phlb.* 16c). Demosthenes speaks of noble stories with contrasting descriptors: 'traditional' (παραδεδομένα) and 'legendary' (μυθώδη) (*Against Aristocrates* 23.65).

[42] Gordon D. Fee, *The First Epistle to the Corinthians*, rev. ed. (Grand Rapids, MI: Eerdmans, 2014), 801, calls it 'technical vocabulary from Paul's Jewish heritage for the transmission of religious instruction'. Fitzmyer, *First Corinthians*, 545, says that Paul 'makes use of the technical Greek terms for tradition, *paradidonai* and *paralambanein*'. Horsley, *1 Corinthians*, 198, says, 'Using what had become almost technical terms for the transmission of creeds and formulae basic to the movement . . . Paul reminds the Corinthians that he had presented to them the basic gospel that had preceded his own ministry and was shared by the movement generally.' Paul uses similar language in 1 Thess. 4:1; 1 Cor. 11:2; and Col. 2:6.

[43] Collins, *First Corinthians*, 526.

[44] Ibid.

to mythologise human activity.⁴⁵ Following this mythologising language are the basics of the mythology of Christ's death 'on behalf of our sins' (ὑπὲρ τῶν ἁμαρτιῶν ἡμῶν) and his resurrection 'on the third day', (τῇ ἡμέρᾳ τῇ τρίτῃ) both 'according to the scriptures' (κατὰ τὰς γραφὰς) (verses 3–4), and Christ's appearance to a list of apostles, Paul being the last (verses 5–11).

Paul writes the recent past, including his own, into the history of Israel by naming all those to whom the risen Christ appeared, including himself last of all (verses 5–9). He also links in the Corinthians through his and his co-workers' proclamation and interpretation of this history (verse 11). These events that Paul discusses are not merely a list of 'historical facts' for the Corinthians, although they are that for Paul.⁴⁶ He imbues them with meaning from the outset, creating the mythological origins for the assembly upon which everything important is built, not the least of which is the very salvation of the assembly members and the consolidation of cosmic rule for god the father. God has enacted these events, in Paul's mind, and so Christ is now ensconced within the history of god's interaction with Israel, expanded beyond the boundaries of Israel proper. In addition, I think it is important to note that the moniker that Paul uses is 'Χριστός', even in describing his death, the most earthly of the events in this passage.⁴⁷ The royal term colours the recipients' understanding of the body of Jesus's significance from earthly death to cosmic enthronement under god the father. It is all one continuous drama, at least as articulated in 1 Corinthians.

The second major term for Jesus that plays into the interwoven history/mythology of Jesus and god is κύριος. The term is often paired with Χριστός or with Ἰησοῦς Χριστός, or simply appears alone. Κύριος is also sometimes blurred with the Septuagint term for god, especially in direct quotations from Israel's scriptures, as in 1 Corinthians 1:31 ('Let the one who boasts boast in the lord'⁴⁸), which, although billed by Paul as a scripture quotation, is actually a summary of LXX Jer. 9:22–3.⁴⁹ In the Jeremiah passage, κύριος clearly means god, but Paul's use of κύριος in 1 Corinthians 1:31 comes after seven previous uses in the chapter, all referring to Jesus. So, while verse 31 probably refers to god, the lines are blurred enough for the Corinthians to infer that lord is a reference to Jesus.

---

⁴⁵ Russell McCutcheon provides an excellent discussion of myth that goes beyond generic description but instead redescribes myth as a process 'whereby societies create the extraordinary from the everyday'. Russell T. McCutcheon, 'Myth', in *The Guide to the Study of Religion*, ed. Willi Braun and Russell T. McCutcheon (London and New York: Continuum, 2000), 200.
⁴⁶ Collins, *First Corinthians*, 526.
⁴⁷ See also 1 Cor. 2:2, where the focus of Paul's 'knowledge' is 'Jesus Christ and him crucified' (Ἰησοῦν Χριστὸν καὶ τοῦτον ἐσταυρωμένον).
⁴⁸ ὁ καυχώμενος ἐν κυρίῳ καυχάσθω. Paul has the same 'quotation' in 2 Cor. 10:17.
⁴⁹ Fitzmyer, *First Corinthians*, 165. For some uses of κύριος where Paul clearly refers to god, see 1 Cor. 3:20 (quoting Ps. 94:11); 10:26 (quoting Ps. 24:1); and 2 Cor. 6:17–18 (part of the possible interpolation that might not be written by Paul).

On a wider scale, κύριος was often used as a metonym for deities in the Hellenistic period. Certain Egyptian deities – such as Isis, Serapis, Bes and Hermes-Thot[50] – are referred to with κύριος/κύρια, as well as some Syrian and Thracian deities.[51] Frenschkowski says, 'When covering a Greek God kyrios usually means the interpretation Graeca of an oriental deity.'[52] During the first century, Corinth had such a mix of deities, with origins from a variety of regions, including the East, that it is not unreasonable to think that the usage of κύριος for a deity would be a recognisable term for the Corinthians. Paul seems to assume so in 1 Corinthians 8:5 when he says 'as in fact there are many gods and many lords' (ὥσπερ εἰσὶν θεοὶ πολλοὶ καὶ κύριοι πολλοί), just before calling for an exclusive allegiance to his one god and one lord. So, with the use of κύριος, not only is there a blurring of god and Jesus at times, but the Corinthians would hear clear indication of his divine status.

One major mythological aspect of κύριος is the fact that the term is used for the risen Jesus to mark his importance to the life of the Corinthians. 1 Corinthians 6:14 states this most clearly: 'And god also raised the lord and will raise us through his power' (ὁ δὲ θεὸς καὶ τὸν κύριον ἤγειρεν καὶ ἡμᾶς ἐξεγερεῖ διὰ τῆς δυνάμεως αὐτοῦ). By virtue of his resurrection, then, Jesus is lord of the Corinthians and so is the foundation of their life together, their social formation as a group. In addition, as we have discussed above, Jesus's resurrection is a key moment in the mythological unfolding of the cosmos for Paul. That event sets the end times in motion; it is the first of many resurrections that culminate in the risen Christ consolidating and handing over the kingdom to god the father. The epithet or metonym κύριος for Jesus constantly reminds the Corinthians of his place in the cosmic drama in which they are involved and which forms the basis of their group life.

But κύριος does not replace Χριστός; it complements it appositionally as a title for Jesus.[53] As Χριστός does, so also κύριος communicates overtones of royal leadership for the Corinthians because the term was also used as a reference to the Roman emperor – not very commonly before Nero, but certainly thereafter. According to Suetonius, Augustus and Tiberius were both reluctant to be called κύριος, or *dominus* or *despotes*, two Latin equivalents.[54] But while Suetonius says that these terms were not looked favourably upon by these two

---

[50] See Giulia Ronchi, *Lexicon theonymon rerumque sacrarum et divinarum ad Aegyptum pertinentium quae in papyris ostracis titulis graecis latinisque in Aegypto repertis laudantur*, vol. 3 (Milan: Istituto editoriale cisalpino-La goliardica, 1975).

[51] Marco Frenschkowski, 'Kyrios in Context: Q 6:46, the Emperor as "Lord", and the Political Implications of Christology in Q', in *Zwischen den Reichen. Neues Testament und Römische Herrschaft. Vorträge auf der Ersten Konferenz der European Association of Biblical Studies*, ed. Michael Labahn and Jürgen Zangenberg (Tübingen: Francke, 2002), 97.

[52] Ibid.

[53] Fitzmyer, *First Corinthians*, 72.

[54] Suet. *Aug.* 53:1; Suet. *Tib.* 27.

emperors, their stances might have been attempts at false humility or efforts to distance their monarchies from tyrannical ones of the past. With Nero, however, the term κύριος starts to appear dramatically more frequently in the Egyptian evidence. According to Frenschkowski,

> We have very few Egyptian instances of kyrios for emperors earlier than [Nero], but there are left-overs from Ptolemaic monarchic language. We can mention one instance for Augustus in 12 BC and perhaps one or two instances for Caligula and Claudius, but after that we encounter a veritable explosion of kyrios-piety. All of a sudden literally hundreds of ostraca and papyri use κύριος ἡμῶν 'our lord' as an abbreviated way of referring to the emperor.[55]

He goes on to say, 'Particularly telling is the extent of ostraca from all levels of society, in which we often also find simply ὁ κύριος for Nero', and he credits it to a 'revitalization of older Hellenistic (Ptolemaic) piety that quickly spread through the empire'.[56] But κύριος was never an official title of the emperor; rather it was an expression of the respect and loyalty the emperor's subjects had for him, starting with Nero. It is unclear why this explosion of evidence for κύριος as a referent for the emperor came to be during Nero's reign, and it would have been a little late for Paul's Corinthians to draw on this sort of convention. So it is hard to tell for sure what specific connotations κύριος would have had for the Corinthians when used as a sole epithet or metonym for Jesus, other than the times when it is blurred with the Septuagint references to god. But when κύριος is combined with Χριστός, it is hard to imagine that they would not have heard the royal overtones in κύριος too. And with the royal overtones of Jesus's most common monikers, the Corinthians are taken to the cosmic/mythological role that he plays in 1 Corinthians 15.

Paul further interweaves the Corinthians into Christ's mythological role by his discussion of resurrection of the dead, using Christ as the paradigm for future resurrections:

> If Christ has not been raised, then both our preaching is empty, and our faith is empty. And we also are found to be false witnesses of god because we witnessed by god (κατὰ τοῦ θεοῦ)[57] that he raised Christ, whom he did not raise if the dead are not indeed raised. (15:14–15)[58]

[55] Frenschkowski, 'Kyrios in Context', 98–9.
[56] Ibid., 99.
[57] See H. W. Smyth, *Greek Grammar*, rev. by Gordon M. Messing (Cambridge, MA: Harvard University Press, 1956), para. 1690c, for this usage of κατά with the genitive for verbs of swearing, in this case μαρτυρέω.
[58] εἰ δὲ Χριστὸς οὐκ ἐγήγερται, κενὸν ἄρα [καὶ] τὸ κήρυγμα ἡμῶν, κενὴ καὶ ἡ πίστις ὑμῶν· εὑρισκόμεθα δὲ καὶ ψευδομάρτυρες τοῦ θεοῦ, ὅτι ἐμαρτυρήσαμεν κατὰ τοῦ θεοῦ ὅτι ἤγειρεν τὸν Χριστόν, ὃν οὐκ ἤγειρεν εἴπερ ἄρα νεκροὶ οὐκ ἐγείρονται.

And further, 'But now Christ has been raised from the dead ones, the first fruits of those who have fallen asleep' (Νυνὶ δὲ Χριστὸς ἐγήγερται ἐκ νεκρῶν ἀπαρχὴ τῶν κεκοιμημένων; verse 20). Paul then launches into his reimagining of the Adam narrative from Genesis with Christ as the counter to the fall that caused death (verses 21–3) and carries it forward into the future by describing 'the end' (τὸ τέλος) when Christ 'hands over the kingdom to the god and father, after he has destroyed every ruler and every authority and power' (εἶτα τὸ τέλος, ὅταν παραδιδῷ τὴν βασιλείαν τῷ θεῷ καὶ πατρί, ὅταν καταργήσῃ πᾶσαν ἀρχὴν καὶ πᾶσαν ἐξουσίαν καὶ δύναμιν; verse 24) 'in order that god might be all in all' (ἵνα ᾖ ὁ θεὸς [τὰ] πάντα ἐν πᾶσιν; verse 28). In short, god raised Christ; Paul and his co-workers witnessed it (the first of many such future resurrections); the resurrected Christ undoes Adamic death; Christ will subjugate all powers to god; and god will reign supreme. The lack of tense parallelism reflects the historical/mythological dynamic of past, present, future. The distant mythological past (the first Adam) is joined with the recent past/present (the advent of Christ, his death, resurrection and current reign over god's kingdom) and extends into the future (the end times, when Christ will destroy god's enemies and hand over the kingdom to the father). God, Christ, Paul and the Corinthians are historically and mythologically bound together in past, present and future moments of Israel's revised foundational story.

**Pneuma**

As I said at the outset of this chapter, I recognise the plurality of perception among the Corinthians when it comes to *pneuma*. It is likely that a few members of the assembly had received some formal education or some other kind of informal exposure to the concept of *pneuma*, which would have included some exposure to materialist philosophical notions of *pneuma*. These people probably would not have understood *pneuma* as an autonomous divine being and so the question of genealogy and history/mythology would be focused only on god and/or Christ Jesus, since *pneuma* was the material stuff of god and/or Christ Jesus.

But what about the genealogy and history/mythology for those who likely were not familiar with *pneuma* in materialist philosophical terms but who were more familiar with it as an autonomous divine being? Back in 1 Corinthians 2, Paul introduced the idea of the Corinthians having received the *pneuma* and therefore becoming spiritual people (πνευματικοί; 2:13) in contrast to physical people (ψυχικοί), aligned and connected with the *pneuma* of god that dwells within the assembly of Corinthians. That is their present collective state based upon the presence of the *pneuma* among them. When Paul describes what will happen with the resurrection of the dead (starting in 15:35), he tells the Corinthians that the transformation will be from a perishable, physical (ψυχικόν) body to an imperishable, spiritual (πνευματικόν) body. Although the *pneuma* is not mentioned explicitly in this description of the transformation of the resurrected body, the similarity of terminology certainly points to its role in this process.[59]

The *pneuma* plays a crucial role, then, in the continuation and culmination of the interaction of god with Israel (that is, the history of Israel) as embodied in the Corinthians. The cosmic drama described in 1 Corinthians 15 begins with the Corinthians (as they hear it), with their transformation from ψυχικοί to πνευματικοί.[60] The Corinthians follow Christ, the first fruits of this transformation, and are the first stage of the process that eventually culminates in Christ subduing all the powers of the world and handing over the kingdom to the father. The *pneuma* is woven into this unfolding history and contributes to the foundational story that guides the assembly into the eschaton. Certainly, a Stoic mechanism of transformation makes sense of Paul's language here, but for those Corinthians who do not know this Stoic concept, the mechanism is more mysterious because the collective language of 1 Corinthians 2 seems to be changed to individual bodies, unless the collective body metaphor carries over from Chapter 12.

The most foundational presentation of these three divine figures interacting in the unfolding history of Israel is Paul's somewhat convoluted argument regarding the nature of his and his co-workers' activity among the Corinthians, described in 2 Corinthians 3. Paul presents to the Corinthians an image of their community as testimony to the success he has had with his activity. He uses the metaphor of a letter of recommendation embodied by the Corinthians (2 Cor. 3:2), but they are 'a letter of Christ . . . written not with ink but with the *pneuma* of the living god' (ἐπιστολὴ Χριστοῦ . . . ἐγγεγραμμένη οὐ μέλανι ἀλλὰ πνεύματι θεοῦ ζῶντος; verse 3). Paul builds on this imagery by claiming that their competence resides in god 'who also has made us competent servants of a new covenant, not of [the] letter but of [the] *pneuma*; for the letter kills, but the *pneuma* makes alive' (verse 6).[61] He goes on to assert that the old covenant's ineffectiveness is symbolised by the veil over Moses's face, necessary

---

[59] Fitzmyer, *First Corinthians*, 596, mentions 1 Cor. 3:1 in discussing the contrast between *pneumatikos* and *sarkikos*, but he gets too caught up in the precise terminology and fails to see the connection between what Paul is proposing in 1 Corinthians 2–3 and 1 Cor. 15:35 ff. But see Troels Engberg-Pedersen, *Cosmology and Self in the Apostle Paul: The Material Spirit* (Oxford: Oxford University Press, 2010), 27–8: 'The latter contrast has been prepared for far back in the letter: at 2:14–15, which Paul distinguished between "psychic man" and "the pneumatic (man)".'

[60] See Engberg-Pedersen, *Cosmology and Self*, 26–37, for a discussion of the Stoic cosmological background to Paul's argument about transformation here.

[61] ὃς καὶ ἱκάνωσεν ἡμᾶς διακόνους καινῆς διαθήκης, οὐ γράμματος ἀλλὰ πνεύματος· τὸ γὰρ γράμμα ἀποκτέννει, τὸ δὲ πνεῦμα ζῳοποιεῖ.

to protect Israel from harm but ultimately obscuring their minds from understanding. The new covenant – brought to the Corinthians through the service of the *pneuma* (διακονία τοῦ πνεύματος; verse 8) – not only leads to life, but it allows something that Israel could never accomplish on its own: full understanding because the veil over their minds has been removed (verses 12–16).

Paul most fundamentally writes the *pneuma* into the mythology of Sinai and of its next chapter enacted by the Corinthians in verse 17. In verse 16, we have a traditional use of κύριος to refer to god: 'Whenever [someone] turns to the lord, the veil is lifted' (ἡνίκα δὲ ἐὰν ἐπιστρέψῃ πρὸς κύριον, περιαιρεῖται τὸ κάλυμμα). But then Paul changes the referent of κύριος in the next two verses, as we have seen above:

> The *pneuma* is the lord, and where [there is] the *pneuma* of the lord, [there is] freedom. We all – with faces that have been unveiled, having gazed upon the same image as in a mirror, the glory of the lord – are being transformed from glory to glory just as from the lord *pneuma*.[62]

Paul has transposed the terminology of κύριος to mean the *pneuma* instead of the god of the Septuagint, or at least he has blurred the boundaries between the two to the extent that now the *pneuma* plays a foundational role in the unfolding of god's interaction with Israel. The *pneuma* is responsible for the unveiling and transformation of the Corinthians through Paul and his co-workers' role as servants of the new covenant. The result is that the Corinthians have become the locus of god's activity in the present, just as the Hebrews were at Sinai in the past. The Corinthians are contrasted with the Hebrews, but for Paul it is all part of a continuum of interaction between god and Israel, with the Corinthians now woven into that continuum through the activity of the lord *pneuma*.

The *pneuma* is a bit trickier to describe genealogically. While there is no direct familial relationship described in the Corinthian correspondence, we have the idea of the *pneuma* being intimately connected with god in several places: the *pneuma* 'seeks after' or 'searches' (ἐραυνᾷ) the 'depths of god' (τὰ βάθη τοῦ θεοῦ; 1 Cor. 2:10); the *pneuma* is 'from god' (τὸ πνεῦμα τὸ ἐκ τοῦ θεοῦ; 1 Cor. 2:12; cf. 6:19),[63] 'god's' (1 Cor. 2:14; 3:16; 7:40; 12:3; cf. 2 Cor. 3:3)[64] and 'of our god' (1 Cor. 6:11). Interestingly, 2 Corinthians 3:17–18 shows

---

[62] ὁ δὲ κύριος τὸ πνεῦμά ἐστιν· οὗ δὲ τὸ πνεῦμα κυρίου, ἐλευθερία. ἡμεῖς δὲ πάντες ἀνακεκαλυμμένῳ προσώπῳ τὴν δόξαν κυρίου κατοπτριζόμενοι τὴν αὐτὴν εἰκόνα μεταμορφούμεθα ἀπὸ δόξης εἰς δόξαν καθάπερ ἀπὸ κυρίου πνεύματος.

[63] Fitzmyer, who is in the minority of commentators, thinks that this phrase refers to the human *pneuma* of the believers that comes from god. Fitzmyer, *First Corinthians*, 181.

[64] All of these are constructions that have θεοῦ modifying πνεῦμα in various cases. Given the range of possibilities for the genitive, some or all of these could be possessive genitives or they could have the overtone of origin.

a similar relationship between the 'lord' (Jesus) and the *pneuma*: 'the lord is the *pneuma*', 'the lord's *pneuma*' and 'the lord, the *pneuma*' all appear here, as we have just seen. This passage is particularly difficult to unravel because of the syntax equating Jesus and the *pneuma* when just before these verses there was a seemingly clear distinction. This passage could be the equivalent to 1 Corinthians 15:45: 'the last Adam [that is, Christ] [turned] into a life-endowing πνεῦμα' (ἐγένετο ... ὁ ἔσχατος Ἀδὰμ εἰς πνεῦμα ζῳοποιοῦν). If so, then any distinction between Christ and the *pneuma* is erased, at least in these two passages. Since the overall presentation of the *pneuma* seems to be as a distinct divine entity working alongside god and Christ,[65] these verses, while difficult, could have been heard by the Corinthians in continuity with the majority of Paul's presentation of the *pneuma*.

The next two examples pretty clearly show the way in which the three are presented as closely connected: 1 Corinthians 12:4–6 is at the beginning of Paul's argument about the way that χαρίσματα are supposed to work to build up the community. Varieties (διαιρέσεις) of χαρίσματα, διακονίαι (services) and ἐνεργήματα (actions) are linked to *pneuma*, lord and god, respectively, in a repetitive tricolon of sentences giving the effect of connectedness in the midst of distinction among the three divine figures. As we saw in Chapter Three above, the *pneuma* is put in parallel with lord and god, with the effect being that the three all have both agency and distinctive but overlapping influence on the Corinthians. But their connectedness is also important to note here because all three are working together to form the Corinthians into a unified body, as Paul goes on to assert, beginning in verse 12. The *pneuma* plays a key role in this formation because 'the one and the same *pneuma* enacts all these things [χαρίσματα]' (πάντα δὲ ταῦτα [χαρίσματα] ἐνεργεῖ τὸ ἓν καὶ τὸ αὐτὸ πνεύματι; 1 Cor. 12:11). Similarly, the blessing at the end of 2 Corinthians links all three: 'The favour (ἡ χάρις) of the lord Jesus Christ and the love of god and the partnership of the holy *pneuma* (ἡ κοινωνία τοῦ ἁγίου πνεύματος) be with you all' (13:13).[66] As I noted in Chapter Three, many commentators want to see a trinitarian bent to this grouping, not surprisingly

---

[65] As we have seen in Chapter Three, there is a school of thought (Engberg-Pedersen, Stowers, Bazzana and Eyl) that sees πνεῦμα as Christ or the substance of god rather than as a distinct entity. While I am sympathetic to this reading when it comes to trying to tease out what Paul had in mind when talking about πνεῦμα, I am convinced that none but a few of the Corinthians would have been sufficiently educated in the fine points of Stoicism to recognise πνεῦμα in this way.

[66] As I did in Chapter Three, I translate the verse somewhat unconventionally because 'grace' (translating χάρις) is now a technical theological term with certain connotations that I do not think are clearly present among early Christ followers. Similarly with 'communion' or 'fellowship' for κοινωνία.

to anticipate the eventual formulation of the doctrine of the Trinity a few centuries later.[67] These attempts to read 13:13 as such are thoroughly theologically anachronistic and say more about the interests of the commentators than about Paul or the Corinthians.

The point in our discussion of 1 Corinthians 12:4–6 and 2 Corinthians 13:13 is to highlight the clear connectedness of the *pneuma* to god and Christ as Paul presents them to the Corinthians. They all have a role to play in the life and social formation of the Corinthian group, but they are also all working together for the benefit of the Corinthians. Although these passages do not represent all three figures in a familial relationship, it shows their connectedness, probably enough for the relationship to sound familiar to the Corinthians, who experienced groups of gods connected in various ways, genealogically and otherwise.

We cannot be sure whether Paul talked in detail about the mythological scenarios he paints in his letters prior to their composition, and he probably did not do so in the specific ways that he does in the letters, since they are integral parts of the written arguments. But this sort of presentation of god the father, Christ and the *pneuma* as crucial to the past, ongoing and future history/mythology of Israel would probably not have been comprehensible to the Corinthians had Paul not communicated this sort of thinking to the community before he wrote such elaborate mythologies in his letter. We cannot know exactly what development happened following his initial encounters with what would later become the collection of Corinthian Christ followers, but these mythological scenarios seem out of place as a primer to the topic of how god, Christ and the *pneuma* work together for the betterment of the Corinthians.

---

[67] Gordon D. Fee, *God's Empowering Presence: The Holy Spirit in the Letters of Paul* (Peabody, MA: Hendrickson, 1994), 362. Fee even goes as far as saying, 'It needs to be noted, finally, how thoroughly and unmistakably Trinitarian this prayer is. That Paul would include the Holy Spirit as an equal member of this triadic formula, and that he would pray to the Spirit on their behalf, says as much about his understanding of the Spirit both as person and as deity as any direct statement of this kind ever could' (364–5). So also Larry W. Hurtado, 'The Binitarian Shape of Early Christian Worship', in *The Jewish Roots of Christological Monotheism: Papers from the St. Andrews Conference on the Historical Origins on the Worship of Jesus*, ed. Carey C. Newman, James R. Davila and Gladys S. Lewis (Leiden: Brill, 1999), 195; Craig S. Keener, *1–2 Corinthians* (Cambridge: Cambridge University Press, 2005), 246. Margaret E. Thrall, *2 Corinthians: A Critical and Exegetical Commentary*, 2 vols (London: T & T Clark, 2004), 2:920, comments, 'It would be possible to see in the Pauline formula one of the starting points of trinitarian development.' C. K. Barrett, *A Commentary on the Second Epistle to the Corinthians*. BNTC (London: Black, 1973), 345, opts for a proto-trinitarian view of the phrase: 'Christ, God, the Spirit, appearing in balanced clauses in one sentence, must stand on one divine level.'

## Cult

We now turn to the cultic dimensions of the Corinthian correspondence. As I described in the Introduction, cult should be understood as framed within the larger cultural practice of reciprocity, meaning that the activity is a give-and-take process: it is not based on obligation but forms the foundation of a mutual, freely exercised relationship. In particular, cult refers to any ritual honour that is given freely to a god or divine figure and in so doing maintains and reinforces the relationship between the god or divine figure and the practitioner, and among the local group of gods of a particular sanctuary or group. There is a danger of defining cultic activity too narrowly as being focused on animal sacrifice, but in reality cultic activities can include ritual offerings (animal, plant and liquid), prayers, singing honorary hymns, other musical performances directed towards the divine world or performed in honour of a deity or deities, purifications specific to a sanctuary as part of the activity to honour a deity, meals, processions, ecstatic behaviour and so on. If one thinks of cultic activity in the larger terms of ancient reciprocity, then the limits of what constitutes this activity can be whatever an individual or collective does to honour a deity.

We have three direct mentions of cultic connections in the Corinthian correspondence that would fit this wider definition of cultic activity: one metaphorical and two ritual. We also have a description of the gatherings of Corinthians that include activities that are supposed to honour Paul's chord of gods, and therefore these activities would be considered cultic activity. The activities during these gatherings are akin to cultic activities in other ancient Mediterranean sanctuaries (civic and domestic), including those in Corinth. First, Paul twice uses metaphorical temple imagery to describe the Corinthian community as the dwelling place of god's *pneuma* (1 Cor. 3:16; 6:19), as I discussed in Chapter Three.[68] We need to examine this imagery from a slightly different perspective than we did earlier. There I focused on the imagery to determine whether or not the *pneuma* could be understood as a distinct divine entity for those unfamiliar with materialist philosophical notions of *pneuma*; here, we need to look at the cultic dimensions of the imagery.

The particular cultic term found in 3:16 and 6:19 is ναός, the building(s) within the (usually larger) sanctuary where the cult statue(s) of its god(s) reside. The space around the *naos* also matters because most common among almost all ancient sanctuaries is the presence of an altar outside the *naos* but virtually connected to it. The altar outside the *naos* to the primary god of the

---

[68] 2 Cor. 6:16 says, 'For we are the temple of the living god' (ἡμεῖς γὰρ ναὸς θεοῦ ἐσμεν ζῶντος). But because this comes from a section of 2 Corinthians whose origins are disputed, I have decided not to treat it here. See Chapter 6 for a discussion of this passage in another context.

sanctuary – often placed on the steps leading up to the *pronaos* but sometimes in front –would frequently be aligned with the front entrance, which was then aligned with the cult statue(s) within the *naos*.[69] Some altars would be used for more than one deity in the *naos*; we know this from inscriptions that refer to the deities as 'altar-sharing'[70] or from altars that have more than one deity named on them.[71] The variety of ritual offerings made at the altar could then be within sight of the deity or deities within the *naos*.

It is hard to overestimate the importance of ritual offerings – traditionally termed 'sacrifices' by scholars – in the context of ancient religion. Robert Parker calls 'sacrifice' 'the central ritual of Greek religion'.[72] Similarly, Beard, Price and North say, 'Animal sacrifice, the ritual killing of an animal and the offering to the gods of parts of its body, burnt on the altar, was a (perhaps the) central element of Roman ritual.'[73] Sacrifice usually refers particularly to animal ritual offerings, but altars were also the place for grain and liquid offerings and sometimes for dedicatory offerings that would remain near the altar or be displayed somewhere else in the sanctuary. Despite – or perhaps because of – the centrality of ritual offerings, most frequently offered near the ναός, the meaning of these offerings is pluriform,[74] and any general theory of ritual offerings will always be inadequate and perhaps misguided.[75] What F. S. Naiden emphasises in his monograph on sacrifice is that the ritual killing and eating of the animal or other offering does not make sense outside of the

---

[69] Many altars in sanctuaries are located near the temple of the god to which the altar is dedicated, but this is not uniform. Altars can sometimes be off to one side of the temple or even free-standing, with no particular temple for the god to which the altar is dedicated. A good example of this is the sanctuary of Asklepios at Epidauros, which has the altar to Asklepios near the Temple of Asklepios, but it also contains numerous altars to other divinities that do not have temples in the sanctuary.

[70] Ξενοκράτεια Κηφισο͂ ἱερὸν ἱδρύσατο ὃν καὶ ἀνέθηκεν ξυνβώμοις τε θεοῖς διδασκαλίας τόδε δῶρον (*IG* II² 4548, 1–4 in Kephisos). See also *IG* XI, 4 1223, *ID* 2128, *ID* 2387 (all from Delos). *IG* XII Suppl. 565 (Euboia) and *IGUR* I 177 (Italy; Magna Graecia) have both συννάος and συμβώμος.

[71] In his description of the oracle of Amphiaraos, Pausanias says that those consulting the oracle must 'make a purificatory offering to the god, but they both make an offering to him and to all whose names are on the altar' (καθάρσιον τῷ θεῷ θύειν, θύοθσι δὲ καὶ αὐτῷ καὶ πᾶσιν ὅσοις ἐστὶν ἐπὶ τῷ βωμῷ τὰ ὀνόματα; 1.34.5). For heroes sharing an altar with a god see *LS* 18, col. I, 46–8; *LSS* 19, 93.

[72] Robert Parker, *On Greek Religion* (Ithaca: Cornell University Press, 2011), 124.

[73] Beard, North and Price, *Religions of Rome*, 2:148.

[74] See Parker, *On Greek Religion*, 124–70, for a fine overview of the options. See also F. S. Naiden, *Smoke Signals for the Gods: Ancient Greek Sacrifice from the Archaic through the Roman Periods* (Oxford: Oxford University Press, 2013), for a recent treatment of the topic, with an excellent history of scholarship in his chapter 1.

[75] See Paul Veyne, 'Inviter les dieux, sacrifier, banqueter: quelques nuances de la religiosité gréco-romaine', *Annales*, 55 (2000): 21–2.

larger context of Greek ritual life.[76] The same could be said about Roman and Jewish ritual life. All of these rituals worked within the context of ongoing attempts to maintain and build reciprocal divine–human relations. Whatever the precise importance of sacrifice (if it can be determined at all), it is less important for us than the fact that it was central to ancient religion across the ancient Mediterranean, and certainly at Corinth.[77] It was a fundamental way of honouring the god(s) and it was often tied directly to a sanctuary, its wider ritual life and its *naos*.

In addition, suppliants often made their requests before the statue of the god in the *naos*;[78] and sometimes they would leave votive offerings within or around the outside of the *naos* to honour the god.[79] These were either displayed in the *cella* (where the cult statue[s] resided) or stored in the *opisthodomos* (a rear porch or storage room in the rear of the naos). The various kinds of offerings and dedications centred around the *naos* were not the only ritual activity that occurred at a sanctuary; hymns, musical performances, ecstatic activity and purifications also took place. But the presence of the god(s) in the temple(s) was certainly central to the life of sanctuary in all its ritual variety. In other words, the *naos* was not a place for the static location of the cult statue. It was a vibrant centre of ritual activity that enriched all those who attended, and offered a place for human and divine to meet and for humans to pay proper honour to the god or gods. And it was the tangible location of the presence of a god or gods, which was a crucial element of ancient religious life across cultures, but certainly in Corinth.

The cultic metaphor of the community as *naos* would have been a powerful one for the Corinthians. The entirety of cultural importance located in the life of a *naos* in ancient Corinth and across the wider Mediterranean world imbued this metaphor with meaning. It is unnecessary and even incorrect to

---

[76] Naiden, *Smoke Signals*.

[77] See Jennifer Wright Knust and Zsuzsanna Várhelyi, eds., *Ancient Mediterranean Sacrifice* (Oxford: Oxford University Press, 2011), for an excellent collection of studies that addresses various ways to think about sacrifice in the ancient Mediterranean world.

[78] Minucius Felix *Octav.* 22.5; Heracles frag. 5; Herodotus 6.61.3. See Sarah Iles Johnston, 'Animating Statues: A Case Study in Ritual', *Arethusa* 41 (2008): 449, for a discussion of the Herodotus passage.

[79] The Asklepios sanctuary at Athens is a good example of this. The sanctuary became so full of votives that at certain points they would have to be removed and stored in another building. See also the Asklepieion at Corinth in the classical period. The temple of Zeus in his sanctuary at Olympia was first constructed in the mid-fifth century BCE, with dedicatory and monumental statues erected on the steps of the temple upon its completion. See Julia Kindt, *Rethinking Greek Religion* (Cambridge: Cambridge University Press, 2012), 131–2, for a discussion of the placement of dedicatory and monumental items at the sanctuary, and the whole chapter for a treatment of the sanctuary, which relies, in part, on the wide variety of votive offerings extant from its remains.

limit these references to the *naos* as referring to the Jerusalem temple exclusively.⁸⁰ Whether or not Paul intended the Jerusalem temple as the referent in his metaphor, the Corinthians' immediate experience of temples would not have sent their imaginations to Jerusalem first.⁸¹ Instead, the variety and scope of cultic activity in local sanctuaries would have resonated with the Corinthians.⁸² With this metaphor, as Fitzmyer says, 'Consequently, they are sacred . . . i.e., dedicated to God's cultic service.'⁸³ This involves a whole variety of activities with the fundamental purpose of honouring their deity or deities, just as happened in ancient Corinthian temples across the region. The metaphor asserts an identity for the assembly as the 'place' of honouring their chord of gods through the presence of the *pneuma*. Although Paul uses the metaphor to exhort the Corinthians to a certain kind of behaviour, the identity produced through the metaphor has a concreteness that allows the Corinthians to understand that their assembly activities should be thought of as sanctuary activities that are supposed to honour their chord of gods. In other words, the assembly has become the location for proper cultic activities honouring their chord of gods, very much in line with how the Corinthians would have experienced their past – and perhaps present – cultic activities in local sanctuaries.

More concretely than the metaphor of *naos*, Paul refers to the ritual of baptism in a few places: 1 Corinthians 1:13–17, 6:11, 12:13 and 15:29. It has been long thought among scholars that baptism was one of the foundational rituals of the early Christ group in general. Over sixty years ago, C. F. D. Moule said, 'There is little doubt as to the universality of practice in the Christian Church.'⁸⁴ The Corinthians probably went through baptism as some sort of

---

⁸⁰ James D. G. Dunn, *The Theology of Paul the Apostle* (Edinburgh: T & T Clark, 1998), 545, mentions nothing of the Corinthian context for the metaphor, but refers only to its Jewish background (Philo, Qumran) and possible antecedents during Jesus's adult life. Gerd Theissen, *The Religion of The Earliest Churches: Creating a Symbolic World* (Minneapolis: Fortress Press, 1999), 279, talks about the 'presence' motif already found in the Hebrew Bible and in 'primitive Christianity'.

⁸¹ Fitzmyer, *First Corinthians*, 203, says, 'Behind Paul's cultic imagery is the OT idea of one place, Jerusalem, where Israel was to worship Yahweh.' I think the imagery goes beyond Jerusalem to the basic experience and meaning of a temple in Corinth and beyond.

⁸² Horsley, *1 Corinthians*, 66, correctly but only briefly comments: 'Paul may have had the Jerusalem temple in mind, but the Corinthians' understanding of temple would surely have been shaped by the many prominent temples in their own city.' Although Fee, *The First Epistle*, 159, focuses most on Pauline intention and the Jewish overtones of his use of temple imagery, he does give a nod to what the Corinthians might have understood by this imagery: 'The imagery of the church as a temple would have been easily understood by the Corinthians, as well, although perhaps not with all of its rich OT overtones. As practicing pagans . . . most of them would have frequented the many pagan temples and shrines (*naoi*) in their city.' Both Fee and Horsley, however, fail to describe in any detail what it meant for the Corinthians to practice their religion in and around local *naoi*.

⁸³ Fitzmyer, *First Corinthians*, 193.

⁸⁴ C. F. D. Moule, *Worship in the New Testament* (Richmond, VA: John Knox Press, 1961), 47.

entry or affirmation ritual,[85] as did other Christ followers across the spectrum of groups, but the details of the ritual and its intention are difficult to reconstruct.[86] Paul's discussions of baptism in the Corinthian correspondence are after-the-fact interpretations of baptism rather than detailed explications of the ritual and its intention. This reflects the developing nature of the group and any associated rituals performed by the group rather than a change of intention or meaning.[87]

1 Corinthians 1:13–17 describes baptism as a ritual that results in some sort of adherence to the person in whose name one is baptised. The issue, widely believed to be the occasion for the letter, is that factions have emerged among the Corinthians. Some are claiming allegiance to Paul, some to Apollos, some to Peter, some to Christ (verse 12). Paul counters the factionalism by recalling for them the point of their baptism. He asks, rhetorically, 'Were you baptized in the name of Paul?' (εἰς τὸ ὄνομα Παῦλος; verse 13)[88] and then gives thanks for not baptising anyone except Crispus and Gaius 'lest anyone says that you were baptised in my name' (εἰς τὸ ἐμὸν ὄνομα; verse 15). The meaning of these baptisms for the Corinthians seems to be at odds with Paul's understanding. The person who did the baptising seems to be more important for the Corinthians than the ritual itself,[89] and the result is group formation around the baptiser – being 'of' the baptiser as Paul says in verse 12. Paul corrects them by pointing out that it is Christ in whose name the Corinthians were baptised, and therefore Christ is the one who deserves their allegiance. The Corinthians seemed to have understood the effects of the ritual – joining

---

[85] Richard E. DeMaris, *The New Testament in its Ritual World* (London: Routledge, 2008), 15, points to 1 Cor. 12:12–13 as the passage that most clearly indicates this in the letter.

[86] Lars Hartman, *'Into the Name of the Lord Jesus': Baptism in the Early Church* (Edinburgh: T&T Clark, 1997), 3, says, 'Baptism is taken for granted and apparently writers need not instruct their readers about it.' However, DeMaris, *The New Testament in its Ritual World*, 16–36, convincingly shows that the ambiguity of the language in most of the references to baptism goes against any clear reading of the practice as a particular kind of ritual, such as initiation or conversion.

[87] See DeMaris, *The New Testament in its Ritual World*, 15, for the consensus view, before he goes on to problematise this view in the following pages.

[88] Richard E. DeMaris, 'Water Ritual', in *The Oxford Handbook of Early Christian Ritual*, ed. Risto Uro, Juliette Day, Richard E. DeMaris and Rikard Roitto (Oxford: Oxford University Press, 2018), 404, says, 'This last question [of v. 13] implicated baptismal practices in the divisiveness that plagued the Corinthian house churches. The lines that immediately follow, in which Paul denied having baptized many at Corinth – he immediately qualifies the denial – were his attempt at damage control (1:14–16). They underscore baptism's ability to create allegiances that could unravel a group's fabric.'

[89] Pheme Perkins, *First Corinthians* (Grand Rapids, MI: Baker Academic, 2012), 49. Anthony C. Thiselton, *The First Epistle to the Corinthians: A Commentary on the Greek Text* (Grand Rapids, MI: Eerdmans, 2000), 140, says, 'A number of Christians at Corinth sought to acquire enhanced status by claiming some special connection with a major, esteemed figure.'

a group – without fully understanding the (ideal) dynamics of the group.[90] In Naiden's framework of sacrificial ritual, where the gods mattered for the ritual far more than the social or psychological effects of it,[91] the Corinthians' understanding of baptism seems to violate the ideal focus of cultic ritual, which is the divine figure. The god matters; in this case, baptism without Christ as the object of the ritual resulted in factions rather than in honouring Christ.

In 1 Corinthians 6:11, Paul talks about the lingering and ongoing effects of this baptism: the Corinthians were 'washed clean ... made holy ... made righteous in the name of the lord Jesus Christ and in the *pneuma* of our god'.[92] Many commentators think that Paul is referring to baptism with ἀπελούσασθε,[93] but James Dunn (and Fee, who follows him) argues against a strictly baptismal reference. Instead, he says that the referent should be wider than baptism, even if it includes baptism, and instead be thought of as a 'conversion-initiation' reference.[94] Thiselton claims that 'Dunn has effectively put an end to an uncritical tradition of interpretation instanced, e.g., in H. L. Goudge's commentary: "But ye were washed, i.e., in baptism."'[95] Whether it is baptism, strictly speaking, or the whole phenomenon of conversion-initiation, as Dunn puts it, there is a ritual context that likely would have been recognised by the Corinthians.

The context of the verse is Paul's admonition of the Corinthians for bringing fellow members of the assembly to court over disputes that they could have handled themselves, as if they were not part of the same group. The shame that he points to in 6:5 reveals that the Corinthians did not understand the ramifications of their participation together in the assembly. Their baptism, as

---

[90] DeMaris, 'Water Ritual', 404, says, 'baptism may have been an ideal ritual for establishing and structuring circles of believers, but it had to be administered carefully, lest it create rival hierarchies'.

[91] Naiden's main point in arguing for his understanding of ancient Greek sacrifice in *Smoke Signals* is in contradistinction to Burkert's focus on the psychological effects of killing the animal and Vernant and Detienne's focus on eating the cooked meat (see Walter Burkert, *Homo Necans: The Anthropology of Ancient Greek Sacrificial Ritual and Myth*, trans. Peter Bing (Berkeley: University of California Press, 1983); J.-P. Vernant and Marcel Detienne, eds., *The Cuisine of Sacrifice among the Greeks*, trans. P. Wissig (Chicago: University of Chicago Press, 1989). Naiden correctly points out that the gods are present and the most important of the participants. Everything in the sacrificial ritual is aimed at pleasing the god or gods to which the ritual is directed. This seems to be Paul's point precisely with respect to baptism, something that seemed to escape some of the Corinthians.

[92] ἀλλ' ἀπελούσασθε, ἀλλ' ἡγιάσθητε, ἀλλ' ἐδικαιώθητε ἐν τῷ ὀνόματι τοῦ κυρίου Ἰησοῦ Χριστοῦ καὶ ἐν τῷ πνεύματι τοῦ θεοῦ ἡμῶν.

[93] For example, Fitzmyer, *First Corinthians*, 258; Collins, *First Corinthians*, 237; Perkins, *First Corinthians*, 97; Richard B. Hays, *First Corinthians* (Louisville, KY: John Knox, 1997), 99–100.

[94] James D. G. Dunn, *Baptism in the Holy Spirit: A Re-examination of the New Testament Teaching on the Gift of the Spirit in Relation to Pentecostalism Today* (Philadelphia: Westminster John Knox, 1970), 104.

[95] Thiselton, *The First Epistle to the Corinthians*, 454.

described in the beginning of the letter – an initiation into a group that honours Christ – means that they were 'washed clean . . . made holy . . . made righteous' but not just in some abstract way. Their actions should honour Christ, not only in the ritual but also afterwards because of the ritual, and not only Christ because the effects of the ritual were 'in the name of the lord Jesus Christ and in the *pneuma* of our god' (6:11). In this one verse, Paul recalls all three members of his chord of gods in reference to the effects of ritual baptism.[96] The baptismal cultic ritual life of the Corinthians is directed towards all three divine figures, and the actions of the assembly members thereafter will either bring shame upon the Corinthians or continue their honour of these divine figures.

The next reference to baptism is 1 Corinthians 12:13, which reads, 'For we have all been baptized by one *pneuma* into one body, whether Jew or Greek or slave or free, and we all were given one *pneuma* to drink.'[97] This verse kicks off the famous discussion of the body of Christ metaphor, but it also comes on the heels of the divisions that Paul describes in the lord's supper, and then his explication of the variety of gifts that have been granted to the Corinthians. Both passages deal with divisions of status – the former apparently based on wealth, the latter on the status that comes from what kind of spiritual gift one has been granted. We will discuss the lord's supper below. The variety of gifts/status connection is squashed by Paul with an appeal to unity because of the source of the gifts – the 'same *pneuma* . . . the same lord . . . the same god' (12:4–6). When he gets to the body of Christ metaphor to reinforce his plea for unity rather than division of status, he introduces it with an appeal to baptism and its effects, in a similar argument to that in 1:13–17. The common experience of baptism is supposed to yield unity because it initiates the individual into a group, and that initiation should result in unity because all have gone through the same ritual together, ideally. Anything else is a dishonour to Christ and, by implication, the *pneuma* and god. Baptism should direct the Corinthians towards these divine figures, who are all working together for their benefit, and create unity of purpose. It should also render irrelevant social status distinctions – Jew/Greek, slave/free. Once again in this letter, the cultic reference to baptism clearly points to a ritual life that has social formation as its foundation: horizontal formation (Corinthians among themselves) and vertical formation (Paul's chord of gods with their Corinthians adherents).[98]

---

[96] Even if, in this case, the three figures might be just two, the reference to god recalls the third. Hays, *First Corinthians*, 100, says, 'note the implicit trinitarian structure of the formula', which I think goes too far, even if he does not capitalise 'trinitarian'.

[97] καὶ γὰρ ἐν ἑνὶ πνεύματι ἡμεῖς πάντες εἰς ἓν σῶμα ἐβαπτίσθημεν, εἴτε Ἰουδαῖοι εἴτε Ἕλληνες εἴτε δοῦλοι εἴτε ἐλεύθεροι, καὶ πάντες ἓν πνεῦμα ἐποτίσθημεν.

[98] DeMaris, 'Water Ritual,' 403, puts it this way: 'In embryonic Christianity, baptism gave those who underwent it entry into a divine relationship and into a symbolic family of believers. One became a daughter or son of a divinity *and* a brother or sister of one's co-believers' (emphasis original).

The last reference to baptism is in 1 Corinthians 15:29, which is a difficult verse to understand.[99] It reads, 'For otherwise, what would those who are baptised on behalf of the dead do? If the dead are not at all raised, why are they baptised on their behalf?'[100] The verse occurs within the context of Paul's argument about the validity and importance of his teaching on the resurrection of the dead (not just the resurrection of Christ). It seems that the practice, whatever the details of it might have been, was designed to include the dead in the hope or expectation that the members of the assembly would share in the transformation that the living were experiencing. As I discussed above, Paul explains to the Corinthians that they received the *pneuma* of god and are thus πνευματικοί (1 Corinthians 2:12–13). This puts them in the same category as Christ, whose body was transformed into a πνεῦμα ζῳοποιοῦν ('life-giving pneuma'; 15:45) with a σῶμα πνευματικόν ('pneumatic body'; 15:44). If this baptismal ritual is to enact the same kind of transformation that Paul describes in 1 Corinthians 2, then it will involve similar dynamics as the baptism that the living Corinthians have undergone: something that honours the divine figures involved and creates unity with them.

We do not learn the details of the ritual of baptism as practised by the Corinthians, but we do learn that it is crucial for the social identity of the assembly, at least in the manner that Paul envisions it. As a ritual honouring the divine figures involved in its practice, it serves a very similar purpose as the cultic ritual acts of honour that the Corinthians would have engaged in with other groups of gods in their sanctuaries and other places of worship.

Next, we have the lord's supper in 1 Corinthians 11:17–34, an assembly ritual, or something on the way to becoming a ritual, that has gone terribly wrong in Paul's eyes.[101] The passage is clearly focused on Jesus, who is referenced in

---

[99] Fitzmyer, *First Corinthians*, 578, says, 'The major problem in this passage is the interpretation of *hoi baptizomenoi hyper tōn nekrōn*, "those who undergo baptism on behalf of the dead," or "in place of the dead" in v. 29.' DeMaris has written several pieces on baptism on behalf of the dead and situates it within the context of what he claims is a preoccupation with the dead, and worship of chthonic deities, in Corinth and Isthmia. See Richard E. DeMaris: 'Demeter in Roman Corinth: Local Development in a Mediterranean Religion,' *Numen* 42, no. 2 (1995): 105–17, and Richard E. DeMaris, 'Corinthian Religion and Baptism for the Dead (1 Corinthians 15:29): Insights from Archaeology and Anthropology', *JBL* 114 (1995): 662–82. His intent to contextualise Paul's Corinthian practice within local Corinthian practice is laudable, but his understanding of Greek religious categories (chthonic/Olympian) relies on an old scholarly model of division that was not as consistent in the ancient world as he assumes. More nuance would have helped his argument.

[100] Ἐπεὶ τί ποιήσουσιν οἱ βαπτιζόμενοι ὑπὲρ τῶν νεκρῶν; εἰ ὅλως νεκροὶ οὐκ ἐγείρονται, τί καὶ βαπτίζονται ὑπὲρ αὐτῶν;

[101] Stanley K. Stowers, 'Kinds of Myth, Meals, and Power: Paul and the Corinthians', in *Redescribing Paul and the Corinthians*, ed. Cameron and Miller (Atlanta: SBL, 2011), 129. Stowers points to the ritualisation of a meal practice in which the Corinthians were engaged. See also Perkins, *First Corinthians*, 143. Raymond Collins in *First Corinthians*, 430–1, repeatedly refers to 'the cup ritual' and 'the bread ritual'.

the passage fourteen times as 'lord', 'lord Jesus' or 'he.' However, Paul identifies the group at Corinth as 'god's assembly', implying that what goes on in this gathering is under the auspices of god, even if the focus is on the lord Jesus. What is at issue in this passage is how the Corinthians gather and celebrate 'the lord's supper', a practice of the assembly that reveals a disconnect between Paul's and the Corinthians' understandings of its purpose.[102] Paul clearly envisions it as a cultic meal that memorialises the history/mythology of the 'lord Jesus's' last meal before his death and imbues it with ongoing significance for the Corinthians.[103] The Corinthians seem to have a different understanding.[104]

Stowers argues that because the Corinthians lived in 'a culture that centered thysia', they would have had the skills associated with a sacrificial meal: '(1) testing and truth-making; (2) group formation and social differentiation skills; (3) skills in interpreting signs and symbols; and (4) skills in relating fragments of mythic narratives to the preceding activities'.[105] Several things in Paul's description of the meal mark it as a cultic meal, and Paul appeals to the Corinthians to recognise it as such since they should have the skills to do so: (1) the liability to divine judgement if the meal is not conducted properly; (2) the interpretation of the actions in the meal in light of a foundational myth; and (3) particular social formation of the action of sharing a cultic meal. The meal, as the Corinthians are celebrating it, divides the assembly of god because they are not 'discerning' the body of Christ (that is, the assembly) in their celebration of the cultic meal. Among Stowers's hypotheses regarding this meal, he argues that there are some non-elite Corinthians who

> resisted full participation in Paul's practices and reacted by experimenting with their own mythmaking and ritual activities based on their strategic locative interests. Thus, 11:21 contrasts genres of meals that the Corinthians are having with the one true, united Lord's supper.[106]

---

[102] See Stowers, 'Kinds of Myth', 127, for a discussion of 'practice' and the indeterminate meanings involved in them. Stowers says: 'Paul's discussion of the Lord's supper, then, can be seen as one interpretation of a broader practice. But the practice belonged to the culture and was not under his control, as various people participated in that activity employing practical skills that may have involved a huge variety of social abilities, bodily skills, beliefs, symbols, and strategic interests.'

[103] Perkins, *First Corinthians*, 144; Collins, *First Corinthians*, 431. Fitzmyer, *First Corinthians*, 429, calls the passage 'a cultic aetiology'.

[104] See Hans Joseph Klauck, *Herrenmahl und hellenistischer Kult. Eine religionsgeschichtliche Untersuchung zum ersten Korintherbrief* (Münster: Aschendorff, 1982), for an extended discussion of Hellenistic meal practices with which the Corinthians would clearly have been familiar.

[105] Stowers, 'Kinds of Myth', 133. Stowers unpacks these skills in a very compelling, comparative interpretation of the meal practice of the Corinthians on pp. 133–8.

[106] Ibid., 141.

This makes good sense to me but, whatever the social divisions, mythic presumptions or stratification of the assembly reflected in this passage, the meal is cultic, in the sense that I described it in the Introduction.[107] And if this meal is a cultic ritual, however poorly performed or non-ideal it is in Paul's eyes, it certainly involves the attempt to honour a deity or deities and reinforce or build the relationship between the deity/deities and those performing the ritual. The lord is the centre of the lord's supper, but because Paul defines the assembly as god's assembly, at least two of the three divine figures from his chord of gods are at play here in this cultic activity.

In 1 Corinthians 12–14, Paul describes the activity of the Corinthians while assembled as the *naos* of god (3:16), among which are the use of the various spiritual gifts activated by god (12:6), ideally for the unity (πρὸς τὸ συμφέρον) of the assembly (12:7). Although Paul mentions a whole host of gift activities in Chapter 12 as a way of setting up his extended metaphor of the body to show that all members of the assembly are important regardless of the gift, his taxonomy of gifts in 12:28–9 clearly shows that certain gifts should be thought of as prioritised over others. But it is not until Chapter 14 that we learn the real problem that Paul has with some in the assembly: the tongue-speakers are dominating the gatherings and building themselves up, rather than considering the rest of the Corinthians gathered (14:1–7). He goes on to compare tongue-speaking to 'lifeless things that give sound' (τὰ ἄψυχα φωνὴν διδόντα; 14:7), as with musical instruments that do not give distinctive notes. Those who hear such sounds do not understand them as music, nor as a call to battle in a military situation (12:8). Tongue-speaking functions the same way, unless the tongue-speaker can also interpret, which allows for prayer or singing with the spirit and with the mind (14:13–15). It also allows for outsiders to understand and be 'called to account by all' gathered (ἀνακρίνεται ὑπὸ πάντων, 14:24), and perhaps even results in the outsider joining in worshipping the Corinthians' new god.

Paul gives his instructions for gathering more clearly in 14:26–33 – instructions that will result in honouring god in proper order. The activities include hymns, teaching, revelations, tongue-speaking and interpretations of the tongue-speaking: all ecstatic activity, with some being more dramatic than others. The sanctuary that is the Corinthians assembled in their particular location defines these activities as cultic activities. Some of these activities would have been familiar to the Corinthians since they were

---

[107] As I explained there, 'cult means any ritual honour that is given to a god or divine figure that maintains and reinforces the relationship between the god or divine figure and the practitioner *and* among the members of local group of gods of a particular sanctuary.' There seems to be general agreement among scholars that 1 Corinthians 11–14 is about how to act properly during Corinthian assembly ritual activities.

common to other sanctuaries, civic and domestic, such as hymn-singing,[108] myth retelling (akin to teaching)[109] and ecstatic behaviour.[110] In other words, Paul is instructing the Corinthians to organise their cultic gatherings within their sanctuary in a way that will give greatest reciprocal honour to his chord of gods.

## Paul's Chord of Gods

Paul's presentation of his god(s) as god (father), Jesus (son, lord, Christ) and, for some, *pneuma* fits the chord of gods practice that we saw in Chapters One and Two above: (1) a small group of divine figures (2) connected by genealogy, mythology and history, (3) with a cultic life centred around the connected deities that works to honour them and form those worshipping. This was normal practice for the Corinthians; when they heard it in Paul's preaching and appeals, it is hard to imagine that what they heard Paul demanding varied radically from their current practice. The only major differences were the particular elements that filled out the practice: the divine figures (god and Christ; or god, Christ and *pneuma*), the particular ways in which these divine figures were honoured (one-time baptism, with ongoing expectations of social unity; a cultic meal that commemorated the central act of two of the group; and the various ecstatic activities during their cultic assemblies) and the location (a sanctuary of Corinthian Jesus followers where the *pneuma*

---

[108] Many sanctuary inscriptions from the ancient Mediterranean are hymns to the deities of the sanctuary. Some examples from William D. Furley and Jan Maarten Bremer, *Greek Hymns*, vol. 1, *The Texts in Translation* (Tübingen: Mohr Siebeck, 2001), demonstrate the importance of hymns in the life of Greek sanctuaries across the ancient Mediterranean: Crete: The Hymn to Zeus at Mount Dikta, likely a fourth- or third-century BCE hymn inscribed in the third century CE (ibid., 1:1); Delphi: the long tradition of the *paian* at the Delphic sanctuary, mostly associated with Apollo, but other gods, like Dionysos, were sometimes the object of praise and worship in these musical forms (ibid., 75–138, with many examples); and the many hymns or *paians* to Asklepios and the gods found at his sanctuaries, for example to Asklepios at Erythrae (with slightly different versions of the same hymn found at Dion and Ptolemais) (ibid., 211–12) and to Hygieia at Epidauros (ibid., 224).

[109] Although it is impossible to identify a particular version of the Demeter–Persephone myth, it is clear that the ritual at the mysteries of Eleusis contain some retelling and/or re-enactment of elements of the story. See Jan N. Bremmer, *Initiation into the Mysteries of the Ancient World* (Berlin: De Gruyter, 2014), 1–20; and Kevin Clinton, 'The Mysteries of Demeter and Kore', in *A Companion to Greek Religion*, ed. Daniel Ogden (Oxford: Blackwell, 2010), 342–56.

[110] See the widespread evidence of maenadism associated with Dionysos, or the self-castration of the Galli associated with the Mother of the Gods.

resided, their cultic activity was carried out and their social unity was nurtured and reinforced). The similar pattern of religious practice, however, seems close enough to postulate strong familiarity between Paul's appeals and the Corinthian socio-religious ethos at all social strata. It is therefore imaginable that the Corinthians were attracted to Paul's appeal because of its familiarity and overlap with their regular practice and experience. I will unpack this conclusion more in the next chapter.

CHAPTER FIVE

# Reimagining the Early Days of Paul's Corinthians

The scholarship on Christian origins is vast and wide. As Joshua Garroway says, 'There has never been a definitive model for depicting the emergence of Christianity, no perfect description to capture what happened.'[1] It has not been the aim of this book to prove Garroway wrong by providing just such a perfect description, but instead to lay the groundwork for plausible socio-religious overlap between the Corinthians and Paul that might have started the ball rolling towards the development of this group. Paula Fredriksen – one of the more recent scholars to attempt a reconstruction of the early success of Paul among Gentiles – correctly says,

> This is a Paul who fits within his Jewish, Greek, and Roman contexts by way of conformation rather than contrast. A Paul who had no idea that his life's work would eventuate – and only long years after his death, as a belated historical phase-change – in gentile Christianity. A Paul whose very success at turning pagans from their gods to his god, the god of Abraham, Isaac, and Jacob, confirmed him in his conviction that he stood at the edge of history's end. A Paul, in other words, who lived his life entirely within his native Judaism.[2]

While I agree that Paul never saw himself as leaving his native Judaism and also saw himself as part of the larger Greek and Roman worlds in which he acted, I believe that Fredricksen does not adequately account for Paul's success with gentiles. She attributes it to surprising luck and to focusing exclusively on a group of gentiles who already had a deep affinity for Jewish practices and

---

[1] Joshua Garroway, *Paul's Gentile-Jews: Neither Jew nor Gentile, but Both* (New York: Palgrave Macmillan, 2012), 49.
[2] Paula Fredriksen, *Paul: The Pagans' Apostle* (New Haven: Yale University Press, 2017), 175.

traditions, namely the god-fearers. A group of god-fearers is a logical and convenient solution to connect Paul the Jew with gentiles, but we need to look closer at the evidence before we can judge the likelihood that god-fearers' 'conversion' was the most likely scenario for Paul's success in Corinth.

## God-Fearers as the Reason for Gentile Success

'God-fearers' or 'Judaisers' were those gentiles who had some association with a local synagogue and adhered to some of the ancestral traditions of Israel without ever becoming fully a part of Israel. The scholarship on this group is extensive.[3] Some scholars focus on the terminology from the evidence to determine whether there is some technical or semi-technical usage that can help identify the group. Shaye J. D. Cohen contextualises the idea of god-fearers within the larger discussion of conversion, and correctly nuances the idea of god-fearers as a widespread phenomenon or group afforded any status by other Jews: 'The example of Aphrodisias, Miletus, and Panticapaeum [inscriptional evidence for god-fearers (*theosebeis*)] . . . hardly proves that everywhere gentile "venerators of God" were accorded recognition by local Jewish communities, much less that they could "join" the communities and become members.'[4] He goes on to point out the local variations for the ways in which 'venerators of God' would have been viewed, and discusses whether they were even seen to be a distinct group in the wider context of general society, thus helpfully resisting generalisation.[5] But Fredriksen is not concerned about the narrow focus of technical terminology and the necessary social and geographical nuances of the evidence, arguing that a wide range of terminology does not necessarily mean that the group did not exist.[6] For her, the terminology to describe this group is only semi-technical at best, but also varying. What is important is the social phenomenon: a group of gentiles who were not only familiar with Judaism but involved in the life of the synagogue in some tangible way. This can include anything from simply being a benefactor to fully embracing the

---

[3] A small sampling: Shaye J. D. Cohen, *The Beginnings of Jewishness: Boundaries, Varieties, Uncertainties* (Berkeley: University of California, 1999), especially chs 5 and 6; Louis H. Feldman, *Jew and Gentile in the Ancient World* (Princeton: Princeton University Press, 1993), ch. 10; Ross S. Kraemer, 'Giving Up the Godfearers', *Journal of Ancient Judaism* 5 (2014): 61–87; Joyce Reynolds and Robert Tannenbaum, *Jews and Godfearers at Aphrodisias* (Cambridge: Cambridge Philological Society, 1987); Judith M. Lieu, 'The Race of the God-Fearers', *Journal of Theological Studies* 46 (1995): 483–501.

[4] Cohen, *The Beginnings of Jewishness*, 172–3.

[5] Ibid., 173.

[6] Fredriksen, *Paul: The Pagan's Apostle*, 55–9; Paula Fredriksen, 'Judaizing the Nations: The Ritual Demands of Paul's Gospel', *NTS* 56 (2010): 242.

practices and teachings of Judaism as expressed in the local context. But one thing is clear in how Fredriksen understands this group: the god-fearers were not full adherents to Judaism but maintained ties to their ancestral gods while simultaneously participating in the local synagogue.

To judge Fredriksen's reconstruction of Paul's success as applied to Corinth, we have to follow Cohen's lead and examine the local context carefully. Is it clear whether or not god-fearers were an actual group in first-century Corinth? Generally speaking, the evidence for them (as described as terminologically inclusively as possible) consists of a combination of inscriptional and literary evidence. The literary evidence comes from a few sources: Juvenal 14.96–106 talks about a pagan who takes on some Jewish practices, particularly giving up pork and observing the Sabbath without forsaking his pagan loyalties. Josephus has a few references: sympathy with Jewish causes (*AJ* 20.195); contributions to the temple by gentiles from Asia Minor and Europe (*AJ* 14.110); 'Judaising' (ἰουδαΐζοντας) gentiles found in the cities of Syria (*BJ* 2.463); gentile wives in Damascus turning to Jewish practice (θρησκεία; *BJ* 2.560); and Greeks who are drawn to the θρησκεία of the Jews in Antioch (*BJ* 7.45). Acts of the Apostles repeatedly refers to the idea of god-fearers, using various terms or phrases. As Levinskaya describes, 'Luke himself used different names for these adherents of the Jewish God: φοβούμενοι τὸν θεόν (Acts 10:1–2; 10:22; 13:16; 13:26), σεβόμενοι τὸν θεόν (13:50; 16:14; 18:6–7), σεβόμενοι (17:4), σεβόμενοι προσήλυτοι (13:43), σεβόμενοι Ἕλληνες (17:17).' She then goes on to admit that 'The abrupt change in terminology is puzzling.'[7] In a narrower and more local focus, the only literary evidence referring to Corinth comes from Acts 18, which mentions Paul attending the synagogue and arguing with Jews and Greeks there, before going to a certain Titius Justus whose house was right next to the synagogue. There is no literary evidence outside of Acts for god-fearers in Corinth in any of the first five centuries CE.

Most of the inscriptional evidence for the general existence of god-fearers is located in Asia Minor and revolves around terminology that might or might not indicate the presence of god-fearers as an identifiable group, at least as Acts describes them.[8] As Levinskaya has stated,

> No such terms as the ones Luke used exist in the Greek inscriptions – the only possible exception known at present is provided by the evidence for cult associations worshipping the Most High God in the imperial period at Tanais (one of the cities in the estuary of the Don, that belonged to the Bosporan Kingdom). These usually employ the term

---

[7] Irina Levinskaya, *The Book of Acts in Its First Century Setting*, vol. 5, *The Book of Acts in Its Diaspora Setting* (Grand Rapids, MI: Eerdmans, 1996), 52.

[8] Kraemer, 'Giving Up the Godfearers', 66.

θεοσεβής, which has been equated with Luke's usage, though such an equation was considered by many as wrong and unproven.[9]

When an ambiguous usage of a term like θεοσεβής in an inscription appears, it is easy to jump quickly to Judaisers or god-fearers as the referent, but 'The main difficulty with the latter conclusion is that here, more than usual, historical research depends upon one's presuppositions, underlying theory and imagination.'[10]

While there might be some consistency in terminology in the inscriptions, it is not clear whether they refer to god-fearers or are just general complimentary descriptors for local people.[11] Context certainly matters, so synagogue inscriptions or overt Jewish symbols on inscriptions more securely refer to god-fearers, although there are not many from synagogues. To give a sense of the range of evidence: *CIJ* I² 202 is very fragmentary and likely has θεοσεβής as one of its terms.[12] It is part of a sarcophagus, and near the inscription is a menorah. Its provenance is Rome. In contrast, *CIJ* I² 500 has an uncertain provenance but a very clear representation of θεοσεβής.[13] The birthplace of the subject is mentioned (Phaena in Syria), but otherwise it is ambiguous as to whether or not it refers to a god-fearer. *CIJ* I² Lifshitz, Prolegomenon 731e from Rhodes was found on an altar with a clear representation of θεοσεβής, but there is no indication of whether it refers to a Jew, a gentile or a god-fearer.[14] The altar location suggests a gentile or god-fearer identification for the subject, but beyond that we cannot say much.[15] *CIJ* II 754, a third-century inscription from Deliler, Lydia, clearly comes from a synagogue and clearly names a θεοσεβής, so it is much less ambiguous.[16] Every inscription has its peculiarities and raises questions about the usage of θεοσεβής.

---

[9] Levinskaya, *The Book of Acts*, 54.
[10] Ibid.
[11] Kraemer, 'Giving Up the Godfearers', 66: '*Theosebes*, in particular, is attested in some ambiguous contexts that invite explication. There is at least as much, if not more, evidence for the use of *theosebes*, especially, in ways that are demonstrably *not* indications of Gentile practice of limited aspects of Judean/Jewish piety. Hard, unambiguous evidence remains quite limited, and comes mostly from a few geographical locations (primarily Asia Minor); is datable to a relatively narrow time-frame (mostly the 3rd–5th centuries C.E., and even this may be generous) and is mostly found in donative and votive contexts' (emphasis original).
[12] *CIJ* I² 500 = [.....Ἰο]υδέα προσή | [λυτος. ... θ]εοσεβή | [ς......] νον | [....] ν.
[13] *CIJ* I² 500 = Ἀγρίππας Φού | σκου Φαινή | σιος θεοσεβής.
[14] *CIJ* I² Lifshitz, Prolegomenon 731e = Εὐφροσύνα θεοσεβής | χρηστὰ χαῖρε.
[15] And maybe we cannot say even that much, since the relationship between Jewish and gentile practice is not as clear cut as it was once believed to be.
[16] *CIJ* II 754 = Τῇ ἁγιοτάτῃ | συναγωγη | τῶν Ἑβραίων | Εὐστάτιος | ὁ θεοσεβὴς | ὑπὲρ μνίας | τοῦ ἀδελφοῦ | Ἑρμοφίλου | τὸν μασκαύ | λην ἀνέθη | κα ἅμα τῇ νύμ | φῃ μου Ἀθανασίᾳ.

The exception is the famous Aphrodisias inscription, which has a list of names under the term on one side of a stone at the door of a synagogue. This is the most unambiguous example of non-literary evidence in existence and, according to Levinskaya, 'changed the picture completely, and has now become the central point of the discussion'.[17] But there are even problems with this inscription in terms of the ramifications for the existence of god-fearers as a clearly defined social group in the first century, especially in Corinth. In 1996, Levinskaya dated the inscription to the third century to represent what most scholars thought then.[18] But since that time the dating has been rethought, and now some scholars think it is better dated to the fourth or fifth century.[19] Aphrodisias is a long way from Corinth,[20] and this inscription is a long time away from the first century.[21] While it might speak to the development of god-fearers as an identifiable group in that area of Asia Minor in the fourth or fifth century, can this be definitive evidence for the existence of the group in all places across the Mediterranean for the previous three or four centuries? That is a stretch at best. Any supposition of god-fearers as a distinct group in Corinth in the mid-first century relies exclusively on Acts (written decades later with a certain theological agenda that Paul did not share), supplemented by inscriptional evidence from centuries later, located hundreds of miles from Corinth.

This key element of Fredriksen's reconstruction of the earliest outreach activity of the Jesus movement – reliance on the existence of god-fearers as the accidental gateway to gentile inclusion in the movement[22] – falls short precisely because of the lack of evidence for god-fearers in Corinth during the time of Paul. There is no extant evidence in Corinth before the late first or early second century CE, depending on when one dates Acts.[23] More generally, Fredriksen

---

[17] Levinskaya, *The Book of Acts*, 56.

[18] The original editors of the Aphrodisias inscription dated it to the third century. See Reynolds and Tannenbaum, *Jews and God-Fearers at Aphrodisias*.

[19] Angelos Chaniotis, 'The Jews of Aphrodisias: New Evidence and Old Problems', *Scripta Classica Israelica* 21 (2002): 209–42; Fredriksen, *Paul: The Pagan's Apostle*, 55.

[20] Over 1500km by car on modern ferries and roads, and 690km by boat and car.

[21] Sometimes modern scholars forget that ancient time actually corresponds to the same register of time that we use. So, relative to United States history, the Aphrodisias inscription was created at least 300 years after Paul was alive and well in Corinth, longer than the United States has been a country, and almost 165 years longer than Minnesota (my home state) has been a state.

[22] The accidental success of early missionaries is in direct contrast to Wayne Meeks's attempt to give a 'non-accidental' explanation for why non-elites were also part of the assemblies of Paul. Wayne Meeks, *The First Urban Christians: The Social World of the Apostle Paul* (New Haven: Yale University Press, 1983), chs 3–6.

[23] This is based on the conventional dating of Acts. Stanley K. Stowers, 'Kinds of Myth, Meals, and Power: Paul and the Corinthians', in *Redescribing Paul and the Corinthians*, ed. Ron Cameron and Merrill P. Miller (Atlanta: SBL, 2011), 108n9: 'The Corinthian letters, unlike Acts, give no

assumes that there were significant numbers of god-fearers in all the synagogues visited by Paul and the other early leaders of the Jesus movement – large enough numbers to account for the spread of the movement and cause the theological reorientation that we find in Paul's undisputed letters and in Acts. Since she never explains if or how other gentiles might have heard of the movement – let alone been convinced enough to leave their ancestral practices to join it – one has to assume that god-fearers were the only gentiles that made up the movement in this early period. But how could this be with so little evidence for widespread groups of god-fearers in the early to mid-first century? Reliance on the god-fearers hypothesis to explain the early development of Corinthian followers of Paul simply does not hold up with such a lack of evidence.

## Alternatives to the God-Fearers as the Reason for Gentile Success

Stanley Stowers agrees that Paul's culture was thoroughly Jewish, but he has a more plausible solution to Paul's success in Corinth than a receptive group of Corinthian god-fearers. He centres his solution on Paul's ability to enlist educated, fairly high-status Corinthians to learn his 'alternative esoteric and exotic *paideia*' and act as his deputies to get others on board with it.[24] For him, Paul is best described as 'a producer and distributor of an alternative esoteric paideia different from the dominant sophistic or philosophical kinds, yet still recognizable as a form of the same broader game of specialized literate learning.'[25]

There is much to say for this scenario, especially the fact that Stowers posits the need for there to be recognisability in Paul's *paideia* among at least some of the Corinthians. On this point Stowers makes clear that the perspectives of Paul's Corinthian interlocutors are as important to consider as Paul's *paideia*. But he is unclear about the specifics of how the non-elite among the Corinthians might have been convinced to join the group. Would they have fallen in line with those of higher status whom Paul had convinced already?

---

hint of the existence of a Jewish community, synagogues, so-called god-fearers, or converted Jews. It is not impossible that there were non-Jews among the Corinthians who had had an interest in things Jewish, but there is little or no evidence for it in the letters except for the coming of Paul and other Jewish teachers.'

[24] Stowers 'Kinds of Myth', 116.
[25] Ibid., 117. Stowers is working within the framework of Pierre Bourdieu's social theory, which posits the technical notion of practices that I discussed in the Introduction. He thinks of Paul's activity in Corinth as part of a wider intellectual practice 'in which specialists employed their skills to compete and "debate" in their production and interpretation of oral and written texts and discourses that contest the truth and legitimacy of both traditions and novel doctrines' (ibid., 116).

If they were not beholden to the higher-status individuals – as slaves or clients – how compelled would they have felt to join? This is an important question because the non-elite were likely the majority of the group, as I discussed in Chapter Three.[26] How would Paul and/or his deputies convince others to join the movement when their education level and social status could not support assent to an exotic *paideia* they might not have understood? Or if they did have the capability to understand Paul's *paideia*, would they likely have the time to contemplate it long enough to understand it and assent to it, given their need to work for their subsistence?

I think the common 'chord of gods' practice described in this study offers a helpful supplement to Stowers's theory. We cannot assume a uniform group of gentiles in the Corinthian assembly, and so there would be a portion of the Corinthians (perhaps even a majority) who were non-elites who initially found something appealing about Paul's movement that was not tied to his possible activity with the elite. The affinity to the chord of gods practice offers a plausible scenario for Paul's success with other Corinthian gentiles, though whether accidental or purposeful on Paul's part is hard to tell. But if this practice was obvious to the Corinthians, then it provided a familiarity and comfortability with at least some of Paul's proposals about his chord of gods and the subsequent demands he was making of those who would join the movement. This would not be the only reason for them wanting to join the movement: social connection, economic improvement and desire for security

---

[26] Bruce W. Longenecker, 'Socio-Economic Profiling of the First Urban Christians', in *After the First Urban Christians: The Social-Scientific Study of Pauline Christianity Twenty-Five Years Later*, ed. Todd D. Still and David G. Horrell (London: T & T Clark, 2009), 36–59. See also Bruce W. Longenecker, *Remember the Poor: Paul, Poverty, and the Greco-Roman World* (Grand Rapids, MI: Eerdmans, 2010). The system of classification of relative wealth and poverty in Roman society that Longenecker uses is a modified version of the one that Steven J. Friesen developed, which involved 'seven distinct "levels" on an economic scale' (Steven J. Friesen, 'Poverty in Pauline Studies: Beyond the So-Called New Consensus', *JSNT* 26 (2004): 323–61). Since Friesen's proposal, Walter Scheidel and Friesen ('The Size of the Economy and the Distribution of Income in the Roman Empire', *JRS* 99 (2009): 61–91), Longenecker (*Remember the Poor*) and Timothy A. Brookins ('Economic Profiling of Early Christian Assemblies', in *Paul and Economics: A Handbook*, ed. Thomas R. Blanton IV and Raymond Pickett (Minneapolis: Fortress, 2017), 57–88) have all offered elaborations and refinements to the model. In a very recent study on poverty and wealth ('Wealth, Poverty, Economy', in *The Oxford Handbook of the Synoptic Gospels*, ed. Stephen P. Ahearne-Kroll (Oxford: Oxford University Press, 2023), 296–319), Blanton offers a further modified version that is based on Raymond Pickett's introduction to *Paul and Economics: A Handbook*, xiii–xxxvi. One problem with trying to get a sense of the makeup of the Pauline group in Corinth through the lens of an economic scale is that issues of education and social status are correlative but not identical to economic status. It is conceivable that an enslaved person, for example, could have the educational level to understand Paul's *paideia* and help facilitate its spread, even though the enslaved person's economic status was not autonomously determined. This enslaved person might be considered 'elite' even if their status with regard to their autonomy was lower than that of a free person. See the discussion in Chapter Three.

could all have contributed to the process. But familiarity and comfortability with the structure of practice would have aided Paul's efforts.

Further, the chord of gods practice might help explain the spread of Paul's *paideia* beyond the elite circles that Stowers posits. Current research on network formation shows that at least two major forces result in social group formation: preferential attachment and homophily.[27] Preferential attachment theory basically states that alliances form as a result of a bandwagoning effect, where alliances grow in number of participants by attraction to the member who has the most centralised organisation and power.[28] It is imaginable that, after Paul's initial success with some of the more educated Corinthians (Gaius or Stephanus, for example, as Stowers argues) in sharing his alternative *paideia*, a small centre of authority formed around Paul that attracted other members to the group, perhaps those already adhered to Gaius or Stephanus as clients, freedmen, enslaved or other less elite members of their households. Even if the newest members were not completely convinced by Paul's Christ-centred mythmaking and thoughts about the eschatological dynamics unfolding in real time, their social connections would have played a role in their adherence to this new *paideia*. Once the node that had formed around Paul grew large enough, others would have been attracted through the social force of homophily – a theory that can be expressed, in short, as 'Similarity breeds connection',[29] a popular ancient concept referred to famously in Plato and Aristotle.[30]

[27] This sort of research is thoroughly modern, so we have to be careful not to assume that all aspects of it hold. But homophily, especially, has been applied to a huge range of social relations and settings and has proven to be highly explanatory of behaviour in these settings. I see no reason to question its usefulness for thinking about formation of the Corinthian Christ group.

[28] 'Thinking of alliance formation or institutional network formation as a bandwagoning process is both simple and intuitive.' Zeev Maoz, 'Preferential Attachment, Homophily, and the Structure of International Networks, 1816–2003', *Conflict Management and Peace Science* 29, no. 3 (2012): 347 (and 343–7 for a more extensive description of the model). Maoz describes this process in the context of international alliances from modern times, but I think that the basic idea of preferential attachment theory can offer something to our discussion. See also Zeev Moaz, Lesley G. Terris, Ranan D. Kuperman and Ilan Talmud, 'What Is the Enemy of My Enemy? Causes and Consequences of Imbalanced International Relations, 1816–2001', *Journal of Politics* 69, no. 1 (2007): 100–15.

[29] Miller J. McPherson, Lynn Smith-Lovin and James M. Cook, 'Birds of a Feather: Homophily in Social Networks', *Annual Review of Sociology* 27 (2001): 415. See also Christopher Weare, Juliet Musso and Kyu-Nahm Jun, 'Cross-Talk: The Role of Homophily and Elite Bias in Civic Associations', *Social Forces* 88, no. 1 (2009): 147–73; Maoz, 'Preferential Attachment', 347–52.

[30] Pl. *Phdr.* 240c: 'The old proverb says, "birds of a feather flock together"; that is, I suppose, equality of age leads them to similar pleasures and through similarity begets friendship' (trans. Harold N. Fowler, *Plato: Euthyphro; Apology; Crito; Phaedo; Phaedrus* (Cambridge, MA: Harvard University Press, 1925), accessed 25 October 2022, www.perseus.tufts.edu). Arist. *Eth. Nic.* 8.6: 'Some define [friendship] as a matter of similarity; they say that we love those who are like ourselves: whence the proverbs "Like finds his like," "Birds of a feather flock together," and so on.' (trans. H. Rackham, *Aristotle: Nicomachean Ethics* (Cambridge, MA: Harvard University Press 1934), accessed 25 October 2022, www.perseus.tufts.edu).

While Aristotle sees that 'significant disparities in wealth or status interfere with conceptions of genuine friendship between people on opposite sides of a class divide' (Arist. *Eth. Nic.* 1158b31–1159a2), these differences were often overridden by connections essential to one's character.[31] Robert Holschuh Simmons argues that, in an ancient Athenian context, a leader could cultivate friendships with social subordinates by seizing on essential similarities or advantageous qualities of the social subordinate and using these as the basis of a friendship. One strong force that enables feelings of connection between social unequals is physical proximity, something that modern sociologists who study interpersonal interaction call propinquity.[32] Simmons appeals to one such incident, namely that of Crito's behaviour towards Archedemus as found in Xenophon's *Memorabilia*. Crito, the social superior to Archedemus, wants to benefit from Archedemus's skill as an orator, despite his relative poverty. The way Crito builds a friendship with Archedemus is not just with gifts; primarily, he invites Archedemus to spend time with him by inviting Archedemus to join him in sacrifices and to take refuge in his home (Xen. *Mem.* 2.9.4–5), which eventually leads Crito to call Archedemus his φίλος (2.9.8). As Simmons says, 'Their inequality in wealth could, in another situation, have interfered with their homophily connection, but Crito's treatment of Archedemus leads the latter to see himself as Crito's equal, and thus his friend.'[33]

These types of connections could plausibly have formed between the elite group of Corinthians to whom Paul taught his *paideia* and the less elite Corinthians, in part because of the homophily of practice that was being offered by Paul and his deputies.[34] The proximity of the socially

---

[31] Robert Holschuh Simmons, '"Men, Friends": The Sociological Mechanics of Xenophontic Leaders in Winning Subordinates as Friends', in *At the Crossroads of Greco-Roman History, Culture, and Religion: Papers in Memory of Carin M. Green*, ed. Sinclair W. Bell and Lora L. Holland (Oxford: Archeopress, 2018), 33–4 (quote at 33).

[32] 'One highly relevant consideration is that both mediation and proximity affect nonverbal immediacy, which refers to a constellation of nonverbal behaviors (e.g., physical proximity, eye contact, touch, body orientation, body lean) that enable sensory immersion and create psychological closeness as well as physical and social presence ... Furthermore, physically copresent interactants may entrain to each other's speech rhythms and nonverbal behavior, coordinating and synchronizing their communication into a unified, smooth-flowing pattern, all seemingly without conscious awareness.' Judee K. Bergoon, Joseph A. Bonito, Artemio Ramirez Jr, Norah E. Dunbar, Karadeen Kam and Jenna Fishcer, 'Testing the Interactivity Principle: Effects of Mediation, Propinquity, and Verbal and Nonverbal Modalities in Interpersonal Interaction', *Journal of Communication* 52 (2002): 661–62.

[33] Simmons, 'Men, Friends', 34.

[34] J. Albert Harrill, *Paul the Apostle: His Life and Legacy in Their Roman Context* (Cambridge: Cambridge University Press, 2012), 50, briefly mentions a plausible social scenario in which Paul reaches out to the local leatherworkers association – his trade – giving him a ready audience for his preaching. But Harrill does not develop this idea at all.

heterogeneous members of the Corinthian group could have created this selective homophily (that is, chord of gods practice), thus creating the bonds necessary for the group to grow in size as they spent more and more time together. There was no need for every one of the Corinthians to buy into Paul's exotic *paidea* for the movement to have grown, nor could have this been possible if the majority of Corinthians did not have the level of education necessary to understand it. However, if the homophily of practice was strong enough, this would have been enough for the group to grow beyond the few elites with the education to understand Paul's *paideia*. And the familiarity of the chord of gods practices would have been a strong draw during the homophily stage of development because these practices had been deeply grounded in the traditions of the Corinthians for many centuries. Analogous to the result of Crito's homophilic overtures to Archedemus, which led to Crito calling Archedemus φίλος, the homophilic overtures of Paul's small elite group to the non-elites via chord of gods practice could have resulted in the elites calling the non-elites ἀδελφός.

## Allegiance to Paul's Chord of Gods

While the demand to change allegiance from one's ancestral gods to the god(s) of Paul was a very difficult ask of the Corinthians, as Fredriksen has noted in much of her work,[35] the chord of gods similarities might have been compelling enough to make joining the group comfortable for the non-elite members of the growing group. Alternatively, there is some sense that at least some of the Corinthian assembly members did not fully grasp that Paul was demanding exclusive allegiance to his god(s), or rejected that demand while still expecting to remain in the group. Take 1 Corinthians 8–10, for example, where Paul tries to explain why eating food sacrificed to other gods might be a problem for the community. One could explain this practice as accidental on the Corinthians' part because they might not have been taking an active part in the worship of other gods and did not realise that even this passive activity was problematic for the assembly. Or it could be evidence that there were some assembly members who simply dismissed the exclusivity of Paul's group practice. If what he presented to the Corinthians was similar enough to what they were used to doing, then they might have seen no problem with continuing their regular practice alongside what Paul introduced.

With regard to the lord's supper as described in 1 Corinthians 11:17–34, Stowers rightly notes that there were some 'less or non-elite Corinthians

---

[35] But see especially in Fredriksen, 'Judaizing the Nations', and *Paul: The Pagans' Apostle*.

[who] resisted full participation in Paul's practices and reacted by experimenting with their own mythmaking and ritual activities based on their strategic and locative interests'.[36] We could easily point to the Corinthians' chord of gods practice and traditions as a strong locative interest, since long-held practices and traditions tied to ethnic identity cannot be shed without difficulty. As there was no exclusivity assumed in conventional chord of gods practice — that is, Corinthians could be affiliated with more than one chord of gods at a time in a variety of settings — it seems quite plausible that they would have seen the lord's supper as one practice among other chord of gods practices, especially if Paul was not explicit about exclusivity in his initial time with the Corinthians. If this is plausible for some with the lord's supper, it is also plausible that some would participate in other practices around other gods — for example, eating food sacrificed to other gods — for similar reasons. So, whether they were actively dismissive or lacking understanding of the practices that Paul was advocating, some of the Corinthians could have been attracted to join and stay in Paul's group by similarity of their traditional chord of gods practice.

There are a few places in the Corinthian correspondence that, when read through the chord of gods lens, help to demonstrate the possibility of Paul's awareness of the Corinthians' problems of exclusive adherence to his god(s). In these passages, Paul draws sharp distinctions between adhering to the traditions of the Corinthians (the tell-tale marker is the use of εἴδωλον as descriptor for the Corinthian gods) and adhering to the developing traditions that he advocates. In these passages, Paul makes no effort to argue for an abandonment of the Corinthians' chord of gods practice; instead, he seems to assume that his chord of father god and (lord) Jesus (Christ), or god, (lord) Jesus (Christ) and the *pneuma* would be an understandable configuration for his Corinthian addressees and argues only for loyalty to *his* chord of gods. I will look briefly at just three examples: 1 Corinthians 8:4–6 and 12:1–11, and 2 Corinthians 6:14–7:1.

In 1 Corinthians 8, Paul is beginning a long section that responds to the issue of whether the Corinthians should be eating 'offerings to idols' (εἰδωλόθυτον). He first dismisses the existence of idols over and against the one god of his tradition by evoking the 'famous commandment ... of ancient Israel', the so-called Shema of Deuteronomy 6:4.[37] As Joseph Fitzmyer points out, the parallel between the two sayings that Paul quotes back to the Corinthians is clearest in the Greek: ὅτι οὐδὲν εἴδωλον ἐν κόσμῳ, καὶ ὅτι οὐδεὶς θεὸς εἰ μὴ εἷς.[38] This parallel sets up a contrast between the lack of even one idol in

---

[36] Stanley K. Stowers, 'Kinds of Myth', 141.
[37] Fitzmyer, *First Corinthians*, 341.
[38] Ibid., 340.

the world with the existence of 'the one' god, that is, the god of Israel.[39] But Pheme Perkins and others go too far by saying that this was about monotheism versus polytheism, even if 'the oneness of the God of Israel was emphasized'.[40] Perkins says, 'The *knowledge* question was based on the monotheistic belief that *no one is God except one* (8:4), which the Corinthians had embraced upon their conversion (cf. 1 Thess. 1:9–10). That conviction is shared by everyone in the church.'[41] She goes on to frame the entirety of this section of the letter in terms of monotheism and polytheism, while trying to explain away the presence of the Lord Jesus Christ as a 'dual confession' of the one god, with no consideration of how the Corinthians might have understood the mention of these two deities.[42] Raymond F. Collins similarly assumes this monotheistic/polytheistic framework, by naming the relevant subsection of his commentary 'The Monotheistic Confession of Faith (8:4–6)'.[43]

I do not agree that the monotheism that Perkins and Collins presuppose was shared by everyone in the assembly at Corinth, or that the theological divide that Perkins, Fitzmyer, Collins and many others presume was even an issue for Paul or the Corinthians. Timothy A. Brookins moves in the right direction by noting that the syntax of 8:4 requires that Paul and the Corinthians both would have 'affirmed that idols in fact *did* exist in the world'.[44] And Paul goes on to assert this in verse 5. So Paul was not interested in theological systems that deny the existence of more than one god in the universe but in the issue of to which god the Corinthians should pledge their allegiance. 'Even if' (εἴπερ) there are gods and lords in heaven and on earth, 'for us' (ἡμῖν) there is something different, says Paul, setting up an 'us vs them' scenario. And what better way to earn allegiance than to negate 'them'? So Paul goes on to disparage the 'many gods and many lords' with λεγόμενοι ('so-called'; 8:5), and to contrast these with his god by defining the divinity more specifically as 'father' in verse 6: 'But for us, there is one god, the father, from whom are all things

[39] In contrast to a statement by Oh-Young Kwon, 'Discovering the Characteristics of Collegia: Collegia Sodalicia and Collegia Tenuiorum in 1 Corinthians 8, 10 and 15', *Horizons in Biblical Theology* 32 (2010): 174–5: 'On the other hand, they affirmed that the God of Jesus is the one true God – and that the idols/emperors were not true gods (8:4) – therefore it did not matter in other respects if they participated in banquets and dinner parties in the wider Corinthian society.' This was not just about the god of Jesus but, more widely, about the god of Israel and Paul, by default.
[40] Fitzmyer, *First Corinthians*, 341.
[41] Pheme Perkins, *First Corinthians* (Grand Rapids, MI: Baker, 2012), 114 (emphasis original).
[42] Ibid., 114–15.
[43] Raymond F. Collins, *First Corinthians* (Collegeville, MN: Liturgical Press, 1999), 313. The blatant presumption that theological difference between monotheistic belief and polytheistic belief drives the divide between Paul and the Corinthians is on full, erroneous display here.
[44] Timothy A. Brookins, *Corinthian Wisdom, Stoic Philosophy, and the Ancient Economy* (Cambridge: Cambridge University Press, 2014), 89n67 (emphasis original).

and we are [going] towards him', and then by distinguishing the many 'lords' from his: 'and one lord Jesus Christ, through whom are all things and we are through him'. Paul calls for an apparent shift from θεοὶ πολλοὶ καὶ κύριοι πολλοί to εἷς θεὸς ὁ πατὴρ ... καὶ εἷς κύριος Ἰησοῦς Χριστός – from the many to the one. But was he calling for a shift from 'polytheism' to 'monotheism', from one theological system to another, to reorient the way in which the Corinthians envisioned their future in relation to their past and perhaps their present?[45] It seems not.

The beginning of verse 6 – ἀλλ' ἡμῖν – differentiates the community from their past (or even current) activity of honouring deities other than the god of Paul's tradition, as he would prefer. If Paul had stopped at εἰς αὐτόν halfway through this verse – or even at the end of 8:4 with his strong assertion of the existence of only the one god of Israel – he would have been on solid ground with the Corinthians in terms of differentiating *their* tradition of honouring 'many' deities from his tradition of (purportedly) honouring only the one god.[46] Instead, he goes on to assert the importance of honouring Jesus Christ as lord (and son; see also 1:9) right alongside the importance of honouring the one god of Israel. While many have probed the theological significance of κύριος as a title for Jesus in comparison to θεός or πατήρ, I think it would not have mattered for the Corinthians, who were used to deities who existed across a spectrum of status, acting together and being honoured in everyday worship.[47] For instance, there is no indication that the presence of Poseidon

---

[45] James D. G. Dunn, *Christology in the Making: A New Testament Inquiry in the Origins of the Doctrine of the Incarnation* (London: SCM, 1989), 180, says that Paul 'splits the Shema' here in a way that has no precedents. See also S. U. Lim, 'The Political Economy of Eating Idol Meat: Practice, Structure, and Subversion in 1 Corinthians 8 through the Sociological Lens of Pierre Bourdieu', *Horizons in Biblical Theology* 34 (2012): 155–72, who repeatedly assumes a monotheistic underpinning of the knowledge difference between the strong ('those who possess knowledge of the monotheistic God', 166) and the weak (those who lack this knowledge), and locates that difference mainly in 1 Cor. 8:4.

[46] As I described in the Introduction, Schäfer has recently and convincingly argued for at least a two-deity configuration in Israel for many centuries up through to late antiquity. See Peter Schäfer, *Two Gods in Heaven: Jewish Concepts of God in Antiquity* (Princeton: Princeton University Press, 2020).

[47] Wilhelm Bousset, *Kyrios Christos: A History of Belief in Christ from the Beginnings of Christianity to Irenaeus* (Waco, TX: Baylor University Press, 2013; first published 1913), began the twentieth-century scholarly discussion about the origins of worship of Christ as a divinity in early Christianity. See also Dunn, *Christology in the Making*, 179–83, and Richard A. Horsley, 'The Background of the Confessional Formula in 1 Kor 8:6', *Zeitschrift für die neutestamentliche Wissenschaft und die Kunde der älteren Kirche* 69 (1978): 130–15. Neil Richardson, *Paul's Language about God* (Sheffield: Sheffield Academic Press, 1994), 300, is helpful here: 'As so often in Paul ... God-phrases and Christ-phrases are simply set side by side, and the relationship between the two is not spelled out.' There is much of relevance in Richardson's book as a whole. All of these studies look at either Pauline intention or from where Paul drew his language or concept of Jesus as lord juxtaposed with the one god of Israel.

and his sons in the same sanctuary meant that Poseidon was the only one who deserved divine honours because he was the father of the Tritons. Similarly, Demeter and Kore as mother and daughter were not of equal status in the hierarchy of deities, but they both received divine honours in their sanctuary on the Acrocorinth. All of these deities were worthy of the honours that the Corinthians gladly offered through their ritual lives.

Paul surely knew this, even if he did not himself participate in these sanctuaries, to our knowledge. He seems to require the Corinthians' allegiance to a particular group of deities, but he does not seem to be calling on the Corinthians to change their basic chord of gods practice. The parts appear interchangeable because the configuration of, say, Demeter as mother and Persephone as daughter simply gets replaced by that of the one god of Israel as father and lord Jesus Christ as son.[48] From the perspective of the Corinthians, there is not a radical shift from polytheism to monotheism when they join this community, but it does require a shift in allegiance to the father and son associated with Paul's tradition, at least at the point of composition of 1 Corinthians.[49] The 'us vs them' scenario that Paul constructs in 8:4–6 points to this contrast of allegiance: Paul's chord of gods or the Corinthians' chords of gods. That is the choice that Paul is putting before them.

Once the issue of monotheism/polytheism is put aside, we can see some of the other dynamics of the following verses a little differently. 1 Corinthians 8:7–13 describes some of the Corinthians' behaviour that Paul is trying to change. This familiar passage discusses the fact that some Corinthians – usually characterised as 'the strong', that is, those with γνῶσις – are still participating in the life of the local sanctuaries, eating the meat from ritual offerings with apparently no concern that what they are doing is affecting anyone.

---

[48] This fits well with William Arnal's critique of Burton Mack and J. Z. Smith: 'The disjunction between Paul and his interlocutors in Corinth ... is, in my view, much exaggerated, both by Mack and by Smith.' William Arnal, 'Bringing Paul and the Corinthians Together? A Rejoinder and Some Proposals on Redescription and Theory', in *Redescribing Paul and the Corinthians*, ed. Cameron and Miller, 80.

[49] Pamela Eisenbaum, *Paul Was Not a Christian: The Original Message of a Misunderstood Apostle* (New York: HarperOne, 2009), 182–3, says, 'Alternatively, I suggest that Paul's preference for the term *kyrios* in reference to Jesus was for the purposes of expedience. As Apostle to the Gentiles, Paul designed his message for the non-Jewish polytheistic world. By repeatedly referring to Jesus as Lord, Paul was trying to instill in his Gentile audience the kind of loyalty required of those who have now chosen to devote themselves to the One God, especially since there were many gods in Greco-Roman society, and people were accustomed to paying homage to more than one. For Gentiles, proper worship of one god did not necessarily imply that one needed to abstain from worshipping all others. Paul's proclamation of Jesus as Lord was likely an essential first step in enabling Gentiles to comprehend the kind of theological exclusivity demanded by Jewish monotheism.' I do not see the issue as Corinthian polytheism versus Jewish monotheism, but I mostly agree with Eisenbaum's basic scenario of Paul demanding loyalty to the god of Israel.

Paul disagrees, of course, because he points out that those who do not have knowledge 'in' them – the 'weak' (ἀσθενής) – might think otherwise and have their consciences 'defiled' (μολύνεται; verse 7). Paul goes on to argue (at least here) that, for the sake of these weaker members of the community, the strong should refrain from eating this food, regardless of what the γνῶσις of the strong might say about the existence of 'idols' (verses 10–13). The premise here is that the strong are eating in local sanctuaries thinking that their γνῶσις protects them from stumbling. What Paul points out is that their actions cause others to stumble, which is just as important.

But what if Paul did not size up the situation correctly? What if his characterisation of those with γνῶσις as using it as a licence to continue to eat at local sanctuaries is not about abuse of γνῶσις but the continuation of the practice of still honouring the gods of these sanctuaries, even if their esteem for the gods of Paul's tradition ranks higher than that for the sanctuary gods? If the strong were understanding Paul correctly and assenting to his demands of exclusivity, then the pull of meat and sanctuary meals must have been very powerful for them to violate Paul's directives. Perhaps the strong never understood Paul's preaching in the ways he describes here, and so the 'slogan' in 8:4 ('there is no idol in the world') does not actually capture the thinking of the Corinthian strong. Instead, it could represent Paul's attempted correction of the γνῶσις that the Corinthians think they have about what he initially preached. Paul is, perhaps, repeating something he has already preached to the Corinthians, which they did not understand correctly the first time, leading them to continue to participate in honouring small groups of gods in local sanctuaries through the meals in which they partook. Or perhaps they did understand, and refused to comply with Paul's wishes. For the Corinthians, Paul's gods would simply have been an addition to their traditional practices rather than a break from them, albeit an addition that required priority over their other gods. Paul's correction, then, was not one of theological framework (monotheism instead of polytheism) but one of exclusive allegiance to his chord of gods.

I have treated 1 Corinthians 12:1–11 already, but I wish to return to it with an eye towards Corinthian chord of gods practice. As with 1 Corinthians 8:1, Paul begins with an item on his laundry list of issues with the Corinthians, this time πνευματικός, spiritual gifts. He draws a contrast between past time when the Corinthians were an ἔθνος (ὅτε ἔθνη ἦτε) and the present time – the former time characterised by Paul as 'being led astray by idols that could not speak' (verse 2). The contrast he draws with the present, however, is with those who speak by the holy *pneuma* of god and say 'Jesus is lord' (verse 3). He then goes on to describe the sources of the varieties of πνευματικοί (that is, the *pneuma*, the lord and god), their purpose (that is, 'in order to bring together', πρὸς τὸ συμφέρον; verse 7) and the πνευματικοί themselves (verses 8–11). We eventually find out that some Corinthians (that is, the tongue-speakers) are using the πνευματικοί as a pretence for superiority. Paul counter-argues that the Corinthians should recognise that the source of the πνευματικοί is the τὸ αὐτὸ πνεῦμα (the same *pneuma*), which, as he mentioned at the outset, is also the source of correct speech about Jesus as lord. Paul's appeal to the Corinthians is to correct their understanding of the πνευματικοί, thus changing their past activity as an ἔθνος, errantly following idols.

As we read this passage with chord of gods practice in mind, Paul's contrast between the Corinthians' time as an ἔθνος and their time in his movement falls along the lines of speech: speech under the influence of idols who could not speak (resulting in errant speech), versus speech under the influence of the *pneuma* of god (resulting in 'true' speech). The former state as an ἔθνος resulted in the Corinthians being led astray; the new state should result in unity amidst variety under the one *pneuma* of god. The former state resulted in chaos whereas the new state leads to order, as expressed in 12:28–31. Obviously, if the Corinthians were in this new state, Paul would not have argued for it so strongly. He clearly calls for a new or renewed allegiance to the ways of his gods in contrast to the Corinthians' former state, and so, in that sense, he calls for an abandonment of the idols who led the Corinthians astray in the past. But he is not calling them from idols to a singular god; he is calling for a shift in loyalties from these idols – perhaps one or more chord of gods – to the *pneuma*, the lord and god (12:4–6) – another chord of gods. Allegiance is the biggest issue for Paul, not the structure of practice, and so the correction is around proper understanding of the new state by which Paul wishes the Corinthians to be governed. These idols, worshipped and adhered to in chords, may be false; Paul's demand of the Corinthians is difficult in the sense of abandoning their traditions, but not in the sense of abandoning their basic mode of practice. In other words, his concerns for them had nothing to do with theology but had everything to do with loyalty and the ensuing ramifications for their life together as followers of Jesus.

Finally, we come to 2 Corinthians 6:14–7:1, which is widely believed to be a fragment of an early letter of Paul to the Corinthians that is no longer extant. However, there is a growing number of scholars who argue for its inclusion in the original 2 Corinthians, while also considering an integrated rather than composite letter.[50] We need not worry too much about partition and interpolation theories because, whether Paul is writing this passage

---

[50] See Philip F. Esler, 'Paul's Explanation of Christ-Movement Identity in 2 Corinthians 6:14–7:1: A Social Identity Approach', *BTB* 51 (2021): 101–18, for a recent take along these lines. For the traditional, and still majority, opinion about the integrity of 2 Corinthians, see Margaret E. Thrall, *2 Corinthians*, 2 vols (London: T & T Clark, 2004), 1:47–9, where she lists the possibilities for partitioning the letter. For a discussion of the possibility of 2 Cor. 6:14–7:1 being an interpolation, even a non-Pauline interpretation, see Murray J. Harris, *The Second Epistle to the Corinthians* (Grand Rapids, MI: William B. Eerdmans, 2005), 15–25.

as part of a greater argument in 2 Corinthians or as part of another letter, the language he uses contrasts the in-group of Jesus followers with those who are associated with idols, much as we saw how idols were used as a dividing line in the arguments of 1 Corinthians 8:4–6 and 12:1–6. In 2 Corinthians 6:14–7:1, the language similarly revolves around the contrast between *pistoi* and *apistoi* (faithful and the unfaithful), expanded to include *dikaiosyne* and *anomia* (righteousness and lawlessness), *phōs* and *skotos* (light and dark) and Christ and Beliar (6:14–15) before the contrast between the temple of god and idols ('What concord is there in the temple of god with idols?'; 6:16). Paul goes on to define the Corinthians as the positive pole of this last contrast: 'For we are the temple of the living god' (ἡμεῖς γὰρ ναὸς θεοῦ ἐσμεν ζῶντος; 6:16) but, given the series of binaries in verses 14–16, all the positive poles can be considered equivalent (righteousness, light, Christ, faithful, temple of god), and all the negative poles can likewise be considered equivalent (lawlessness, darkness, Beliar, unfaithful, idols).

The rest of the passage is Paul's further call to separate from those associated with the negative pole. He does this through a chain of citations from the Hebrew Bible (6:16–18) – Leviticus 26:12; Ezekiel 37:27; 2 Samuel 7:14; and Isaiah 52:11 and 43:6 – which then culminates in a call to 'purify ourselves from all defilement of flesh and spirit, by perfecting holiness in fear of god' (7:1). Purification and separation are the overall exhortation in this passage, with imagery that evokes the Corinthians' traditions of worship of their gods as a negative. Clearly, Paul wants the Corinthians to have nothing to do with these traditional gods, but, again, we see every indication that the call to separation is a call to allegiance to his gods because he invokes both Christ and father god in this call. There is no call to shift the basic structure of chord of gods practice.

All three of these passages demonstrate that, when given the clear chance to distinguish between Corinthian traditional chord of gods practice and Paul's desired practice, the only thing that Paul called for was a change of allegiance to favour his chord of gods. Clearly, the Corinthians had no problems mingling their traditions and their life as Christ followers or else Paul would not have been calling for this shift in allegiance. To me, this could indicate that the similarities in chord of gods practice were great enough that the Corinthians chose to integrate Paul's chord of gods with their own traditional chords of gods rather than choosing between the chords. There was continuity of practice between Corinthian tradition and Paul's growing tradition, in other words, rather than a discontinuity in practice – a similarity of doings and sayings, in Schatzki's terms. And Paul called for nothing other than a change of allegiance to another chord of gods – certainly a difficult demand but not a wholesale, systematic theological shift or shift in practice.

CHAPTER SIX

# A Chord of Gods as a 'Tool' for Rupture

We started out this investigation with the task of imagining what it would be like for the Corinthians to encounter Paul's discourse about his god(s), to see what the appeal might have been and what might have caused the Corinthians to join the Christ movement as a result of Paul's work. I argued along the way that the framework of practice of the Corinthians would have shaped their reception of Paul's discourse around the father god, his son (Jesus, Christ, the lord) and the *pneuma* (for some Corinthians), meaning that they understood Paul's god(s) as a chord of gods rather than as a singular god – a small group of gods that usually shared a common mythological/genealogical/historical connection, as well as a shared cultic life in a particular local context. These chords of gods were often envisioned as working together for and with their human adherents in a reciprocal relationship of mutual exchange for the betterment of all parties involved. Most of this book has involved imagining the picture from the Corinthians' side rather than arguing for Pauline intention in the literary evidence of the Corinthian correspondence. This was done to show the likelihood that Paul's discourse would have reasonably been understood within the framework of chord of gods practice so universally familiar to ancients in the Mediterranean world, including in Corinth.

Obviously, we cannot know with certainty what motivated the Corinthian gentiles to respond favourably to Paul and join the movement. If nothing else, the chord of gods scenario for which I have argued in this book gives us a reasonable, historically based context for the understandability of the group practices that Paul was advocating. As we saw in the Introduction, 'monotheism' and 'polytheism' are really unhelpful and inaccurate terms to describe the religious landscape of the ancient world because they artificially divide that world into two groups that had little in common and were therefore at odds with each other in every way – both false characterisations. So, transitioning from a polytheistic to a monotheistic religious worldview was not the dynamic at play between the Corinthians and Paul. Perhaps, thinking in smaller terms along the lines of chords of gods can give a more accurate picture of how religious practice worked in the ancient world – somewhere between 'monotheism' and 'polytheism' – and how Paul and his adherents in Corinth overlapped in their religious sensibilities, doings and sayings. If we can imagine this overlap more concretely, as I have done here, we can identify possible reasons for Paul's success in convincing gentiles to join his movement, and we can also understand more accurately why it would have adversely affected Paul and the assembly for some to ignore the exclusivity that Paul was demanding.

I argued in Chapter Five for a plausible scenario of the transition from Corinthian gentiles to Corinthian followers of Christ at Paul's initiative. This scenario was based on Stanley Stowers's model of Paul teaching an exotic, alternative *paideia* to a small group of elite Corinthians, which interested and convinced them to become part of Paul's movement. Because Stowers's model does not adequately account for the growth of the group among non-elite Corinthians, I posited a model based on modern sociological theory (but also evident in the ancient world) that started with a small node of authoritative elites around Paul but then grew based on the two forces evident in current research on network formation – preferential attachment and homophily. Preferential attachment would account for those attracted to this small node of authoritative elites because of their centralised organisation and power. As this small node attracted some Corinthians, other Corinthians would be attracted to the group through a selective homophily centred on chord of gods religious practice. This homophily need not have been only for those of similar social status and/or wealth, but could have been developed through the essential similarity of chord of gods religious practice, which would allow members of varying social classes to develop close relationships because of this practice.

However, Paul demanded exclusive allegiance to his chord of gods, so the Corinthians would have had to leave behind their ancestral traditions to be a part of Paul's movement. If we read Paul's (father) god and (lord Jesus) Christ, or god, (lord Jesus) Christ and *pneuma*, as a chord of gods similar in structure to prevailing ancient Mediterranean religious practice, then some of the conflict between Paul and the Corinthians would be centred on exclusive allegiance rather than on belief or conversion to nascent Christianity based on monotheistic Judaism or some other theological category. Whether Paul taught about his demand for exclusive allegiance from the beginning is hard to tell, but it is possible that the Corinthian correspondence contains, in part, his attempt to correct or clarify this demand for exclusive allegiance to his chord of gods in place of the Corinthians' traditional chords of gods. In other words, the most difficult aspect of being a part of Paul's group did not centre on theological categories of belief in the one god of Israel, but on exclusive allegiance to the chord of gods that Paul presented the Corinthians. It becomes more imaginable for the Corinthians to join the movement if the chord of gods religious practices were similar. It also becomes more imaginable for there to be a need for Paul to clarify or re-explain the need for exclusive allegiance to his chord of gods as an element of these practices.

Because of this scenario and the way in which ancient religion worked in Corinth and its surroundings, we can leave behind the notions that the Corinthians were backsliding into 'sinful' activities related to their inherently sinful polytheism, as so many modern commentators presume. These presumptions of a sinful polytheistic group of Corinthians being corrected by Paul the righteous monotheist inevitably morphs into valorising the supposed monotheism as the superior 'religion'. Given the chord of gods religious practice I described in Chapters One and Two, it is clear that the valorisation of monotheism is a projection of modern concerns onto Paul and his Corinthians rather than a historically plausible portrayal of the situation in Corinth.

I would like to reflect here on the ramifications in the modern world of reimagining Christian origins. Pierre Bourdieu said,

> This is why there is no more potent tool for rupture than the reconstruction of genesis: by bringing back into view the conflicts and confrontations of the early beginnings and therefore all the discarded possibles, it retrieves the possibility that things could have been (and still could be) otherwise.[1]

This quote has nothing to do with Christian origins. It has to do with the genesis of the state and the dangers of the state's ability to 'exert symbolic violence'.[2] But what better way to think of Christian origins than as the beginnings of what would later become the Christian state? Reconstructing these early years of what would later become Christianity is not just an academic exercise but a 'tool for rupture'. Rupturing the prevailing views about the earliest years is necessary for several reasons. The popular view of 'the persecutor Paul struck from his horse only to be rehabilitated by Christ to start the church by convicting Jews and gentiles of the truth of the gospel and folly of the law' simply does not stand up in the face of close analysis. This view has also spearheaded atrocities against Jews over the centuries and has separated Christian from Christian for more than five hundred years, with no end in sight in some circles of modern Christianity. The popular view has also generated a sense of Christian exceptionalism that has spawned centuries of Christians thinking of themselves as superior to adherents of other religions – a view that still colours all sorts of political and social conflict across the globe.

---

[1] Pierre Bourdieu, 'Rethinking the State: Genesis and Structure of the Bureaucratic Field', trans. Loic J. D. Wacquant and Samar Farage, *Sociological Theory* 12, no. 1 (1991): 4.
[2] Ibid., 3.

Recasting these early years will not undo the cultural forces that unfolded over the course of history, but it can help unravel the exceptionalism and superiority complex that plagues Christians, blocking them from embracing the perspectives of those from other religious persuasions as legitimate ways of interacting and honouring the divine as they perceive it.

I think there is a good argument to be made that scholarship that maintains the valorisation of ancient monotheism and the exceptionalism of the origins of Christianity in the first century (as erroneously conceived in modern circles) contributes significantly to the continued attitudes of Christian exceptionalism among many Christian scholars and non-scholars alike. Whatever positive efforts are made in modern cultures towards pluralism and valuing various religions and religious practices equally are indeed seriously undermined when Christian scholars implicitly or explicitly endorse a picture of the founding moments of its movement as one that was fundamentally distinct and 'truer' than the 'other' in its midst. While the exclusivity called for by Paul was real, the actual social dynamics of his assemblies were much more complex than 'us (monotheistic, right, virtuous, saved)' versus 'them (polytheistic, wrong, sinful, condemned)' and need to be accounted for in much more robust ways than have been done by many scholars. It is well past time to develop tools for rupture so that we can reconstruct and redescribe the genesis of the early days of the Christ movement, to paraphrase Bourdieu. There have been lengthy strides made along this road over the past forty years, but more work must be done. Hopefully, this book advances us down the road a little further.

# Appendix

## The Pergamene *Lex Sacra* from the Cult of Asklepios, turn of the first and second centuries CE

After *IvP* III 161A; transcribed from the Packard Humanities Institute Database of Greek Inscriptions (http://epigraphy.packhum.org/inscriptions/). The translation is a slight modification from Alexa Petsalis-Diomidis, *'Truly Beyond Wonders': Aelius Aristides and the Cult of Asklepios* (Oxford: Oxford University Press, 2010), 225–6.

[— — — — — — — — — — — — — — — — —] καὶ τραπεζούσθω σκ[έ]-
[λος δεξιὸν κ]αὶ σπλάγχνα κα[ὶ] λαβὼν ἄλλον στέφανον ἐλάας π[ρο]-
[θυέσθω Διὶ] Ἀποτροπαίωι πόπανον ῥαβδωτὸν ἐννεόμφαλον καὶ *vac.*
[Διὶ Μειλιχίω]ι πόπανον ῥαβδωτὸν ἐννεόμφαλον καὶ Ἀρτέμιδ[ι]
[..c.7..] καὶ Ἀρτέμιδι Προθυραίαι καὶ Γῆι ἑκάστηι πόπανον *vac*?    [5]
[ἐννεόμφ]αλον. *vac.* ταῦτα δὲ ποήσας θυέτω χοῖρον γαλαθηνὸν *vac.*
[τῶι Ἀσκλ]ηπιῶι ἐπὶ τοῦ βωμοῦ καὶ τραπεζούσθω σκέλος δεξ[ι]-
[ὸν καὶ σπ]λάγχνα. ἐμβαλλέτω δὲ εἰς τὸν θησαυρὸν ὀβολοὺς τρεῖ[ς].
[εἰς δὲ τὴ]ν ἑσπέραν ἐπιβαλλέ[σ]θω πόπανα τρία ἐννεόμφαλα,
[τούτων μὲ]ν δύο ἐπὶ τὴν ἔξω θυμέλην Τύχηι καὶ Μνημοσύνηι, *vac*?    [10]
[τὸ δὲ τρίτ]ον ἐν τῶι ἐγκοιμητηρίωι Θέμιδι. *vac.* ἁγνευέτω δὲ ὁ *vac.*
[εἰσπορευ]όμενος εἰς τὸ ἐγκοιμητήριον ἀπό τε τῶν προειρημέ- *vac*?
[νων πάν]των καὶ ἀφροδισίων καὶ αἰγείου κρέως καὶ τυροῦ κα[ὶ]
[..c.7..]ΙΑΜΙΔΟΣ τριταῖος. *vac.* τὸν δὲ στέφανον ὁ ἐγκοιμώμενος
[ἀποτιθέμ]ενος καταλειπέτω ἐπὶ τῆς στιβάδος. *vac.* ἐὰν δέ τις βού-    [15]
[ληται ὑπὲρ] τοῦ αὐτοῦ ἐπερωτᾶν πλεονάκις, προθυέσθω χοῖρο[ν],
[ἐὰν δὲ καὶ] ὑπὲρ ἄλλου πράγματος ἐπερωτᾶι, προθυέσθω χοῖρο[ν]
[ἄλλον κατὰ] τὰ προγεγραμμένα. εἰς δὲ τὸ μικρὸν ἐγκοιμητήριον
[ὁ εἰσιὼν ἁγ]νείαν ἁγνευέτω τὴν αὐτήν. *vac.* προθυέσθω δὲ Διὶ Ἀποτ[ρο]-
[παίωι πόπ]ανον ῥαβδωτὸν ἐννεόμφαλον καὶ Διὶ Μειλιχίωι πόπ[α]-    [20]
[νον ῥαβδω]τὸν ἐννεόμφαλον καὶ Ἀρτέμιδι Προθυραίαι καὶ Ἀρτέμι-

[δι...c.6..]ι καὶ Γῇ ἑκάστηι πόπανον ἐννεόμφαλον. ἐμβαλλέ-
[τω δὲ καὶ] εἰς τὸν θησαυρὸν ὀβολὸς τρεῖς. περιθυέσθωσαν
[δὲ πελανο(?)]ῖς μέλιτι καὶ ἐλαίωι δεδευμένοις καὶ λιβανωτῶι
[πάντες οἱ θ]εραπεύοντες τὸν θεὸν ἑπόμενοι τῶι ἱερεῖ καὶ ΙΕ[.?]         [25]
[...c.9...]. vac. εἰς δὲ τὴν ἑσπέραν ἐπιβαλλέσθωσαν οἵ τε ΠΡΟ[.?]
[...c.8... ε]ἰς τὸ ἐγκοιμητήριον καὶ οἱ περιθυσάμενοι πάν-
[τες πόπα]να τρία ἐννεόμφαλα Θέμιδι, Τύχηι, Μνημοσύνηι ἑ-
[κάστηι πό]πανον. vac. καθιστάτωσαν δὲ ἐγγύους τῶν ἰατρείων τῶ[ι]
[θεῶι, ἃ ἂν α]ὐτοὺς πράσσηται, ἀποδώσειν ἐντὸς ἐνιαυτοῦ. Vac         [30]
[...c.8...] ἴατρα μὴ νεώτερα ἐνιαυσίων. vac. ἐμβαλέτωσαν δὲ vac?
[εἰς τὸν θησ]αυρὸν τοῦ Ἀσκληπιοῦ τὰ ἴατρα, Φωκαΐδα τῶι Ἀπό[λ]-
[λωνι καὶ Φ]ωκαΐδα τῶι Ἀσκληπιῶι, ὑγιεῖς γενόμενοι καὶ ἐάν τι
[ἄλλο αὐτ]οὺς αἰτή{ι}σηι {αἰτήσηι} ὁ θεός. vac
[.c.2. Κ]λώδιος Γλύκων
[ἱερ]ονομῶν ἀνέθηκεν.


[vacat] and he is to set on the table
[the right] leg and entrails and once he has taken another wreath of olive
he is [to make a preliminary offering to Zeus] Apotropaios of a nine-knobbed, ribbed round cake and [vacat]
to [Zeus Meilichios] a nine-knobbed, ribbed round cake and to Artemis         [5]
[c. 7 letters] . . . and to Artemis Prothyraia and to Gē, to each a [nine-]knobbed, round cake [vacat?]
[vacat] Then having done this he is to sacrifice a suckling pig [vacat]
[to Askl]epios on the altar and set on the table the right leg
and entrails. Then he is to put three obols into the offertory box.
[At] evening he is to add three nine-knobbed, round cakes,         [10]
of [these first] two on the outdoors altar for burning to Tychē and Mnēmosynē [vacat]
[and then the third] to Themis in the incubation chamber. [vacat] He who [vacat]
[enters] the incubation chamber is to keep himself pure from all things mentioned above [vacat]
And from sex and from goat meat and cheese and
[c. 14 letters] . . .on the third day. [vacat] The incubant is then to         [15]
[lay aside] the wreath and leave it on his straw bed. [vacat] If someone wants
to inquire several times about the same thing, he is to make a preliminary sacrifice of a pig,
[and if he also] makes an inquiry about another matter, he is to make a preliminary sacrifice of [another pig],
[according] to the above instructions. He who [enters] the small incubation chamber
is to observe the same rules of purity. [vacat] And he is to make a preliminary offering to Zeus Apotropaios         [20]
of a nine-knobbed, ribbed round cake and to Zeus Meilichios of a [ribbed] round cake with nine knobs, and to Artemis Prothyraia and Artemis
[c. 6 letters] . . . and to Gē, to each a nine-knobbed, round cake.
[And he is also to] put three obols into the offertory box.

All those worshipping the god are to perform a sacrifice in a circle with [cakes?] dipped in honey and oil and with incense following the priest and [. . .] [vacat] [25]
[c. 9 letters] [vacat] At evening those who [. . .] [vacat]
[c. 8 letters] . . . into the incubation chamber and those who have sacrificed in a circle [vacat]
are all to add three nine-knobbed, round cakes to Themis, Tychē, Mnēmosynē [vacat?]
[to each one] round cake. [vacat] They are to bring forward guarantors [to the god] for any healing fee
which he exacts from them, that they will pay it within a year [vacat?] [30]
[c. 8 letters] . . . healing offering not younger than one year. [vacat] And then they are to put [vacat?]
the payment for the cure [into] the offertory box of Asklepios, a Phokaian hekte to Apollo
and a Phokaian hekte to Asklepios, once they have become healthy, and if the god should ask them for anything [else] [. . .]
[c. 2 letters C]lodius Glykon
The sacred official set this up.

# Bibliography

Adams, Edward. *The Earliest Christian Meeting Places: Almost Exclusively Houses?* Rev. ed. London: T & T Clark, 2016.
Ahearne-Kroll, Stephen P. 'Mnēmosynē at the Asklepieia'. *CP* 109 (2014): 99–118.
Ahearne-Kroll, Stephen P. *The Psalms of Lament in Mark's Passion: Jesus' Davidic Suffering*. Society for New Testament Studies monograph series 142. Cambridge: Cambridge University Press, 2007.
Ahearne-Kroll, Stephen P. 'Remembering the Loaves'. In *Scripture and Justice: Catholic and Ecumenical Essays*, edited by Gregory E. Sterling and Anathea E. Portier-Young, 143–58. Minneapolis: Fortress Academic Press, 2018.
Aicher, Peter. *Rome Alive: A Source Guide to the Ancient City*. Vol. 1. Mundelein, IL: Bolchazy-Carducci, 2004.
Amandry, M. *Le Monnayage des duovirs corinthiens*. BCH supplement 15. Paris: École française d'Athènes, 1988.
Arnal, William E. 'Bringing Paul and the Corinthians Together? A Rejoinder and Some Proposals on Redescription and Theory'. In *Redescribing Paul and the Corinthians*, edited by Ron Cameron and Merrill P. Miller, 75–104. Early Christianity and Its Literature 5. Atlanta: SBL, 2011.
Arnold, Dieter. *Temples of the Last Pharaohs*. Oxford: Oxford University Press., 1999.
Ashton, John. *The Religion of Paul the Apostle*. New Haven: Yale University Press, 2000.
Assmann, Jan. *Der König als Sonnenpriester. Ein kosmographischer Begleittext zur kultischen Sonnenhymnik*. ADAIK 7. Glückstadt: J. J. Augustin, 1970.
Assmann, Jan. 'Die Macht der Bilder: Rahmenbedingungen ikonischen Handelns im Alten Ägypten'. *Visible Religion: Annual for Religious Iconography* 7 (1990): 1–20.
Assmann, Jan. 'Der Tempel der ägyptischen Spätzeit als Kanonisierung kultureller Identität'. In *The Heritage of Ancient Egypt: Studies in Honour of Erik Iversen*, edited by Jürgen Osing and Erland Kolding Nielsen, 9–25. Carsten Niebuhr Institute of Ancient Near Eastern Studies Publications 13. Copenhagen: Museum Tusculanum Press, 1992.
Barclay, John M. G. *Paul and the Gift*. Grand Rapids, MI: Eerdmans, 2015.
Barrett, C. K. *A Commentary on the Second Epistle to the Corinthians*. BNTC. London: Black, 1973.

Barringer, Judith M. 'Zeus at Olympia'. In *The Gods of Ancient Greece*, edited by Jan N. Bremmer and Andrew Erskine, 155–77. Edinburgh: Edinburgh University Press, 2010.

Bauckham, Richard. *God Crucified: Monotheism and Christology in the New Testament*. Carlisle: Paternoster, 1998.

Bazzana, Giovanni B. 'The Challenges of Comparison: A Response to Peter Struck'. In *Synergistic Pneumatic: A Syndicate Symposium*, 29 June 2021. Accessed 26 August 2022. https://syndicate.network/symposia/theology/synergistic-pneumata/

Bazzana, Giovanni B. *Having the Spirit of Christ: Spirit Possession and Exorcism in the Early Christ Groups*. New Haven: Yale University Press, 2020.

Beard, Mary, John North and Simon Price. *Religions of Rome*, 2 vols. Cambridge: Cambridge University Press, 1998.

Becker, Jürgen. *Christian Beginnings*. Louisville, KY: Westminster/John Knox, 1993.

Bell, Catherine. *Ritual: Perspectives and Dimensions*. Oxford: Oxford University Press, 1997.

Bell, Catherine. *Ritual Theory, Ritual Practice*. Oxford: Oxford University Press, 1992.

Bergoon, Judee K., Joseph A. Bonito, Artemio Ramirez Jr, Norah E. Dunbar, Karadeen Kam and Jenna Fischer. 'Testing the Interactivity Principle: Effects of Mediation, Propinquity, and Verbal and Nonverbal Modalities in Interpersonal Interaction'. *Journal of Communication* 52 (2002): 657–77.

Berlin, Andrea M. 'Herod, Augustus, and the Augusteum at the Paneion'. In *Ehud Netzer*, special issue, *Eretz-Israel: Archaeological, Historical and Geographical Studies* 31 (2015), 1*–11*.

Berlin, Andrea M. 'The Archaeology of Ritual: The Sanctuary of Pan at Banias/Caesarea Philippi'. *BASOR* 315 (1999): 27–45.

Blanton, Thomas R., IV. 'Wealth, Poverty, Economy'. In *The Oxford Handbook of the Synoptic Gospels*, edited by Stephen P. Ahearne-Kroll, 296–319. Oxford: Oxford University Press, 2023.

Boccaccini, Gabriele, and Carlos A. Segovia. *Paul the Jew: Rereading the Apostle as a Figure of Second Temple Judaism*. Minneapolis: Fortress Press, 2016.

Bodel, John. 'Cicero's Minerva, *Penates*, and the Mother of the *Lares*: An Outline of Roman Domestic Religion'. In *Household and Family Religion in Antiquity*, edited by John Bodel and Saul M. Olyan, 248–75. Oxford: Blackwell, 2008.

Bookidis, Nancy. 'Religion in Corinth: 146 BCE to 100 CE'. In *Urban Religion in Roman Corinth*, edited by D. N. Schowalter and S. J. Friesen, 141–64. Harvard Theological Studies 53. Cambridge, MA: Harvard University Press, 2005.

Bookidis, Nancy. 'The Sanctuaries of Corinth'. In *Corinth: The Centenary*, edited by C. K. Williams II and N. Bookidis, 247–60. Corinth 20. Princeton: ASCSA, 2003.

Bookidis, Nancy and Ronald S. Stroud. *The Sanctuary of Demeter and Kore: Topography and Architecture*. Corinth 18.3. Princeton: ASCSA, 1997.

Borgeaud, Phillippe. *The Cult of Pan in Ancient Greece*. Chicago: University of Chicago Press, 1988.

Bourdieu, Pierre. 'Rethinking the State: Genesis and Structure of the Bureaucratic Field'. Translated by Loïc J. D. Wacquant and Samar Farage. *Sociological Theory* 12, no. 1 (1991): 1–18.

Bourdieu, Pierre. *Outline of a Theory of Practice*. Translated by Richard Nice. Cambridge: Cambridge University Press, 1977.

Bousset, Wilhelm. *Kyrios Christos: A History of Belief in Christ from the Beginnings of Christianity to Irenaeus*. Waco, TX: Baylor University Press, 2013. First published 1913.

Boyarin, Daniel. *Border Lines: The Partition of Judaeo-Christianity*. Philadelphia: University of Pennsylvania Press, 2006.

Boyarin, Daniel. *The Jewish Gospels: The Story of Jesus Christ*. New York: The New Press, 2012.

Boyarin, Daniel. *A Radical Jew: Paul and the Politics of Identity*. Berkeley: University of California Press, 1994.

Braun, Willi. 'Amnesia in the Production of (Christian) History'. *Council of Societies for the Study of Religion Bulletin* 28, no. 1 (1999): 3–8.

Bremmer, Jan N. *Initiation into the Mysteries of the Ancient World*. Berlin: De Gruyter, 2014.

Bremmer, Jan J. *The Rise of Christianity through the Eyes of Gibbon, Harnack and Rodney Stark*. Groningen: Barkhuis, 2010.

Brookins, Timothy A. *Corinthian Wisdom, Stoic Philosophy, and the Ancient Economy*. Society for New Testament Studies monograph series 159. Cambridge: Cambridge University Press, 2014.

Brookins, Timothy A. 'Economic Profiling of Early Christian Assemblies'. In *Paul and Economics: A Handbook*, edited by Thomas R. Blanton IV and Raymond Pickett, 57–88. Minneapolis: Fortress, 2017.

Brookins, Timothy A., and Bruce W. Longenecker. *I Corinthians 1–9: A Handbook on the Greek Text*. Waco, TX: Baylor University Press, 2016.

Broneer, Oscar. *Isthmia*. Vol. 1, *Temple of Poseidon*. Princeton: ASCSA, 1971.

Broneer, Oscar. *Isthmia*. Vol. 2, *Topography and Architecture*. Princeton: ASCSA, 1973.

Brown, Ian Phillip. 'The *Pepaideumenoi* and Jesus: Ancient Education and Marginal Intellectuals in Paul's Corinth and the Gospel of Thomas'. PhD diss., University of Toronto, 2020.

Brown, Peter. *The World of Late Antiquity*. London: Thames & Hudson, 1971.

Budin, Stephanie L. 'A Reconstruction of the Aphrodite-Ashtart Syncretism'. *Numen* 51 (2004): 95–145.

Budin, Stephanie L. 'Sacred Prostitution in the First Person'. In *Prostitutes and Courtesans in the Ancient World*, edited by C. Faraone and L. McLure, 77–94. Madison: University of Wisconsin Press, 2006.

Buraselis, K. and S. Aneziri. 'Die griechische und hellenistische Apotheose'. *ThesCRA* (2004): 158–86.

Burkert, Walter. *Homo Necans: The Anthropology of Ancient Greek Sacrificial Ritual and Myth*. Translated by Peter Bing. Berkeley: University of California Press, 1983. First published in German 1972.

Cameron, Ron, and Merrill P. Miller. *Redescribing Paul and the Corinthians*. Early Christianity and Its Literature. Atlanta: SBL, 2011.

Caneva, S. 'Queens and Ruler Cults in Early Hellenism: Observations on Festivals, and on the Administration and Ideological Meaning of Cults'. *Kernos* 25 (2012): 75–102.

Cauville, Sylvie. *Offerings to the Gods in Egyptian Temples*. Translated by Bram Calcoen. Leuven: Peeters, 2012.
Cauville, Sylvie. 'Le pantheon d'Edfou à Dendera'. *Bulletin de l'Institut Français d'Archéologie Orientale* 88 (1988): 7–23.
Cauville, Sylvie. *Le Temple de Dendera. Guide archéologique*. Cairo: l'Institut Français d'Archéologie Orientale du Caire, 1990.
Cauville, Sylvie, and Didier Devauchelle. *Le Temple d'Edfou*. Cairo: l'Institut Français d'Archéologie Orientale du Caire, 1984.
Chaniotis, Angelos. 'The Divinity of Hellenistic Rulers'. In *A Companion to the Hellenistic World*, edited by A. Erskine, 431–46. Malden, MA: Blackwell, 2003.
Chaniotis, Angelos. 'The Jews of Aphrodisias: New Evidence and Old Problems'. *Scripta Classica Israelica* 21 (2002): 209–42.
Christensen, Thomas J., and Jack Snyder. 'Chain Gangs and Passed Bucks: Predicting Alliance Pattern in Multipolarity'. *International Organization* 51 (1990): 65–98.
Clinton, Kevin. 'The Epidauria and the Arrival of Asclepius in Athens'. In *Ancient Greek Cult Practice from the Epigraphical Evidence*, edited by R. Hägg, 17–34. Stockholm: Swedish Institute at Athens, 1994.
Clinton, Kevin. 'The Mysteries of Demeter and Kore'. In *A Companion to Greek Religion*, edited by Daniel Ogden, 342–56. Oxford: Blackwell, 2010.
Cohen, Shaye J. D. *The Beginnings of Jewishness: Boundaries, Varieties, Uncertainties*. Berkeley: University of California, 1999.
Collins, Raymond F. *First Corinthians*. Sacra Pagina. Collegeville, MN: Liturgical Press, 1999.
Concannon, Cavin W. 'The Matter of Class: Assemblages, Networks, and the Shape of the Pauline Collectives'. In *The Struggle over Class: Socioeconomic Analysis of Ancient Christian Texts*, edited by G. Anthony Keddie, Michael Flexsenhar III, and Steven J. Friesen, 53–72. Atlanta: SBL, 2021.
Conway-Jones, Ann. 'The New Testament: Jewish or Gentile?' *Expository Times* 130 (2019): 237–42.
Conzelmann, Hans. *1 Corinthians: A Commentary on the First Epistle to the Corinthians*. Hermeneia. Philadelphia: Fortress, 1975.
Corté Copete, J. M. *Elio Aristides. Un sofista griego en el imperio romano*. Madrid, 1995.
Coşkun, A. 'Dionysiac Associations among the Dedicants of Ho-sios kai Dikaios: Revisiting Recently Published Inscriptions from the Mihalıççık District in North-West Galatia'. *Gephyra* 19 (2020): 111–33.
Crosby, Nicholas E. 'A Basrelief from Phaleron (Plate XII)'. *AJA* 9 (1894): 202–5.
Cuchet, Violaine Sebillotte. 'Families et société à Athènes à l'époque classique: un éclairage par les études de genre'. In *Pallas. Famille et société dans le monde grec, en Italie et à Rome du Ve au IIe siècle avant J.-C.*, 71–90. Toulouse: Presses universitaires du Midi, 2017.
Currarini, Sergio, Matthew O. Jackson and Paolo Pin. 'An Economic Model of Friendship: Homophily, Minorities, and Segregation'. *Econometrica* 77, no. 4 (2009): 1003–45.
de Angelis, Francesco. 'Decoration and Attention in the Forum of Augustus: The Agency of Ancient Imagery between Ritual and Routine'. In *Principles of*

Decoration in the Roman World, edited by Annette Haug and M. Taylor Lauritsen, 15–32. Berlin: De Gruyter, 2021.

Deissmann, G. Adolf. *Light from the Ancient East: The New Testament Illustrated by Recently Discovered Texts of the Greco-Roman World*. London: Hodder & Stoughton, 1910.

DeMaris, Richard E. 'Corinthian Religion and Baptism for the Dead (1 Corinthians 15:29): Insights from Archaeology and Anthropology'. *JBL* 114 (1995): 662–82.

DeMaris, Richard E. 'Demeter in Roman Corinth: Local Development in a Mediterranean Religion'. *Numen* 42, no. 2 (1995): 105–17.

DeMaris, Richard E. *The New Testament in Its Ritual World*. London: Routledge, 2008.

DeMaris, Richard E. 'Water Ritual'. In *The Oxford Handbook of Early Christian Ritual*, edited by Risto Uro, Juliette Day, Richard E. DeMaris and Rikard Roitto, 391–408. Oxford: Oxford University Press, 2018.

Doniger, Wendy. *The Implied Spider: Politics and Theology in Myth*. New York: Columbia University Press, 1998.

Dowden, Ken. 'Religious Practices of the Individual and Family: Rome'. In *Religions of the Ancient World: A Guide*, edited by Sarah Iles Johnston, 435–6. Cambridge, MA: Belknap Press of Harvard University Press, 2004.

Droge, Arthur J. 'Finding His Niche: On the "Autoapotheiosis" of Augustus'. *Memoirs of the American Academy in Rome* 56/57 (2011/2012): 85–112.

Duff, Paul Brooks. 'The Mind of the Redactor: 2 Cor. 6:14–7:1 in Its Secondary Context'. *Novum Testamentum* 35 (1993): 168–80.

Dunn, James D. G. *Baptism in the Holy Spirit: A Re-examination of the New Testament Teaching on the Gift of the Spirit in Relation to Pentecostalism Today*. Philadelphia: Westminster John Knox, 1970.

Dunn, James D. G. *Christology in the Making: A New Testament Inquiry in the Origins of the Doctrine of the Incarnation*. London: SCM, 1989.

Dunn, James D. G. *Jesus and the Spirit: A Study of the Religious and Charismatic Experience of Jesus and the First Christians as Reflected in the New Testament*. London: SCM Press, 1975.

Dunn, James D. G. *The Theology of Paul the Apostle*. Edinburgh: T & T Clark, 1998.

Eaton, Katherine. *Ancient Egyptian Temple Ritual: Performance, Pattern, and Practice*. London: Routledge, 2013.

Ebel, Eva. *Die Attraktivität früher christlicher Gemeinden. Die Gemeinde von Korinth im Spiegel griechisch-römischer Vereine*. WUNT II, 178. Tübingen: Mohr Siebeck, 2004.

Eisenbaum, Pamela Michelle. *Paul Was Not a Christian: The Original Message of a Misunderstood Apostle*. New York: HarperOne, 2009.

Ekroth, Gunnel. *The Sacrificial Rituals of Greek Hero-Cults*. Liège: Centre international d'étude de la religion grecque antique, 2002.

Elderkin, G. W. 'The Cults of the Erectheion'. *Hesperia* 10 (1941): 113–24.

Engberg-Pedersen, Troels. *Cosmology and Self in the Apostle Paul: The Material Spirit*. Oxford: Oxford University Press, 2010.

Engberg-Pedersen, Troels. 'The Material Spirit: Cosmology and Ethics in Paul'. *NTS* 55 (2009): 179–97.

Engberg-Pedersen, Troels. *Paul and the Stoics*. Louisville, KY: Westminster John Knox, 2000.

Esler, Philip F. 'Paul's Explanation of Christ-Movement Identity in 2 Corinthians 6:14–7:1: A Social Identity Approach'. *BTB* 51 (2021): 101–18.

Eyl, Jennifer. *Signs, Wonders, and Gifts: Divination in the Letters of Paul*. Oxford: Oxford University Press, 2019.

Falconer, W. A., ed. and trans. *Cicero*. Vol. 20, *De senectute; De amicitia; De divinatione*. LCL 154. Cambridge, MA: Harvard University Press, 1923.

Faraone, Christopher A. 'Curses, Crime Detection, and Conflict Resolution at the Festival of Demeter Thesmophoria'. *JHS* 131 (2011): 25–44.

Farnell, Brenda. 'Getting Out of the Habitus: An Alternative Model of Dynamically Embodied Social Action'. *Journal of the Royal Anthropological Institute* 6 (2000): 397–418.

Feldman, Louis H. *Jew and Gentile in the Ancient World*. Princeton: Princeton University Press, 1993.

Fatehi, Mehrdad. *The Spirit's Relation to the Risen Lord in Paul: An Examination of Its Christological Implications*. WUNT II, 128. Tübingen: Mohr Siebeck, 2000.

Fee, Gordon D. *The First Epistle to the Corinthians*. Rev. ed. New International Commentary on the New Testament. Grand Rapids, MI: Eerdmans, 2014.

Fee, Gordon D. *God's Empowering Presence: The Holy Spirit in the Letters of Paul*. Peabody, MA: Hendrickson, 1994.

Feldman, Louis H. *Jew and Gentile in the Ancient World*. Princeton: Princeton University Press, 1996.

Ferguson, William Scott. 'The Attic Orgeones and the Cult of Heroes'. *HTR* 37 (1944): 61–140.

Finnestad, Ragnhild Bjerre. 'Temples of Ptolemaic and Roman Periods: Ancient Traditions in New Contexts'. In *Temples of Ancient Egypt*, edited by Byron Shafer, 185–239. Ithaca: Cornell University Press, 1997.

Fishwick, Duncan. 'Genius and Numen'. In *Studies in the Ruler Cult of the Western Provinces of the Roman Empire*, Part 2.1, 373–87. Leiden: Brill, 1990. Accessed October 15, 2023. https://doi.org/10.1163/9789004295759_002.

Fishwick, Duncan. '"Sanctissimum numen": Emperor or God?' *ZPE* 89 (1991): 196–200.

Fishwick, Duncan. 'The Statue of Julius Caesar in the Pantheon'. *Latomus* 51 (1992): 329–36.

Fitzmyer, Joseph A. *First Corinthians*. Anchor Yale Bible 32. New Haven: Yale University Press, 2008.

Fitzmyer, Joseph A. *The One Who Is to Come*. Grand Rapids, MI: Eerdmans, 2007.

Flower, Harriet I. *The Dancing Lares and the Serpent in the Garden: Religion at the Roman Street Corner*. Princeton: Princeton University Press, 2017.

Förtsch, Reinhard, and Walter Eder. 'Capitolium'. In *Brill's New Pauly*, Antiquity volumes edited by Hubert Cancik and Helmuth Schneider, English edition by Christine F. Salazar; Classical Tradition volumes edited by Manfred Landfester, English edition by Francis G. Gentry. Accessed 16 October 2023. https://doi.org/10.1163/1574-9347_bnp_e12220600.

Fowler, Harold N., ed. and trans. *Plato: Euthyphro; Apology; Crito; Phaedo; Phaedrus*. LCL 36. Cambridge, MA: Harvard University Press/London: William Heinemann Ltd, 1925.

Fredriksen, Paula. 'If It Looks like a Duck, and It Quacks like a Duck . . .: On Not Giving Up the Godfearers'. In *A Most Reliable Witness: Essays in Honor of Ross Shepard Kraemer*, edited by Susan Ashbrook Harvey, Nathaniel P. DesRosiers, Shira L. Lander, Jacqueline Z. Pastis and Daniel Ullucci, 25–34. Providence: Brown University Press, 2015.

Fredriksen, Paula. 'Judaizing the Nations: The Ritual Demands of Paul's Gospel'. *NTS* 56 (2010): 232–52.

Fredriksen, Paula. 'Mandatory Retirement: Ideas in the Study of Christian Origins Whose Time Has Come to Go'. *Studies in Religion/Sciences Religieuses* 35 (2006): 231–46.

Fredriksen, Paula. 'Why Should a "Law-Free" Mission Mean a "Law-Free" Apostle?' *JBL* 134 (2015): 637–50.

Fredriksen, Paula. *Paul: The Pagans' Apostle*. New Haven: Yale University Press, 2017.

Fredriksen, Paula. *When Christians Were Jews: The First Generation*. New Haven: Yale University Press, 2018.

Frenschkowski, Marco. 'Kyrios in Context: Q 6:46, the Emperor as "Lord", and the Political Implications of Christology in Q'. In *Zwischen den Reichen. Neues Testament und Römische Herrschaft. Vorträge auf der Ersten Konferenz der European Association of Biblical Studies*, edited by Michael Labahn and Jürgen Zangenberg, 95–118. Texte und Arbeiten zum neutestamentlichen Zeitalter 36. Tübingen: Francke, 2002.

Friedland, Elise A. *The Roman Marble Sculptures from the Sanctuary of Pan at Caesarea Philippi/Panias (Israel)*. Boston: ASOR, 2012.

Friesen, Steven. 'Poverty in Pauline Studies: Beyond the So-Called New Consensus'. *JSNT* 26 (2004): 323–61.

Frölich, Thomas. *Lararien- und Fassadenbilder in den Vesuvstädten. Untersuchungen sur 'volkstümlichen' pompejanischen Malerei*. Mainz: P. von Zabern, 1991.

Furley, William D., and Jan Maarten Bremer. *Greek Hymns*. Vol. 1, *The Texts in Translation*. Tübingen: Mohr Siebeck, 2001.

Gaca, Kathy L. Review of *Paul and the Stoics* by Troels Engberg-Pedersen. *RBL* (2002). Accessed 31 January 2024. https://www.sblcentral.org/API/Reviews/2893_2913.pdf

Gager, John G. *Reinventing Paul*. Oxford: Oxford University Press, 2000.

Gager, John G. *Who Made Early Christianity? The Jewish Lives of the Apostle Paul*. New York: Columbia University Press, 2015.

Ganzert, J. *Im Allerheiligsten des Augustusforums. Fokus 'oikoumenischer Akkulturation'*. Mainz: Verlag Philipp von Zabern, 2000.

Garroway, Joshua D. *The Beginning of the Gospel: Paul, Philippi, and the Origins of Christianity*. New York: Palgrave Macmillan, 2018.

Garroway, Joshua D. *Paul's Gentile-Jews: Neither Jew nor Gentile, but Both*. New York: Palgrave Macmillan, 2012.

Gebhard, Elizabeth R. 'The Isthmian Games and the Sanctuary of Poseidon in the Early Empire'. In *The Corinthia in the Roman Period: Including the Papers Given at a Symposium Held at The Ohio State University on 7–9 March, 1991*, edited by Timothy E. Gregory, 78–94. JRA Supplemental Series 8. Ann Arbor, MI: JRA, 1993.

Gebhard, Elizabeth R. 'Rites for Melikertes-Palaimon in the Early Roman Corinthia'. In *Urban Religion in Roman Corinth*, edited by Daniel N. Schowalter and Steven J. Friesen, 165–204. Harvard Theological Studies 53. Cambridge, MA: Harvard University Press, 2005.

Gebhard, Elizabeth R., and Timothy E. Gregory, eds. *Bridge of the Untiring Sea: The Corinthian Isthmus from Prehistory to Late Antiquity*. Hesperia Supplement 48. Athens: American School of Classical Studies, 2015.

Geiger, Joseph. *The First Hall of Fame: A Study of the Statues in the Forum Augustum*. Leiden: Brill, 2008.

Gerding, Henrik. 'The Erechtheion and the Panathenaic Procession'. *AJA* 110 (2006): 389–401.

Gordon, Richard L. 'Apis'. *Oxford Classical Dictionary*. 4th ed. Oxford: Oxford University Press, 2012.

Gordon, Richard L. 'Isis'. *Oxford Classical Dictionary*. 4th ed. Oxford: Oxford University Press, 2012.

Gordon, Richard L. 'Sarapis'. *Oxford Classical Dictionary*. 4th ed. Oxford: Oxford University Press, 2012.

Gowing, Alain M. *Empire and Memory: The Representation of the Roman Republic in Imperial Culture*. Cambridge: Cambridge University Press, 2005.

Graf, Fritz, and Sarah Iles Johnston. *Ritual Texts for the Afterlife: Orpheus and the Bacchic Gold Tablets*. 2nd ed. London: Routledge, 2013.

Graml, Constanze. 'Wandering Maidens in the Acropolis Propylaia: Some Considerations on the Spatial Setting of the Cults of the Charites, Artemis and Hermes, Their Administration and Related Cult Images'. *JHS* 142 (2022): 274–97.

Green, Carin M. C. *Roman Religion and the Cult of Diana at Aricia*. Cambridge: Cambridge University Press, 2007.

Grigoropoulos, Dimitris. 'The Piraeus from 86 BC to Late Antiquity: Continuity and Change in the Landscape, Function and Economy of the Port of Roman Athens'. *Annals of the British School at Athens* 111 (2016): 239–68.

Gummere, Richard M., ed. and trans. *Seneca: Epistles*. Vol. 1, *Epistles 1–65*. LCL 75. Cambridge, MA: Harvard University Press, 1917.

Güney, Hale. 'New Inscriptions from Northeast Phrygia: The Cult of Hosios and Dikaios'. *Gephyra* 15 (2018): 101–17.

Gunkel, Hermann. *The Influence of the Holy Spirit: The Popular View of the Apostolic Age and the Teaching of the Apostle Paul*. Translated by Roy A. Harrisville and Philip A. Quanbeck II. Philadelphia: Fortress, 1979. First published in German 1888.

Harnack, Adolf von. *Die Mission und Ausbreitung des Christentums in den Ersten Drei Jahrhunderten*. Leipzig: J. C. Hinrichs, 1906.

Harrill, J. Albert. *Paul the Apostle: His Life and Legacy in Their Roman Context*. Cambridge: Cambridge University Press, 2012.

Harris, Murray J. *The Second Epistle to the Corinthians*. NIGTC. Grand Rapids, MI: William B. Eerdmans, 2005.

Harris, William V. *Ancient Literacy*. Cambridge, MA: Harvard University Press, 1989.

Hartman, Lars. *'Into the Name of the Lord Jesus': Baptism in the Early Church*. Edinburgh: T & T Clark, 1997.

Hawthorne, John G. 'The Myth of Palaemon'. *TAPA* 89 (1958): 92–8.
Hays, Richard B. 'Christ Prays the Psalms'. In *The Conversion of the Imagination: Paul as Interpreter of Israel's Scripture*, 101–18. Grand Rapids, MI: Eerdmans, 2005.
Hays, Richard B. *First Corinthians*. Interpretation. Louisville, KY: John Knox, 1997.
Hays, Richard B. 'Three Dramatic Roles: The Law in Romans 3–4'. In *The Conversion of the Imagination: Paul as Interpreter of Israel's Scripture*, 85–100. Grand Rapids, MI: Eerdmans, 2005.
Heller, Robert. 'Pneuma in Early Stoicism'. PhD diss., Royal Holloway, University of London, 2018.
Hermann, Ingo. *Kyrios und Pneuma. Studien zur Christologie der paulinischen Hauptbriefe*. Studien zum Alten und Neuen Testament 2. Munich: Kösel, 1961.
Hölbl, Günther. *A History of the Ptolemaic Empire*. London: Routledge, 2001.
Hollinshead, Mary B. 'The North Court of the Erectheion and the Ritual of the Plynteria'. *AJA* 119 (2015): 117–90.
Holum, Kenneth G. 'The Gods of Sebastos: King Herod's Harbor Temple at Caesarea Maritima'. In *Ehud Netzer*, special issue, *Eretz-Israel: Archaeological, Historical and Geographical Studies* 31 (2015): 51–68.
Hooks, S. M. 'Sacred Prostitution in Israel and the Ancient Near East'. PhD diss., Hebrew Union College, 1985.
Horn, Friedrich Wilhelm. *Das Angeld des Geistes. Studien zur paulinischen Pneumatologie*. Göttingen: Vandenhoek & Ruprecht, 1992.
Hornung, Erik. *Der Eine und die Vielen*. Darmstadt: Wissenschaftliche Buchgesellschaft, 1971. Translated by John Baines as *Conceptions of God in Ancient Egypt: The One and the Many*. Ithaca: Cornell University Press, 1982.
Horrell, David. 'Domestic Space and Christian Meetings at Corinth: Imagining New Contexts and the Buildings East of the Theatre'. *NTS* 50 (2004): 349–69.
Horsley, Richard A. 'The Background of the Confessional Formula in 1 Kor 8:6'. *Zeitschrift für die neutestamentliche Wissenschaft und die Kunde der älteren Kirche* 69 (1978): 130–15.
Horsley, Richard A. *1 Corinthians*. ANTC. Nashville: Abingdon, 1998.
Howgego, C. J. 'After the Colt Has Bolted: A Review of Amandry on Roman Corinth'. *NC* 149 (1989): 199–208.
Hunter, R. L., ed. and trans. *Theocritus: Encomium of Ptolemy Philadelphus. Text and Translation with Introduction and Commentary*. Berkeley: University of California Press, 2003.
Hurtado, Larry W. 'The Binitarian Shape of Early Christian Worship'. In *The Jewish Roots of Christological Monotheism: Papers from the St. Andrews Conference on the Historical Origins on the Worship of Jesus*, edited by Carey C. Newman, James R. Davila and Gladys S. Lewis, 187–213. Leiden: Brill, 1999.
Hurtado, Larry W. *Lord Jesus Christ*. Grand Rapids, MI: Eerdmans, 2003.
Hurtado, Larry W. *One God, One Lord: Early Christian Devotion and Ancient Jewish Monotheism*. Philadelphia: Fortress Press, 1988.
Hurwit, Jeffrey M. *The Athenian Acropolis: History, Myth, and Archaeology from the Neolithic Era to the Present*. Cambridge: Cambridge University Press, 1999.
Imhoof-Blumer, Friedrich, and Percy Gardner. *A Numismatic Commentary on Pausanias*. Charleston, SC: Nabu Press, 2012. First published 1855.

Iossif, P., A. S. Chankowski and C. C. Lorber, eds. *More than Men, Less than Gods: Studies on Royal Cult and Imperial Worship*. Leuven: Peters, 2011.
Ismail, Fatma Talaat. *Cult and Ritual in Persian Period Egypt: An Analysis of the Decoration of the Cult Chapels of the Temple of Hibis at Kharga Oasis*. New Haven: Yale Egyptology, 2019.
Jackson-McCabe, Matt, ed. *Jewish Christianity Reconsidered: Rethinking Ancient Groups and Texts*. Minneapolis: Fortress Press, 2007.
Jameson, Michael H. 'The Ritual of the Athena Nike Parapet'. In *Ritual, Finance, Politics: Democratic Accounts Presented to David Lewis*, edited by R. Osborne and S. Hornblower, 307–24. Oxford: Oxford University Press, 1994. Repr. in Michael H. Jameson, *Cults and Rites in Ancient Greece: Essays on Religion and Society*, edited by Allaire B. Stallsmith, 127–44. Cambridge: Cambridge University Press, 2014.
Jameson, Michael H. 'The Spectacular and the Obscure in Athenian Religion'. In *Performance Culture and Athenian Democracy*, edited by S. Goldhill and R. Osborne, 321–40. Cambridge: Cambridge University Press, 1999.
Johnson Hodge, Caroline. *If Sons, Then Heirs: A Study of Kinship and Ethnicity in the Letters of Paul*. Oxford: Oxford University Press, 2007.
Johnston, Sarah Iles. 'Animating Statues: A Case Study in Ritual'. *Arethusa* 41 (2008): 445–77.
Johnston, Sarah Iles. *Restless Dead: Encounters between the Living and the Dead in Ancient Greece*. Berkeley: University of California Press, 1999.
Jones, C. P. 'Aelius Aristides and the Asklepieion'. In *Pergamon: Citadel of the Gods: Archaeological Record, Literary Description, and Religious Development*, edited by Helmut Koester, 63–76. Harvard Theological Studies 46. Harrisburg, PA: Trinity Press International, 1998.
Jost, M. 'Pan'. *Oxford Classical Dictionary*. 4th ed. Oxford: Oxford University Press, 2012.
Kamlah, E. 'πνεῦμα'. In *NIDNTT*, 3:690.
Kaufmann-Heinimann, Annemarie. 'Religion in the House'. In *A Companion to Roman Religion*, edited by Jörg Rüpke, 188–201. Chichester: Wiley-Blackwell, 2011.
Kearns, Emily. *The Heroes of Attica*. London: University of London, Institute of Classical Studies, 1989.
Keener, Craig S. *1–2 Corinthians*. New Cambridge Bible Commentary. Cambridge: Cambridge University Press, 2005.
Keener, Craig S. *The Mind of the Spirit: Paul's Approach to Transformed Thinking*. Grand Rapids, MI: Baker Academic, 2016.
Keesling, Catherine M. *The Votive Statues of the Athenian Acropolis*. Cambridge: Cambridge University Press, 2003.
Kent, J. H. *Corinth*. Vol. VIII.3, *The Inscriptions (1926–1950)*. Princeton: ASCSA, 1966.
Kindt, Julia. *Rethinking Greek Religion*. Cambridge: Cambridge University Press, 2012.
Klauck, Hans Josef. *Herrenmahl und hellenistischer Kult. Eine religionsgeschichtliche Untersuchung zum ersten Korintherbrief*. Münster: Aschendorff, 1982.

Kleinknecht, H. 'πνεῦμα'. In *TDNT*, 6:357.
Kloppenborg, John S. *Christ Associations: Connecting and Belonging in the Ancient City*. New Haven: Yale University Press, 2019.
Kloppenborg, John S. 'Greco-Roman Thiasoi, the Ekklesia at Corinth, and Conflict Management'. In *Redescribing Paul and the Corinthians*, edited by Ron Cameron and Merrill P. Miller, 187–218. Early Christianity and Its Literature 5. Atlanta: SBL, 2011.
Kloppenborg, John S., and Richard S. Ascough. *Greco-Roman Associations: Texts, Translations, and Commentary*. Vol. 1, *Attica, Central Greece, Macedonia, Thrace*. Berlin: De Gruyter, 2011.
Knust, Jennifer Wright, and Zsuzsanna Várhelyi, eds. *Ancient Mediterranean Sacrifice*. Oxford: Oxford University Press, 2011.
Kopestonsky, Theodora. 'The Greek Cult of the Nymphs at Corinth'. *Hesperia* 85 (2016): 711–77.
Kotrosits, Maia. *Rethinking Early Christian Identity: Affect, Violence, and Belonging*. Minneapolis: Fortress, 2015.
Kraemer, Ross S. 'Giving Up the Godfearers'. *Journal of Ancient Judaism* 5 (2014): 61–87.
Kreutz, N. *Zeus und die griechischen Poleis*. Tübingen: Marie Leidorf, 2007.
Kwon, Oh-Young. 'Discovering the Characteristics of Collegia: Collegia Sodalicia and Collegia Tenuiorum in 1 Corinthians 8, 10 and 15'. *Horizons in Biblical Theology* 32 (2010): 166–82.
La Rocca, E. 'La nuova imagine dei Fori Imperiali: appunti in margine degli scavi'. *RM* 108 (2001), 184–95.
Laird, Margaret L. 'The Emperor in a Roman Town: The Base of the Augustales in the Forum at Corinth'. In *Corinth in Context: Comparative Studies on Religion and Society*, edited by Steven J. Friesen, Daniel N. Schowalter and James C. Walters, 67–116. Leiden: Brill, 2010.
Lamont, Jessica. 'Asklepios in the Piraeus and the Mechanisms of Cult Appropriations'. In *Autopsy in Athens: Recent Archaeological Research on Athens and Attica*, edited by Margaret M. Miles, 37–50. Oxford: Oxbow, 2015.
Lanci, John R. *A New Temple for Corinth: Rhetorical and Archaeological Approaches to Pauline Imagery*. New York: Peter Lang, 1997.
Lebreton, Sylvain. 'Zeus Polieus à Athènes: les Bouphonies et au-delà'. *Kernos* 28 (2015): 85–110.
Lehmann, Clayton M., and Kenneth G. Holum. *The Greek and Latin Inscriptions of Caesarea Maritima: Joint Expeditions to Caesarea Maritima*. Vol. 5. Boston: ASOR, 2000.
Leisegang, H. *Der heilige Geist. Das Wesen und Werden der mystisch-intuitiven Erhenntnis in der Philosophie und Religion der Griechen*. Leipzig: Teubner, 1919. Repr. Darmstadt: Wissenschaftliche Buchgesellschaft, 1967.
Leisegang, H. *Pneuma Hagion. Der Ursprung des Geistbegriffs der synoptischen Evangelien aus der griechischen Mystik*. Leipzig: J. C. Hinrichs, 1922. Repr. Hildesheim: Georg Olms, 1970.
Levinskaya, Irina. *The Book of Acts in Its First Century Setting*. Vol. 5, *The Book of Acts in Its Diaspora Setting*. Grand Rapids, MI: Eerdmans, 1996.

Levison, John R. *Filled with the Spirit*. Grand Rapids, MI: Eerdmans, 2009.
Lieu, Judith M. 'The Race of the God-Fearers'. *Journal of Theological Studies* 46 (1995): 483–501.
Lim, S. U. 'The Political Economy of Eating Idol Meat: Practice, Structure, and Subversion in 1 Corinthians 8 through the Sociological Lens of Pierre Bourdieu'. *Horizons in Biblical Theology* 34 (2012): 155–72.
Lincoln, Bruce. *Apples and Oranges: Explorations In, On, and With Comparison*. Chicago: University of Chicago Press, 2018.
Lincoln, Bruce. *Between History and Myth: Stories of Harald Fairhair and the Founding of the State*. Chicago: University of Chicago Press, 2014.
Lincoln, Bruce. *Discourse and the Construction of Society*. 2nd ed. New York: Oxford University Press, 2014.
Lincoln, Bruce. *Myth, Cosmos, and Society: Indo-European Themes of Creation and Destruction*. Cambridge, MA: Harvard University Press, 1986.
Lincoln, Bruce. *Theorizing Myth*. Chicago: University of Chicago Press, 1999.
Lincoln, Bruce. 'Theses on Comparison'. In *Comparer en historie does religions antiques*, edited by Claude Calame and Bruce Lincoln, 99–110. Liège: Presses universitaires de Liège, 2012. Accessed 18 August 2022. https://books.openedition.org/pulg/8058
Littlewood, R. Joy. 'Fortune'. In *The Oxford Encyclopedia of Ancient Greece and Rome*, edited by Michael Gagarin. Oxford: Oxford University Press, 2010. Online edition. Accessed 23 January 2024. https://www.oxfordreference.com/display/10.1093/acref/9780195170726.001.0001/acref-9780195170726-e-495?rskey=winxQS&result=494
Long, A. A., and D. N. Sedley. *The Hellenistic Philosophers*. 2 vols. Cambridge: Cambridge University Press, 1987.
Longenecker, Bruce W. 'Exposing the Economic Middle: A Revised Economy Scale for the Study of Early Urban Christianity'. *JSNT* 31 (2009): 243–78.
Longenecker, Bruce W. *Remember the Poor: Paul, Poverty, and the Greco-Roman World*. Grand Rapids, MI: Eerdmans, 2010.
Longenecker, Bruce W. 'Socio-Economic Profiling of the First Urban Christians'. In *After the First Urban Christians: The Social-Scientific Study of Pauline Christianity Twenty-Five Years Later*, edited by Todd D. Still and David G. Horrell, 36–59. London: T & T Clark, 2009.
Lundgreen, Birte. 'A Methodological Enquiry: The Great Bronze Athena by Pheidias'. *JHS* 117 (1997): 190–7.
Luke, Trevor S. *Ushering in a New Republic: Theologies of Arrival at Rome in the First Century BCE*. Ann Arbor: University of Michigan Press, 2014.
MacMullen, Ramsay. *Paganism in the Roman Empire*. New Haven: Yale University Press, 1981.
Maharam, Wolfram-Aslan. 'Genius'. In *Brill's New Pauly*. English edition edited by Francis G. Gentry. Accessed 11 October 2023. doi: https://doi.org/10.1163/1574-9347_bnp_e421560
Malherbe, Abraham. *Social Aspects of Early Christianity*. Philadelphia: Fortress Press, 1977.
Maoz, Zeev. 'Preferential Attachment, Homophily, and the Structure of International Networks, 1816–2003'. *Conflict Management and Peace Science* 29, no. 3 (2012): 341–69.

Maoz, Zeev, Lesley G. Terris, Ranan D. Kuperman, and Ilan Talmud. 'What Is the Enemy of My Enemy? Causes and Consequences of Imbalanced International Relations, 1816–2001'. *Journal of Politics* 69, no. 1 (2007): 100–15.

Mark, Ira S. *The Sanctuary of Athena Nike in Athens: Architectural Stages and Chronology*. Princeton: ASCSA, 1993.

Martin, Dale B. *The Corinthian Body*. New Haven: Yale University Press, 1995.

Matera, Frank J. *II Corinthians: A Commentary*. Louisville, KY: Westminster John Knox, 2003.

Mauss, Marcel. *Sociology and Psychology: Essays*. Translated by Ben Brewster. London: Routledge & Kegan Paul, 1979. Originally published as *Sociologie et anthropologie*. Presses universitaires de France, 1950.

McCutcheon, Russell T. 'Myth'. In *The Guide to the Study of Religion*, edited by Willi Braun and Russell T. McCutcheon, 190–208. London: Continuum, 2000.

McPherson, Miller J., Lynn Smith-Lovin and James M. Cook. 'Birds of a Feather: Homophily in Social Networks'. *Annual Review of Sociology* 27 (2001): 415–44.

Meeks, Wayne. *The First Urban Christians: The Social World of the Apostle Paul*. New Haven: Yale University Press, 1983.

Melfi, Milena. 'Rebuilding the Myth of Asklepios at Epidauros in the Roman Period'. In *Roman Peloponnese*. Vol. 3, *Society, Economy and Culture under the Roman Empire: Continuity and Innovation*, edited by A. D. Rizakis and C. E. Lepenioti, 329–40. Athens: Nationale Hellenic Research Foundation, 2010.

Michigan State University. 'The Michigan State University Excavations at Isthmia'. Accessed 26 January 2024. https://msuisthmia.org

Millis, Benjamin W. 'The Social and Ethnic Origins of the Colonists in Early Roman Corinth'. In *Corinth in Context: Comparative Studies on Religion and Society*, edited by Steven J. Friesen, Daniel N. Schowalter and James C. Walters, 13–35. Leiden: Brill, 2011.

Mitchell, Margaret M. *Paul and the Rhetoric of Reconciliation: An Exegetical Investigation of the Language and Composition of 1 Corinthians*. Tübingen: Mohr Siebeck, 1992.

Mitchell, Stephen. *Anatolia: Land, Men, and Gods*. 2 vols. Oxford: Oxford University Press, 1993.

Momigliano, Arnoldo. *On Pagans, Jews, and Christians*. Middletown, CT: Wesleyan University Press, 1987.

Montague, George T. *The Holy Spirit: Growth of a Biblical Tradition*. New York: Paulist Press, 1976.

Morgan, Theresa. *Literate Education in the Hellenistic and Roman Worlds*. Cambridge Classical Studies. New York: Cambridge University Press, 1998.

Moule, C. F. D. *Worship in the New Testament*. Richmond, VA: John Knox Press, 1961.

Naiden, F. S. 2013. *Smoke Signals for the Gods: Ancient Greek Sacrifice from the Archaic through Roman Periods*. Oxford: Oxford University Press, 2013.

Nanos, Mark D., and Magnus Zetterholm, eds. *Paul within Judaism: Restoring the First-Century Context to the Apostle*. Minneapolis: Fortress Press, 2015.

Netzer, Ehud. *The Architecture of Herod, the Great Builder*. Tübingen: Mohr Siebeck, 2006.

Newlands, Carole E. *Playing with Time: Ovid and the Fasti*. Ithaca: Cornell University Press, 1995.

Nicholae, Maria-Corina. 'The Capitoline Triad in Roman Dacia'. In *Volum dedicat lui Florin Topoleanu la a 60-a aniversare*, special issue, *Peuce*, n.s. 9 (2011): 291–304.
Nongbri, Brent. 'The Concept of Religion and the Study of the Apostle Paul'. *Journal of the Jesus Movement in Its Jewish Setting* 2 (2015): 1–26.
Oakes, Peter. 'Constructing Poverty Scales for Graeco-Roman Society: A Response to Steven Friesen's 'Poverty in Pauline Studies''. *JSNT* 26 (2004): 367–71.
Olyan, Saul M. 'Is Isaiah 40–55 Really Monotheistic?' *Journal of Ancient Near Eastern Religion* 12 (2012): 190–201.
Pack, Roger, ed. *Artimidori Daldiani Onirocriticon Libri V* (Leipzig: Teubner, 1963).
Paige, Terence. 'Who Believes in "Spirit"? Πνεῦμα in Pagan Usage and Implications for the Gentile Christian Mission'. *HTR* 95 (2002): 417–36.
Parker, Holt N. *The Birthday Book: Censorinus*. Chicago: University of Chicago Press, 2007.
Parker, Robert. *Greek Gods Abroad: Names, Natures, and Transformations*. Berkeley: University of California Press, 2017.
Parker, Robert. *On Greek Religion*. Ithaca: Cornell University Press, 2011.
Parker, Robert. 'Pleasing Thighs: Reciprocity in Greek Religion'. In *Reciprocity in Ancient Greece*, edited by Christopher Gill, Norman Postlethwaite and Richard Seaford, 105–26. Oxford: Oxford University Press, 1998.
Parker, Robert. *Polytheism and Society at Athens*. Oxford: Oxford University Press, 2005.
Patterson, John R. *Landscapes and Cities: Rural Settlement and Civic Transformation in Early Imperial Italy*. Oxford: Oxford University Press, 2006.
Pellam, Gregory. 'Ceres, the Plebs, and "Libertas" in the Roman Republic'. *Historia: Zeitschrift für Alte Geschichte* 63 (2014): 74–95.
Peppard, Michael. 'Brother against Brother: Controversiae about Inheritance Disputes and 1 Corinthians 6:1–11'. *JBL* 133 (2014): 179–92.
Perkins, Pheme. *First Corinthians*. Paideia Commentaries on the New Testament. Grand Rapids, MI: Baker Academic, 2012.
Petrovic, Ivana. 'Deification: Gods or Men?' In *The Oxford Handbook of Ancient Greek Religion*, edited by Esther Eidinow and Julia Kindt, 429–43. Oxford: Oxford University Press, 2015.
Petrovic, Ivana. 'Transforming Artemis: From the Goddess of the Outdoors to City Goddess'. In *The Gods of Ancient Greece: Identities and Transformations*, edited by Jan N. Bremmer and Andrew Erskine, 209–27. Edinburgh: Edinburgh University Press, 2010.
Petsalis-Diomidis, Alexia. *'Truly Beyond Wonders': Aelius Aristides and the Cult of Asklepios*. Oxford: Oxford University Press, 2010.
Pfeiffer, Stefan. *Herrscher- und Dynastiekulte im Ptolemäerreich. Systematik und Einordnung der Kultformen*. Münchener Beiträge zur Papyrusforschung und antiken Rechtsgeschichte 98. Munich: C. H. Beck, 2008.
Philip, Finny. *The Origins of Pauline Pneumatology*. WUNT II, 194. Tübingen: Mohr Siebeck, 2005.
Phillips, Darryl A. 'The Temple of Divus Iulius and the Restoration of Legislative Assemblies under Augustus'. *Phoenix* 65, nos. 3–4 (2011): 371–92.
Pötscher, Walter. '"Numen" und "Numen Augusti"'. *ANRW* II 16.1, 355–92. Berlin: De Gruyter, 1978.

Prescendi, Francesca (Geneva). 'Numen'. In *Brill's New Pauly*, edited by Hubert Cancik and, Helmuth Schneider. English edition edited by Francis G. Gentry. Accessed 13 October 2023. doi: https://doi.org/10.1163/1574-9347_bnp_e826240.

Price, Simon R. F. *Rituals and Power: The Roman Imperial Cult in Asia Minor*. Cambridge: Cambridge University Press, 1984.

Prusac, Marina. 'Personifications of *Eudaimonia, Felicitas* and *Fortuna* in Greek and Roman Art'. *Symbolae Osloenses* 85 (2011). Accessed 5 July 2023. https://doi-org.ezp3.lib.umn.edu/10.1080/00397679.2011.631365

Rabens, Volker. *The Holy Spirit and Ethics in Paul: Transforming and Empowering for Religious-Ethical Life*. 2nd ed. Minneapolis: Fortress Press, 2013.

Rabens, Volker. 'Power from In Between: The Relational Experience of the Holy Spirit and Spiritual Gifts in Paul's Churches'. In *The Spirit and Christ in the New Testament and Christian Theology: Essays in Honor of Max Turner*, edited by I. Howard Marshall, Volker Rabens and Cornelis Bennema, 138–55. Grand Rapids, MI: Eerdmans, 2012.

Rackham, H., ed. and trans. *Aristotle: Nicomachean Ethics*. LCL 73. Cambridge, MA: Harvard University Press/London: William Heinemann Ltd, 1934.

Rawson, Elizabeth. *Intellectual Life in the Late Roman Republic*. Baltimore: Johns Hopkins University Press, 1985.

Renberg, Gil H. 'Was Incubation Practiced in the Latin West?' *Archiv für Religionsgeschichte* 8 (2006): 105–47.

Reynolds, Joyce and Robert Tannenbaum. *Jews and God-Fearers at Aphrodisias: Greek Inscriptions with Commentary*. Cambridge: Cambridge Philological Society, 1987.

Rhodes, Robin Francis. *Architecture and Meaning on the Athenian Acropolis*. Cambridge: Cambridge University Press, 1995.

Richardson, Neil. *Paul's Language about God*. JSNT Supplement Series 99. Sheffield: Sheffield Academic Press, 1994.

Ricl, Marijana. 'Hosios kai Dikaios. Première partie: catalogue des inscriptions'. *Epigraphica Anatolica* 18 (1991): 1–70.

Ricl, Marijana. 'Newly Published and Unpublished Inscriptions for Hosios and Dikaios and Their Contribution to the Study of the Cult'. In *Vom Euphrat bis zum Bosphorus. Kleinasien in der Antike. Festschrift für Elmar Schwertheim zum 65. Gebürtstag*, edited by Engelbert Winter, 563–79. Asia Minor Studien 65. Bonn: Habelt, 2008.

Rife, Joseph L. 'Religion and Society at Roman Kenchreai'. In *Corinth in Context: Comparative Studies on Religion and Society*, edited by Steven J. Friesen, Daniel N. Schowalter and James C. Walters, 391–432. Leiden: Brill, 2010.

Rives, James B. *Religion in the Roman Empire*. Malden, MA: Blackwell, 2007.

Roebuck, Carl. *The Asklepieion and Lerna*. Corinth 14. Athens: American School of Classical Studies, 1951.

Roetzel, Calvin J. *Paul: The Man and the Myth*. Minneapolis: Augsburg Fortress Press, 1999.

Ronchi, Giulia. *Lexicon theonymon rerumque sacrarum et divinarum ad Aegyptum pertinentium quae in papyris ostracis titulis graecis latinisque in Aegypto repertis laudantur*. Vol. 3. Milan: Istituto editoriale cisalpino-La goliardica, 1975.

Rookhuijzen, J. Z. van. 'The Erechtheion on the Acropolis of Athens'. *Kernos* 34 (2021): 69–121.

Rosen-Zvi, Ishay, and Adi Ophir. 'Paul and the Invention of the Gentiles'. *Jewish Quarterly Review* 105 (2015): 1–41.
Rüpke, Jörg. *Religion of the Romans*. Translated and edited by Richard Gordon. Cambridge: Polity Press, 2007.
Salmon, J. B. *Wealthy Corinth: A History of the City to 338 B.C.* Oxford: Oxford University Press, 1984.
Sambursky, Samuel. *The Physical World of Late Antiquity*. Princeton: Princeton University Press, 1962.
Sanders, E. P. *Paul and Palestinian Judaism: A Comparison of Patterns of Religion.* Minneapolis: Fortress Press, 1977.
Sandin, Pär Ola. 'Life and Death on the East Frieze of the Parthenon'. *Symbolai Osloenses* 96 (2022). Accessed 23 January 2024. https://doi.org/10.1080/00397679.2023.2175502.
Schäfer, Peter. *Two Gods in Heaven: Jewish Concepts of God in Antiquity*. Princeton: Princeton University Press, 2020.
Schalit, A. *König Herodes. Der Mann und sein Werk*. 2nd ed. Berlin: De Gruyter, 2001.
Schatzki, Theodore R. 'Practices and Actions: A Wittgensteinianism Critique of Bourdieu and Giddens'. *Philosophy of the Social Sciences* 27 (1997): 283–308.
Schatzki, Theodore R. *The Site of the Social: A Philosophical Account of the Constitution of Social Life and Change*. University Park, PA: Pennsylvania State University Press, 2002.
Scheid, John. *The Gods, the State, and the Individual: Reflections on Civic Religion in Rome*. Translated with a foreword by Clifford Ando. Philadelphia: University of Pennsylvania Press, 2016.
Scheid, John. *An Introduction to Roman Religion*. Translated by Janey Lloyd. Bloomington, IN: Indiana University Press, 2003.
Scheid, John. 'Luna'. *Oxford Classical Dictionary*. 4th ed. Oxford: Oxford University Press, 2012.
Scheidel, Walter, and Steven J. Freisen. 'The Size of the Economy and the Distribution of Income in the Roman Empire'. *JRS* 99 (2009): 61–91.
Schrage, Wolfgang. *Der erste Brief an die Korinther*. Evangelisch-Katholischer Kommentar zum Neuen Testament 7/1–4. Zurich: Benziger, 1991–2001.
Schultz, Peter. 'The Akroteria of the Temple of Athena Nike'. *Hesperia* 70 (2001): 1–47.
Scully, Stephen. *Plato's* Phaedrus: *A Translation with Notes, Glossary, Appendices, Interpretive Essay and Introduction*. Newburyport, MA: Focus, 2003.
Shapiro, H. A. 'The Attic Deity Basile'. *ZPE* 63 (1986): 134–36.
Shaya, Josephine. 'The Public Life of Monuments: The *Summi Viri* of the Forum of Augustus'. *AJA* 117 (2013): 83–110.
Shear, Julia L. *Serving Athena: The Festival of the Panathenaia and the Construction of Athenian Identities*. Cambridge: Cambridge University Press, 2021.
Shear, T. Leslie. *Trophies of Victory: Public Building in Periklean Athens*. Princeton: Princeton University Press, 2016.
Shelton, James B. 'Delphi and Jerusalem: Two Spirits or Holy Spirit?' *Pneuma* 33 (2011): 47–58.
Simmons, Robert Holschuh. '"Men, Friends": The Sociological Mechanics of Xenophontic Leaders in Winning Subordinates as Friends'. In *At the Crossroads*

*of Greco-Roman History, Culture, and Religion: Papers in Memory of Carin M. Green,* edited by Sinclair W. Bell and Lora L. Holland, 31–44. Oxford: Archeopress, 2018.

Simon, Erika. *The Gods of the Greeks.* 4th ed. Translated by Alan Shapiro. Wisconsin Studies in Classics. Madison: University of Wisconsin Press, 2021.

Smith, Jonathan Z. 'In Comparison a Magic Dwells'. In *Imagining Religion: From Babylon to Jonestown,* 19–35. Chicago: University of Chicago Press, 1988.

Smith, Jonathan Z. 'Differential Equations: On Constructing the Other'. In *Relating Religion: Essays in the Study of Religion,* 230–50. Chicago: University of Chicago Press, 2004.

Smith, Jonathan Z. *Drudgery Divine: On the Comparison of Early Christianities and the Religions of Late Antiquity.* Chicago: University of Chicago Press, 1990.

Smith, Jonathan Z. 'What a Difference a Difference Makes'. In *Relating Religion: Essays in the Study of Religion,* 251–302. Chicago: University of Chicago Press, 2004.

Smyth, H. W. *Greek Grammar.* Revised by Gordon M. Messing. Cambridge, MA: Harvard University Press, 1956. First published 1920.

Sinn, U. 'Die Stellung der Wettkämpfe im Kult des Zeus Olympios'. *Nikephoros* 4 (1991): 31–54.

Spaeth, Barbette Stanley. 'Greek Gods or Roman? The Corinthian Archaistic Blocks and Religion in Roman Corinth'. *AJA* 121 (2017): 397–423.

Stafford, Emma. 'Visualizing Creation in Ancient Greece'. *Religion and the Arts* 13 (2009): 419–47.

Stalder, Kurt. *Das Werk des Geistes in der Heilgung bei Paulus.* Zurich: EVZ-Verlag, 1962.

Stamatopoulou, Zoe. 'Weaving Titans for Athena: Euripides and the Panathenaic Peplos (*Hec.* 466–74 and *IT* 218–24)'. *CQ* 62 (2012): 72–80.

Stendahl, Krister. 'The Apostle Paul and the Introspective Conscience of the West'. *HTR* 56 (1963): 199–215.

Steuernagel, Dirk. 'Synnaos Theos: Images of Roman Emperors in Greek Temples'. In *Divine Images and Human Imaginations in Ancient Greece and Rome,* edited by Joannis Mylonopoulos, 241–55. Leiden: Brill, 2010.

Stirling, Lea M. 'Pagan Statuettes in Late Antique Corinth: Sculpture from the Panayia Domus'. *Hesperia* 77 (2008): 89–161.

Stowers, Stanley K. 'Does Pauline Christianity Resemble a Hellenistic Philosophy?' In *Redescribing Paul and the Corinthians,* edited by Ron Cameron and Merrill P. Miller, 219–44. Early Christianity and Its Literature 5. Atlanta: SBL, 2011.

Stowers, Stanley K. 'Kinds of Myth, Meals, and Power: Paul and the Corinthians'. In *Redescribing Paul and the Corinthians,* edited by Ron Cameron and Merrill P. Miller, 105–50. Early Christianity and Its Literature 5. Atlanta: SBL, 2011.

Stowers, Stanley K. 'Matter and Spirit, or What is Pauline Participation in Christ?' In *The Holy Spirit: Classic and Contemporary Readings,* edited by Eugene F. Rogers Jr, 91–108. Chichester: Wiley-Blackwell, 2009.

Stowers, Stanley K. 'Religion as a Social Kind'. Unpublished paper given to the Redescribing Christian Origins group at the SBL Annual Meeting, 2020.

Stowers, Stanley K. 'The Religion of Plant and Animal Offerings Versus the Religion of Meanings, Essences, and Textual Mysteries'. In *Ancient Mediterranean Sacrifice,*

edited by Jennifer Wright Knust and Zsuzsanna Várhelyi, 35–56. Oxford: Oxford University Press, 2011.
Stowers, Stanley K. *A Rereading of Romans: Justice, Jews, and Gentiles*. New Haven: Yale University Press, 1994.
Stowers, Stanley K. 'Why "Common Judaism" Does Not Look Like Mediterranean Religion'. In *Strength to Strength: Essays in Honor of Shaye J. D. Cohen*, edited by Michael L. Satlow, 235–55. Brown Judaic Studies. Atlanta: SBL, 2018.
Strelan, Rick. 'What Might a Pagan Have Understood by "Holy Spirit"?' *Colloquium* 42 (2010): 151–72.
Stroud, Ronald S. *The Sanctuary of Demeter and Kore: The Inscriptions*. Corinth 18.6. Princeton: ASCSA, 2013.
Sturgeon, Mary C. 'New Sculptures from the Isthmian Palaimonion'. In *Bridge of the Untiring Sea: The Corinthian Isthmus from Prehistory to Late Antiquity*, edited by Elizabeth R. Gebhard and Timothy E. Gregory, 159–92. Hesperia Supplement 48. Princeton: ASCSA, 2015.
Swetnam-Burland, Molly. *Egypt in Italy: Visions of Egypt in Roman Imperial Culture*. Cambridge: Cambridge University Press, 2015.
Theissen, Gerd. *The Religion of The Earliest Churches: Creating a Symbolic World*. Minneapolis: Fortress Press, 1999.
Theissen, Gerd. *The Social Setting of Pauline Christianity*. Translated by John H. Schütz. Edinburgh: T & T Clark, 1982.
Thiselton, Anthony C. *The First Epistle to the Corinthians: A Commentary on the Greek Text*. NIGTC. Grand Rapids, MI: Eerdmans, 2000.
Thomas, Christine M. 'Greek Heritage in Roman Corinth and Ephesos: Hybrid Identities and Strategies of Display in the Material Record of Traditional Mediterranean Religions'. In *Corinth in Context: Comparative Studies on Religion and Society*, edited by Steven J. Friesen, Daniel N. Schowalter and James C. Walters, 117–47. Leiden: Brill, 2010.
Thrall, Margaret E. *2 Corinthians: A Critical and Exegetical Commentary*. 2 vols. ICC. London: T & T Clark, 2004.
Thrall, Margaret E. 'The Initial Attraction of Paul's Mission in Corinth and of the Church He Founded There'. In *Paul, Luke and the Graeco-Roman World: Essays in Honour of Alexander J. M. Wedderburn*, edited by Alf Christophersen, Carsten Claussen, Jörg Frey and Bruce Longenecker, 59–74. JSNT Supplement 217. Sheffield: Sheffield Academic Press, 2002.
Tibbs, C. *Religious Experience of Pneuma: Communication with the Spirit World in 1 Corinthians 12 and 14*. WUNT II, 230. Tübingen: Mohr Siebeck, 2007.
Tiverios, Michalis. 'Artemis, Dionysos und Eleusinische Gottheiten'. *Mitteilungen* 119 (2004): 147–60.
Turner, Max. *The Holy Spirit and Spiritual Gifts, Then and Now*. Carlisle: Paternoster, 1996.
Ullucci, Daniel. *The Christian Rejection of Animal Sacrifice*. Oxford: Oxford University Press, 2012.
Verela, C. R. 'Cartesianism Revisited: The Ghost in the Moving Machine or the Lived Body'. In *Human Action Signs in Cultural Context: The Visible and the Invisible*

*in Movement and Dance*, edited by B. Farnell, 216–93. Metuchen, NJ: Scarecrow Press, 1995.

Vernant, J.-P., and Marcel Detienne, eds. *The Cuisine of Sacrifice among the Greeks*. Translated by P. Wissig. Chicago: University of Chicago Press, 1989. First published in French 1979.

Veyne, Paul. 'Inviter les dieux, sacrifier, banqueter: quelques nuances de la religiosité gréco-romaine'. *Annales*, 55 (2000): 3–42.

Veyne, Paul. 'The Roman Empire'. In *A History of Private Life*. Vol. 1, *From Pagan Rome to Byzantium*, edited by Paul Veyne, 5–234. Cambridge, MA: Belknap Press of Harvard University Press, 1987.

Waele, Jos de. *The Propylaia of the Akropolis in Athens: The Project of Mnesikles*. Amsterdam: J. C. Gieben, 1990.

Wagner, Claudia. 'The Worship of Athena on the Athenian Acropolis: Dedications of Plaques and Plates'. In *Athena in the Classical World*, edited by Susan Deacy and Alexandra Villing, 95–104. Leiden: Brill, 2001.

Walbank, Mary E. Hoskins. 'Evidence for the Imperial Cult in Julio-Claudian Corinth'. In *Subject and Rule: The Cult of the Ruling Power in Classical Antiquity*, edited by A. Small, 201–14. Ann Arbor: JRA, 1996.

Walsh, Robyn Faith. *The Origins of Early Christian Literature: Contextualizing the New Testament within Greco-Roman Literary Culture*. Cambridge: Cambridge University Press, 2021.

Wasserman, Emma. Review of Troels Engberg-Pedersen, *Cosmology and Self in the Apostle Paul: The Material Spirit*, *Catholic Biblical Quarterly* 77 (2015): 368–70.

Weare, Christopher, Juliet Musso and Kyu-Nahm Jun. 'Cross-Talk: The Role of Homophily and Elite Bias in Civic Associations'. *Social Forces* 88, no. 1 (2009): 147–73.

Welborn, L. L. *An End to Enmity: Paul and the 'Wrongdoer' of Second Corinthians*. Berlin: De Gruyter, 2011.

Welborn, L. L. Review of Bruce W. Longenecker, *Remember the Poor*. RBL (July 2012). Accessed 31 January 2024. https://www.sblcentral.org/API/Reviews/7899_9350.pdf

Wells, Colin. *The Roman Empire*. 2nd ed. Cambridge, MA: Harvard University Press, 1993.

Wendt, Hans Heinrich. *Die Begriffe Fleisch und Geist im biblischen Sprachgebrauch*. Gotha: Berthes, 1878.

West, Allen Brown. *Corinth*. Vol. VIII.2, *The Latin Inscriptions*. Cambridge, MA: Harvard University Press for ASCSA, 1931.

Wickkiser, Bronwen L. 'Asklepios in Greek and Roman Corinth'. In *Corinth in Context: Comparative Studies on Religion and Society*, edited by Steven J. Friesen, Daniel N. Schowalter and James C. Walters, 37–66. Leiden: Brill, 2010.

Wickkiser, Bronwen L. *Asklepios, Medicine, and the Politics of Healing in Fifth-Century Athens: Between Craft and Cult*. Baltimore: Johns Hopkins University Press, 2008.

Williams, Kaufman. 'The City of Corinth and Its Domestic Religion'. *Hesperia* 50 (1981): 408–21.

Williams, Kaufman, and O. H. Zervos. 'Corinth, 1982: East of the Theater'. *Hesperia* 52 (1983): 1–17.

Wilson, P. 'The Politics of Dance: Dithyrambic Contest and Social Order'. In *Sport and Festival in the Ancient Greek World*, edited by D. J. Phillips and D. Pritchard, 163–96. Swansea: Classical Press of Wales, 2003.

Winter, Bruce W. *Divine Honours for the Caesars: The First Christians' Responses*. Grand Rapids, MI: Eerdmans, 2015.

Wörrle, M. 'Die Lex Sacra von der Hallenstrasse (Inv. 1963, 20)'. In *AvP* VIII.3, *Die Inschriften des Asklepieions*, edited by Christian Habicht, 167–90. Berlin: De Gruyter, 1969.

Wright, N. T. *Paul and the Faithfulness of God*. 2 vols. Minneapolis: Fortress Press, 2013.

Wuellner, W. H. 'The Sociological Implications of I Corinthians 1:26–28 Reconsidered'. In *Studia Evangelica VI*, edited by Elizabeth A. Livingstone, 666–72. Berlin: Akademie Verlag, 1972.

Yarbro Collins, Adela, and John J. Collins. *King and Messiah as Son of God: Divine, Human, and Angelic Figures in Biblical and Related Literature*. Grand Rapids, MI: Eerdmans, 2008.

Yates, John W. *The Spirit and Creation in Paul*. WUNT II, 251. Tübingen: Mohr Siebeck, 2008.

Zanker, Paul. *The Power of Images in the Age of Augustus*. Ann Arbor: University of Michigan Press, 1998.

Zetterholm, Magnus. *Approaches to Paul: A Student's Guide to Recent Scholarship*. Minneapolis: Fortress Press, 2009.

Zsengellér, József. *Rewritten Bible after Fifty Years: Texts, Terms, or Techniques? A Last Dialogue with Geza Vermes*. Supplements to *JSJ* 166. Leiden: Brill, 2014.

# Index

**Introductory Note:** References such as '178–9' indicate (not necessarily continuous) discussion of a topic across a range of pages. Wherever possible in the case of topics with many references, these have either been divided into sub-topics or only the most significant discussions of the topic are listed. Because the entire work is about the 'Corinthian Christ group', the use of this term (and certain others which occur constantly throughout the book) as an entry point has been restricted. Information will be found under the corresponding detailed topics. Cross-references in a form such as 'gods *see also individual names*' direct the reader to headings in a particular class (e.g. in this case 'Zeus') rather than a specific *'individual names'* entry.

Aaron, 132
Abel, 133
Abraham, 196
*absent*, 4, 119, 169
Abydos, 32, 34
Achaia, 106, 108
Achelous, 61
Acrocorinth, 82, 88–9, 94, 101, 209
   north slope, 101, 103
Acrocorinthian Aphrodite, 82–7
Acropolis, 49–59
Adam, 158–9, 172, 179, 182
Adams, Edward, 151–2
adoption, 118
Adrastos, 171
Aegira, 126
Aelius Aristides, 42, 217
Aeneas, 66–71
Aeschylus, 99
Aesculapius, 80
affectivity, 12
agency, 10–11, 67, 127, 158–9, 182

Agora, Athenian, 60–1
Akeso, 57
akroteria, 51
Alba Longa, 67
Alcmena, 64
Alexander the Great, 169–70
allegiance
   exclusive, 177, 205, 210, 214–15
   to Paul's chord of gods, 205–12
Alpheius, 64
altars, 46–8, 58–61, 63–4, 75–6, 86–7, 136, 138, 184–5
Ἄλτις, 64
Amphiaraos, 185
Amphitrite, 86, 95, 97–9, 140–1
Amynos, 58–9
analysis, categories, 18–23
Anatolia, 25, 41–8, 101
anatomical votive offerings, 56, 100–1, 157, 208
ancestral gods, 198, 205
ancestral traditions, 197, 214

ancient Jewish monotheism, 3–4, 166, 209
ancient religion, 1–5, 21–2, 185–6, 215
animal sacrifice, 7, 21–3, 184–5
anthropomorphic forms, 139–41
Antiochus III, 169
Aphrodisias, 197, 200
  inscription, 200
Aphrodite, 40–1, 53, 82–3, 86–7, 97, 101
  Acrocorinthian, 82–7
Apollo, 18, 21, 40–2, 44–8, 101–2, 106–7, 126, 170
  and Asklepios, 18, 21, 101
  sanctuary, 21, 48, 101
Apollo Pythios, 61
Apphia, 47
apses, 68–9, 71, 73
Apteros Nike, 51
Aquilla, 3, 134
Arcadia, 139
archaeological evidence, 5, 102
Archedemus, 204–5
Areopagos, 58–60
*Argonautica*, 87
Argos, 126
Aricia, 141
Aristides, 127
Aristotle, 203–4
Arnal, William, 209
Arnobius, 74
Arnold, Dieter, 27–8, 30
Artemidorus, 125, 130
Artemis, 40–1, 48, 50–3, 63, 88–90, 92–3, 141, 218
Artemis Alphiaias, 90
Artemis Brauronia, 52
Artemis Eileithyia, 50
Artemis Epipyrgidia, 52
Artemis Hekate, 52
Artemis Lochia, 61
Artemis Prothyraia, 44–5, 218
Artemis Rospigliosi, 40
Asclepiades, 131
Asclepius, 58
Ascough, Richard S., 58–60
Ascyltos, 74

Asia Minor, 24, 35, 107, 170, 198–200
Asklepieia, 18, 23, 41–2, 44–5, 56–8, 100–3, 186
Asklepios, 18, 21, 40–5, 56–9, 99–103, 109, 185–6, 217
assembly, 116–17, 119–20, 151, 155–8, 160–1, 187, 189, 191–3
assembly members, 117, 159, 176, 190, 205
Assmann, Jan, 26–7, 32
associations, 15, 19, 59–60, 86, 89, 139, 167, 197
Astarte, 87
Athamas, 99
Athena, 40, 47, 49–51, 53–6, 63–4, 79, 132, 139–40
Athena Hygieia, 52, 55
Athena Nike, 50–2, 54–5
Athena Parthenos, 55
Athena Polias, 53–5
Athena Promachos, 54
Athenian Agora, 60–1
Athenians, 50–1, 53–6
Athens, 5, 48–50, 52–63, 88–90, 97, 101, 186
Atia, 170
attachment, preferential, 203, 214
Attica, 52–3, 56, 58–61
audiences, 6, 113, 118, 128, 131–2, 148–9, 152–3, 204
*Augustales*, 35, 108
Augustan Forum, 65–71, 77
Augusteum, 39
Augustus, 34–7, 39, 41, 65–71, 75, 106–8, 170–1, 177–8
autonomy, 134, 202

Bacchus, 80
bandwagoning, 203
banquets, 78, 207
baptism, 117, 187–91, 194
Barrett, C. K., 160, 183
Barthes, Roland, 20
Basile, 60–1
Bazzana, Giovanni B., 7, 15–16, 114, 117–20, 182

Beard, Mary, 65, 67–9, 72, 79–80, 170, 185
Beelzeboul, 133–4
believers, 115–17, 157, 181, 189–90
  fellow Christ, 119–20
Berlin, Andrea M., 37–41
Bes, 31, 177
bias, 16, 83
Bible, Hebrew, 114, 173, 187, 212
birthing houses, 28, 31, 34
Bithynia, 45
Blanton, Thomas R. IV, 144, 150–1, 202
blessings, 117–18, 166–8, 182
blurring of distinctions, 20, 159, 164–5, 177
Bodel, John, 5, 74, 77
Bookidis, Nancy, 83, 86, 88, 90–2, 94, 107–8, 110
Bosporan Kingdom, 198
Bourdieu, Pierre, 8–12, 201, 208, 215–16
Boutis, 53, 55
Boyarin, Daniel, 3
Braun, Willi, 20, 176
Brauron, 52–3
Briareus, 83
Broneer, Oscar, 97–8
Brookins, Timothy A., 157, 202, 207
Brown, Ian Phillip, 146
Brutus, 65
building metaphor, 155–7
Burkert, Walter, 189

Caesar, Julius, 65, 68–71, 105–6, 170–1
Caesarea Maritima, 34–7, 39, 142
Caesarea Philippi, 35, 37, 40–1
cakes, round, 218–19
Caligula, 178
canonical gospels, 133–4
Capitoline Triad, 78–82, 104, 107, 112
Capitolium, 78–9
Caria, 48
Cassius, 65–6, 131
Castor, 80
categories of analysis, 18–23
Catholicism, 14
causal powers theory, 11

Cauville, Sylvie, 27–8, 31, 33
*cellae*, 68, 79, 102, 107, 186
Celsus, 124, 128
Cenchreae, 82
Censorinus, 135
Ceres, 91, 93, 103–5
chaos, 32–3, 211
chapels, 30, 34, 48
chariot sculptures, 67
chariots, 60, 97, 139–40, 142
Charites, 51–2
childbirth/child rearing, 50, 63
children, 57, 61, 72–3, 87, 139, 141, 171, 175
chords of gods, 5, 8, 187, 190, 193–4, 205–6, 209–12, 214–15; *see also* Introductory Note
  allegiance to, 205–12
  around the mediterranean, 27–81
  practice, 194, 202–3, 205–6, 211–13
  as tool for rupture, 213–16
Christ
  death, 120, 173, 176
  groups, 145–6, 150, 168
  movement, 1, 6–8, 13, 153, 213, 216
  risen, 119, 163–4, 176
  *see also* Jesus
Christian exceptionalism, 215–16
Christian origins, 1, 196, 215
Christianity, 1, 4, 7, 14, 101, 121, 208, 215–16
Christians, 3, 20, 128–9, 132, 134, 156, 188, 215
  early, 7, 14, 160, 182
  modern, 4, 173
Chryseros, 47
Chrysippus, 123, 125
Cicero, 5, 72–4, 77, 126, 130–1
cities, 50–1, 58–9, 70, 86, 90–1, 100–1, 109–10, 187
Claros, 126
class, 143, 145, 204
classical period, 25, 82, 97, 99, 102, 126, 186
Claudius, 134, 178
Cleopatra VII, 28

clients, 202–3
Clinton, Kevin, 58, 194
Cohen, Shaye J. D., 197–8
coins, 54, 86, 102, 104, 106, 148
*collegia*, 15, 153
Collins, Raymond, 156, 166, 168–9, 174–6, 189, 191–2, 207
colonial protective divinities, 103–5
colonies, 79, 86, 104–7; *see also* Corinth
colonisation, 82, 88, 90–1, 93, 101–2
colonists, 148
colossus, 54, 97
columns, 27, 94
commentators, 123, 130, 156–7, 160, 174–5, 181–3, 189
communion, 160, 182
communities, 2–3, 15, 152–3, 156, 180, 182–3, 186, 208–10
comparative approaches to *pneuma*, 115–20
Concannon, Cavan, 143, 145–6, 150
configurations, 5, 41, 63, 75, 78, 108–9, 206, 208–9
connectedness, 182–3
contextualisation, 13, 114, 191
continuity, 9, 40, 56, 82, 113, 155, 163, 170
   architectural, 26
   of practice, 212
conversational realism, 11
conversion, 115, 173, 188–9, 197, 207, 214
core education, 148, 152, 154
Corinth, 81–3, 86, 90–5, 103–13, 134–5, 151–2, 186–8, 200–2
   forum, 108–9
   maps, 83–4
   Roman colonisation, 82, 88, 90–1, 93, 101–2
   sacking, 90, 101
   sanctuaries, 94, 110
   temples, 156, 187
Corinthian assembly, 15, 151–2, 154–5, 158, 160, 166–7, 172, 179
   members, 205
   ritual activities, 193
Corinthian gentiles, 1, 202, 213–14
Corinthian Jesus followers, 183, 194, 203

Corinthian letters, 24, 134, 136, 160, 163, 165, 184, 213–14
Corinthian region, 82, 95, 99
Corinthian sanctuary, 93–4, 101, 103, 110
Corinthian society, 149, 151, 207
Corinthians
   elite, 151–3, 203–4, 214
   non-educated, 130–1, 135, 155
   non-elite, 192, 205, 214
   Paul's, 15, 17, 134, 143, 164, 168, 178, 196–211
cornucopias, 77, 136
correction, Paul's, 210–11
correspondence *see* letters
cosmic drama, 177, 180
cosmology, 32, 34, 115–17, 123, 154
cosmos, 16, 33, 123, 128, 165–7, 177
counter-gifts, 22–3; *see also* gifts
co-workers, 158, 165, 176, 179–81
Crito, 203–5
crossroads, 78, 110, 136, 204
Cult of Asklepios, 42, 59, 102, 217
cult statues/statuettes, 39, 51, 54–5, 68–9, 71, 97, 108–9, 184–6
cultic activity, 21, 23, 40, 74, 108–9, 184, 187, 193
cultic life, 27, 35, 40, 48, 81, 105, 108, 140
cultic meal, 192, 194
cultic practice, 18, 23, 26, 52
cultic ritual, 52, 189, 193
cultic worship, 4, 51, 87–8
cults, 30–1, 86–7, 91–2, 99–100, 104–6, 112–13, 141, 184–94
cultures, 6–7, 13, 16, 37, 147, 149, 186, 192
   Egyptian, 31
   Greek, 91, 169
   religious, 35, 64, 112
   Roman, 37, 78–80, 93, 105, 148–9, 169
Curetes, 64
curse tablets, 91–2
Cyclopes, 97
Cyprus, 40, 171

*daimōn*, 125, 128–9, 132–4, 154
datives, 157–8, 172
Davila, James R., 160, 183

de Angelis, Francesco, 66–7
*De defectu oraculorum*, 128, 134
*De divinatione*, 72, 126
death, 123, 128, 135, 172–4, 176, 179, 192, 196
　Christ's, 1, 132, 173, 176
dedications, 45, 48, 55, 59–60, 63–4, 71, 78, 171
dedicatory offerings/objects, 52, 55, 64, 185
Deissmann, G. Adolf, 143
deities, 31–2, 93–4, 101–2, 135–6, 138–9, 177, 183–5, 207–9; see also *individual names*
　personified, 124, 160
Deleuze, Giles, 145
Deliler, 199
Delos, 126, 185
Delphi, 21, 52, 95, 101, 114, 122, 126–7, 194
DeMaris, Richard E., 188–91
Demeter, 83, 87–94, 101, 103, 112, 139, 194, 209
　Lady, 91, 93
　sanctuaries, 83, 87–94, 101, 103, 109
Demosthenes, 175
Dendera, 26–34
designators, 165–6, 168
Dexios, 59
Diana, 141
*didaskaloi*, 147
Didyma, 48, 126
Dikaios, 42, 45–8
Dikeos, 46–7
Dinarchus, 175
Diodokoi, 169
Diodorus, 88
Diogenes of Oenoanda, 131
Dion, 194
Dionysius son of Dionysius, 171
Dionysos, 40, 46, 64, 88–93, 99, 109, 112, 194
　Theatre of, 52, 57
dispositions, 6, 10–11, 146
divination, 7, 126–7
divine communities, 49–50, 81, 112
divine entities, 132, 136, 155, 157–8, 163, 165, 182, 184
divine figures, 23, 34–5, 57–8, 164–5, 167–70, 184, 189–91, 193–4
　groupings of, 71, 160–1, 194
divine honours, 37, 41, 169–70, 209
divine intermediaries, 124, 129
divine status, 35, 68, 139, 170, 177
divine world, 5, 33, 64, 77, 184
divinities, 4, 28, 37, 45, 91, 185, 190, 207–8
　colonial/state protective, 103–5
*divus Iulius*, 71, 106, 170
Dodona, 122, 127
doings, 9, 12, 21, 26, 112, 212, 214; see also sayings, and doings
domestic contexts, 74–8, 110, 112, 136
domestic religion, 109–11
*Domus Augusta*, 106
*Domus Augustus*, 106
Doniger, Wendy, 18–19
doors, 32–4, 70, 122
Droge, Arthur J., 67–9, 71
Dunn, James, 114, 187, 189, 208

early Christ movement, 6–8, 14–15
early Christianity, 2, 4, 14, 129, 143, 208
east frieze of the Parthenon, 50, 52–3
Echelidai, 60–1
Echelos, 60–1
economic scale, 150, 153–4, 202
economic security, 153–4, 163
economic status, 147, 202
ecstatic activities/behaviour, 120, 126–7, 184, 186, 193–4
Edfu, 26, 28–34
　Horus of, 28, 30
education, 130, 146–50, 163, 202, 205
　core, 148, 152, 154
　formal, 24, 130, 147–8, 150–2, 154–5, 163, 179
　level of, 146, 152, 162, 202, 205
　peripheral, 147, 152
　philosophical, 147–8
Egypt, 24, 26–8, 30–1, 33–4, 80, 94, 169, 174
　temples, 26, 28, 31, 34

Egyptian gods, 34
Eisenbaum, Pamela, 209
Eitea, 60
Eleans, 63–4
Eleusis, 73, 89, 91, 194
elites, 5, 117, 131, 143–4, 148–55, 202, 205
  Corinthian, 151–3, 203–4, 214
emperors, 35, 37, 47, 69–70, 107–8, 138–9, 170–1, 177–8; *see also individual names*
empire, 69, 72, 77, 79, 145, 149, 151, 170
  early, 106, 144, 146, 148
*encyclia paideia*, 147
Engberg-Pedersen, Troels, 115–18, 120, 123, 180, 182
Enneads, 30–2, 34
Enoch, 133
enslaved persons *see* slaves
Ephesos, 40, 91
Ephyra, 126
Epictetus, 130
Epicureanism, 131
Epidauria, 58
Epidauros, 23, 57, 101, 103, 185, 194
Epimedes, 64
Epipyrgidia, 52
epithets, 32, 42, 44, 50–1, 77, 90–1, 177–8
Erchia, 60
Erechtheion, 53–4
Erechtheus, 53–5
Ergane, 64
Eros, 40, 53, 86–7
Erosa shrine, 110
ES4-7 levels, 152–3
ethnicity, 4–5, 7, 117–18, 148–9, 206
Eueteria, 92
events, 13, 18, 56, 88, 98, 164–6, 173, 175–6
exceptionalism, Christian, 215–16
exclusive allegiance, 177, 205, 210, 214–15
exclusivity, 14, 205–6, 209–10, 214, 216
existential transition, 32–3
Eyl, Jennifer, 7, 15, 182
Ezekiel, 212

factions, 120, 168, 188–9
fame, 44, 64–6, 95
familial relationship, 18, 168, 183
familiarity, 1, 129–30, 154, 195, 202–3, 205
family, 46–7, 57, 61, 71, 74–5, 77–8, 111, 168–9
  members, 45, 58, 103, 118
Farnell, Brenda, 8, 10–11, 13
*Fasti*, 66, 68–70
fathers, 113–14, 160–1, 165–9, 175–7, 179–80, 206–7, 209, 212–14
Fee, Gordon D., 114, 156–7, 160, 175, 183, 187, 189
fellowship, 160, 182
festivals, 28, 33, 52, 55–6, 58, 63, 89, 93–4
fifth century BCE, 41–2, 47, 56, 59–60, 80, 186
fifth century CE, 37, 41, 92
filial relationship, 167–8
Finnestad, Ragnhild Bjerre, 26–8, 32–3
Fishwick, Duncan, 68, 135–6, 138
Fitzmyer, Joseph A., 156–7, 163, 167–8, 175–7, 180–1, 187, 191–2, 206–7
*flamen Augusti*, 108
*flamen divi Iulii*, 106, 108
flesh, 116, 132, 212
Flower, Harriet I., 74–5, 77, 135–6
food, 32, 77, 153, 165, 205–6, 210
  spiritual, 174–5
formal education, 24, 130, 147–8, 150–2, 154–5, 163, 179
Fortuna Primigenia, 68, 104–5, 142
  temple, 72–4
forums, 65–71, 77, 79, 91, 94, 99, 104, 108–10
founders, 68–9, 97, 106
fourth century BCE, 59, 88, 101, 110, 140
fourth century CE, 42, 91, 109, 111
fragmentary inscriptions, 35, 106
Fredriksen, Paula, 3–4, 196–8, 200, 205
freedmen, 35, 144, 147–9, 152, 203
Frenschkowski, Marco, 177–8
Friedland, Elise A., 37, 39–41
Friesen, Steven J., 83–4, 86, 91–2, 98, 100, 143–5, 148–51, 202

Gaios, 47
Gaius, 153, 188, 203
Gaius Flavius Figulus, 171
Galatians, 115, 118
Galen, 123–5
games, 37, 79, 95, 98–9, 139, 201
Ganzert, J., 68
gardens, 74, 77, 135
Garroway, Joshua D., 2–3, 7, 196
Ge, 44–5, 63–4, 93, 218
*gebaute Erinnerung*, 26
genealogy, 18, 20, 32, 112–13, 162, 164–6, 179, 194–5
genesis, 1, 6, 179, 215–16
genetic approaches to *pneuma*, 120–30
genitive, 138, 159, 178, 181
*genius*, 75, 77–8, 135–9
Genius Augusti, 108, 135, 138
*genius urbis Romae*, 135
genres, 6, 16, 18, 61, 121, 192
Gens Iulia, worship of, 105–8
gentiles, 1–4, 7, 117–18, 129, 196–9, 201–2, 209, 214–15
  Corinthian, 1, 202, 213–14
  reception/understandings, 114, 117, 128–9
geographical locations, 5, 24–5, 162, 199; *see also individual places*
Geraza, 134
gifts, 3, 7, 15, 21–3, 157, 165, 189–90, 193; *see also* counter-gifts
  battle of, 53
  spiritual, 129, 157, 193, 210
gigantomachy, 49, 55–6
glory, 64, 181
gnomic sayings, 130, 148
γνῶσις, 209–10
goats, 39, 41, 139–40, 218
goddesses, 40, 52, 55, 82–3, 86, 88, 111, 139–40; *see also individual names*
god-fearers, 197–201
  alternatives to, 201–5
gods, 3–6, 23–35, 37–83, 111–14, 138–40, 165–72, 183–7, 205–15; *see also individual names*
  ancestral, 198, 205
  in Corinth, 82, 109, 112, 164
  Egyptian, 34
  Greek, 41, 51, 91, 104, 177
  household, 74, 77, 111
  nature, 139
  personifications *see* personifications
  Roman, 35, 92, 104–5
  small groups of, 5–6, 8–9, 11–12, 18, 24–5, 78–9, 111–13, 162–4
  traditional, 175, 212
Gordon, Richard L., 79, 94–5, 142
gospels, 2, 7, 133–4, 143, 146, 172–3, 175, 215
Graml, Constanze, 51–2
Greece, 24, 48–64, 91, 93, 100–1, 108, 122
Greek gods, 41, 51, 91, 104, 177; *see also individual names*
Greek inscriptions, 37, 198, 217
Greek religion, 5, 21–2, 25, 50, 58, 64, 185, 194
Greek traditions, 40, 82, 120
Greek world, 80, 94–5
Green, Carin, 141
groupings of divine figures, 71, 160–1, 194
growth, 1–2, 100, 114, 214
  agrarian, 73
Güney, Hale, 46–7
gymnasia, 42, 171

*habitus*, 8–12
Hadrian, 39, 42–4, 104, 107, 138
Hammadi, Nag, 164
harbours, 35–6, 112
Harpocrates, 80
Harrill, Albert J., 2, 204
Hathor, 28, 30–1, 33
Hays, Richard B., 173, 189
healing, 23, 58–9, 100–1, 219
heaven, 4, 116, 133, 207–8
Hebrew Bible, 114, 173, 187, 212
Hebrews, 174–5, 181; *see also* Jews
Hedjhotep, 33
Heliopolis, 31
Helios, 46, 57, 83, 86–7, 139–42

Hellenistic period, 40, 100–1, 110–11, 177
hemicycles, 65, 69
Hephaestus, 53, 55, 64
Hera, 48, 99
Hera Bounaia, 83
Hera Olympias, 64
Herakles, 40, 64, 109, 169
Herculaneum, 103
Hermes, 51–2, 57, 60, 64, 83, 93, 99
Hermes Enagonios, 64
Hermes-Thot, 177
Herod, 35, 37, 39, 41
Herod Philip, 37, 40
heroes, 43, 54, 58, 60–1, 65, 111, 185
heroines, 60–1, 111
Hestia, 61, 63, 78
hierarchies, 133, 157, 209
history, and mythology, 164–83
Hollinshead, Mary B., 53–4
Holum, Kenneth, 35, 37
holy spirit, 114, 122, 124, 127, 129, 133, 157, 183
Homer, 53, 147
Homonoia, 64
homophily, 203–5, 214
honey, 72, 219
Honos, 142
Horrell, David G., 143, 151, 202
horses, 46, 50, 139–40, 142, 215
Horsley, Richard A., 156, 175, 187, 208
Horus, 28, 30–1, 33, 94, 169
*Hosion kai Dikaion*, 45
Hosios, 42, 45–8
household gods, 74, 77, 111; *see also Lares*; *Penates*
households, 15, 74, 77–8, 111, 118, 135–6, 149, 151–3
　leaders, 151
　structure, 111
houses, 5, 65, 74–9, 107, 109–11, 151–2, 169–70, 198
　birthing, 28, 31, 34
human activity, 8, 12, 20, 51, 176
Hurtado, Larry W., 3–4, 160, 166, 183
Hygieia, 42, 45, 56, 58, 102–3, 194

*Hymn to Demeter*, 87, 139
hymns, 32, 87, 98, 139, 186, 193–4
hypostyle halls, 28, 34

Iasile, 61
Iasos, 57, 64
iconography, 46, 68, 75, 78, 86, 135–6, 139, 142
Idas, 64
identification, 4, 60, 91, 97
identity, 42, 44, 55, 110–11, 115, 117, 133–4, 187
ideology, 19–20, 26–7, 125, 169–70, 174
idols, 206–7, 210–12
imagery, 56, 67, 104, 156–8, 168, 180, 184, 187
　temple, 157, 163, 187
imaginations, 16, 187, 199
immortals, 22–3, 121, 169
imperial cult, 35, 43, 105–8, 170
imperial family, 43, 105–6
incense, 32, 92, 219
incomes, 150–2
incubation, 44–5, 101
　chambers, 44, 57, 218–19
individualism, 11, 156
individuation of *pneuma*, 156–8
Ino, 99
inscriptions, 31, 39–40, 42–8, 56–61, 89–91, 106–8, 148–9, 197–200
　fragmentary, 35, 106
　Greek, 37, 198, 217
　Latin, 37, 94, 108
inspiration, 121–2, 126–7
institutions, 104–5, 162, 164
instructions, 193, 218
intelligibility, 6, 12, 21
intentions, 66, 114, 117–18, 159, 188
　Pauline, 117, 187, 208, 213
intermediaries, divine, 124, 129
Isaac, 196
Isaiah, 212
Ishtar, 87
Isis, 30, 80, 83, 94–5, 177
Isis Pelagia, 83, 94
Isis-Fortuna, 77–8

Israel, 34–5, 37, 117–18, 165–6, 174–6, 179–81, 197, 207–9
Isthmia, 82, 92, 95–9, 112, 140, 191
　canal, 98
　Poseidon sanctuary, 86
Isthmian Games, 95, 97–9
Italy, 40, 72, 80, 153, 185

Jacob, 196
Jameson, Michael, 50–1, 55
Jerusalem, 114, 133, 187
　temple, 156, 187
Jesus, 3–4, 133–4, 158–60, 167–8, 172–4, 176–9, 182–3, 206–9; *see also* Christ
　followers, 143, 212
　as Messiah, 7
　movement, 200–1
Jewish monotheism, 3–4, 166, 209
Jewish practices, 196, 198
Jews, 2–4, 7, 129, 132, 134–5, 164–5, 190, 196–200; *see also* Hebrews
Johnson Hodge, Caroline, 117–18
Josephus, 35, 37, 164, 198
Judaisers/Judaising, 197–9
Judaism, 3–4, 13, 34, 197–8
　early, 4–5
　Paul's, 2–3, 196
Julius Caesar, 65, 68–71, 105–6, 170–1
Juno, 72–4, 77–80, 104, 135, 139, 141
Jupiter, 71–3, 78–80, 104, 139
justice, 45–8, 93
Justitia, 142
Juvenal, 198

Kairos, 64
Kaliteknos, 42
Kalliphanes, 60
Kallirhoe, 61
Kallynteria, 53
Katrosits, Maia, 7
Kearns, Emily, 58–61
Kekrops, 53–5
Kenchreai, 92, 94–5, 112
Kephisos, 49, 61–3, 139, 185
*kharis*, 22–3
Khepri, 32

Kibyratis, 45
kings, 67, 79, 168–70, 172; *see also* individual names
Kloppenborg, John S., 15, 58, 60
Knidos, 92
knowledge, 131, 147, 165, 176, 207–8, 210
Kodros, 60
κοινωνία, 160, 168, 182
Kore, 48, 112, 194, 209
　sanctuaries, 83, 87–94, 101, 103, 109
κύριος, 158–9, 176–8, 181, 208
Kos, 101
*kyrios*, 158, 178, 209

Laird, Margaret L., 108
Lambek, Michael, 119
lamps, 40–1, 92
landscapes, 40, 49, 56, 82, 107, 153
　religious, 48, 128, 213
language, 20, 113, 119, 121, 126, 154–6, 174–5, 212
　Paul's, 114, 119, 152, 162, 167, 180, 208
Laouas, 47
Lapethos, 170
larariums, 75–6, 78
Lares, 5, 74–5, 77–8, 111, 136; *see also* household gods; *Penates*
　Augusti, 108
Latin, 104, 141, 148–9
　inscriptions, 37, 94, 108
Latium, 64–81
Lavinium, 80
leaders, 15, 133–4, 141, 151, 154, 201, 204
Lebreton, Sylvain, 54
legal status, 145, 150
Leisegang, H., 120–1, 126
Lentrini, 90
Leto, 61, 63
letters, 154–6, 158–9, 163–4, 166–8, 180, 183, 188, 218–19
　Corinthian, 24, 134, 136, 160, 163, 165, 184, 213–14
Leukothea, 97–9

levels
  economic, 146, 149, 202
  of education, 146, 152, 162, 202, 205
  of society, 5, 8, 178
Levinskaya, Irina, 198–200
Leviticus, 212
*Lex sacra*, 44, 57, 217
libations, 32, 77, 128, 136
Liber, 91, 93, 103–5
Libera, 91, 93, 103–5
*libertas*, 104–5, 142
life force, 130, 132
light, 33, 212
  of knowledge, 165
  natural, 33
Lim, S. U., 208
Lincoln, Bruce, 16–20, 128, 164–5, 174
literary evidence, 17, 52, 87, 95, 102, 147, 198, 213
Littlewood, R. Joy, 73
Lloyd, Janet, 22, 65
local groups, 20, 23, 165, 184, 193
local sanctuaries, 52, 63, 95, 187, 209–10; *see also individual sanctuaries*
Longenecker, Bruce W., 143–5, 149–54, 157, 202
lord, 159, 166–7, 175–7, 181–2, 190, 192–4, 206–11, 213
loyalty, 178, 206, 209, 211
Lucan, 127
Lucilius, 127
Lucius Verus, 86, 102
*ludi Augustales*, 37
*Ludi Plebei*, 79
*Ludi Romani*, 79
Luke, 2, 133, 198–9
Luna, 141–2
Lydia, 45, 199

McCutcheon, Russell, 18, 20, 176
Macedonia, 45, 58
Mack, Burton, 8, 20, 209
MacMullen, Ramsay, 130
madness, 122, 127
Maleatas, 57
μανία, 121–3, 127, 133

Maoz, Zeev, 203
maps, 82, 145, 150, 157
marble
  reliefs, 61
  statues/statuettes, 68–9, 110
  throne, 52
Marcus Aurelius, 86, 98
Mars Ultor, 71
Marsyas, 47–8
Martin, Dale B., 8, 125–6, 154–5
material substances, 116, 121, 123–4, 127, 130, 155
materialist notions, 125–6, 146, 148, 154–5, 159, 161, 163, 179
Matthew, 133
Mauss, Marcel, 8–10, 19, 23
meals, 6, 77, 117, 184, 191–3, 200, 210
meat, 55, 189, 209–10
mediating figures, 4
medicine, 58, 100, 125, 131, 155
Meeks, Wayne A., 8, 143, 151, 153, 200
Melikertes-Palaimon, 95, 97–9
Memphis, 94
Messiah, Jesus as, 7
*Metamorphoses*, 87, 94
metaphors, 28, 128, 155–6, 158–9, 180, 186–7
Metis, 79
metonyms, 177–8
Micaiah, 132
middling groups, 149–51, 155
Midrash, 164
Millis, Benjamin W., 148–9
mind, state of, 22, 44, 127
Minerva, 77–80, 104
Mitchell, Stephen, 25, 46, 48
Mnemosyne, 23, 44–5, 57, 101, 218–19
Moirai, 90, 93
monotheism, 2–5, 28, 161, 166, 207–10, 213–15
  Jewish *see* Jewish monotheism
  and polytheism, 3, 5, 161, 207, 209
  valorisation of, 215–16
monuments, 35, 48, 58, 65, 67, 97, 108, 149
moon, 27, 116, 141–2

Morai, 83, 91
Morgan, Theresa, 147, 152
Morgantina, 92
mortals, and immortals, 22–3
Moses, 132, 159, 174–5, 180
mothers, 61, 63–4, 68, 73–4, 83, 87, 89, 209
Moule, C. F. D., 187
municipal elites, 144
Muses, 40, 64, 122
Musonius Rufus, 130
Mysia, 45
mysteries, 2, 14, 41, 89, 165, 194
mythmakers, 19–20, 164
mythmaking, 18, 20, 168, 192, 206
mythological connections, 73, 78, 93, 95, 99, 112
mythology, 16, 18–20, 37, 41, 61, 65, 69–70, 162
   and history, 164–83
   Paul's, 164, 166
Mytilene, 92

Naiden, F. S., 185–6, 189
*naos*, 184–7, 193
Naso, Lucius Axius, 171
nature gods, 139
ναός, 88, 156–7, 184–5
Neleus, 60, 97
Nemesis, 39–41
Neon Phaleron, 60
Nereids, 99, 141
Nero, 98, 106, 177–8
Netzer, Ehud, 35
New Testament, 3, 5, 25, 114, 121, 145, 187–8
nexus of sayings and doings, 9, 12, 21, 26, 112
Nice, Richard, 10
niches, 39–40, 43, 67–8, 71, 76, 80
Nike, 50–1, 55, 64, 110
Nike Apteros, 51
non-educated Corinthians, 130–1, 135, 155
non-elites, 143, 151, 192, 200–2, 205, 214
Northeast Phrygia, 46–7

*numen*, 87, 135–6, 138, 191
Numen Augusti, 138
numismatic evidence *see* coins
Nutton, Vivian, 125
nymphs, 39–41, 60, 64, 112

offerings, 21–3, 31–2, 48, 57, 60–1, 77–9, 136, 184–6
   anatomical, 56, 100–1, 157, 208
   dedicatory, 52, 55, 64, 185
   miniature, 110
   terracotta, 63, 100–1, 203
offertory box, 218–19
Olympia, 55, 63–4, 95, 186
open-air sanctuaries/shrines, 58, 104–5
oracles, 41, 48, 52, 63, 72, 74, 126–8, 185
oracular activity, 120, 126
orators, 130, 175, 204
*orgeōnes*, 58–60
Origen, 124, 128
Orpheus, 40, 89, 93
Osiris, 30, 33–4, 80, 94–5, 169
Osiris-Apis, 94
Ovid, 66, 68–71, 87

pagans, 2, 121–2, 127, 129, 132, 187, 198
   writings, 121, 125
*paideia*, 117, 132, 147–8, 150–3, 201–5, 214
Paige, Terence, 121–9, 132–4
Paionaios, 64
Palaimon, 95–9
   temple, 97, 99
Palatine, 68
Palestine, 34–41, 48, 107, 128
Pan, 37–41, 109, 139–40
Panakeia, 57
*Panathenaea*, 55–6
Pandion, 54–5
Panias, 37–41
Panion, 37
pantheons, 5, 28, 31, 34, 46, 68, 78, 80
   Roman, 34, 43, 170
parallelism, 158, 179
χαρίσματα, 158, 182
Parker, Robert, 5, 22–3, 25, 50–1, 55–6, 58, 61, 185

Parthenon, 49, 51–3, 55, 140
  east frieze, 50, 52–3
  Periclean, 49
Parthians, 65
partnerships, 50, 60, 160, 182
*paterfamilias*, 75, 78, 136
Patrae, 108
patron deities, 49, 82, 107
Patterson, John, 153
Paul
  appeals, 1–2, 6, 24, 195, 211
  Corinthians, 15, 17, 134, 143, 164, 168, 178, 196–211
  correction, 210–11
  initial audiences, 117, 146, 148
  initial conversations, 113, 152, 155, 161
  Judaism, 2–3, 196
  language, 114, 119, 152, 162, 167, 180, 208
  letters *see* letters
  mythology, 164, 166
  and *pneuma*, 154–61
  preaching, 146, 152, 161, 194, 210
  success, 151, 196–8, 201–2, 214
  theology, 114, 119
Pauline intention, 117, 187, 208, 213
Pausanias, 52, 54–5, 63–4, 82–3, 86–7, 94–5, 97–9, 101–2
pediments, 46–7, 49, 67–8, 140, 170
Pelagia, Isis, 83, 94
Pellam, Gregory, 104–5
Penates, 5, 67, 74, 77–8; *see also* household gods; Penates
*pepaideumenoi*, 146–8
*peplos*, 55–6
Peppard, Michael, 170–1
Pergamene *Lex sacra*, 217
Pergamon, 21, 41–4, 48, 57, 101, 103
Pergamon Asklepieion, 42–5, 107
Periclean Parthenon, 49
peripheral education, 147, 152
peristyles, 77, 109
Perkins, Pheme, 188–9, 191–2, 207
Persephone, 73, 87, 89, 91, 93, 139, 194, 209
Persians, 50, 53, 169

personifications, 68, 72, 132–4, 136, 139–42, 158–60
Peter, 3, 188
Petsalis-Diomidis, Alexa, 42–3, 217
*Phaedrus*, 121–3, 203
Phaleron, 60–1
Pheidias, 54–5
Philippi, 7, 65
Philo, 120–1, 164, 187
philosophers, 130, 135, 155
philosophical education, 147–8
philosophical maxims, 130, 147
philosophical notions, 130, 154
philosophy, 11, 130–1, 146, 148, 155
Philotis, 94
Phoenicia, 128
Phokaian hekte, 219
Phrygia, 42, 45–8
physicians, 58, 131
piety, 67, 110–11, 178, 199
pigs, 23, 60, 136, 218
pilgrims, 44, 72
*pinax*, 88–90
Piraeus, 23, 56–9, 103
*pistis*, 115
plaques, 23, 55, 63–4
Plataea, 50
Plato, 120–2, 127, 175, 203
Platonism, 154
plebians, 104–5
Plutarch, 123, 126–8, 134, 155
Plynteria, 53–4
πνευματικοί, 179–80, 191, 210–11
*pneuma*, 24, 113–65, 175, 179–83, 189–91, 194, 210–11, 213–14
  comparative approaches, 115–20
  genetic approaches, 120–30
  individuation, 156–8
  in Paul, 154–61
  range of meanings, 130–9
  scholarly approaches, 113–14
Pneumatists, 125
Pnyx, 58
poetry, 19, 122, 127, 158
Pollux, 80
Polybius, 37

polytheism, 3–5, 28, 161, 207–10, 213–15
pomerium, 69–70
Pompeii, 75–6, 80, 136–7
Poseidon, 49–50, 53–5, 140–1, 208–9
    sanctuary at Isthmia, 86, 95–9
possession, 119–20, 122–3, 126, 133
Potamo, 67
pottery, 39–41, 55
poverty, 144–5, 202, 204
power, 6–7, 35, 37, 51, 106–7, 151, 170, 179–80
practice, 6–10, 12–13, 17–18, 23–8, 77–8, 191–2, 201–6, 210–16
    chord of gods, 194, 202–3, 205–6, 211–13
    cultic, 18, 23, 26, 52
    homophily of, 204–5
    meal, 191–2
    patterns of, 8, 21, 113, 154, 162, 195
    Paul's, 9, 192, 205–6
    social, 1, 8, 14–15, 81–2, 112
    social theory of, 8–13
    universality of, 187
Praeneste, 72
prayers, 124, 160, 183–4, 193
preaching, 112, 178, 204
    Paul's, 146, 152, 161, 194, 210
preferential attachment, 203, 214
Prescendi, Francesca, 138
Price, Simon, 35, 37, 65, 67–9, 72, 79–80, 170, 185
priestesses, 105, 122, 127
priests, 32, 52–3, 56, 97, 128, 170–1, 219
Priscilla, 3, 134
χριστός, 168–9, 172, 174, 176–8
processions, 32, 52, 55–6, 58, 66, 79, 89, 135
Propertius, 77
property, 52, 60, 124–5
prophecy, 122, 124, 126, 128
prophetess, 122, 127
prophets, 128, 132, 165
Propylaia, 50–2, 54
prostitution, sacred, 87
proto-trinitarian views, 160, 183
psalms, 173–4
Ptolemaic period, 26–8, 32–3, 95, 178

Ptolemaic religion, 26–8, 32
Ptolemais, 194
Ptolemies, 26–8, 169
purifications, 184, 186, 212
Pythia, 126–8

quadrigas, 46, 67

Rancière, Jacques, 145
Raphael, 133
Raphia, 169
Rawson, Elizabeth, 130–1
reality, 119, 123–4, 128, 157
rebirth, 33
reciprocity, 7, 22–3, 55, 112, 184, 213
reconstructions, 14, 20, 24, 51, 82, 87, 196, 200
relationships, 18, 21–3, 34, 37, 164, 173–4, 182–4, 193
    filial, 167–8
    reciprocal, 23, 112, 213
reliefs, 27, 31, 44, 60–1, 68, 91, 103–4
religious acts, 21–2
religious cultures, 35, 64, 112
religious landscape, 48, 128, 213
religious practice *see* practice
Reno, Joshua, 131
resurrection, 94, 116, 120, 164, 172–4, 176–9, 191
rhetoric, 131, 146, 148, 152, 154, 156
Rhodes, 92, 199
rites, 98, 138, 175
ritual activities, 23, 186, 192, 206
ritual honour, 23, 184, 193
ritual life, 27–8, 31–2, 34, 44–5, 57, 60, 63, 186
ritual offerings *see* offerings
rituals, 31–5, 37–40, 44, 50–1, 92–3, 186, 188–91, 193–4
    cultic, 52, 189, 193
    sacrificial, 111, 189
Roebuck, Carl, 101–2
Roma, 34–7, 39–41, 66, 68, 107, 109–10
    statuette, 110
Roman colonisation, 82, 88, 90–1, 93, 101–2

Roman culture, 37, 78–80, 93, 105, 148–9, 169
Roman Empire *see* empire
Roman gods, 35, 92, 104–5; *see also individual names*
Roman history, 65–6, 69, 108, 131
Roman Pantheon, 34, 43, 170
Roman period, 26–8, 32–3, 39, 41–2, 88–93, 95, 100, 102
Roman sanctuaries, 31, 102
Roman society, 145, 148–9, 202
Roman temples, 32, 68, 79–80
Romans, 3, 5, 25–6, 79, 118, 139–40, 142, 173
Rome, 37, 61, 64–82, 104–5, 131, 138, 141, 170
Romulus, 66–71
round cakes, 218–19
royal overtones, 168–9, 178
rupture, chord of gods as tool for, 213–16
*rustici Stoici*, 131

Sabbath, 198
sacking of Corinth, 90, 101
sacred prostitution, 87
sacrifices, 21, 35, 55, 71, 78, 185–6, 189, 218–19
    animal, 7, 21–3, 184–5
sacrificial rituals, 111, 189
salvation, 1–2, 176
sanctuaries, 39–46, 48–55, 57–9, 63–5, 79–83, 86–95, 97–103, 184–6
    of Aphrodite, 82, 101
    of Apollo, 21, 48, 101
    of Asklepios, 21, 43, 57, 99–103, 185–6
    Corinthian, 93–4, 101, 103, 110
    Demeter and Kore, 83, 87–94, 101, 103, 109
    life, 172, 186
    local, 52, 63, 95, 187, 209–10
    open-air, 58, 104–5
    of Palaimon, 95, 97
    of Poseidon, 86, 95–9
    of Zeus, 48, 54, 63–4
Saqqara, 94
Sarapis, 48, 83, 94–5

Saturnus Augustus, 108
satyrs, 40, 47
sayings, 6, 9, 12, 21, 26, 206, 212, 214
    and doings, nexus of, 9, 12, 21, 26, 112
    gnomic, 130, 148
Schäfer, Peter, 3–4, 208
Schatzki, Theodore R., 8–9, 11–13, 21, 26, 81, 112, 212
Scheid, John, 22, 64–5, 72, 75, 77–81, 105, 141
Scheidel, Walter, 144, 149–51, 202
scriptures, 2, 164–5, 172–3, 175
sculptures, 17, 40, 50–1, 64, 67–8, 104, 109
sea, 35, 97–9, 174
second century BCE, 59, 72, 94, 141
second century CE, 28, 63, 86, 93, 95, 102–3, 128, 200
Second Temple period, 2–3, 114, 132–3, 164
security, economic, 153–4, 163
selective homophily, 205, 214
self, 116, 125, 154
Selinous, 92
Senate, 67, 69, 71, 78–9, 135, 150–1
Seneca, 79, 127
Septuagint, 120, 132–3, 155, 159, 173, 176, 178, 181
Serapis, 177
serpents, 53, 55, 74, 135, 170
Seth, 169
shields, 55, 68
shrines, 30, 32, 37, 39, 70, 74–5, 77, 110–11; *see also individual deities*
    open-air, 58
    oracular, 41, 72
    roadside, 112
    rural, 37
    stele, 110–11
    urban, 5
Simmons, Robert Holschuh, 204
Sinai, 159, 181
sins, 165, 172, 176
Sisyphus, 97
skills, 147, 192, 201
slaves, 46–7, 136, 145, 150–1, 190, 202
small groups of gods, 5–6, 8–9, 11–12, 18, 24–5, 78–9, 111–13, 162–4

Smith, Jonathan Z., 8, 14–16, 20, 209
social constitution of Paul's Corinthians, 143–54
social formation, 20, 168, 177, 183, 190, 192
social patterns, 8, 10
social practice, 1, 8, 14–15, 81–2, 112
social status, 143–4, 147, 202, 214
social theory of practice, 8–13
social unity, 194–5
society, 9, 11, 142, 176, 197
    Corinthian, 149, 151, 207
    levels of, 5, 8, 178
    Roman, 145, 148–9, 202
Society of Biblical Literature, 8, 91
Socrates, 121–2
Sol, 141–2; *see also* sun
Somtus, 31
sons, 45–6, 61, 63–4, 87, 102–3, 117–18, 166–71, 208–9
souls, 122–3
Spaeth, Barbette, 91–3, 103–5
spears, 54–5, 68
speech, 132, 134, 157, 204, 211
*sphagia*, 50–1
spirit, 7, 114, 118–19, 124–9, 132–4, 156–7, 160, 183
    possession, 7, 114, 117–19
spiritual gifts, 129, 157, 193, 210
stars, 27, 116
state protective divinities, 103–5
states of mind, 22, 44, 127
statues, 43, 54–7, 64–9, 71–4, 97–8, 102, 106–10, 171
    colossal, 39, 108
    cult, 39, 51, 54–5, 68–9, 71, 80, 97, 184–6
statuettes, 56, 74, 78, 109–10
status, 67, 69, 143, 145, 150–1, 190, 201–2, 204
    economic, 147, 202
    legal, 145, 150
    social, 143–4, 147, 202, 214
stele, 60–1, 63, 83, 139
    shrines, 110–11
Stephanas, 151–3, 203

Stirling, Lea M., 109–10
Stoicism, 114–19, 121, 123–5, 127, 129, 131, 180, 182
Stowers, Stanley K., 3–6, 117, 151–3, 162, 191–2, 200–1, 203, 205–6
Strabo, 126–7
Strelan, Rick, 122, 127, 129
Stroud, Ronald S., 83, 89–90, 92–4
students, 146–7
subsistence level, 144, 149–50, 152–4, 202
substance(s), 11, 21, 119, 123–7, 131, 139, 155, 182
Suetonius, 39, 41, 71, 147, 170, 177
sun, 27, 32–3, 116, 139, 141–2
superiority, 14, 122, 166, 211, 216
suppliants, 44–5, 186
symbols, 11, 20, 27, 68–9, 187, 190, 192, 199
synagogues, 134, 197–201
Syria, 40, 198–9

tablets, 92–3
    curse, 91–2
Tanais, 198
taxonomy, 19, 193
Telemachos, 58
Telesphoros, 42, 45, 102–3
temples, 26–37, 41–4, 50–4, 67–72, 90–2, 106–7, 156–7, 184–7; *see also* sanctuaries; shrines
    of Apollo, 106, 170
    of Artemis, 53
    complexes, 26, 31, 34
    in Corinth, 156, 187
    Edfu, 26, 28
    Egyptian, 26, 28, 31, 34
    Fortuna Primigenia, 72–4
    of Hera, 48
    imagery, 157, 163, 187
    Jerusalem, 156, 187
    of Mars Ultor, 65–71
    of Palaimon, 97, 99
    of Pan, 39–40
    of Poseidon, 97–8, 140
    of Ptolemaic and Roman Periods, 27–8, 32–3

Roman, 32, 68, 79–80
  of Zeus, 39–40
  of Zeus Asklepios, 42–3
θεοσεβής, 199
θεοῦ, ναὸς, 156
θεοῦ Σεβαστοῦ υἱῶι, 171
terminology, 17, 126, 174, 180–1, 197–9
terracotta offerings, 63, 100–1, 203
θεός, 129, 158, 167, 208, 218
thanksgiving, 22–3, 48, 101
theatre(s), 42, 52, 57, 72, 94, 110, 131, 151
Theissen, Gert, 143
Themis, 44–5, 64, 218–19
Theoi Dikaioi, 45
Theokritos, 169
theology, 28, 129, 211
  Augustan, 69
  Paul's, 114, 119
*theos*, 158
Thesmophoria, 93
third century BCE, 37, 39, 88, 95
third century CE, 54, 194
thrones, 83, 94, 132, 169–70
Tiberius, 106–7, 138, 171, 177
Tiberius Augustus, 171
Timoleon, 88
Titius Justus, 198
tongue-speakers, 157, 193, 210
Toronto, 146
trades, 145–6, 204
traditions, 19–21, 26–8, 170, 174–5, 197, 205–6, 208, 211–12
  local, 5, 40, 81
  long, 18, 86, 175, 194
  Roman, 65, 135
Trajan, 31, 39
transformation, 10, 51–2, 57, 94, 116, 153, 179–81, 191
transition, 77, 213–14
  existential, 32–3
triads, 31, 79, 91, 104–5, 160, 165, 183
tridents, 53, 140
trinitarian doctrines, 4, 114, 160, 166, 182–3, 190
Tritons, 95, 98–9, 139–41, 209
Trophonius, 126

truth, 2, 20, 114, 119, 201, 215
Tychē, 44–5, 107, 218–19
Tyrannos, 46

Ullucci, Daniel, 7, 21–3
underworld, 50, 93
uniqueness, 1, 14–15, 128
unity, 14, 54, 120, 190–1, 193–5, 211
  social, 194–5
universality of practice, 187
universe, 123–5, 130, 159, 166–7, 207
us vs. them scenario, 207, 209

valorisation of monotheism, 215–16
vapours, 126–7
Varela, C. R., 11
Varro, 74, 141
Venus, 68–72, 74, 77–8, 80, 99
Vespasian, 35, 37, 190
Vesta, 77
Vesuvius, 74, 109
villages, 5, 45, 81
Virtus, 142
Vitruvius, 70
votive offerings *see* offerings

Walbank, Mary E. Hoskins, 105–8
Wasserman, Emma, 116–17, 154
water, 35, 99, 123, 175
wealth, 78, 144–6, 150–1, 190, 202, 204, 214
Welborn, L. L., 8, 144–5
whips, 46, 60
Wickkiser, Bronwen L., 58–9, 100–1
wilderness, 41, 165
Williams, Kaufman, 104, 110–11
Winter, Bruce, 132, 170, 175
wisdom, 4, 120, 132, 165
Wittgenstein, Ludwig, 12
women, 7, 15, 42–3, 59, 92, 135, 141, 144
worship, 5, 8, 25–6, 51, 59–60, 79–82, 105–8, 111–12
  cultic, 4, 51, 87–8

Xenocrateia, 61–2
Xenophon, 204

Zeno, 123
Zervos, 110–11
Zeus, 39–40, 46, 48, 50, 53–5, 63–4, 132, 139
Zeus Apotropaios, 44–5, 218
Zeus Ares, 64
Zeus Asklepios, 42–3
Zeus Asklepios Soter, 107
Zeus Chthonios, 50, 64
Zeus Hera, 48
Zeus Karios, 48
Zeus Kataibates, 53, 64
Zeus Katharisios, 64
Zeus Meilichios, 44–5, 57, 218
Zeus Panamaros, 48
Zeus Philios, 57
Zeus Polieus, 54
Zeus Thebaieus, 50

EU Authorised Representative:
Easy Access System Europe Mustamäe tee 50, 10621 Tallinn, Estonia
gpsr.requests@easproject.com

Printed and bound by CPI Group (UK) Ltd, Croydon, CR0 4YY
02/03/2026
02063700-0001